A Tale of New England

PUBLISHING FOR THE WORLD
125 Years
THE JOHNS HOPKINS UNIVERSITY PRESS

A Tale of New England

The Diaries of Hiram Harwood,
Vermont Farmer, 1810–1837

ROBERT E. SHALHOPE

THE JOHNS HOPKINS UNIVERSITY PRESS
Baltimore & London

© 2003 The Johns Hopkins University Press
All rights reserved. Published 2003
Printed in the United States of America on acid-free paper
9 8 7 6 5 4 3 2 1

The Johns Hopkins University Press
2715 North Charles Street
Baltimore, Maryland 21218-4363
www.press.jhu.edu

Library of Congress Cataloging-in-Publication Data

Shalhope, Robert E., 1941–
    A tale of New England : the diaries of Hiram Harwood, Vermont farmer,
1810–1837 / Robert E. Shalhope.
        p. cm.
Diaries were started by Benjamin Harwood in 1805 and continued by his son,
Hiram Harwood, in 1808.
Includes bibliographical references and index.
    ISBN 0-8018-7127-1 (alk. paper)
    1. Harwood, Hiram, 1788–1839. 2. Pioneers — Vermont — Bennington Region —
Biography. 3. Farmers — Vermont — Bennington Region — Biography. 4. Harwood,
Hiram, 1788–1839 — Diaries. 5. Bennington Region (Vt.) — Biography.
6. Bennington Region (Vt.) — Social life and customs — 18th century. 7. Bennington
Region (Vt.) — Social life and customs — 19th century. 8. Farm life — Vermont —
Bennington Region. 9. Harwood, Benjamin, 1762–1851. 10. Harwood, Benjamin,
1762–1851 — Diaries. I. Title: Diaries of Hiram Harwood, Vermont farmer, 1810–
1837. II. Harwood, Hiram, 1788–1839. III. Harwood, Benjamin, 1762–1851.
IV. Title.
F59.B4 S535 2002
974.3′8 — dc21
2002006466

A catalog record for this book is available from the British Library.

For Emma

Contents

Acknowledgments

It is with great pleasure and a deep sense of gratitude that I acknowledge the individuals and institutions that contributed so much toward bringing this book to fruition. The College of Arts and Sciences at the University of Oklahoma provided a sabbatical leave that gave me valuable time free of other academic responsibilities. A National Endowment for the Humanities–American Antiquarian Society fellowship made that time all the more productive. The academic year spent at the American Antiquarian Society was one of the most fruitful and pleasant experiences of my professional career. I thank all the members of the AAS staff for their kindness during my time there. John Hench and Caroline Sloat merit special thanks; I greatly appreciate their good fellowship and wise counsel. My work at the AAS could not have been nearly as fruitful as it was without the help of two individuals: John Carnahan and Steven Miller. As president of the board of trustees of the Brattleboro Retreat, John provided me with copies of Hiram Harwood's medical records while a patient at the Vermont Asylum for the Insane; Steven, then executive director of the Bennington Museum, granted me permission to copy the typescript version of the Harwood diaries. These documents were vital to my research. I must thank two other individuals from the Bennington Museum who contributed greatly to my undertaking: Joseph Parks assumed full responsibility for having the diaries photocopied, and Ruth Levin provided me access to the original handwritten journals and helped supply illustrations from the museum's collection.

A number of scholars who critiqued portions of my work along the way deserve commendation. Robert Gross provided helpful insights when I delivered a paper at an annual meeting of the Omohundro Institute of Early American History and Culture. Members of the faculty seminar in early American history at the University of Oklahoma offered additional provocative suggestions when we met to discuss Hiram Harwood's mental and physical problems. Charles Rosenberg gave even more helpful advice when I delivered a paper on this same subject at a symposium held at Oregon State University. Two other scholars merit special thanks. My colleague Cathy Kelly read the entire manuscript and provided me with the keen perspective of a wonderfully astute social historian. James Kloppenberg also read the entire manuscript. His provocative insights into matters of both style and substance were of inestimable value. He is an exceptional scholar and a good friend. I would also like to express my appreciation to Robert Brugger, whose editorial patience and perseverance has made this a much better book. The same is certainly true of Lois Crum; her work as a copy editor was truly extraordinary.

My greatest debt of gratitude is to my family. My parents have always supported my scholarly endeavors; my daughter Adelaide made one of my trips to Bennington a special treat; and my son Robert's pride in me and my work is a wonderful source of comfort. Most of all, I thank my wife, Emma, for her constant love and support. Without her, no book would be worth writing; no life would be worth living.

A Tale of New England

Introduction

On March 3, 1808, Peter Harwood, patriarch of the Harwood family living on Tanbrook Creek, several miles south of the meetinghouse in Bennington, Vermont, gathered his family about him to announce a momentous decision. It was a moment that all family members had awaited with much apprehension and that some may have hoped to postpone indefinitely. To his assembled family Peter declared that his youngest son, Ira, who had returned in broken health the previous year from an attempt to clear a farm near Hopkinton, New York, would henceforth live in a nearby family house, replacing his older brother Benjamin and his family, who currently occupied it. Later that same day Ira, his wife, Theodosia, and their two-year-old daughter, Catherine, obediently took up residence in the old slab house where Benjamin and his family had resided for seventeen years. The forty-six-year-old Benjamin now had to move, settling his own wife, Diadama, his son, Hiram, and his two daughters, Lydia and Diadama, into the two-story frame residence occupied by his seventy-three-year-old father, his stepmother, Mary, and his thirty-year-old sister, Lucy. Describing this as "an event of considerable consequence," Benjamin observed that "my family are now in my father's house." Then, always the dutiful son, he announced that the two families "will be consider'd as one for the future, and as long as he lives [my father] will be it's [*sic*] head."[1]

A month later Benjamin's filial respect remained strong, but whatever personal satisfaction he once enjoyed had disappeared entirely. He now described himself as "unhappy and dissatisfied with my situation." Rather than create a "difficulty in the family," Benjamin would not state the reasons for his discontent. He did, however, venture to observe that "never since the 3d of last March have I enjoyed myself so well as I us'd to." To say more would be to question his father's authority. Instead, he meant "to content myself as well as I can." Nonetheless, before the end of the year, Benjamin took steps to alleviate the distress he felt at sharing his father's home. With Peter's approval, he hired a carpenter to divide the lower floor of the house into separate apartments and to put up a temporary partition in the kitchen "to try the effect & importance of a permanent one." Now, even while living under his father's roof, Benjamin could once again gather his family in his own kitchen and sit at the head of his own table.[2]

 ⤳ Benjamin's *filiopiety* — his ingrained respect for his father and his way of doing things — and the presence of several generations living within the same household were not exceptional among the Harwoods or other New England farm families of the day. These traits had characterized the Harwood family experience from the time Nathaniel Harwood first arrived in Boston and then settled in Concord as a cordwainer sometime after 1665.[3] So, too, had the Harwoods' manner of transferring property from one generation to the next. Shunning the practice of partible inheritance predominant throughout New England, the Harwoods remained steadfastly loyal to the custom of impartible inheritance so common in their native village of Cranleigh on the eastern fringe of England's champion (open-field) country. Because they were intent upon maintaining intact whatever land they managed to acquire, the land itself — the farm — became the end for which all family members sacrificed. Consequently, Harwood parents turned over all their landed property and their homesteads to a single son on the condition that he support them for the remainder of their lives. Upon their death the deed to the property would pass to the chosen son.[4] In this manner the Harwoods perpetuated a family tradition of patriarchy.[5]

Throughout the years since Nathaniel Harwood settled in Concord, an attenuated version of patriarchy gradually prevailed, not only among the Harwoods but throughout most of rural New England as well. No longer did a dominating figure rule by fiat; instead the head of the household guided the family by means of a far more subtly nuanced set of reciprocal relationships between father and children, husband and wife, male and female, old and young. Mutual respect rather than abject submissiveness characterized these relationships. Nevertheless, certain traditional attitudes continued to shape the life and thought of the Harwoods: the family, with its titular head, remained the central focus in their lives and continued to bear responsibility for socializing all its members; it molded their beliefs, shaped their behavioral patterns, and imbued them with their morals and their manners. At the same time, though, as the head of the household aged and had to relinquish more and more responsibilities to his chosen heir, patriarchal power assumed a far more fluctuating and relational character. Most important of all, these patriarchal attitudes affected male as well as female members of the family. Intense pressure was placed on the favored heir to live up to the expectations of the family. The patriarch's primary responsibility was to direct that son's upbringing in such a manner as to ensure that he would mature into a responsible steward of the family's fortunes. Above all else, the chosen son must be capable of sustaining the prosperity of the farm and the family.

Because decisions about land and its transfer normally were made after Harwood parents were past their prime, elder sons rarely inherited the farm. They had long since married and, eager to establish separate households, set out on their own. To experience a protracted adolescence by remaining within their father's home long after reaching maturity would have been difficult for them; intergenerational friction might have created intolerable tensions. Generally, then, the Harwood family homestead included the aging parents, their unmarried daughters and younger sons, and the family of the middle son who was to take over the farm. This was the case when Peter Harwood made the vital decision demanded of all Harwood patriarchs: Benjamin was to assume ownership of the farm upon his parents' death. Until that time he would remain on the farm and work it with his father.[6]

Once it was decided that he was to be the chosen son, the maintenance and improvement of his father's farm, which one day would belong to him and then to his only son, Hiram, became the center of Benjamin's world. The very rhythms of his life sprang from the seasonal demands of agriculture. This was never so apparent as when, in the spring of 1805, he began to keep a "minute book," a daily log of farm activities that gradually evolved into a journal serving not only as a farm daybook but also as a window into Benjamin's world. When Hiram assumed responsibility for keeping the journal five years later, it blossomed into an expansive, wide-ranging diary that opened not only outward to a far wider world, but also inward to a deeply introspective, private space. By the time Hiram made his last entry on October 23, 1837, the diary had consumed fourteen large leather-bound volumes.

❧ The original hand-written volumes of this remarkable diary are now located in the vault of the Bennington Museum. Thirteen large black books — typewritten copies of the diaries — rest on the shelves of the museum's library. Two things immediately become apparent upon perusing these volumes. First is their immensity; the diaries consist of more than four thousand pages of single-spaced typescript. Next is their immense value to anyone interested in New England culture in the early nineteenth century. The diaries provide a wonderful window into the social, political, economic, and religious life of Bennington and of the entire region. Between the years 1805 and 1837, Benjamin, and then Hiram, wrote in detail about their own lives as well as the lives of their immediate family members, their neighbors, and the residents of the larger community. Sometimes as outside observers, but more often as actual participants, they revealed valuable insights into the changes and continuities of life in New England throughout the early nine-teenth century. One can observe their village grow into a prosperous marketplace and then gradually begin its transformation into a manu-facturing center. At the same time the town's Jeffersonian Republicans battle their Federalist opponents in town meeting after town meeting until the Federalists finally gain the ascendancy. Divisive concepts such as temperance, sabbatarianism, abolitionism, and moral reform exacer-bated such political differences and set ordinary individuals against one another. There are few issues of even the slightest significance to the cultural life of New Englanders during this time that escape notice in the Harwood diaries and for which they fail to provide insightful observations.

Upon close reading, the diaries disclose even more provocative in-sights. Hiram's entries include far more than personal discussions of politics, religion, and economics; they are replete with introspection, with personal hopes, fears, and anxieties. Through his diary, one gains access to the inner life of a common citizen living in early-nineteenth-century America. The reader becomes privy to Hiram's fondness for music; his fascination with books and newspapers; his love of itinerant lectures, traveling exhibitions, and the theater; and his intense loyalty to American republicanism. One also becomes intimately acquainted with Hiram's severe lack of self-confidence, his fear of failure, his obsessive concern with his public persona, and above all else his constant struggle to come to grips with his own sense of masculinity. As Benjamin's sole heir, Hiram experienced an unrelenting pressure to become the sort of mature, responsible male capable of perpetuating the family farm.

The more intensely one studies Hiram's diaries, the clearer it becomes that they contain a multiplicity of stories dealing with the social, political, economic, and religious lives of the Harwoods, their neighbors, and rural inhabitants throughout New England. This book focuses on one story: Hiram's struggle to attain his own individual identity — to achieve a sense of his own manhood — in a changing world and within the confines of a restrictive familial environment. In one way or another, however, this story incorporates important elements of all the others. Readers can, for example, clearly see the tensions — familial, economic, political, and religious — brought about by the transition from small-scale, diversified family farming to large-scale commercial dairy farming in New England. Most of all, Hiram's story reveals the personal price exacted of him by the Harwood family's belief in patriarchy.

ᕙ Benjamin Harwood began his minute book on March 25, 1805, with a simple observation: "Prun'd my Orchard — ." We will enter the diary at a much more poignant moment, one far more resonant with meaning for understanding the intimate relationship between father and son. The event is Hiram's twenty-first birthday; the notation reveals Benjamin's feelings on this occasion.

A Man of Business

My son this day became twenty one years of age — An awkward fellow he is too, he never frequents company of any sort — has very little ambition about work — not at all ingenious about getting along with business, not having acquainted himself with many little arts that are necessary for the quick dispatch of many sorts of work. He has a moderate love for reading, but a memory like — or too much like a looking glass to profit much by what he reads. He writes a middling hand — possesses some knowledge of English Grammar — writes in a style agreeable to his character — Is fond of music — and a bungling performer on the fife & flute. After all his faults & oddities he is an inoffensive fellow — wishes every one to enjoy all the happiness they can find in this world. I am sorry to add that in arithmetic his knowledge reaches far short of the rule of three. And farther to do him justice I must mention, that he is acquainted in a very limited degree with geography — still less with history & is a would be politician. — Thus much to describe the character of my son — it can't be expected that a father should as impartially delineate the character of a son — an only son, whom he dearly loves; as an indifferent person can.[1]

Despite such candor, Benjamin Harwood's words did not capture the full intensity of his feelings toward his son Hiram. The task of shaping Hiram into an industrious worker and responsible participant in the family's efforts to maintain and improve the Harwood farm never ceased to trouble Benjamin. His daily journal echoed a perpetual re-frain: "Hiram worked very poorly at chopping today"; "Hiram did but little"; "Hiram did nothing worthy of notice"; "Hiram earnt his bread and I don't know how much more"; and "Hiram did little or nothing . . .

having a poor disposition to work." Once, in total exasperation, he even scribbled, "Hiram aint you ashamed you great lazy luber."[2]

Even in the face of such constant disappointment, Benjamin remained resolute in his determination to instill proper work habits in his son. When Hiram balked at cutting hay, Benjamin observed firmly that even though his son was "awkward about the business, and dislikes it much, however he must submit to it—whether it suits him or not." Another time, after Hiram once again "might have done much more than he did, had it been his mind to do so," Benjamin "strongly hinted my displeasure toward his conduct, which I hope may alter him for the better."[3]

And yet all Benjamin's effort seemed for naught. One night a group of neighborhood youths held a party that did not break up until nearly daybreak. The revelers lost nearly a whole night's sleep. Sorrowfully, Benjamin had to note that Hiram was among these irresponsible young people. It may have been just such an occasion as this that led Hiram to disappoint his father yet again. When all hands were hard at work reaping, Hiram "gave way to his feelings so much as even to lie down in the field." His excuse was that he had "suffered much in the two previous nights for want of sleep." Finally, after observing how awkward Hiram was at mowing hay, Benjamin admitted that his son was "a poor recommendation for a young man of 22." He could only conclude that if Hiram had "the spirits of others at that age, he would soon overcome a difficulty of this kind." Nonetheless, although he still had hope for his son, Benjamin had to confess that "it rests on a sandy foundation."[4]

Regardless of such misgivings, Benjamin persevered. His efforts to stamp out Hiram's laziness, ineptitude, and general indifference to farm work never abated; instead, they intensified with the passage of time. The grim determination with which Benjamin went about the task of molding Hiram's behavior went far beyond anything that might normally have been expected of a father's efforts to shape the character of his son. Such single-minded intensity emanated from Benjamin's own life experience, which drew strength and meaning from the Harwood family's belief in patriarchy. To comprehend the relationship between father and son, and to gain insight into the son's efforts to achieve manhood in a ceaselessly changing environment, it is necessary first to know the world that produced the father.

To understand Benjamin's world, one must understand that of his father, Peter, and his grandfather, Benjamin. Born April 30, 1713, the elder Benjamin grew to manhood on his father's farm in Concord. In May 1733 he married Bridget Brown, the daughter of a neighboring family. Four years later his father moved to a substantial farm six miles northwest of Concord in Littleton, Massachusetts. Well before that time, Benjamin's two eldest brothers had already settled with their families in Lunenburg and Uxbridge. Since his next eldest brother was to take over the farm in Littleton, Benjamin, after struggling to make a living on various small plots of land in Concord, migrated to the frontier town of Hardwick (originally Lambstown) with Bridget and their two-year-old son Peter.[5] There he attempted to gain a living as a "worsted weaver" and by farming a small plot of rocky land. In an attempt to better himself and his heirs, he also made a small speculative purchase of wilderness lands on the New Hampshire Grants (present-day Vermont).[6]

While residing in Hardwick, Benjamin became caught up in the momentous wave of religious enthusiasm sweeping over New England. Preaching "the Rule of Equity" — a principle rooted in the "natural equality of mankind"[7] — evangelists such as George Whitefield and Gilbert Tennent attacked Congregational ministers and church members who had not had a personal saving experience. Exalting the vernacular, they associated virtue with ordinary people rather than with an educated elite; they empowered common individuals by valuing their deepest spiritual impulses over the orthodox doctrine of the learned clergy.

This message engulfed Hardwick in October 1740 when George Whitefield spoke to hundreds of avid listeners in an open field in nearby Brookfield. Many who heard Whitefield returned to Hardwick filled with the spirit and eager to hear more of God's redeeming grace from the pulpit of their own church. Experiencing only disappointment and frustration, they began to absent themselves from church services and refused to share Communion with the unconverted. As a result, on July 25, 1749, church members voted to call a council of ministers to advise them whether to dismiss the "dissatisfied brethren" — Samuel Robinson, James Fay, Benjamin Harwood, Silas Pratt, and George Abbott Jr. — or to "censure them as irregular, disorderly members." Only Silas Pratt accepted the council's advice; Benjamin Harwood — deemed a "zealous Separate" by orthodox authorities — and the others firmly "declared their non-compliance." Over the next several years, an increasing number of "dissatisfied brethren" were called to account by the church. Finally, on November 14, 1753, church members selected a committee to meet with the individuals who had "sepa-rated from this church" in order "to propose some reconciling methods to them."[8]

The church's efforts proved fruitless. Benjamin Harwood and his fellow New Lights ardently believed in the old ways; they cherished the covenant of grace and a church composed exclusively of visible saints. Intent upon keeping alive the fervent spirit manifested so plainly in the public professions of their individual conversion experiences, these people were equally determined to preserve the same sort of simple equality within their church that had characterized their civil affairs since the incorporation of the town in 1739. More important still, the message of the New Light ministers had greatly intensified their sense of localism — their belief that they should control their own lives. Con-sequently, the separation of Benjamin Harwood and some thirty other individuals from the old church became irrevocable on August 29, 1750. On that date the church voted to seat its members within the town's newly finished meetinghouse — "the highest payers in the high-est seats."[9] No longer willing to accept this traditional means of rein-forcing the social hierarchy of the secular world within the church, Hardwick's New Lights broke away, formed a separate church, and erected a meetinghouse on Samuel Robinson's farm, where they shared in the blessed spirit with a lay exhorter and elected Samuel Robinson, James Fay, and John Fassett to serve as their deacons.

By 1758 Benjamin, no longer able to support his wife and children in Hardwick, had moved his family, which now consisted of five sons and two daughters, to Amherst. There they joined the families of Timothy and Samuel Pratt, fellow Separates who had migrated to Amherst sev-eral years earlier. Within a year after settling there, Benjamin died while serving with the local militia in the French and Indian war.[10]

Upon Benjamin's death, Peter and his younger brother Eleazer became executors of their father's estate and assumed responsibility for the care of their mother, their brothers Stephen and Zechariah, and their sisters Mary, Abigail, and Hepzibah.[11] Peter took over the eighteen-acre farm and its livestock.[12] Within a matter of months, he married Margaret Clark of Colerain, Massachusetts, and brought her to the farm in Amherst. In May 1760 Margaret gave birth to a son, Clark. Exactly one year later, Eleazer married Elizabeth Montague of Sunderland, but he did not bring her to the farm.[13] Instead, they joined Peter's family, the remaining Harwoods, the Pratt families, and their old Hardwick neighbors Leonard and Samuel Robinson Jr. in a migration northward. Following a trail marked only by blazed trees, this small band of Separates—twenty-two men, women, and children—made their way toward the wilderness township of Bennington on the New Hampshire Grants, where they hoped to start anew under more favorable circumstances. For men like Peter and Eleazer, whose family had become nearly impoverished, this was particularly important. It was their chance to obtain an independent livelihood—a competency. More than that, it was an opportunity to become respectable members of a new community—to regain the stature the Harwood family had enjoyed in Concord and Littleton.

Immediately upon their arrival, the Harwood men began the arduous task of clearing a homesite and constructing a two-story home out of slabs hewn from trees felled in the area. In the meantime the family lived in lean-tos made of pine boughs, and the women cooked over open fires. Whenever labor could be spared from the immediate tasks at hand, all members of the family helped to plant grain in whatever open areas could be found in the dense forest that surrounded them. By the onset of winter, the slab house, with its massive stone fireplace, had been completed. This was fortunate, for on January 12 Margaret gave birth to Benjamin. By this time, too, Samuel Robinson Sr., the leading proprietor of the new township, had arrived with thirty more families from Hardwick, Sunderland, Ware, and Amherst. Peter Harwood purchased his land—190 acres, several miles south of the spot where the village meetinghouse was to stand—from the senior member of the Robinson family.[14] Improving this land held the key to achieving the prosperity and respectability his family had lost when his father did not inherit the farm in Littleton.

Over the next several decades, Peter's household changed considerably. Bridget Harwood died November 8, 1762. With the death of his mother, Peter became the titular head of the Harwood family, which at that time included his wife, Margaret, and their two sons, Clark and Benjamin, Peter's brothers Zechariah and Stephen, and his sisters Abigail and Hepzibah. Eleazer and his family lived on a fifty-five-acre farm adjoining Peter's land.[15] In subsequent years Margaret gave birth to six more boys, Ebenezer, Abijah, Asa, Peter, Jonas, and Ira, and two girls, Sarah and Lucy. Peter's brothers and sisters married and established their own households in neighboring townships.[16] Throughout most of this time, Peter's growing family resided in separate homes built nearly side-by-side: the original slab house and a commodious two-story frame structure built in 1769.

By 1790 Peter's household once again included three generations. Benjamin had married Diadama Dewey four years earlier, and their first child, Hiram, had been born in 1788. By the time Benjamin's family took up exclusive residence in the old slab house in 1791, the decision that Benjamin was to assume ownership of the farm upon his parents' death had been made. At this time Peter was fifty-six years old and Benjamin twenty-nine; Benjamin's elder brother Clark, who had married six years earlier, had already moved to Rutland, where he owned his own farm. Ebenezer, too, had married, and he had taken up farming in Sunderland, Vermont. Abijah and Peter were dead; this left Asa, Jonas, Sarah, Lucy, and Ira to live in the frame house with their parents. Then in 1794 their mother, Margaret, died. Within a year Peter married Mary Doty, a widow from an old Hardwick family. The following year Asa married and began farming in New York.[17]

~ Upon becoming the chosen son, Benjamin took up the quest pursued by his father and his grandfather before him — the quest to achieve prosperity and respectability for the Harwood family through hard work and perseverance. The farm — the only means by which these goals could be achieved — became the very center of his world. The farm itself consisted of 100 acres of improved land and 55 acres of woodlands.[18] The family kept 34 acres of improved land under cultivation. These fields produced wheat, corn, rye, barley, oats, and potatoes. Hay meadows and orchards occupied the remainder of the improved property. The farm's animals generally included one yoke of oxen, six horses, more than twenty cows and calves, fifty-some sheep, two dozen or so hogs, and flocks of chickens and geese.[19]

Benjamin did not tend the farm alone; he had his father, his brothers Jonas and Ira, and his son, Hiram, to assist him. Ira lived with his wife and daughter in his father's house. In return for the support given his family, he cut wood for Peter's fireplace and owed a number of days' labor to Benjamin.[20] Jonas resided with his wife and four daughters on a farm that he rented nearby; he exchanged labor with Benjamin and received produce from a portion of the Harwood garden. The farm also depended upon the labor of the Harwood women — Benjamin's wife, his mother, his sister Lucy, his daughters, Lydia and Diadama, and Ira's wife, Theodosia. They cooked, cleaned, made butter and cheese, spun wool, wove cloth, sewed clothing, tended the garden, and helped the men in the fields and orchards whenever needed. And yet Benjamin made no mention of such labor in his journal. Although he kept a close accounting of the comings and goings of every male member of the family, Benjamin never mentioned the contributions made by the Harwood women to the welfare of the family. His silence may have represented the influence of his patriarchal beliefs—his unthinking assumptions about the role of women in any family.[21] These beliefs gained strength from biblical teachings long honored by the Harwoods. Among these, Eve's treachery in the Garden of Eden and the Apostle Paul's strictures (particularly his letter to the Colossians) perpetuated traditional suspicions that the feminine constitution was inherently corrupt and that wives were helpmeets rather than equal partners with their husbands.[22]

During the spring months, the Harwoods performed tasks about the farm that varied from year to year only in response to vagaries in the weather. In early April the men cut and prepared posts and rails in order to keep the farm's fences in good repair, turned the livestock into the pastures, tended their apple orchards, and sowed summer wheat, barley, oats, and flax. During this same time they attempted each day to transport ten to twelve cartloads of manure onto their fields. Later in the month, with the assistance of the women, they planted an extensive garden. In May they turned their attention to planting corn, potatoes, and beans. At the end of May, the sheep had to be gathered up, driven to a neighboring millpond, and washed. After that the animals were shorn and the wool turned over to the women, first to be spun into thread and then to be woven into cloth. By early June, as the corn began to sprout, the men turned their attention to cultivating their cornfields in order to keep them free of weeds. Throughout all of the spring months, Hiram and Ira dug and transported stone to wherever Jonas and Benjamin were constructing a wall. Beyond that, many garden plants, as well as Peter's tobacco, had to be transplanted during this same period.[23]

At all times, regardless of the task at hand, Benjamin measured the worth of each day by whether or not it had been "a good day for business."[24] A rigidly disciplined worker, he put business before all creature comforts and even before his own health. Thus, upon arising early one particularly nasty morning, he thought to himself, "had I possess'd property enough I should have kept in the house in stead of going in to the fields to work." Without another thought, of course, he warmed himself behind the plow rather than by the fire. On another occasion, "if pure necessity had not drove me to it, I should have suspended my personal labors today, for I was more fit to be on the bed than behind the plow." Nevertheless, despite eating nothing the entire day and suffering a "sick headache," Benjamin performed what he considered to be "a pretty good days work at plowing." He pushed himself particularly hard while shearing sheep, because it was the "sort of business which I always disliked; and therefore knew but little about." Still, having sheared sixteen sheep to his father's fourteen, he concluded, "I must not censure myself for not doing a greater days work than that which I performed today; for it exceeds any that I have ever done before at the same kind of business."[25]

The fact that he took Peter's production as the standard by which he measured his own reflected Benjamin's desire to please his father — to prove himself worthy of upholding the patriarchal tradition of the Harwoods. And yet this was not easy for Benjamin; Peter — a seemingly tireless worker even in his seventies — set an exacting standard. One afternoon the old man became so intent upon repairing a piece of fence that he became "almost angry that he had been called away to dinner." Such behavior characterized the son as well. It was not unusual for Benjamin to skip supper and keep working until dark. During a brief halt from plowing, Benjamin "finished a piece of wall which was left undone" while the others refreshed themselves and their teams. When rain prevented heavy work in the fields, Benjamin would "garden between showers."[26]

If Benjamin pushed himself, he expected a great deal of others as well. When a neighbor came over with his sons to hoe corn, Benjamin wondered when the father would prove himself more by action than by words, and finally, after correcting their work for two days, he sent the youngest boys off, because "their hoeing offended me very much." When another neighbor sent his apprentice to hoe corn, Benjamin felt obliged to watch him "pretty closely," or his corn would have been "badly hoed."[27]

Benjamin treated his work animals in much the same manner. He would never overwork his oxen in the heat and was considerate of his draft horses. If, however, during the press of an arduous season, one of his animals misbehaved, it suffered the full force of his temper. Such befell a young mare that refused to move when attached to the sweep of the cider mill. After nothing else seemed to work, Benjamin "plied her smartly with the lash." When this caused her to back up and break the sweep, Benjamin became "not a little heated with passion" and, determined that she should behave, "took her out of the gears & gave her a very severe dressing." A short time later, after the animal had broken several sweeps, Benjamin's anger "was raised to a very high pitch — and I suppose I was not very merciful to the beast."[28]

Peter's temperament was every bit as explosive. When Hiram mistakenly unloaded a cartload of potatoes in the wrong spot, Peter went into "such a violent passion that he could hardly contain himself." Although Hiram was "accustomed to his way of speaking on such occasions," the startled young man recalled that his grandfather "delivered his expressions so forcibly this morning that I almost trembled with fear, though he stood a number of rods from me." Fortunately, Peter's "passion soon subsided" and "all went right after that."[29]

At times, then, the pressing needs and expenses of the farm combined to cause Benjamin great anxiety. He lamented that "sometimes when I get thinking over my affairs I almost lose my patience." But his inner drive would not allow such feelings to linger. Most of the time, he wrote with pride of his accomplishments — accomplishments that reflected his most basic concerns. Thus, when it came time to cease construction of a stone wall in order to begin the harvest season, Benjamin quit, knowing that the wall would be "a lasting monument to our labour." In fact it would "show what can be done by perseverance & labour." More importantly, "it will show what I have done on this farm in the year 1806."[30] Such an accomplishment stood as solid testimony to Benjamin's worthiness to inherit the mantle of the patriarch.

Just as Benjamin rarely worked alone, his life on the Harwood farm was not one of isolation. He and his family existed within a network of interdependent relationships that, like a spiderweb, spread outward in ever widening and attenuated concentric strands. At the center stood the Harwood homestead and the Tanbrook neighborhood of which it was an integral part. Two miles to the north lay the village of Bennington, where the Harwoods attended church, transacted whatever business was necessary at the county courthouse or the local newspaper, and dealt with whichever one of several merchants, attorneys, tavernkeepers, artisans, or blacksmiths was appropriate to the needs of the moment. They patronized sawmills, gristmills, and fulling mills located along Paran Creek several miles north of the village and on the Walloomsac River a mile to the east of Bennington. They also traded from time to time with the operators of a sawmill in Pownal, five miles to the south. Beyond that they rarely ventured. Exceptions included a twenty-mile journey to Wilmington twice a year to deliver and retrieve their sheep from farmers with whom they had arranged to pasture their flock for the summer season; an occasional twenty-five-mile ride to Manchester to attend countywide political gatherings or militia musters; and seasonal trips covering the thirty miles to Troy, New York, to market their crops and to purchase necessary items that were either unavailable in Bennington or deemed a better purchase in Troy.

Although daily life for the Harwoods focused on their own farm, they could not separate themselves from their Tanbrook neighbors. Contact with these people was the most frequent, relationships the most familiar, and loyalties the most intense. For the Harwoods — bred within the Separate Congregational tradition of intense localism — Tanbrook was a small community whose members supported one another as well as the good of the whole. They exchanged labor; traded animals, tools, and individual expertise; shared meals; sheltered those caught out in a storm; tended one another's sick; and helped those among them who had fallen on hard times.

No one within this community was entirely self-sufficient; each depended upon others. Whenever possible, Benjamin "changed works" (traded labor) with his neighbors in order to pay for a needed bit of help. Thus, while a neighbor sheared his sheep, Benjamin "helped his boys plant a field of corn." When Benjamin, Ira, and Hiram split wood for William Norton's pottery kiln, their work was "to be paid for in hoeing." Benjamin always kept a careful record of such transactions; when one of Norton's apprentices finished a day of hoeing, Benjamin noted in his journal that a day and a half's labor still remained due him.[31] From time to time, Benjamin or another of the Harwood men would split wood for a local widow, deliver food to a family in distress, or cut and transport firewood to the district schoolhouse. On these occasions Benjamin expected nothing in return. The Calvinist rule of equity and law of charity, observed by the Harwood family for years, shaped Benjamin's behavior. Like his father's before him, his household would honor these revered traditions.

The Harwoods did require a modicum of goods and services for which they could not exchange labor. Captain John Norton grafted their fruit trees, Major William Norton did all their blacksmithing and sharpened their plow irons, Stephen Harwood made wooden farm implements and furniture for them, Captain Isaiah Hendryx sewed clothing for the family, Stephen Robinson tended to the veterinarian requirements of the farm, Elisha Waters handled most of their carpentry work, Timothy Palmer gradually took over the bulk of their weaving, and various merchants supplied salt, nails, glassware, and other necessary household items. These people generally received payment in farm produce. Stephen Harwood, for example, received a barrel of cider and eight bushels of potatoes in exchange for a bureau and a bookcase, and individuals who helped butcher Benjamin's cattle and pigs received a share of the meat in return for their labor.

Twice a year neighbors — willing or not — came together to work on the roads in their district. Paid at the rate of $.75 per day in the spring and $.50 per day in the fall, all residents were required to work off the tax rate assessed against them by the town. Having been selected by the annual town meeting in 1808 as surveyor of roads and highways for the southern district of Bennington, Benjamin Harwood called out his neighbors and went to work. Applying the same strict standards to repairing public roads as he did to work on his own property, he believed that most of those who turned out did as much as could be "reasonably expected from men who love to hear and tell stories, and boys who had much rather stand still, than work." Nonetheless, Benjamin did manage to get the roads in his district up to the common standard: plowed, scraped reasonably clear of rocks, and mounded in the middle. After three days of work, he carefully calculated his own expenses — a span of horses at $.50 each per day, a cart and a plow at $.20 each per day, and himself, Ira, and Hiram at $.75 each per day — to be $8.65. Since his tax amounted to only $7.23, he calculated that there was "a little due me now."[32]

Just as Benjamin worked diligently as road surveyor, he strove to be a good neighbor. He promptly repaired weaknesses in his fences and offered immediate restitution whenever any of his stock broke into a neighbor's field and destroyed a portion of the man's crops. In addition, he stood ready to help his neighbors whenever asked. One hot day in July, having finished the backbreaking work of hoeing his own fields, Benjamin observed that "perhaps if a neighbor should be in distress about getting his work along, I might turn out and hoe for him a day, otherwise I don't think I shall do any more of that business this season."[33] A firm advocate of the Golden Rule, Benjamin expected his neighbors to abide by the same principle. Whenever they did not, he could become extremely provoked. Just such an occasion arose when a neighbor's flock of geese entered one of his fields and consumed a great deal of wheat. When confronted, all the satisfaction the man would give was that he was "SORRY"; he offered no restitution for a loss that Benjamin estimated to be at least four bushels of grain. Furious, Benjamin scribbled in his journal that had he "caught a dozen or 2 of them biting off heads of wheat—and rung their necks stoutly—I don't believe I should have felt a 'bit sorry.' "[34]

By venting his anger in his journal rather than upon his neighbor, Benjamin behaved quite characteristically. He may have displayed his wrath with recalcitrant animals, but he always tried to curb his temper when dealing with neighbors. A dispute with Captain Thomas Hinman over the status of an old barn proved just how difficult this could be. When Hinman accosted Benjamin, "he was so very angry as to be unable to utter a syllable, he however said a word or 2 which very much spoil'd my temper." Benjamin "said but very little to him but kept about my work," and the captain went away. Three days later Hinman returned to vent his anger yet again. Benjamin saluted him with a hearty "Good morning" but, to avoid a quarrel, would say no more. Instead he simply kept on with his work. Four additional days passed before the two men, both "cool and deliberate," met and reached an agreeable compromise. When Hinman claimed to own a piece of land that Benjamin knew to be a part of Peter's farm, however, he defied the captain to take the land by any measure he could. Hinman immediately relented and the two men parted "good natur'dly."[35]

When Captain Hinman died just a year later, Benjamin sat up all night, accompanied by a neighbor, to watch the corpse. Adherence to this practice characterized Benjamin's deep loyalty to the traditional customs of localism that bound him and his neighbors together. Watching the dead was an essential element of this bond of community, this ligament that drew the inhabitants of Tanbrook together into a neighborhood.[36] In spite of past arguments, Benjamin could do no less for the man who had long been his neighbor.[37]

If any other institution or set of values held Benjamin's loyalties with the intensity that linked him to Tanbrook, it was the Congregational Church in Bennington and the Harwood family's devotion to traditional New Light religious principles. His grandfather had been a "zealous Separate" at a time when such people often suffered harsh treatment at the hands of town authorities; his father had been a member of the rugged band of Separates that first settled Bennington as well as a charter member of Bennington's Old First Church, where his Uncle Eleazer served as one of the original deacons. Since he had not undergone a personal conversion experience himself, Benjamin could not be a member of the church; he was, however, a devout member of the Congregational Society.[38] The traditions and beliefs of the church were an integral part of his world, and he meant to impart them to members of his family. They were to keep the Sabbath and to live by the teachings of the Bible and the Calvinist moral law that sprang from the revivals of the 1740s.

Upon the opening of Bennington's new meetinghouse in 1805, it was Benjamin who attended the vendue and purchased pew number nineteen in his name for seventy dollars. And of all the family members living in the Tanbrook household, Benjamin was the most diligent about church attendance. Yet he was not overbearing with family members who chose not to attend; whether his wife and children accompanied him was their decision. It was so unusual for his son, Hiram, to accompany him to church that it merited special notice when he did go. One Sunday Benjamin noted that Hiram's attendance was "what he hasn't never done before since Dedication day"; another time he commented that his son's "head has not been within the walls of a church for more than 12 months before" but said nothing more.[39]

Benjamin firmly believed that "every man in this country is allowed to think and speak for himself."[40] Although generally tolerant of all persuasions, Benjamin could be critical of those who particularly offended his basic beliefs. Elitists truly upset him. Thus, upon leaving a service performed at the Bennington meetinghouse by a visiting minister, Benjamin declared that the man "went on much like our New England federalists extolling the piety of that country" and recommending for political office "men of the greatest zeal and piety in religious affairs." Most offensive to Benjamin's Separatist heritage, the man was one "who would be glad to see Church & State firmly united."[41] Consequently, Benjamin gave his full support to Daniel Marsh, a plainspoken individual with only a common-school education, who was installed as minister of Bennington's Congregational Church in March 1806. It was to hear Marsh, a democrat of simple tastes and manners — a New Light egalitarian — that Benjamin suspended his labor each Sunday morning to make the trip to the meetinghouse.

⌒ Activity on the Harwood farm picked up considerably in July, August, and September. During these months cornfields required a second and third hoeing, hay must be cut and stored away securely for the winter, flax had to be pulled, and wheat, barley, and rye needed to be harvested and brought to the barn. Since these tasks necessitated additional labor, Benjamin hired three or four extra hands during harvesttime. He generally paid them in wheat or hay, but some worked only for cash. A good hand might be paid as much as eighteen dollars for a month's labor. Such a man truly earned his pay; the work was intense and, in order to keep the harvested crops from being damaged by rain, the hours long. At the end of one particularly grueling day, even Benjamin noted that he was "more overcome with fatigue than I have been at any time for six months past." The pressure became so acute one harvest season that Benjamin, driven by "necessity," did "what I have never done before in my life": he worked on Sunday. Nonetheless, even at the height of harvesttime, Benjamin did not hesitate to assist others. When a neighboring tenant got "very much behind hand," Benjamin and his boys spent three days helping him harvest his oats. The end of Benjamin's harvest was, therefore, cause for celebration.[42]

The completion of the hay and grain harvest in early August hardly meant the end of the work season for the Harwoods. September ushered in an equally grueling work schedule. This was the time to begin harvesting corn, digging potatoes, and picking apples. During this same period, Benjamin also penned up hogs to be fattened for slaughter and turned selected cows into the meadow in order "to make beef of them — which will be the chief article I shall have to pay my debts with." During this season rain did not cause the consternation to Benjamin that it did in August, although bad weather in September "affords farmers no time to rest." When not in their fields, they "can go to [their] barn[s] & there work at a very profitable rate." By this he meant that farmers could make good use of their time by beating their flax and threshing and winnowing their wheat, rye, and barley.[43]

On several days during the summer months, Benjamin lost the labor of Ira and Hiram because of their obligation to attend militia training. From time to time Benjamin himself — like so many of his neighbors — would take the opportunity to watch the local regimental muster. There were three days that Benjamin particularly honored: July 4, August 16, and the first Tuesday in September — freeman's day. On the Fourth of July he regularly joined a procession of "democratic republicans" as they marched from the State Arms Tavern on Courthouse Hill to the meetinghouse to hear a prayer by Reverend Marsh, a reading of the Declaration of Independence by a prominent town leader, and songs from the galleries. Following that, the procession returned to the State Arms to sing patriotic songs, enjoy a hearty banquet, and drink "genuine republican" toasts to the accompaniment of cannons discharged by the local artillery company. The celebration of the battle of Bennington on August 16 generally followed the same routine, but since celebrants attended from surrounding towns, it often involved greater numbers of people. Although the press of "business" occasionally kept Benjamin from participating in either of these celebrations, he never missed the freemen's meeting in September, where he unfailingly cast his "weight" on the "democratic side of the scales."[44]

Benjamin's undeviating loyalty to the "democratic" party sprang from an intense devotion to the egalitarian principles of republicanism bred into him by Harwood family tradition. For the Harwoods, as for so many of their Bennington neighbors, republicanism existed as a social fact — a habit or a way of thought that helped to shape both their consciousness and their behavior. As Benjamin saw it, fidelity to American republicanism and allegiance to the Democratic-Republican Party of Thomas Jefferson were one and the same. For this reason he expressed disillusionment after the freemen's meeting in 1805 when "in this town it seems that Federalism is gaining ground."[45]

Federalist activities prior to the annual town meetings, held the last Wednesday of March, created increased consternation for Benjamin. Before one such meeting, Colonel David Robinson, a stalwart Republican, rode up "in great haste" to warn Benjamin that Captain Moses Robinson Jr., one of the town's leading Federalists, was actively campaigning to be elected first selectman. The colonel wanted to be certain that Benjamin had not been taken in by the captain's sly tactics. Knowing the captain to be an "Adams federalist," Benjamin swore that "men of that description I shall ever oppose as candidates for any office whatever."[46] Nonetheless, much to the chagrin of Benjamin, Robinson won the position he sought. The following year brought even greater political distress for Benjamin. He considered all elections that year — presidential, congressional, gubernatorial, and state legislative — vulnerable to Federalist manipulations of the volatile issue of the Embargo of 1807.[47] Much to his chagrin, while visiting Troy on business, he found "such a display of federalism here, that I felt quite disgusted with it." In fact, he believed that were the merchants of Troy compared "with those virtuous patriots who in 1774 agreed not [to] import any goods from England or her dependencies — until she would restore the rights of the people of America, which they had so unjustly invaded [we] shall find a most shameful degeneracy in the conduct of this class of men." In Benjamin's view the present times were alarming; since Federalists clearly meant to go to any lengths to regain power, "Republicans must be vigilant — self-government is our sole dependence — Reason must combat with passion — and we must take care that the former is not defeated by the latter."[48]

The following year Benjamin had every reason to be optimistic. When attendance at the Republican celebration of August 16, 1809, far exceeded that of the Federalist gathering, he proudly declared, "Democracy was triumphant this day." He exulted at being "among the enemies of aristocracy and monarchy—and the friends of the rights of man." When his close friend Anthony Haswell, editor of Bennington's Republican newspaper, read a letter from John Stark, commander of the American forces during the battle of Bennington, Benjamin praised its sentiments as "rousing to every republican who breathes american air." Although he joined in the procession to the State Arms Tavern, he found himself "among those who felt the want of pocket lining so much that I considered myself unable to be at the expense of a public dinner." Nonetheless, he stayed to take a glass of wine with his "brethren" and to join in toasts and songs that cheered the soul of every "true whig."[49] Such sentiments apparently swayed the majority of Bennington freemen that September—Isaac Tichenor failed to carry the town in his bid for reelection—but the Federalist leader did win the statewide vote by a handsome margin. Clearly, Federalism would remain a constant irritant to Benjamin's peace of mind.

෴ Work required on the farm during the months of October and November quickly diverted Benjamin's mind from politics. The fall harvest not only involved arduous labor but was itself a race against time; a variety of crops vital to the well-being of the farm had to be secured before the onset of winter. Hundreds of bushels of potatoes must be dug, thousands of beans must be pulled, flax must be dressed, and cartloads of pumpkins must be gathered. Above all, fields of corn had to be harvested, and thousands of bushels of apples must be picked and stored for the winter or pressed into cider. During bad weather the Harwood men would thresh the grain crops that had been gathered and stored in the barn during the summer months. Cornhuskings composed of neighborhood men and boys often lasted until midnight.

All of these tasks coming within the space of a few weeks put added pressure on Benjamin, a man constantly aware that the "deadly yellow" of the surrounding forests was a sure sign that winter was not far off.[50] Of all the chores facing him, it was the cider business that drove him most unmercifully. Very often he and his help had to pick by moonlight in order to get an orchard cleared of apples. Just as often, after "much solicitation," he was able to obtain "some assistance from the females in this business." It seemed, however, that whenever he took his eye off the young people helping him, "in a few moments all was play." Worse, his father occasionally found trees that had been overlooked and never hesitated to express "much displeasure to think that so much must have been lost if he had not made a search and found them." As a result Benjamin felt "much harried by my work at present."[51]

The cider mill itself caused Benjamin the most grief. By constantly breaking down, it "brought on more plagues and hinderances that greatly harrassed my mind." Such problems usually happened when there were a thousand bushels of apples waiting to be made into cider for anxious customers. Little wonder then that Benjamin felt "hurried out of my senses." Finally, one day, with three acres of corn yet to be harvested, manure to be spread, wood to be cut, and all of his cider as well as that of a neighbor's to be pressed before the advent of winter, he confessed that "my business drives me terribly." He considered it a "plague to be so harrassed and drove about by work, as I am now"; under such conditions "a man does not enjoy himself day nor night."[52]

Even before the season's cider had been pressed, Benjamin, his brothers, and Hiram were busy storing it in casks in the cellars of their own houses, selling it to nearby merchants, delivering it to individual customers, or taking it to nearby stills to have it made into brandy. Only when this was completed could Benjamin feel that he would "not be driven so much as in past weeks."[53] Regardless of the intensity of the harvest season, Benjamin never failed to acknowledge with pride that August 18 was the day in 1761 that Peter first settled in Bennington and that the "farm on which we reside is the same one the old gentleman pitched upon." Nor did he ignore how hard his father continued to work on the farm. Benjamin swore that Peter often "takes hold of business as though he had just entered his 25th year."[54]

The fact that he could not describe his own son's work habits in the same manner never ceased to trouble Benjamin. Sharing his father's fierce commitment to develop the farm, he faced a difficult problem. When Peter decided that Benjamin would assume responsibility for the farm, he made his choice from among seven sons. Benjamin did not enjoy such an option; Hiram was his only son. The pressure upon Benjamin was thereby intense. He must mold Hiram into an industrious, responsible worker in order to ensure the perpetuation of the Harwood farm — the family's very reason for being. Benjamin must shape Hiram into a man. Manhood for Benjamin meant becoming a husband and father, securing a competence, and developing into a responsible member of the community. Most of all, though, it meant hard work. As he saw it, work formed the very core of adult manhood. Diligence—the steadfast pursuit of useful labor—marked the man. When a man lost the ability to contribute to the well-being of his family and his community, but most particularly his family, he became a useless dependent. He was for all intents and purposes emasculated.[55]

Not only Hiram's lack of ambition, but also his carelessness in matters of business, which often led to the loss of time or equipment, or both, was a constant source of frustration for Benjamin—a man who carefully calculated his margin of profit and loss. Benjamin's anxiety over the financial welfare of the farm became particularly acute during the fall harvest season, when he had to stay abreast of grain prices in Troy that largely determined his margin of profit for the entire year. And yet, in some years the pressure of mounting debts forced him to sell his grain in a bad market. Thus, in September 1806, even though the price of wheat in Troy was unusually low, Benjamin believed that he must carry his grain there in order "to stop the mouths of my creditors."[56] The following month Ira made three trips to Troy with a total of 65 bushels of wheat and 9 bushels of rye and flaxseed. After the final trip, nearly one-half of the Harwood debt to merchants in Troy, which amounted to $60.00, had been paid. When Benjamin took a load of 24 bushels of wheat to Troy early in November, he paid off the entirety of this debt. At the same time, though, after purchasing essential items such as salt, sugar, tea, pepper, spices, and ginger, he left Troy owing various merchants a total of $28.00, "payable next spring." In an effort to reduce that debt, Benjamin made two trips to Troy in February with a total of 52 bushels of wheat. However, when he discovered the price to be lower than expected, he stored his grain with a local merchant to await a rise in the price.[57]

Marketing grain in Troy was not the only means by which the Harwoods gained an income. Benjamin sold seed wheat—calculated at the current price at Troy—to neighbors and marketed meat to merchants and private individuals in town. His wife and daughters sold "a considerable quantity of butter" to merchants as well. To his consternation, Benjamin could never be certain how much butter had been sold, because "the women have the care of that," and like so many farm women in New England, they kept no records.[58] The cider mill was also the source of a steady income, although most of Benjamin's neighbors paid him in goods or services rather than cash. Even when he sold numerous hogsheads of cider to local merchants, he generally took payment partly in cash and partly in goods. As a consequence, he did not handle much money. Quite often this posed a serious problem. In order to pay his property taxes, his ministerial rate, and merchants in Bennington and Troy, Benjamin needed cash. The farm annually brought in from $200 to $300, but much of this was in goods and services.[59] Therefore, he often had to borrow money on short-term credit from one affluent Bennington resident to pay another. So he found himself perpetually in debt.

Regardless of their own financial situation, the Harwoods never wavered in their commitment to Christian charity. Whether it was an "old drunken man" quite "noisy and saucy," young men looking for work, a "crazy person" in the form of a "distressed looking" woman, or traveling peddlers, the Harwoods turned no one away from their door.[60] All received food and drink; those who needed lodging enjoyed it as well. Since peddlers were men of business, the Harwoods generally asked them to pay for having their animals foddered. An individual's race, status, or ethnic background mattered not at all: Ishmael Titus, a "man of color," joined the Harwoods for dinner after having been turned away by more affluent neighbors; they examined the credentials of an Italian man soliciting aid for several of his countrymen imprisoned in Algiers and immediately gave him twenty-five cents in specie; a tenant on the Van Rensselaer manor in New York whose house had been destroyed by fire received their aid even though she had no credentials to support her story.[61]

Although he was always willing to open his home to strangers and to help his neighbors in any manner he could, Benjamin's charity was not always judgment-free. When two Connecticut peddlers dealing in patent medicine left his house one morning, he mused: "Jockies — I conclude — all jockies come from pious Connecticut." Another time, when a family visited in a carriage driven by a white servant, Benjamin recalled that "these words have just popped into my head; slavery — hide thy hideous head — thou who makest unnatural distinctions between men!" Benjamin saved his strongest condemnation, however, for individuals who drank to excess. When he hired two men to dress flax for him, he soon observed that they "cannot allow cider to remain confined in the cask, but will let it run down their parched throats." Indeed, they "liberated" more than three gallons of his cider in the space of a single afternoon. Benjamin was not upset about the cider — he always supplied his workers with rum or cider — but he did object mightily to "how like beasts they will act, when they do not govern themselves." On another occasion, while splitting wood for a neighbor,

Benjamin suffered some "very insipid company" when two "drunken vagabonds" called at the Nortons' and "filled themselves with cider." Benjamin deeply resented how such men "sink themselves beneath the dignity of beasts by yielding to some ignoble passion." It was his distinct opinion that "some place of confinement ought to be provided for such worthless people." Were that done, "we should be rid of their company" and would then be able "to confer our charity on those that merit it more."[62]

❧ The variety of tasks performed on the Harwood farm during the winter months of December, January, February, and March shrank considerably; the amount of labor and time expended upon these chores depended entirely upon weather conditions. Three primary duties had to be accomplished during this season: cutting and transporting firewood, tending the livestock, and threshing the grain stored in the barn. It was not unusual during this time for Benjamin simply to recall a day being "so stormy that I did no business except to cut some wood and take care of my cattle."[63]

Wood was a constant source of concern. The two houses consumed more than one hundred loads of wood each year, which involved much time and effort. It also created anxiety over future shortages of wood for fuel and building purposes. One way in which Benjamin attempted to conserve fuel was to move the occupants of his house upstairs early in December. The women could use the fireplace in the main kitchen on the ground floor only on "washing days." Although this certainly saved firewood, it caused the women considerable inconvenience and created cramped quarters for everyone concerned. Finally, one day early in March, when Diadama's "uneasiness could stand it no longer," she and the other women moved back downstairs. Unalterably opposed to such action and convinced that wood "is scarce especially on this farm and if we are not very saving in the use of it in a few years we shall have none at all," Benjamin was determined that his family "should be willing to dispense with many conveniences for the sake of saving wood." He therefore "wholly disapprove[d] of Mrs. Harwood's conduct in moving into this room at this time." Diadama remained adamant in her determination to move the entire family downstairs. And, Benjamin's objections aside, there all members remained. The power of the patriarch apparently did not extend its sway over the domestic hearth.[64]

The winter season brought anxieties about Benjamin's supply of fuel and fodder, but it also brought with it a measure of relaxation and celebration. The first Thursday in December, a day of thanksgiving annually proclaimed by Vermont's governor, meant special services in the meetinghouse and a bountiful turkey dinner at home with the family and guests gathered around the table. The season also included sleigh rides and visits with neighbors. It was not unusual for Benjamin's house to be "uncommonly thronged with company." In the course of such neighborly visits, there were singing, music, and storytelling that often made "a 12 o'clock evening short." During slack times Hiram even had time to attend exhibitions at the courthouse or to view "a noted criminal" standing in the pillory or receiving stripes at the whipping post.[65]

Often during stormy winter days, after the cattle had been foddered and enough wood had been split to keep the fires going, Benjamin would either read or listen as Hiram read aloud to the entire family. History books held a particular fascination for Benjamin and his son. When Hiram returned their borrowed copy of William Gordon's history of the American Revolution, he brought back a history of Connecticut. Two years later, Benjamin acquired his own copy of Gordon, a particular favorite of his, while trading in Troy. During other visits to that town, he purchased a large quarto Bible, Jedidiah Morse's gazetteers, and William Perry's dictionary. For a man who carefully watched every expenditure, these volumes must have been as "necessary for every good housekeeper" as the salt, sugar, tea, pepper, spice, and ginger he went into debt to obtain.[66]

Newspapers were even more essential to Benjamin's life than books were. He took seriously his obligation to be an informed citizen and believed that every freeman had a responsibility to read as widely in newspapers as possible. As a result, he seriously doubted a neighbor who attempted to tell him about an incident in one of the Carolinas because the man "takes no newspapers, and therefore may have been imposed upon." When another man, who did not "inquire into the state of political affairs much," informed him during the furor over the embargo that he did not read newspapers because they were so full of lies, Benjamin was appalled. Convinced that such behavior played directly into Federalist hands, he was sure that should Federalists ever succeed in keeping newspapers away from the general populace, they would soon be able to "accomplish that [which] they now know to be impossible [political control of the nation]." To prevent this, "every man that feels himself interested in the cause of liberty will take a newspaper."[67]

Benjamin subscribed to the *Republican Farmer*, a Danbury, Connecticut, paper pledged to support "true republican principles," and the *Vermont Gazette*, Bennington's own Jeffersonian newspaper, edited by Anthony Haswell, an egalitarian democrat. He also had ready access to the *Philadelphia Aurora*, which Hiram borrowed regularly from Colonel Fay. In addition, he read individual issues of a wide variety of newspapers that neighbors managed to acquire in their travels.

Firmly committed to the importance of an informed citizenry, Benjamin intended that his children should be well educated and therefore took his responsibility as a resident of the local school district quite seriously. He always made it a point to attend the annual district meeting responsible for selecting the district's teacher and establishing that individual's salary. In addition, he supplied firewood to the schoolhouse during the term, which usually lasted from early December into the first week of February.

Benjamin would not, however, be imposed upon. When a rump session of Federalists appointed a teacher without calling a general meeting of the district, Benjamin withdrew his children from the school. Principle and interest coincided in this decision: he objected to the fact that the school commenced in so undemocratic a manner and did not wish to pay the disproportionate share of the teacher's salary that would fall to him when the majority of his neighbors refused to send their children to the school. Shortly after taking Hiram, Lydia, and Diadama out of school, Benjamin attended a very full meeting that discontinued the school set up by a "small part of the district only and against the minds of the majority of which I was one."[68]

Benjamin and his neighbors would not tolerate elitists, nor would they suffer fools. Not long after a new schoolmaster, who had presented himself as a scholar of both English and Latin grammar, began to teach their children, district residents manifested serious second thoughts. When the Norton family asked the new teacher to read aloud during a visit to their house, he blushed upon taking the book and "made a wretched work of reading — hamming — stammering & spelling & hitching along in a cruel manner — like a beginner." Students often reported how easily they could trip up their teacher regarding the rules of English grammar, and Benjamin himself was appalled at the man's spelling when he wrote out exercises for the students to copy. For "holy" he wrote "holey," for "Sabbath" "saboth," for "few" "fue," for "Hiram" "Hyram." Believing that "never were men worse imposed upon than those of this school district," Benjamin and the families involved called a special school meeting to discuss the matter. The assembled men closely examined the teacher's handwriting and spelling and unanimously voted to dismiss the schoolmaster immediately.[69]

Since Hiram was his only son and would thereby take over the farm one day, Benjamin was determined that he should be as well educated as possible. He continued to send him to district school even after Hiram turned twenty-one. However, fully aware of the deficiencies of many local schoolmasters and equally conscious of the necessity for young men to learn grammar if they were to improve their position in society, Benjamin made special arrangements for Hiram to study English grammar with Dr. Noadiah Swift's store clerk.[70] Benjamin took personal responsibility for teaching Hiram mathematics. Each evening, whether common school was in session or not, Benjamin drilled his son in arithmetic.

Benjamin's determination to improve Hiram was unceasing. Perhaps nowhere was this more evident than in the manner in which he kept his journal. Claiming to be "a plain old farmer," Benjamin declared that he kept his diary "for myself, not for the public or individuals."[71] In this statement Benjamin was not being entirely candid; Hiram remained very much on his mind. In fact, during the summer of 1806, Benjamin made a decision that transformed the journal into yet another method of instilling discipline into his son: he made Hiram his scribe. From this time on, Hiram assumed responsibility for transcribing Benjamin's every thought into the diary, either from notes or from dictation.

The anxiety now suffered by Hiram was even greater than Benjamin's constant distress over his efforts to shape his son into a disciplined worker. Every day now he had to enter into the journal observations such as "Hiram did but little," "Hiram did nothing worthy of notice," or Hiram was "careless," had a "poor disposition to work," and was "a poor recommendation for a young man of 22." Not only must he record that his father's hopes for him rested "on a sandy foundation," but he also had to enter the utterly frank opinions his father expressed on the occasion of his twenty-first birthday. Like Benjamin, the journal became an unrelenting taskmaster.

The same mixture of love and stern utilitarianism that characterized Benjamin's relationship with Hiram also shaped his behavior toward Ira, Jonas, and his youngest sister, Lucy. Jonas and Ira were the mainstay of Benjamin's labor force, but since they would not inherit any of Peter's land, they had to make their own way in the world. Consequently, in

February 1807 both men loaded their families and all their worldly goods on sleds and left for Hopkinton, New York, where they intended to take up their own farms. Prior to their departure, Benjamin did everything he could to help them. This included borrowing eighty-five dollars to purchase needed supplies and to help get them settled on their new farms. Nearly a month passed before word came that Ira and Jonas had arrived safely in Hopkinton and moved their families into "comfortable" houses. Because Ira had been in poor health before his departure, Benjamin and his family were particularly relieved to hear of his safe arrival. Three months later, however, their relief turned to concern upon receiving news that Ira lay "at the point of death." Nearly a month after that, they learned that after having been delirious since late April, Ira was growing better and intended to return home to regain his health. Benjamin received this news with mixed emotions. He rejoiced to hear that Ira was still alive, but "how much greater my joy would be to hear of his having recovered so as to be able to provide for his family." From a purely practical point of view, Benjamin realized that "his misfortunes are mine & my misfortunes are my own." In any event he felt that he had no choice except to "resign myself entirely to the will of providence — If my lot be hard, I must submit to it cheerfully."[72]

While Benjamin pondered the economic future of the farm, Peter traveled to Hopkinton to bring his youngest son home. They arrived a week later with Ira much fatigued and in bad health. Indeed, Ira was a "good deal unwell — crazy at night." Gradually he regained his health and by mid-August was able to help out with the harvest, although not with his previous vigor. As a result, most of the labor fell to Benjamin and Hiram. At the end of a particularly hard day, Benjamin felt "much fatigued & low spirited." He began worrying about the "many debts I shall be obliged to pay within a few months & how little my income — and how much there is of helping my brothers — the gloomy prospect of getting anything to do it with." Such "thoughts made a deep impression on my mind today — so much that I felt much dejected."[73]

Just when matters seemed so desperate, Benjamin received a letter from Jonas complaining of poor crops and requesting aid to purchase wheat so that his family would not have to subsist on Indian corn. Benjamin decided not to acquiesce. He believed that Jonas "can live without wheat this year as well as myself — he must pinch a little." Since Jonas "used to keep a richer table here than I thought I was able to support, especially in his situation of life — without any farm," Benjamin resolved to "let him see the effects of it." It was "not that I would have him or his family suffer for the necessaries of life, but let him be taught that people can & do live without every luxury the world affords."[74] Doubtless these words were meant as much for his scribe as for Jonas.

The next day "a very important question presented itself" to Benjamin's mind: would it be best for Ira to return to Hopkinton, or should his family be moved back to the homestead? When he presented this matter to his father and then to the other family members, they all agreed "for the good of the whole that his family should be brought back to reside in this place." Everyone believed that "Ira's constitution" was simply "too slender to admit of his clearing up a new farm."[75]

On March 1, 1808, Ira's family arrived at the farm and two days later assumed occupancy of the old slab house. Within a month of their return, Benjamin, already distressed about the decision that moved him and his family into his father's house, became seriously concerned about his brother's health. Ira worked diligently at plowing one morning but could do no work that afternoon. Knowing that Ira had labored extremely hard the previous day, Benjamin worried that he had "perhaps took some cold which has brought on some of his former pains occasioned by the sickness he underwent last spring." In any event, it was clear to Benjamin that Ira's "constitution was so much impaired at that time, that he will never be able to endure hard labor, or the inclemency of the weather as he could before."[76]

Matters soon became even more troubling. Benjamin began to receive letters from merchants in Troy threatening to prosecute Jonas if his debts were not paid. Intent upon shielding his brother from legal action, Benjamin traveled to Troy, only to discover that Jonas owed much more there than he had been led to believe. He paid what he could and signed notes for the rest. Very upset, Benjamin vowed that had Jonas "been unfortunate — his crops blasted — his family sick, or distressed by fire — in any such case I should have no reason to feel as I do — But it was not so — he has been lavish and imprudent — and were it not for his family's sake he might suffer the consequences of it without receiving any assistance from me."[77] Again, his hope may have been that his words would not be lost on his son.

Benjamin assumed an equally critical and even more patriarchal stance toward his sister Lucy's relationship with James Waterman, a journeyman shoemaker who had been employed for a time by their neighbor Thomas Parsons. Against the advice of friends and family, Lucy was determined to marry the young man. After she obtained permission from Peter, who had never met Waterman, Benjamin felt compelled to speak candidly with her. He told her in no uncertain terms that if she married Waterman, "she was ruined — if she had any property it would go to pay his debts." In addition, Benjamin pointed out that even though the man had accumulated many debts, he "earned very little if anything through the whole winter — idling away his time in drinking — and making poor bargains." Worse, he was "fond of being in company — which precipitated him into many foolish extravagances — detrimental to his character & interest."[78] In spite of this and against the advice of Benjamin's wife Diadama, Lucy remained adamant. A thirty-one-year-old woman with no other prospects, she fully intended to marry Waterman.[79]

The wedding took place on February 6, 1809, in the front room of Peter Harwood's house. As Benjamin recalled the event, "in the evening there was a wedding in our house, at which I was not present because it was not agreeable to me." He simply "could not bear to be a witness of the compact, which according to my feelings was to be the consequence of turning my sister away from a good home to depend on a husband, whom if one may judge from his past conduct, is scarcely able of supporting himself decently."[80] The day after the wedding, Waterman left for Cooperstown, New York, where he intended to take up farming.

Regardless of his feelings about the wedding, Benjamin considered himself duty-bound to live up to the agreement he had made with his father years before when it was decided that he was to have the farm. He had paid all the heirs except Lucy the shares decided upon at that time and subsequently remained proprietor of her property. Now that Lucy was married, Peter objected to giving her any property, but Benjamin remained determined to fulfill his obligation. However, knowing that Waterman's creditors would likely seize whatever goods he gave to Lucy, he had her sign an agreement witnessed by three neighbors that she received this property as a loan. Believing that he had protected the wagonload of household goods by legally retaining them in his own name, Benjamin sent Lucy off with a driver to join her husband in New York. He then proceeded to the meetinghouse to attend a special service of fasting and prayer called by the Congregational Church.

Several hours later Ira entered the church and informed Benjamin that the sheriff had stopped Lucy on the road and brought her and the wagon back into town in response to a complaint brought by Jonathan Hunt, one of Bennington's most affluent merchants. Benjamin hurried to the wagon, where he found Hunt rummaging through its contents. He informed the man of the status of the goods, but Hunt ignored him and even went so far as to pry up the lid of a chest that had been nailed down. Determined to behave in a lawful manner, Benjamin sought the advice of an attorney, who advised him that he was on solid legal grounds and should let the law take its course. Nonetheless, when Peter learned of the matter, he went into a "most violent passion — he re-nounced Mr. Hunt at once — on whom he used to bestow some favors — but now declared that these should never be renewed." In addition, "Waterman shared equally the lash of his tongue. He had never entertained with him — and always was strenuously opposed to giving Lucy anything — after she was married to him." Benjamin him-self remained deeply troubled. "A great many things came into my mind after I went to bed, so that sleep was driven from my eyes. All this work was new to me — having never had a lawsuit against any man before in my life, but I found myself now in a situation where it was almost impossible for me to avoid it."[81]

When the two men met on the street the following day, Hunt of-fered to relinquish two-thirds of the debt if Benjamin would pay the remaining third. Benjamin refused; he simply would have no part of Waterman's debts. Instead, he proceeded to his attorney's office and engaged the man to take out a writ against Hunt if he failed to return the property. As the matter dragged on, Benjamin remained anxious to solve the problem out of court and went to see Mr. Hunt personally. The man remained determined "to stand a lawsuit," and Benjamin left the meeting with the same resolution: "Fairly, I settle; unfairly, I leave it to an impartial jury to decide." On the day the matter was to be taken up in court, though, Hunt drew Benjamin aside and suggested that the matter go to referees instead. After consulting his attorney, Benjamin agreed. Finally, on May 22, 1810, Hunt came to Benjamin and agreed to return all the goods that he had taken. Each man would pay his own counsel. Benjamin consented and immediately wrote Waterman that he could have the goods on the same terms as previously outlined. He also informed the young man that he had best not show his face in Bennington unless he was able to pay all his creditors. On August 21, 1810, Lucy set out with the goods to join her husband at their home near Cooperstown, New York.[82]

⌒ This, then, was the world of Benjamin Harwood — a world de-voted to the Harwood farm and bounded largely by the parameters of

Tanbrook. Its customs sprang from the time-honored and deeply entrenched traditions of localism, Strict Congregationalism, republicanism, and patriarchy. The values attributed to these traditions were the values Benjamin wished to pass on to his son. Given his intense devotion to the future existence of the farm, however, the standards that Benjamin associated most closely with patriarchy assumed particular saliency for him at this time. In order to prepare Hiram to assume the role of the patriarch — so essential to the perpetuation of the Harwood farm — Benjamin believed he had to ingrain within him a sense of responsibility to the land and to the family. To accomplish this, he must transmit his own single-minded intensity, his highly disciplined work ethic, to his son. These were the personal characteristics he most wanted to instill in Hiram.

And yet, Benjamin probably conveyed more to his son than simply his intense will to preserve the farm. What, for example, must have passed through Hiram's mind when asked one December day to transcribe his father's description of the weather as a "picture of human life — the sky being clear in the morning — the sun gently warming the air — everything wearing the pleasantest aspect that can be conceived at this season; but this was succeeded by clouds before midday — by raw chilly wind in the P.M. & ended in thick clouds & rain with the day."[83] The fatalism embedded within such an observation, combined with the melancholic temperament from which it sprang, may have been as much a part of Benjamin's legacy to his son as his disciplined work ethic and iron-willed devotion to the success of the Harwood farm. Only time would reveal which of the father's traits would most deeply affect the son.

2

A Man of Pleasure

Twenty two — hah — and not better educated, better informed of the ways of mankind than if he had inhabited some lonely cottage on the Green Mountain — What! I keep a journal of such a life as I live! without anything of an enterprising nature to record — must I bear witness against myself — of my folly — ignorance and sloth — Yes, perhaps by keeping these things in remembrance, I shall learn to shun some snares that, without this admonition, I might heedlessly fall into. I certainly desire to improve in every undertaking that I may pursue.[1]

    With this observation, made on his twenty-second birthday, October 23, 1810, Hiram assumed complete responsibility for the journal begun by his father over five years earlier. And yet the imprint of the father remained clearly visible in the son's entry. To describe himself as lacking in enterprise — as foolish, ignorant, and slothful — was to adopt as his own the very characterizations employed by his father over the previous five years. Hiram even used Benjamin's precise language when he noted that no matter how bungling his effort to maintain a journal might be, it certainly "keeps me out of mischief."[2] If by having Hiram serve as his scribe for several years, Benjamin failed to instill a well-disciplined work ethic in his son, he had certainly succeeded in impressing upon the young man an acute awareness of his own shortcomings. Living with his parents in his grandfather's home, Hiram was a painfully self-conscious twenty-two-year-old adolescent entirely shorn of self-confidence.

    In Hiram's hands the journal begun by Benjamin gradually assumed the character of a personal diary and commonplace book rather than a farm daybook.[3] Attention to weather conditions, crop prices, and the condition of the livestock increasingly gave way to personal introspection. Hiram's hopes, fears, anxieties, and self-appraisals occupied more and more of his attention; in many ways these personal concerns unfolded not simply in the journal but through it. His journal became more and more a book or text of self, an instrument of self-fashioning in which he attempted to find or create a personal identity.[4] As in so many commonplace books and diaries of the time, the tone of Hiram's writing could have resulted from inner conflicts that reflected the tension between his father's expectations of him and his own personal desires and sensibilities. Viewed from this perspective, the diary represented an effort either to resolve or to hold in check this disequilibrium in his life.[5] Above all else, it revealed Hiram's efforts to achieve manhood — to take his place as an adult member of the Harwood household.

Regardless of who kept the journal or the form that it assumed, farm work remained the consuming occupation of all the Harwoods. Hiram may have written about them less, but he still had to perform the same day-to-day tasks as always. Determined by the seasons and altered only by the weather, these duties were unrelenting. So, too, were his parents and his grandfather. The fact that he had reached his majority made no difference to them; he continued to be subject to their critical judgment. Even at the age of twenty-two, Hiram had by no means achieved the status of an independent adult.[6]

Benjamin and his father never hesitated to criticize Hiram's work habits or to reprimand him for personal behavior that they considered irresponsible. Neither man could understand Hiram's careless attitude toward "business." When asked to drive a flock of sheep out of the wheat field, he enjoyed "a sweet solitary march in the forest"; when attending the local school with his sisters, he simply turned their horse loose — saddle, bridle, and all — to find its way home and to run the risk of being lost or stolen; when asked to bring in the sheep, he lagged far behind playing a tune on his flute, with no concern for where his charges might be; when asked to watch a flock of lambs, his carelessness allowed one to be bitten to death by a horse.[7]

Such behavior exasperated the older men. Frustrated by his son's attitude toward work, Benjamin exploded in anger at the dinner table when Hiram expressed regret at missing the local performance of several plays because he had to attend to business on the farm that day.

Then one Sunday morning, when charged with bringing water from the brook for the family's tea, Hiram stopped off at Ira's house to read. The "tide of anger" ran so high against him at home that Benjamin came to Ira's, tore the pail from Hiram's grasp, and, despite his son's protestations, fetched the water himself. Another time, when Hiram's slackness caused extended delays in getting the day's work started, his father became so angry that he flung the yoke over the barnyard gate when he went to harness the oxen.[8]

It was work in the fields, however, that most concerned Benjamin and Peter. Once, during the rush at the end of a long day in the hayfield, Benjamin, declaring that he could throw the load on much quicker, ripped Hiram's pitchfork out of his hands and took over his son's task. This gave Peter the perfect opportunity to deride Hiram about his ability as a worker. Expressing disbelief that a man of fifty could pitch hay faster than a man of twenty-three, he exclaimed that he once pitched a ton of hay in five minutes when it looked like rain. Such an outburst was not uncommon; Peter nearly always blamed Hiram's laziness for the family's failure to get hay in before a shower.[9] But it was the very example of his father and his grandfather that most troubled Hiram. Their tireless industry, their intense devotion to farm and family, stood as a constant indictment of him. To disciples of the Old Testament like the Harwoods, laziness was one of the gravest of sins.

Whether Hiram viewed himself as a sinner or not, he did very much want to please his father. He was therefore extremely sensitive to Benjamin's reactions to his blunders about the farm. At times Hiram described the temper his father vented upon him as a "high pitch of flaming wrath," the "highest possible pitch of enthusiastic rage," or delivered in such a manner as to be "impossible for me to do anything like describing." At other times Benjamin responded in a more subtle manner. Once, when Hiram arrived late for work in the morning, Benjamin observed only that Hiram must be a "man of business" to be so hurried in his affairs. "Sensible to the keenness of the ironical gibe," Hiram went directly to work.[10]

Subtle or direct, Benjamin's critique of Hiram struck home. The son internalized his father's expressed perceptions and developed a low opinion of his own character and abilities. Called before his father once for lingering in town rather than attending to chores on the farm, Hiram recalled that "when I appeared before my judge I was suffered to pass with a slight blessing — perhaps not the half of what I deserved." Another day he felt "low-spirited — thought very meanly of my performance in the business of the day—believed my father had reason for hating his son on that account."[11]

So thoroughly did Hiram absorb his father's criticism that he confided to his diary that he intended to record some things "characteristic of myself." He then proceeded to describe an incident that occurred one evening after the sheep had been sheared. His grandfather, fearful that a rainstorm was coming that night, wanted the sheep gathered up and brought into the barn. "Tired and full of vexation," he approached Hiram, who was "enjoying the pleasures flowing from the sound of the flute," and in a "hard tone" asked why he was lying about "whistling" when there was urgent work to be done. Taking his flute with him, Hiram obeyed his grandfather's command to bring the sheep in before nightfall. After a leisurely stroll, Hiram finally found the flock and got it headed in the general direction of the barn. He did not, however, pay close attention. Instead he concentrated on playing his flute while the sheep scattered about once more. Well after dark, Hiram, with the fortuitous help of a friend, managed to get the sheep into the barn. After the flock had been secured, Hiram's father turned to him and exclaimed, "If you had been a boy—you would have had a fine shaking"; he angrily concluded by advising Hiram to "try to be a man or a boy—I would be one or the other." Seemingly unaware of the passive-aggressive nature of his response to his grandfather's demands, Hiram confided to his diary only that the incident "reflects disgrace on its author."[12]

Hiram's mother, too, did not hesitate to criticize her son openly and often. If his father had shaken Hiram when he misbehaved as a boy, his mother had been more severe. Describing himself as a "bad boy" when young, Hiram recalled "deserving and getting many floggings" from his mother.[13] In any event, Diadama, like her husband, no longer punished Hiram like a child; instead she delivered telling verbal stripes. When, for example, he dallied at Ira's instead of bringing water for the family's morning tea, Hiram arrived home fully expecting to find an "enraged mother." Instead, employing a number of "ironical expressions," she promised to inform one of Hiram's female friends of his "unmanly behavior in this as well as in other instances." Another time, taking the same approach, Diadama upbraided him for his shiftlessness and lectured him on how such conduct would affect the feelings of a wife, "were I ever to have one." Then she threatened that if she could ever discover who that woman might be, she would "describe my character to her in full." Hiram's worst blow, however, came when he and his mother had a conversation concerning his "abilities as to getting a living in the world" and she "rated them rather low." Since he always felt himself to be a "good way behind my contemporaries," Hiram was not able to take "very high ground" when defending himself to his mother. But "to be pushed down lower than the meanest of them all, was more than I could bear."[14]

When Hiram's mother spoke openly of his "unmanly behavior," threatened to share these attitudes with potential marriage partners, and "rated" his "abilities" "rather low," she was actively attempting to shame him into altering his behavior. When Benjamin tore the rake out of Hiram's hand and his grandfather scornfully observed that an old man of fifty could outperform a young man of twenty-three, they, too, were following the traditional practice of "shaming" employed by so many New England parents.[15] All of these actions paled in comparison to the excruciating experience Hiram began to endure when obliged to record his father's disparaging observations on his character as well as Benjamin's lack of confidence in his future. No doubt having his son serve as his scribe had also been a conscious tactic adopted by Benjamin to form his son's character, to shape him into a man.

Whatever sense of guilt or disappointment such efforts engendered in Hiram was compounded by his love for his mother and father. He deeply revered and respected his parents and desperately wanted to live up to their expectations. More important, he never doubted their love for him. His mother was particularly solicitous of him. When he suffered a debilitating ache in his jaw, she made a bed for him in front of the fire, tucked him in, and asked if he believed he would ever find a wife who would do as much for him. He replied that he did not think he ever would. On another occasion, when Hiram fell ill, Diadama comforted him in such a kindly manner that tears gushed to his eyes as he struggled to declare: "What a good thing it is to have so kind a mother."[16]

The death of Hiram's grandmother in October 1810 brought him even closer to his mother.[17] Impressed with the stolid patience with which Mary bore her sickness, Hiram observed that in her final hour, "when her soul was summoned to depart her body and fly to regions unknown — whence millions have gone and not one returned to tell us how they were received," she appeared "perfectly willing to go." She seemed even to "rejoice in death." Witnessing this "solemn scene — this picture of what we all must sooner or later be" — Hiram gained strength from those around him. Even though he had never seen a corpse, Hiram claimed that the sight of Mary did not "strike such a dread to me as I had always conceived that it would." Nonetheless, on the night following his grandmother's funeral, Hiram welcomed the opportunity to sit up late with his mother to discuss their mutual feelings about death. He drew welcome consolation from their similarity of sentiments and deeply appreciated his mother's sympathetic companionship on such occasions.[18]

Whenever Hiram ruminated about his deceased grandmother and his widowed grandfather, he desperately needed to "enjoy the present hour." In such moments, feelings for his family provided Hiram the most solace. Believing himself "blessed with a kind father, a tender mother and two sisters very dear to me," Hiram felt his family to be "placed here to associate together to alleviate the pains of an aged Father & Grandfather and administer comfort to him in his declining years."[19] If the family was a comfort to his grandfather, Hiram viewed it as the primary source of his own happiness and security — a safe haven in a world filled with challenges he felt incompetent to meet. And yet home and family bore different meanings for Hiram than for his grandfather and his father. To Benjamin and Peter these terms meant work, duty, and the achievement of a competency; for Hiram they meant above all else shared sensibilities.

Whatever the Harwood household meant to its family members, it was a place of hospitality for friends, relatives, and needy strangers who shared meals with the family and frequently spent the night with them as well. Such occasions could be quite enjoyable for Hiram; just as often, however, they became uncomfortable or embarrassing for him. Visits by Amos Bingham, an elder in the Congregational Church and a zealous advocate of New Light religious beliefs, were particularly upsetting to Hiram. The man always attempted to engage whomever he could in dialogues regarding the sanctity of their souls — a subject of particular dread for Hiram. For this reason he tried to avoid extended contact with the man whenever he was in the house.

One day this simply was not possible. When the family gathered for their ritual of morning prayer, Bingham read aloud from the Bible and expounded on the meaning of his chosen passage. Then, as Hiram later recalled, "prayer and breakfast being over, I thought myself at liberty to go about my business and, taking my hat, made off as fast as I could." Not so easily foiled, Bingham followed Hiram out of the kitchen, cornered him on the stoop, and facetiously asked if he belonged to the

Harwood family. Was he really Benjamin's son? Could he actually be Peter's grandson? When Hiram answered in the affirmative, Bingham expressed mock surprise. Why, then, was he so rarely seen in church? What did he truly think about religion? Did he not know that a "rational attention" must be paid to such matters? When Hiram replied that "no one could make himself a christian," that "every one acted, with respect to religion, as he thought right," Bingham vehemently declared that "a man's thinking himself right, did not make him so; sin was not justifiable; the carnal mind was at enmity against God; repentence and faith were necessary to the salvation of the soul." Hiram defended himself by pleading that he "never meant to be stubborn about the matter"; in all honesty, he genuinely "wished to be a believer."[20]

With this confrontation Bingham broached an extremely sensitive matter for Hiram. Was he ever to become a believer? Would he experience the saving grace that alone could bring him into the church covenant and save his soul? His grandfather was a founding member of the Bennington church, his father a stalwart in the Congregational Society. Would he ever take his place beside them? He did not want to disappoint them; he wanted to be a "believer." And yet, when or how would this come about? Worse yet, what was his fate if he did not, or could not, experience salvation?

Thoughts about death and eternity — the "unknown regions" to which "millions have gone and not one returned," the "solemn scene . . . of what we all must sooner or later be" — caused Hiram constant distress. Once, during a conversation with his cousin Ruth about the "Day of Judgement," his emotions became raised to "such a pitch as caused my blood to prickle in my veins."[21] And yet, just as he could not or would not become a disciplined worker no matter how much he wanted to please his father, Hiram could not bring himself to follow a conventional religious routine. On Sundays he read or wrote in his journal. On those rare occasions when he did attend church, often he "easily and unconsciously dropped into a pleasant sleep" during Reverend Marsh's sermons.[22] When not sleeping, he browsed through books he had brought with him or read his favorite newspaper. Such ambivalent behavior, so similar to his manner of responding to his grandfather's demands on the farm, may have been Hiram's way of dealing with the issue of saving grace and church membership.[23]

Hiram wanted to believe and, given his family's religious heritage as well as his respect for his parents' beliefs, was uncomfortable in his disbelief. When his sister Lydia jokingly asked him if the fanning mill being transported in a wagon he was driving was the Ark of the Covenant, he laughed and said it was. That night, however, the incident bothered him. Alone with his journal, he confessed that this was "joking a little too far—it was wicked and I am sorry for it." On other occasions, too, he could be moved—even by Reverend Marsh. During a funeral oration, the pastor "addressed himself so much to the passions" that Hiram "could not refrain from shedding tears."[24] But such instances were rare. Caught between Amos Bingham's insistence that he prepare himself for salvation by rigid adherence to formal church practices and Marsh's demands for ardent personal prayer, Hiram did neither. Convinced that every man should act "with respect to religion, as he thought right," Hiram did not know what was right. He realized full well how Amos Bingham demanded that he act. He also knew how his father and grandfather wanted him to behave on the farm. And yet, somehow, he could not. His personal impulses were at variance with their definitions of duty.

Quite often, even in the busiest of times, Hiram gave way to his own spontaneous inclinations and simply followed wherever they might lead. Just such a thing occurred one morning during harvest season when Hiram found himself charged with husking corn before breakfast. Having completed his task, he "felt an itching for music" and stopped off at Ira's house, where he "touched off" several favorite tunes on the flute. When his son arrived late at the breakfast table, Benjamin, anxious to get on with the main tasks of the day, sardonically remarked, "You are greatly hurried in your business—you ought to take an apprentice." Then, more directly: "You ought to be here at mealtime because it takes you longer to eat, than anybody in the family." Hiram realized that he had disappointed his father, and yet he believed, "like other young people, when they feel a strong desire for anything—it must be gratified,—to speak the language of their hearts."[25]

On Thanksgiving Day, a month later, Hiram declined his father's invitation to accompany him to church. Instead, he read a favorite book, wrote in his journal, copied tunes for his flute from a borrowed songbook, and sewed his file of the local newspaper into a single volume. When the family and guests sat down to dinner later in the day, Hiram slipped off to Ira's with his tune-book and flute. After taking supper with the children, Hiram spent a long time in Ira's house alone with his music. Later that evening, however, he confided to his diary that "I didn't feel right—somehow my mind was in an uneasy pickle."[26]

In attempting to articulate this sensation, he suggested that he was like other young people, who had a strong desire "to speak the language of their hearts." And yet even that did not adequately describe Hiram's feelings. Once, on a day in which he had felt "extremely dejected and down-hearted," Hiram arrived home "very much dissatisfied with my walk not having found that phantom which I so eagerly pursued."[27]

When Hiram claimed his mind to be in a "pickle," described his search after an elusive "phantom," or expressed his desire to speak the "language of his heart," he was doing his best to describe his feelings, to express the inner turmoil that plagued him constantly. In a time when a growing number of people were able to make lives for themselves that had not been possible previously, Hiram had no options except to remain a farmer. As lifelong friends and acquaintances broke away from their parents and left Bennington to attempt new and different careers, Hiram stayed on the family farm.[28] A sensitive young man who loved music, books, and plays — an individual whose intellectual curiosity led him to seek out whatever exhibitions came to Bennington — Hiram was severely conflicted. Regardless of his own personal desires or capabilities, as Benjamin's only son he was obligated to stay on the farm and devote his life to its future well-being. Always the loyal son, Hiram wanted desperately to please his parents. At the same time, he experienced the powerful urges of his own feelings. Trapped in a protracted adolescence, Hiram struggled to deal with this conflict — to maintain emotional stability and to forge a viable sense of self.

Whatever personal stability and self-identity Hiram did manage to achieve at this point in his life depended largely on his relationship with his Uncle Ira, his love of music and books, and the time he spent alone with his diary. Very often, when his mind was in a "pickle," Hiram sought out the solitude of Ira's house. Only five years older than Hiram, Ira occupied an anomalous position within the Harwood family quite similar to that of his nephew. Both had adult responsibilities in their work roles on the farm and yet occupied subordinate roles within the larger household. Even though married and ostensibly the head of his own house, Ira was at best only semiautonomous. He worked for shares and, like Hiram, faced the wrath of Benjamin and Peter whenever mistakes occurred or work did not go quite as efficiently as these men felt it should. Over time, a close bond developed between Hiram and his uncle, whose friendship and support helped immeasurably in Hiram's efforts to maintain his personal sense of well-being.[29]

The two men shared a passion for books and music, which were vital to Hiram's emotional stability. It was not unusual on Sundays for Hiram to take a table drawer with pen and ink, his flute, and a newspaper or book and simply go out into the woods to write, read, and play music for hours on end. When time or weather would not permit such an escape, he sought out Ira's house, where he spent many happy hours alone with his music and his thoughts. If Ira and his family happened to be home, Hiram still enjoyed himself immensely; his uncle welcomed the chance to read aloud with him, and Ira's family and friends danced enthusiastically to Hiram's favorite tunes on the flute.

Music was his "favorite amusement," but Hiram also found reading absolutely "delightful."[30] Of all the members of the Harwood family, Hiram was the most avid reader; he rarely went anywhere without taking reading material with him or seeking it out wherever he might stop. Although he was always happy to share his books with others and eager to investigate whatever reading material he might find elsewhere, Hiram did most of his reading in or around the family homestead. During the busy seasons, he snatched moments to read before breakfast, at noon, and by candlelight in the evening hours. Sundays and rainy days always meant ample leisure time; it was the long nights and stormy days of winter, though, that afforded him the best opportunity for reading.

Day in and day out, regardless of the season, Hiram was an inveterate newspaper reader. His father subscribed to the *Green Mountain Farmer* (published in Bennington in 1809–16 under the editorship of Anthony Haswell), and Judge David Fay gave Hiram all of his back issues of the *Philadelphia Aurora*. Hiram also obtained copies of the *National Intelligencer* on a regular basis from either Judge Fay or Jonathan Robinson. In addition, he read whatever other newspapers he managed to acquire. Hiram was not undiscriminating, however; he was a devoted Jeffersonian Republican. For that reason he particularly enjoyed Anthony Haswell's local paper and declared that he would not trade the *Aurora's* editor, William Duane, "for all the federal and many of the democratic editors on this Continent."[31] Hiram displayed amazing discipline and concern—quite unlike his attitude toward farm work—over the maintenance of his newspaper collection. On one occasion, when he went to sew his file of *Auroras* together, he discovered a single issue missing. Distraught, he "spent much precious time endeavoring to find it." When he could not locate it, he hurried over to Thomas Parsons' shop, where he often shared newspapers, and "ransacked one of his cupboards without being able to lay my paw on it."

Finally, he discovered the missing issue in his own newspaper chest. Only then could he get on with his day's business.[32]

Hiram was such an enthusiastic Jeffersonian that he even preserved a file of *Auroras* printed in the 1790s that he obtained from a neighbor. He enjoyed reading about the conflict between Thomas Jefferson and Alexander Hamilton over the National Bank. Consequently, when a neighbor loaned him a copy of the *Newsletter* (a Federalist paper published in Bennington during the years 1811–15), which he praised for its candor, Hiram disdainfully observed that the paper was only "as candid as the language of disappointed officer seekers could make it." He had the same low opinion of a Federalist orator's Independence Day address that he borrowed from a Federalist acquaintance. This diatribe against Thomas Jefferson seemed to him a "gloomy thing" indeed.[33]

When Hiram had time for more intensive reading, he turned to his favorite subjects—history, geography, and travel. He spent hours with William Guthrie's *New System of Modern Geography*, David Ramsay's *Life of General Washington*, and Jedidiah Morse's *American Gazetteer* (books owned by the Harwoods) and borrowed many others from individuals in Bennington or from one of the small lending libraries kept on an irregular basis in various stores on the Hill (Bennington village). From these sources he obtained even more works of history and travel accounts. One book of quite a different nature absolutely fascinated Hiram: *Coelebs in Search of a Wife*, a novel that he considered "in many parts too religious to suit a person of my taste" but nonetheless one that "accurately portray[ed] the human heart."[34]

What Hiram read did not differ much from what other individuals in New England read at this time.[35] The manner in which he read this material, however, did distinguish him from many others. Hiram's emphasis upon the heart and his love of history, geography, and travel accounts of exotic places exhibited a restive yearning—a strong desire that must somehow be gratified, a desire for something that he could not quite identify. In this respect Hiram's situation closely resembled that of any number of young male apprentices scattered throughout Vermont and its neighboring states. But there were important differences between Hiram and these young apprentices. The restless yearnings of these young men were those of an autonomous group of individuals potentially free to follow wherever their talents might lead.[36] This was not the case with Hiram; he remained enmeshed in a patriarchal culture. His choices in life, unlike those of many apprentices, were severely limited. Consequently, his reading, unlike theirs, became a temporary escape from the narrowly defined role prescribed by tradition rather than a guide marking out a pathway to a new life.

This escape into the solitude of his own imagination helped ease the anxiety resulting from the conflicted situation in which he found himself. Further, it accomplished this without threatening the patriarchal family tradition that he simultaneously respected and resisted. This may have been the primary reason that *Coelebs* so appealed to him. Although it presented patriarchal domesticity in a favorable light, this novel also fashioned an image of masculinity that appealed to Hiram. Both Coelebs and Mr. Francis Stanley (the novel's male protagonists) were portrayed as men of feelings; the author never dissociated manliness from emotional sensibilities. Coelebs appeared as a man of reason, but he was also emotional — quite capable of tears at the thought of his departed parents. Such characteristics clearly represented manliness in the novel; so, too, was it considered manly to be considerate, thoughtful, and reasonable. Indeed, all the personal sensibilities that Hiram felt — that caused him such conflict when contrasted to his father's perception of manhood — appeared in *Coelebs* to epitomize true manliness and thus may have provided some comfort to Hiram. At the same time, though, his reading, with its constant emphasis upon the self — self-government, self-culture, self-reliance, self-improvement, self-interest — heightened the tension that Hiram felt between his inner desires and his familial obligations.[37]

Thoughts of the future, of his maturity, of the time when he would be expected to take his place at the head of his own household and to assume full responsibility for the Harwood farm, worried Hiram constantly. He feared that "all attempts to metamorphose me into anything good — that is, a right, sprightly, discerning, pretty behaved, sociable, sensible, well educated young man, would prove fruitless." He often worried that he might be "determined to be a poor man all my days"; his "writing, composition and [a] slight view of myself, all considered — makes me feel exceedingly dejected." He longed to become "a vigilant, enterprising, well-educated young man." That he was so critical of himself was not surprising; he learned this from his father. And yet his father's hope was that criticism would prompt change. Hiram harbored this same aspiration; his criticism formed the negative portion of a conversation with himself. His diary became a persistent dialogue of self-fashioning — a dialogue aimed at improvement, self-mastery, and manhood. Fully aware that he was not a "vigilant, enterprising, well-educated young man," Hiram aspired to be just that sort of man.[38]

In December 1810, with the harvest season completed, Hiram took steps to augment his education. Certain that a knowledge of grammar was essential to becoming an "enterprising, well-educated" individual, he asked Samuel Young, a local attorney, if he could study grammar with him. With Young's permission, Hiram made daily trips to town, where he read Murray's *English Grammar* in the lawyer's office. He found the book slow going, even though he had learned all its rules four years earlier when his father had paid Noadiah Swift's clerk to teach him grammar. Nonetheless, he kept at it: he recited pages from Murray to friends who dropped in at Young's office, stayed late to repeat his lessons to himself, "parsed" verbs with men in the office, and even studied his grammar lessons while en route to a funeral in nearby Hoosick Falls, New York. When Young examined him, Hiram had done much better than Young had expected. However, the attorney felt that if Hiram were to become a "grammarian," he "must commit Alexander's rules to memory." The very next day Hiram purchased Caleb Alexander's *Grammatical Elements* and studied it on his own for the next several months. He even took it to church with him. In April he paid Samuel Young twenty cents for the several weeks he had spent in his office during December and January.[39] By this time farm work had picked up, and he had little time to devote to grammar.

Even while in Young's office, Hiram had not been able to devote himself entirely to grammar. Despite his good intentions, his mind easily strayed: he often read the *Spectator* or other works he found on Young's bookshelves; at other times he chatted with friends. His greatest distraction, however, was music. When alone he could not resist singing, playing the flute, or copying "The Devil's Dream" and "Washington's Reel" out of *The Fifer's Companion*, a tune-book he borrowed from an acquaintance.

Music was important to Hiram. His love of music may have been an intrinsic component of the "phantom" — the resolution of the inner conflict between the life he was supposed to live and the life he would like to live — that he pursued so urgently. That tension between business and pleasure remained omnipresent. Late one afternoon, during an unusually active day, Benjamin left the farm to get a cart wheel mended. Later Hiram instructed his diary to "see how worldly [Benjamin's] son was in his absence. See him alone in Ira's kitchen with his notes before him and flute to his lips — puffing away half an hour — till darkness obscures his notes so that he can no longer see them, which puts him in mind of what he is to do, that which ought to have been done before." Then he wondered: "Now is this living a good life — is this improving one's time to the best advantage?" Only one practical answer could be made to such a query, and Hiram knew what it was. Nonetheless, he reasoned that "there is but little time in this life to enjoy pleasure and that, while young, and if I can catch a few flying moments and spend them in so pleasing a manner . . . it cheers up my desponding soul — and dispels the fog which gathers round it." Well aware that he was "not much troubled with fog as yet," Hiram could nevertheless see "a great cloud rising" in the near future. Consequently, he concluded "now is the time for me to enjoy life."[40]

The very next day Hiram shoveled dung from dawn to dusk — a task that "didn't set right to my bones." Late that night he engaged in a dialogue with himself: "Don't you know how long you was gone this morning at Mr Parsons when you went to borrow his shovel? — There you saw Huntington's *Apollo Harmony* which had beside rules for singing — instructions for the Flute & Bass Viol — and view'd it some time?" The response: "Yes-yes, I know it well." Then: "What, take up your time so — in the midst of business when the days are so short and winter just at hand — does this look like a man of business?" The reply: "I care nothing about the man of business — I am a man of pleasure."[41] Never had Hiram drawn such a clear distinction between the man Benjamin wanted him to be and the man he so desired to become.

Music was a growing source of satisfaction for Hiram, and his flute became his constant companion on walks, at work, or when visiting friends. It provided the most solace, however, when depression overcame him. He admitted to an acquaintance that he had "hitherto lived a happy life, but futurity look'd dark to me — my prospects not at all bright — felt quite low-spirited." He was all the more dejected because the day was Sunday, and out of respect for Benjamin's observance of the Sabbath, he could not "take a touch or two on the flute." When that "curious creature called Happiness" seemed to be slipping beyond his reach, Hiram yearned to "enjoy the present hour . . . let me innocently indulge myself with the charming sound of the flute." Very often, then, when Hiram thought of the future, "scenes too serious for my imagination to dwell long upon without wishing myself back again to days of youth and carelessness, when I had no care for tomorrow," flashed before his eyes. At these times he determined that he would sing "Banish Sorrows" and go to bed, or "at least I'll promise myself the pleasure of giving it a touch on the flute."[42]

As music became integral to Hiram's life, he devoted hours not only to playing the flute but also to copying songs from music books that he borrowed wherever he could find them. Whenever he managed to obtain collections like *The Songster's Museum*, he spent all the time he could transcribing the notes of special tunes to his own growing collection of hand-written sheets of music. It was not uncommon for him to stay "up late pricking tunes." When Heman Fay loaned him a book of martial music, Hiram became so excited that he "performed no more business than I could handsomely avoid," in order to copy as many songs as possible before being obliged to return the book. Recalling that he was "very busy writing music in the evening," Hiram noted another ominous fact: "Father disliked my employment." When Hiram was still at this task two days later, Benjamin became "hotly incensed against me for taking so fine an opportunity for pursuing necessary business, to indulge myself in such a frivolous, unprofitable employment — and said so much that I quitted it and attended to other concerns until evening." At the first opportunity, though, he slipped away to a neighbor's house and finished transcribing the desired tunes. He then proceeded to the Fays', where he fluted while Heman Fay played the violin. When the concert ended, Judge Fay complimented Hiram on his musical talents. After "talking of the excellence of music" with the Fays, Hiram, thrilled with the way he had been received in the Fay home, left and spent the night with Nathaniel Locke at the Parsonses' shop.[43]

◠◡ Although it was the source of occasional tension between him and his father, the flute eased Hiram's relations with acquaintances his own age. Such was certainly the case one afternoon when his sister Lydia informed him that young people from the neighborhood were coming to the house that evening. "To avoid the company, I went to Ira's; but had to steal privately into our house, after they arrived, to get my flute — notes — grammar-book etc. before I became fairly settled down." It was not long, however, before several young men came over and insisted that Hiram join the party. He consented to come back to the house but refused to "go into the room amongst the gentlemen and ladies." Finally, several of his friends grabbed him and carried him into the party, where he reluctantly took part in the games. Even then he was often "in the kitchen alone with my flute" or playing it for others. The "last scene they exhibited was dancing to the music of my flute, which seem'd to please them a good deal tho' indifferently performed."[44]

Abjectly self-conscious and lacking in self-confidence, Hiram depended upon the flute to sustain him in awkward social situations. During a visit at the Nortons', after settling into a chair in the family parlor, Hiram "felt that kind of awkwardness which is known only to a true Yankee." In the face of what he perceived to be such genteel company, he simply did not know "what to begin with, for I had nothing to say, and thought [it] would not do to set up a howl with the flute without some time intervening between my entry and the beginning of some sort of conversation or amusement." As a result he sat "gnawing awhile the end of my musical instrument" until Clarissa Norton said good evening. That was all Hiram needed; he immediately began playing the flute and "played so long I must have made the company sick by the time I ended."[45] By playing the flute, Hiram avoided having to engage in conversation or participate fully in whatever activities were taking place; the flute had become a social crutch for him.

Hiram's uneasiness in social circumstances involving individuals and groups beyond his immediate family stemmed from an acute awareness of his own lack of social skills as well as an extreme sensitivity to his social status in the community. Both of these matters weighed heavily on his mind. Once, during an extended conversation with his parents "concerning the manner in which I was brought up," Hiram blurted out that "they had suffered me to remain too much at home, which caused me to feel great diffidence abroad." Willing to shoulder a part of the blame himself, he believed that "I have erred in not going among people more than I have." This resulted in a marked "ignorance of manners" on his part. The fact that "persons in my situation know much better than they speak or write" did not help; Hiram always feared that he would make a fool of himself in public.[46]

Even though Peter Harwood had been one of the town's original settlers and the Harwoods owned a farm of more than one hundred acres, members of the Harwood family retained a markedly humble view of their station in the community. When Hiram and Lydia participated in a conversation with their mother and father that "chiefly concern'd what class of people it would be best for us to go into to make choice of our partners," Diadama favored "hired men and hired girls of good reputation, industrious habits and agreeable dispositions." For his part, Benjamin did not wish "to estimate the standing of his children in the world too low." It was not that he "despised such persons as mother had mentioned, but he would have them consider themselves as good as their neighbors notwithstanding their neighbors being a little better educated and in their manners more polished." Reacting to his father's observation, Hiram concluded: "Manners and education — there is the stick with me — possessed of these I might gain respectability among my neighbors and acquaintances."[47]

Hiram's intense desire to achieve "respectability" made him particularly sensitive to the manner in which he dressed and acted when in the presence of those "more polished" than he. Once, after coming out of the field at the end of the day, Hiram put on Ira's jacket, "calculated for wearing suspenders," instead of his own. Since he was not wearing suspenders, there was quite a gap showing between the bottom of the jacket and the top of his trousers. Dressed in this casual manner, "with the greatest confidence and freedom, not suspecting whom I should see," Hiram strode into his father's kitchen. To his chagrin he encountered Lucretia Norton and Harriot Mellen, the daughters of two of the neighborhood's best families. He quickly backed out of the room, ran to Ira's, and returned only after putting on his own long coat. Another day Hiram went for a walk with his uncles Clark and Jonas. Believing they were simply going to view their neighbors' crops, Hiram wore a "coarse pair of cow-hide shoes of my fathers; dirty overalls — jacket and coat ditto, under which was a chequered woolen shirt unchanged that day — and a coarse every day hat." Great was his mortification upon discovering that his uncles intended to visit the Nortons. "In this plight did I appear on the Holy Sabbath day at a neighbours house, not only in the presence of my elders — but in that of a young gentleman and lady of the house and that eagle eyed old maid Miss Polly Thayer."[48]

Although Hiram constantly agonized over his own appearance, he was even more conscious of the way respectable people behaved toward him. His insecurity regarding the Harwood family's status in the community sensitized him to the slightest hint that others might be patronizing him or looking down on him in any way. Whenever he was in the company of gentlefolk, he vigilantly gauged their behavior toward him. For example, he carefully noted that "I was treated very handsomely during my tarry at Mr. Doty's," or "I was very politely treated by Miss Sophia."[49]

Other incidents did not leave Hiram with such pleasant feelings. One evening he put on his best hat and strolled down the road "very warmly engaged" playing his flute with no expectation of meeting another living soul. To his consternation, he approached "a row of white gowns stretching across the whole breadth of the cart-way — at one end of which was attached a fine Beau and in whose rear was another Beau, with one or two more ladies." Hiram instantly ceased playing, and just as he was "sneaking away . . . to the opposite of the road," one of the gentlemen bade him good evening. Too embarrassed even to turn his head to see who it might be, Hiram returned the compliment. He then detected what he was certain to be "not a little snickering among the ladies."[50] Later that evening, he discovered that Moses D. Robinson — the son of the wealthiest man in Bennington and a student at Williams College — had been one of the "beaux" he had encountered on the road. Acutely conscious of his own common-school education, Hiram resented the thought that attendance at college should confer any special status. He firmly believed that if the inhabitants of Vermont ever accepted the idea that a man must have a college education in order to serve as governor of the state, then "we should be getting in to aristocracy in earnest."[51]

Even with all his insecurities, Hiram did begin attending gatherings of young people held in various homes around the neighborhood. At first, preferring to remain in the background, he was hesitant to participate fully in the festivities. This was certainly true when he sought out his sister Lydia at a neighbor's house one night. He discovered her in a circle of young men and women deeply engaged in playing games. Hiram "hoped to remain an idle spectator, but a young lady came up to me and invited me into the ring." When he told her that he did not belong to the "band," everyone insisted that he join them. He did, and when "they had done with running round, singing and kissing, we, and those who were bound this way, moved in the sleigh for home." Another time, when the group began to play "The Farmer," Hiram "join'd the ring, but didn't attempt to go through all the maneuvers at first." Thus he did not "sow, stamp with my foot, nor clap my hands, but only sang with them & turned on my heel."[52]

As Hiram gradually grew more comfortable at these parties, he participated more fully in the activities. He played such games as "Button," "Proud and Scornful," "Wink'em slyly," and "Neighbor." And yet, during an evening at the Fays', where he "was treated with respect by every one in the company," Hiram carefully avoided showing "any partiality among the fair sex"; he talked first with one lady and then another.[53]

With the passage of time, Hiram actually started to enjoy these parties and games. As he became increasingly familiar with the young men and women who attended them, he even began to look forward to such gatherings. He adamantly refused, however, to attend any "balls" held in the neighborhood. He was certain that whenever he was "acquainted with a young lady and can be placed in a thin company, where there is not so much use for form and parade, I can find enough to talk about." However, "out me in a ball-chamber and there I am wound up at once . . . besides being frightened to death."[54] Not only was the "thin company" of parties comfortable; so, too, were the games. These exuberant activities involving round dances and kissing games allowed young people of both sexes to mix freely. Such ritualized behavior encouraged young men and women to enjoy each other's company but did not require them to commit themselves to a more serious relationship. Playfully moving from one woman to another in such a setting did not bother Hiram. A "ball," or dance, however, was quite a different matter; it forced an entirely different set of requirements on him. He would be expected to pair off in a formal manner with an individual woman, and he was simply not ready for that. Such a prospect triggered all his insecurities about proper manners and polish; worse still, it heightened his self-consciousness regarding the kind of woman with whom he could or should become involved.

Hiram's self-consciousness even affected his relations with a number of people with whom he associated regularly. This was particularly true of the Nortons. Hiram had the utmost regard for Captain John Norton and his large family and often observed that he could "frequent no company more pleasing to me." As portrayed in Hiram's diary, the captain bore a striking resemblance to Mr. Francis Stanley, the patriarch Hiram so admired in *Coelebs*. Following a visit with the captain and his family, Hiram observed in language reminiscent of the novel that he loved "to see a man sit down quietly in the bosom of an enlightened, industrious family. — at night after discharging his duty to himself and them, in his particular vocation — where he enjoys the only happiness this sublunary world can afford." Even in the midst of such reverie, however, Hiram lamented that "I am myself not at all calculated to form an ingredient in such an agreeable composition as was formed at this house that evening."[55] Another time, after spending an evening "rather uneasily" at the Norton home, Hiram observed that even though he had been "us'd as courteously as I ever wish to be," he "felt somehow dissatisfied with myself — just as I do a great deal of my time — when I compare other people with myself — to find them so much better than I."[56]

Hiram became particularly anxious around the Norton girls. On the one hand, because he considered Laura, Clarissa, and Lucretia "truly

engaging, judicious, and well-informed young ladies," he became extremely ill at ease when Lucretia fell into such "dull untoward, roguish,
tasteless, unpleasing company as mine." On the other hand, Hiram was
"never more pleased with anyone's company and conversation in my
life." He also felt that he did not know "a person of her sex that is more
easy in her behavior and more lively in her conversation" than Laura
Norton. And yet, when Hiram was in her company, he hid behind a fa-
cade. Recalling a time when they performed a play under the tutelage of
their schoolmaster, Heman Fay, Hiram constantly called Laura his
"aunt." Quite often they assumed these roles in their conversation. It
was the same with the other Norton sisters. From time to time Lucretia
pretended to be Laura's old-maid relative when the three of them were
together; other times Hiram and Clarissa "feigned great grief at parting
with one another"; still other times Hiram would have a "funny conversation" with Laura or write her a "letter of nonsense." He simply could
not be himself; he was afraid to associate with such genteel women on
an equal footing. Consequently he studiously avoided ever linking his
name with theirs in a serious way. Although he might advise Lydia to
consider John Norton Jr. as a mate, he could never bring himself to
admit that he desired a similar association with any one of John's sisters. Perhaps Hiram was the most honest with himself regarding any
of the Norton girls one day when he saw a "neat swelled bureau"
standing outside the Norton home. Assuming that it belonged to Clarissa, he thought to himself, "That'll do for me—that'll do for me."
Whether he meant the bureau, Clarissa, or both, Hiram never made
clear. His attraction to the Norton girls and their way of life was,
however, manifest.[57]

Even though Hiram managed to repress whatever thoughts he may
have entertained regarding a serious relationship with any of the Norton women, he could not avoid the issue of marriage for long. Now that
he had reached maturity, Benjamin expected him to marry, to have
a family, and eventually to take over the Harwood property. These
assumptions about the future—the much dreaded "bye and bye"—
caused Hiram deep anxiety. And yet, try as he might to avoid facing
this eventuality, he could not. One day, while helping him break and
swingle flax, Luther Bliss, a near neighbor, began to talk about a match
between his daughter Emily and Hiram. Two days later he "again spoke
greatly in favor of my making a bride of his daughter Emily." Bliss's
wife favored the idea, and Emily, who was away visiting relatives, would
certainly give her consent. Since he was a respected landowner him-

self, Bliss could not imagine any "objections could exist on the part of my parents." Several days later Mr. Bliss reported that he had written Emily and suggested Hiram as a "suitor."[58]

In the face of this sudden turn of events, Hiram remained as non-committal as possible; Emily's absence provided him with a much appreciated breathing space. He did, however, engage Thomas Parsons in a serious conversation regarding the subject of marriage. Parsons swore that if he were in Hiram's situation, he would never marry. The problem with such advice was that Parsons vacillated so on this very issue. Sometimes he told Hiram "that it was natural for us to wish for a fair friend with whom we may divide the pleasures and cares of life, that we ought to follow the dictates of this inclination." But at other times, when he considered "how carelessly happy I liv'd at a father's house, he has talk'd as much the other way." Hiram himself knew only one thing for sure: "I shouldn't like much to be an odd, unsociable, whimsical, peevish, hateful, friendless and frozen old bachellor." Nonetheless, "I should rather live so, than to be obliged to live with some women."[59]

At last the day came that Hiram so desperately wished to avoid: Emily Bliss had returned to Bennington, and her father visited the Harwoods for the express purpose of telling Hiram that his daughter would be happy to be "gallanted" by him to a neighborhood party the following evening. When Hiram told him that this "would never do," Bliss exclaimed: "Why, damnit, I am in earnest about this matter," but he let the matter drop. The very next morning, however, he returned to buy grain from Benjamin. As soon as he finished this business, he asked Hiram if he would escort his daughter to a neighborhood party being held that night. Hiram laughed and tried to make light of the matter. For his part, Bliss assured Hiram that he was in earnest and that there was not another young man in town that he would rather have in his household. Hiram responded that he would be very sorry to lose his friendship, but that he was sure that Bliss could surely find a more suitable partner for his daughter. Certain that Emily "knew more than forty of me," Hiram asked Bliss to present his compliments to her and to tell her that he hoped that she would choose an "enterprizing, well educated, active young man for a partner." Taking a different approach, Bliss responded by inviting Hiram to come to his house at any time to borrow whatever books he might want. Also, he should be certain to drop by and pick up a file of newspapers printed in the 1790s that he had previously promised to Hiram. After some weeks, when he could be reasonably certain that it was safe to visit the Bliss household, Hiram did stop by and pick up the file of old newspapers. Mercifully, Mr. Bliss did not mention his daughter.[60]

The personal insecurities that constantly plagued Hiram, combined with the uneasiness he suffered around women whom he considered to be somewhat above him, contributed considerably to Hiram's hesitancy to become involved with Emily Bliss. Always more comfortable around hired girls and apprentices, Hiram's closest companions beyond his own family were Nathaniel Locke — apprenticed to Thomas Parsons — and Sophia Waters, who lived with the Harwoods until she was nineteen and then began to work out in the factories and households of Bennington. Hiram spent many hours perfectly at ease with these two. He did not feel pressured to be something or someone he was not around them; they did not expect anything of him beyond simple friendship. By the time Luther Bliss began to press his daughter upon Hiram, Rebecca Cutler had come to work for Mrs. Parsons and was spending a lot of time at the Harwood house visiting Lydia and Sophia Waters. It was not unusual for her to spend the night with her new friends. When she was not at his house, Hiram saw Rebecca during frequent trips to the Parsonses' shop, where he visited Nathaniel Locke. She became a part of his close circle of neighborhood friends; he felt far more secure with Rebecca than he ever could with Emily Bliss.

As he grew increasingly comfortable around Rebecca, Hiram spent more time alone with her. In his shy, awkward way, Hiram began to court her. At first he serenaded the Parsons house with the flute in the evenings, then he began walking Rebecca to the village when she had jobs to perform for various townspeople. If she was not at home and he could not see her in town, Hiram often sat on a hill above the Parsons home and played the flute for hours. One particular evening, when "the sky was serene and the moon gave us a full quarter of her light," Hiram called for Rebecca in town and walked her to the bridge north of the courthouse. "After a few moments innocent there," they returned to town, where they read a travel account of Indian widows burning themselves alive. All this made several hours "fly away so agreeably as scarcely to be perceived."[61]

Hiram was smitten. He forgot his insecurities and let himself enjoy Rebecca's company without agonizing over how he might embarrass himself around her. His flute-playing lost its melancholy nature and took on a much happier tone. And then, one day Mr. Parsons "put a certain letter in my hands that excited in me both pity and contempt for its author." Rebecca had broken off their relationship.[62]

Rebecca's rejection devastated Hiram. His entire network of friends and acquaintances throughout the neighborhood knew of his courtship. To be spurned was to suffer public humiliation, to be publicly shamed. Deeply hurt by Rebecca's behavior, Hiram turned to Lydia for comfort. The two had always been extremely close; Hiram often noted that he and his sister enjoyed "a right down clever chat" or that he had "spent a long and pleasant evening conversing with sister Lydia." Once, when Lydia and her father had set off for an extended trip, Hiram recalled that he and his sister could only look "each other in the face and laugh as she launched off. We have never lived apart without seeing each other more than three days, since we were born." Now he appreciated Lydia more than ever and affectionately recorded how "an evening never was more agreeably talked away in my life than this which I spent with my oldest sister in my grandfather's kitchen lighted by a low fire."[63]

Hiram remained close with Sophia Waters as well. When she turned nineteen and was soon to leave the Harwood house, Hiram "sat down in the evening with her before the kitchen fire . . . and conversed with her on her future destination in life." He told her that she would probably feel homesick at first but that "that would soon wear off if she were industrious and behaved herself agreeably so as to merit and gain the good will of her employers." Then he "noticed the disadvantages of the situation in which such girls as are obliged to work abroad for wages are placed and advised her, to get out of it (provided she could make a happy choice) to get married." When Sophia began working at the Paran Creek Cotton Factory in the northern part of the township, Hiram kept up a correspondence with her and "cautioned her respecting her conduct in her new station." In a lighter vein, he addressed her as "Miss Cotton Factory." When she came to visit the Harwoods to ask their advice as to whether she should work at Stephen Hinsdill's woolen factory or let herself out as a spinster, Hiram and the rest of the family strongly recommended the later. Taking their advice, she began working in various homes around the Tanbrook neighborhood and became a regular visitor in the Harwood house. Hiram remained her steadfast and sympathetic friend.[64]

The same could not be said of Rebecca Cutler. Within a month after writing her letter to Hiram, Rebecca began hinting very strongly that she would like to renew their relationship. Whenever she came to the Harwood home, Hiram behaved politely toward her but remained aloof. Then one evening she contrived matters so that Hiram walked her home. Once there, he leaned on the gate and chatted with her for nearly an hour, "but not altogether on the subject which she wished to agitate" (marriage). Instead, he "talked of many things as foreign to that, as I could think of, only now and then giving her a direct answer, and then would fly to something I had not thought of before in these years." He finally "dwelt sometime on the bad side of my own character which I fell at without mercy, keeping strictly within what I esteemed the bound of truth." Then, "having ended this blessing with some advice to my lady as to the course I should pursue respecting a young man having such a character, I returned to the Harwood Castle." As kindly as possible, Hiram had told Rebecca to seek another mate.[65]

Rebecca refused to accept the rebuff. A week later, with Lydia's help, she arranged matters so that she and Hiram could have a private conversation in his father's apple orchard. Perhaps to shield himself from his own emotions, Hiram recorded the encounter in the third person; it sounded like the literature with which he was so familiar. Thus, one "evening, a young man's sister gave him an invitation to take his flute and walk with another young gentleman, herself, and four other ladies up to her father's young orchard; which he without a moment's hesitation accepted." Once there, "this young man and a lady about his age with whom he had formerly been acquainted conversed apart from the others on old affairs which had turned up since the commencement of their intimacy." There was, of course, "nothing indecent or unbecoming which at any former period or at that time passed between them." It soon became apparent that "while the lady stood stripping off leaves . . . and the gentleman sat on a bit of an old rail, playing on his flute & carelessly attending to what w's sd, she was soliciting what she had once slighted and rejected, what the young man honestly considered as her's till it was fairly and explicitly acknowledged by her that she retained it no longer, after which he resolved never again to restore it to her." In vain did the young lady attempt "to gain his favor as she had once possessed it." As might well be supposed, "their conversation was not of the most pleasing nature, tho' the young man attached very little importance to it and suffered himself not to be moved by passion." The "interview" ended with the young man "gallanting" the young lady home."[66]

Hiram's diary entry belied his true feelings. Pressured by his father to marry, he had managed to subdue his insecurities to such an extent as to contemplate matrimony with Rebecca. It seemed for a time that he might actually be able to overcome his dread of the "bye and bye" and meet Benjamin's expectations. Now, following Rebecca's rejection of him and the personal shame and humiliation he suffered, he had no idea how to behave. All he knew of intimate relationships between men and women came from his reading; that explains the stilted and emotionless "story" related in his diary as well as his stubborn refusal to renew his relationship with Rebecca. She had not behaved like the ideal woman described in the books he read. In his naïveté he assumed that Rebecca's rejection of him, however fleeting or for whatever reason, meant that she could never become a steadfast, loyal mate like Lucille Stanley, the heroine of *Coelebs*. He had no choice but to soldier on without her.

Such fortitude was not easy. Nathaniel Locke began to escort Rebecca to gatherings of young people in the neighborhood, and Hiram often found himself in their company. His only solace was the hope that he might find comfort in the conviviality of his other friends. Consequently, one afternoon while harvesting potatoes, Hiram "was foolish enough to indulge myself in fanciful dreams of the pleasure I should enjoy in the evening at Mr. House's among my young friends who were to assemble there." However, "the matter took a different coloring at night," when Hiram, "very much staggered" by the news, discovered that the anticipated gathering was to be a ball rather than a friendly neighborhood party. Excited by this prospect, Nathaniel Locke "drove off with his ladies in triumph." That Rebecca was one of the ladies made Hiram's distress all the worse. Nonetheless, with his "usual dronish celerity," he dressed himself in his best and, "with no other company than a flute found my way to House's tavern." So strong was his need to be around friends that he steeled himself to endure the stiff formalities of a ball.[67]

Once in the ballroom, Hiram seated himself "without taking an active part in anything for some time." He observed the participants for a time, then went downstairs and played the flute with several of his friends. When he returned to the dance floor, he accompanied the musician playing for the dancers before returning to his seat. Still, he could find no peace. Even though in a "lively and well-regulated company and personally acquainted from my youth with most of them and well treated by them," Hiram felt "so foolish, whimsical or whatever it may be termed, as to suffer some very melancholy thoughts to steal into my heart which I am not learned enough to express."[68]

The next morning Hiram felt no better. "Extremely dejected and down-hearted—I could not rid myself of it in any manner whatever. I seemed to myself a disappointed, forsaken, spiritless—torpid being;

destitute of every social virtue or feeling." Nor did he improve with the passage of time. Two weeks later, unable to sleep, he crept out of the house at midnight and walked to a spot near the Parsonses', where he "was seated a long time blowing out tunes."[69]

Thoughts of marriage, stimulated by his relationship with Rebecca, remained very much on Hiram's mind and troubled him greatly. All the time he participated in an apple-paring at a neighbor's house amid "a convivial group of people," Hiram "wished I had been at home with Coelebs—Ah—that book I do like." He could not get the image of the ideal marriage relationship portrayed in *Coelebs* out of his thoughts. When he visited Elisha Waters the next day, he encountered Mrs. Waters surrounded by four small children, "all whimpering, prating, running & jumping, keeping the woman in continual watchfulness and vexatious agitation." Upon viewing this "sad, gloomy picture of matrimonial happiness," Hiram exclaimed to himself: "Merciful Providence, must I ever come to this?" Then, however, he visited another part of the house, where an old man lay sick in bed, "kindly nursed by a snug, handsome little wife." Reflecting on his visit, Hiram observed that "in the one case I saw the galling inconveniences of marriage, in the other the beneficial effects of it."[70]

Hiram's uncertainties regarding marriage, intensified by his experience with Rebecca, caused all his old insecurities to return, now magnified. His state of mind suffered a severe setback two days after his visit to the Waterses when Benjamin, feeling "as if the whole world were tumbling in pieces about his ears" because of the backward state of the harvest, "very candidly and dispassionately lectured me on my careless, indolent, thoughtless, indulgent, ill-regulated manner of life." Coming as it did when Hiram was feeling most vulnerable, his father's ill-timed lecture "almost determined me to keep on, without attempting to turn either to the right hand or to the left, in the cold, gloomy, solitary, silent path of celibacy. I was greatly depressed in my mind."[71]

Humiliated by his experience with Rebecca and shamed by his father's criticism of his unmanly behavior about the farm, Hiram became despondent. He needed, above all else, to find some way to establish his manhood—to assume a responsible place within the Harwood household. Ironically, another source of anxiety for Hiram—war between the United States and Great Britain—provided just such an opportunity. To become a soldier might be a way for Hiram to master the insecurity he felt about his own manhood.[72] Consequently, when Captain Samuel Blackmer mustered his militia company in order to fill the required quota of the one-hundred-thousand-man force called for by President Madison on April 10, Hiram and his good friend Nathaniel Locke enthusiastically volunteered.[73]

Having signed on for military service did seem to provide Hiram with a modicum of self-esteem. Sufficiently confident to spend time alone with a woman, he even observed with a note of cockiness that he was "perhaps the cause of a young lady's going abroad . . . against the inclination of her mother." In this case the young woman was Theodosia Montague, daughter of a respectable neighbor family, whom Hiram had once described as a "vivifying little animal." The same sense of self-assurance may have prompted Hiram's reaction to his father one evening when Benjamin, fearful that Hiram would not be fit for work the following day, suggested that he not go out that night. Hiram "harkened not to him, but pursued that course which accorded best with my present desires." He even noted that "such occurrences became more frequent with me in those days than when I was in my twentieth year."[74]

As he neared his twenty-fourth birthday, Hiram did seem to be assuming a more mature, adult character. And with American troops beginning to muster all over the nation, the day did not appear far off when he would have the opportunity to prove to himself as well as to his parents that he was fully capable of assuming the full responsibilities of manhood. For all his apparent confidence, though, military service remained a disquieting thought.

3

A Soldier's Life

With no inconsiderable degree of pleasure I worked with my team in the furrowed field — Perhaps I never relished that employment better, because I soon expected to be called in to a field far less pleasing to me — and one which produces a certain imaginary vegetable that every farmer cannot reap — and rather doubted my ability to perform so difficult a task — however as I had volunteered could see no reasonable way or honorable way of backing out. Received Orders from Sergt Green Blackmer to march to Henry Huntington's in Shaftsbury on the 10th inst.[1]

For Hiram to describe work in the field as pleasurable, his impending military service must have weighed heavily on his mind indeed. From the moment he volunteered in early June, he had dreaded the day he would be called into service. Now that day — September 10 — was less than a week away. Nonetheless, when Henry Mellen, a neighbor and a veteran of the Revolutionary War, stopped by to inquire about Hiram's state of mind, he assured the man that it was "regular and serene." Throughout the afternoon of that same day, while gathered on Courthouse Hill with others who were to serve in the detached militia, he attempted to keep up the same brave front.[2] Whenever townspeople asked him if he really meant to serve, he responded positively. Privately, though, he "felt rather too serious for a brave Volunteer" and feared that he lacked "muscular government enough to prevent some bad passages being read in my long fiz." Finally, when an old school friend engaged him in a lengthy conversation about the prospect of becoming a soldier, Hiram "owned how reluctantly I should leave home." Mustering a modicum of courage, however, he managed to declare that "it were as proper to be me as any other person." Later, before leaving town, Hiram purchased a blank book so that he could keep a journal of his military experience. That evening, in an effort to put thoughts of war out of his mind, Hiram joined a group of neighborhood friends gathered at Ira's house. To his relief, he not only enjoyed the company but also had the pleasure of "gallanting" Theodosia Montague home that night.[3]

The next day Hiram made quite an extraordinary entry in his diary: "Having spent the day most agreeably in the field, attended a ball at Mr House's in the evening." For Hiram to depict his day in the field as "most agreeable" was certainly unusual, but then to describe the affair at House's as "quite a scrumptious Ball" was totally out of character. September 10 — now just two days away — must have loomed truly ominous in his imagination.[4]

Finally, when the dreaded day arrived, Hiram confessed that he had indeed been suffering from a "melancholy frame of mind" for several days. Now, however, as he joined his family in making preparations for the anticipated campaign, he became more cheerful and "thought as little as I could of parting with my friends." During this time Hiram felt especially close to his father, who offered his particularly "kind assistance." When ready to depart, he took an "affectionate leave of my aged Grandfather." Peter, a veteran of the battle of Bennington, shared a few bits of soldierly advice with Hiram, and then, adding that "it is not likely you will ever see me again," the old man declared: "I wish you well." The emotional power of the moment caused Hiram "to struggle with all my might against a torrent of suppressed tears which I was determined should not fall at this time." In an attempt to stem those tears, Hiram avoided shaking hands or looking others directly in the face but instead departed as fast as he could. One image, however, remained with him and "tried my feelings almost equal to anything that took place that day." As he turned to leave, Hiram caught sight of his sister Lydia "bathed in tears."[5]

After leaving the house, Hiram joined Nathaniel Locke in a wagon driven by Benjamin, who was to take them to Shaftsbury. En route they stopped on Courthouse Hill to take on military supplies that the Bennington selectmen had asked them to deliver to Shaftsbury. While others loaded this material, Hiram remained seated in the wagon, "pondering rather too much on the business before me." When friends came by to wish him well, they invariably asked him if he felt "heart-whole" about serving. He always responded affirmatively, but he knew they could "read very differently in my fore-head."[6]

Soon after leaving Courthouse Hill, the men stopped for a short visit at the home of Benjamin's uncle, Zechariah Harwood. Zechariah had fought at the battle of Bennington, and his son, Hiram, was on active duty as a sergeant in the regular army.[7] After drinking cider and discussing life in the military with Zechariah and his family, Hiram paid his relatives a soldier's farewell and Benjamin guided the wagon toward Shaftsbury.

Shortly after their arrival at Huntington's Tavern in Shaftsbury, Hiram bade his father a heartfelt good-bye and quickly became caught up in the events of the day. Lieutenant Samuel Lacy paraded Hiram and other early arrivals in front of the tavern, marched them into Huntington's orchard, mustered them in, and marched them to the meetinghouse and back to the tavern, where he stood a treat and then dismissed them. Shortly thereafter the company commander, Captain Samuel Cross, accepted Hiram to be his fifer. Even though he had sought this position, performing for an entire company made him extremely nervous.[8] He was much relieved to discover a fifer and drummer among the detachment from Pownal that arrived late that afternoon; now the burden for supplying the company's music would no longer rest entirely upon his shoulders. Along with the Pownal men came a large contingent of draftees from Bennington, who brought forward substitutes whom Captain Cross quickly accepted and mustered into service.[9]

By late evening quite a crowd of townspeople from Bennington had assembled around Huntington's Tavern. Certain that the detached regiment would become part of an American army being formed to attack Montreal, these people vigorously circulated a rumor that twelve thousand "regular Portuguese troops" had gathered in the vicinity of that city. Hiram managed to put such talk out of his mind by lodging with Nehemiah Russell, the Pownal fifer, at the home of Oliver Whipple, "whose hospitality afforded us a good supper." After the meal the two men played their flutes for two ladies and a number of militiamen, who passed away the remainder of the evening singing psalms.[10]

The following morning Hiram and his Bennington comrades ate a breakfast of baked mutton and returned to their company, which paraded for a time and then prepared to march northward. Before the company departed, Hiram's new friend Nehemiah Russell passed his hat among the spectators and collected $1.60, with which he treated his fellow soldiers. Shortly after leaving Huntington's, the company wheeled to the left and, with "the music playing—or rather making attempts to play to the Gen'ls Salute," marched through rows of spectators lining both sides of the road leading to the meetinghouse. The men proceeded onward until they came to Governor Jonas Galusha's house, where "the music badly executed the salute" as the company wheeled to the left, repassed the house, wheeled again, and halted in front of the governor's home. Here Governor Galusha delivered a "short but patriotic address calculated to soothe and prepare our minds to meet whatever obstacles might be thrown in our way." His speech completed, the governor "brought on his bottle with the contents of which the comp'y was well served." One of the "hearty toasts" offered by spectators was given by Samuel Young, Bennington attorney and prominent figure in the Democratic Party. He "hoped we should execute our business speedily and successfully and return with our faces shining as Moses' did when he came down from the Mount." As the crowd dispersed, the company marched off toward Manchester.[11]

Although Hiram had made a number of new acquaintances, he very much missed his good friend Nathaniel Locke, who had been dispatched to help guard the baggage wagon. Nonetheless, Hiram was not without companionship; many Bennington acquaintances, including Samuel Young, accompanied the men all the way to Manchester. Shortly before Hiram completed this twenty-mile march, the high bailiff of Manchester fell in with him, and the two passed away the remaining distance in friendly conversation. The bailiff was "greatly encouraged about taking possession of the Canada's—said they could not raise over 10 thousand regulars—and I think he said including Militia—not more than 30,000." When the company reached its destination—Roache's Tavern in Manchester—confusion reigned as soldiers attempted to get settled and the crowd of well-wishers who had accompanied them from Bennington departed for home. Hiram ate a "soldier's supper" and retired for the night on a mound of hay in Roache's barn.[12]

"Owing to a new way of lodging," the night seemed long to Hiram, even though he managed a tolerable rest. After breakfast he walked over to view a detachment of U.S. regulars and "tho't they appeared well." Then the captain of the artillery of Hiram's own First Regiment of detached militia fired a salute as his company marched off, with their musicians playing "Yankee Doodle" in a most lively manner. When Hiram's company moved out, Captain Cross ordered his musicians to follow suit, "but unfortunately it was not in their power and their attempt at it was worse than if they had . . . disobeyed orders."[13]

Following a six-mile march to Dorset, the company rendezvoused with some recently drafted militiamen and Colonel Stephen Martindale, who assumed command of the regiment. Quite a number of townspeople also turned out to greet the troops, and "all conversation was on war—nothing else could be heard among the crowd." After passing friendly greetings with several of his relatives living in Rupert, Hiram retreated to the back of the tavern.[14] Away from the throng, he sat down next to a well and amused himself by playing the flute. Much to the pleasure of the crowd, he struck up his favorite tune, "Gillicrankie." Anxious to learn the piece, a young bystander asked Hiram for the notes. Since he did not have the music with him, Hiram promised that once he reached Burlington, he would take down the notes from memory and mail them to him. Satisfied with this, the young man persuaded Hiram and a local fiddler to move into the ball chamber and play for the crowd of soldiers and citizens, "who promiscuously joined together and shuffled away all their heavy thoughts." Early in the afternoon, the regiment marched to Freeman's Tavern, also in Rupert, where the men halted to receive a treat from another group of enthusiastic citizens. Soldiers and citizens joined in singing the "Canada Hymn."[15] After this short celebration, the troops completed an eight-mile march to Fitch's Tavern in Pawlet, where they encamped for the night. Hiram and a friend lodged near the tavern in the home of a young lawyer and his wife. That evening Hiram enjoyed playing the flute for the lady of the house, who sang beautifully, but, much to his chagrin, "our boys were lewd and noisy on the road—too much so to be within the bounds of decency or candor."[16]

When it came time to depart the next morning, Hiram's generous hosts refused to take any payment. Captain Cross's company left Fitch's at eight o'clock in the morning and marched the six miles to Robert's Tavern in Granville, where the men halted to refresh themselves. Hiram purchased a dinner of bread, butter, crackers, cheese, and cider, "after which my spirits were revived having been fatigued on the march." The company halted again six miles up the road at a tavern in Poultney, where Hiram "saw a couple of fine girls." The men stopped for the night at Beaman's Tavern, several miles further north. As soon as time permitted, they prepared their supper with borrowed utensils over fires built on the road. A kind lady let Hiram and his friends have as many potatoes as they desired, as well as a plate full of pickled cucumbers. In addition, she directed them to another lady, who supplied them with green cucumbers. Even more fortunately, this lady allowed Hiram and his companions to lodge in her home that cold and rainy night "without being taxed a cent for it." The day had been a good one for Hiram: agreeable to his increasingly genteel sensibilities, the "Company behaved themselves with great propriety on the road for which I will give them credit"; he enjoyed hearing a good flutist perform before going to bed that night; and he slept well, "except being disturbed sometime by two or three young bucks in an adjoining shoemaker's chamber who were fixing off one of their companions to join the Detached Militia."[17]

Early the following morning, Captain Cross gathered his men to choose an orderly sergeant. He gave them a choice between electing one of the company's sergeants or drawing lots among these same individuals. The men chose the latter and were on the march by seven o'clock. After several miles they stopped at a house where a woman gave them "as many wild plums, apples and cucumbers [as] we could wish for and likewise cold water in abundance." Hiram partook only of water but was "pleased to see how merry the young lads were while conversing with the ladies who were far from being bashful." Later that morning the men stopped to refresh themselves at a tavern in Castleton and then pushed on to Meeker's Tavern in Hubbardton, where they ate dinner. From that point the march proceeded along a "very dreary and lonesome road" toward Sudbury.[18]

Not far south of Sudbury, Hiram and his friend Sam Whipple stopped at a house near the road and enjoyed a dish of bread and milk. The man of the house "felt spirited enough in the cause [and] talked like a hearty Whig." Hiram and Sam thanked him for his generosity and moved on. They proceeded a half-mile north of Hyde's Tavern in Sudbury, where the company had encamped, and spent the night at a private home. Here they met "a very lively sociable lass . . . who appeared to be greatly interested in the fate of the young drafted soldiers — seemed anxious to do them every kindness in her power." Sam Whipple sang the "new Canadian hymn" for her and a young neighbor lady, and then Hiram played a few pieces on the flute for them as well. Unfortunately, Hiram's flute-playing "carried my thoughts swiftly back to Bennington, where I had so often played [these tunes] in undisturbed solitude." It was a difficult time for him; indeed, only "those who have experienced sensations of that kind can more easily conceive than I or anyone can describe them — the state of my mind at this time."[19]

When they arose in the morning, Hiram and Sam offered to pay their host, but he would take nothing. Thanking him, the two joined their company, which marched five miles to Whiting, where the captain called a halt for breakfast at a local inn. While there, Hiram and his companions managed to obtain some apples, which they "fryed for sauce." Others ascended to a bower between the tavern's signposts and sang the Canadian hymn with gusto. After this brief respite, the company reformed and marched another ten miles to Cornwall, where the men ate dinner. While at Foote's Tavern in Cornwall, Hiram met several Bennington acquaintances. One "appeared to be in high spirits and hearty in the present contest between America and G.B."; another "expressed great warmth in the business of taking Canada, and with a great many more expressed violent indignation at the conduct of Gen. Hull."[20]

After his men finished dinner, Captain Cross had them on the move again toward Middlebury. When they were within a short distance of that village, he called a halt, and the troops rested under whatever shade they could find. A number of regimental officers, who had assembled in Middlebury earlier in the day, rode out to confer with Captain Cross about the manner in which his company should enter the town. A short time later, the company reformed and marched to within a quarter-mile of the village; there the men encountered "a handsome band of martial music—good players and handsomely dressed—in whose rear followed in files the commissioned officers of the Reg't in full uniform." Captain Cross commanded his company to fall in behind the regimental officers, who formed immediately behind the band. He ordered Hiram to take up a position at the very head of the entire parade. Hiram "never desired more in my life [to] be away from any place than I did from this, for beside being in the midst of strangers, a considerable distance from home, I had the mortification of being placed by the side of friend Russel in front of all the music." To make matters worse, the band members were "handsome performers and elegantly dressed, while I was a mere scholar in the art and but meanly and dirtily cloathed." Consequently, during the entire time that he marched with the Middlebury band, Hiram, "as white as death," did not play a single note. He was totally humiliated, and his "spirits sunk to a low pitch" during the halt in Middlebury. An additional five-mile march to the falls near Weybridge did not help. After walking a total of nearly twenty miles that day and suffering through the torment at Middlebury, he collapsed on a mound of hay. Others in the company "were so foolish as to suffer a violin and a few ladies to rob them of nearly a whole night's repose." Not Hiram: "I felt the effects of the march so much that I had no sort of relish for amusement of any kind."[21]

The next day Hiram and the others ate breakfast at a local tavern and resumed their march on a cold, foggy day. By late morning they arrived in Vergennes, where Captain Cross allowed them to rest for nearly an hour. Hiram spent his time browsing in a bookstore and viewing the town's celebrated waterfalls. He also spoke with a number of people who were "opposed to and disheartened about taking the Canada's." From Vergennes the company marched toward Charlotte. Before reaching that village, Hiram, suffering from exhaustion, left his company to stop at a private home, where he asked a young lady for a bowl of milk and some bread. "She immediately brought on a fine wheaten loaf, plenty of milk, good biscuit with excellent butter and cheese on which I fed bountifully." The generous lady also supplied him with some excellent apples. Revived, he offered to pay her, but she refused to take any money. After this brief respite, Hiram hurried on to Wheeler's Tavern in Charlotte, where he found his company halted for the night. After viewing Lake Champlain, Hiram slept alone that night in a nearby barn.[22]

Shortly after Hiram walked into Peter Wheeler's kitchen the next morning, he heard Mrs. Wheeler asking whether Ben Harwood's son was in the company. When Hiram identified himself, she appeared surprised and immediately asked how his mother felt about his being in the service. He responded that he "presumed it tried her feelings powerfully but that she would bear up under them with firmness." Hiram himself, though, felt "rather downcast" and said very little more on the subject. Mr. Wheeler, who "entertained a very hostile disposition towards the present movements," asked Hiram how the townspeople of Bennington felt about the war. He responded as best he could that some were for it and others against it. Soon thereafter, the company took up its march toward Burlington.[23]

A short distance south of Shelburne, the men halted, tightened their formation, and marched onto the common in front of the meetinghouse, where they remained for several hours awaiting the arrival of the remaining companies in the regiment. When they did not appear, Colonel Martindale ordered a slow advance toward Burlington. Upon reaching a public house several miles south of that town, he ordered a halt until all the companies arrived. Once the entire regiment had been formed, Martindale ordered his men forward; marching by platoons, they entered Burlington at sunset amid a large crowd of spectators. Much to his relief, Hiram encountered Nathaniel Locke shortly after entering the town. When Captain Cross dismissed his company, Hiram accompanied Nathaniel to his quarters in the barracks, where he deposited his knapsack. Then the two friends sought out the quarters of Captain Cross's company in order to get something to eat. Failing that, they found lodging in the house of a local judge, who came home "a little intoxicated & very musical." Although bothered by the fact that "an Oath was no vexation at all to him," Hiram did feel that the judge's conversation "was not barren of many bright ideas with regard to various subjects."[24]

When Hiram left the next morning, he paid the lady of the house twelve and one-half cents for his lodging and went in search of his company. After a time he found his companions at Widow Susan Fay's boardinghouse. Soon after his arrival there, he wrote a letter to his parents, but it "savoured so strongly of melancholy, that I suppressed it—a fine acknowledgment for a brave Volunteer to make, I must confess." A private from Pownal saw Hiram composing this letter and asked him to write one for him to his wife and two sick children. When Hiram read the man what he had written, the soldier broke into tears, "not because the style or words were artfully exprest, but his mind was carried back into the midst of his dearest and most tender connexcions on this side the grave." Confronted with such emotions, Hiram "could not resist the impulse of nature sufficient to keep the tears from stealing down my cheeks, altho' I had no family of my own." Soon after this, "being a musician," Hiram felt the need of some "standard to go by" and proceeded to a bookstore, where he purchased *The Fifer's Companion* for one dollar. As he left the store, he worried that he had spent too much money to support his position as a fifer.[25]

That night Hiram slept uncomfortably cold in Mrs. Fay's barn. In the morning he wrote a letter to Lydia detailing all the events of his march from Shaftsbury to Burlington. After that he wrote a letter for another of his comrades and breakfasted on moldy bread that had been brought from Bennington. Shortly thereafter Captain Cross marched his company onto the parade ground, where the men spent several hours to minimal effect. While there, Hiram visited with a number of young people from Williston who were familiar with his Uncle Ebenezer, a resident of that town. Early in the afternoon, Colonel Martindale marched the regiment to the common in front of the college.[26] From there each captain marched his company to their respective quarters. Since Cross's company had never been divided into messes, which had caused the men no end of confusion at meal times, the orderly sergeant divided the men into groups of six members each. From that time on, "our fare . . . generally continued to be good wheat bread [and] fresh beef which was well prepared by our cooks." After being assigned to a mess, Hiram wrote a letter for a sixty-year-old substitute from Shaftsbury. The old man wanted Hiram to tell his wife and children that he had survived the march and was in good health. When Hiram "seriously surveyed the old man's case the tears stood in my eyes I was so affected."[27]

Hiram spent most of the next day with his journal and writing letters for his fellow soldiers. He also wrote another letter to his own father, "not so much tinctured with gloominess as that which I first wrote." However, the following day he did not attend regimental drill, and when he accompanied Nathaniel Locke and another soldier to the lakeshore to do their mess's laundry, "discontent haunted me too much for my comfort." By the end of the day, he shook off this depression the best he could by playing his flute, chatting with messmates, and listening to the songs of his companions.[28]

Early the following morning, Captain Cross ordered his men to sling their knapsacks and march down to the parade ground on the bank of Lake Champlain, where they were to move into tents that should be ready for them. Upon their arrival the men found no tents, so the captain ordered his troops back to their old quarters. In the afternoon all the militia units that had bivouacked in Burlington met on the parade ground, where General Orms conducted an inspection. Hiram, who "did not march with the music, but carried a sick man's gun," believed the assembled troops showed "strength and determination."[29]

The day after this parade, the members of Captain Cross's company finally moved into their tents. Initially Hiram and his companions were not well impressed with their new quarters. However, after a few days, "it was found much more comfortable lying in them than in barns, although at best it was rather chilly lodging."[30]

When Major Bullard organized the regiment's music, Hiram participated in the exercise. After the major dismissed the men, Hiram strolled down to the lakeshore, where he went aboard a large sloop tied up at the wharf. Tired of drinking well water, he filled his canteen from a bucket of fresh water he found on the sloop. After that he wandered along the wharf until he came to a building that had formerly been occupied by an old acquaintance from Bennington. Conversing with the present occupant about his old friend seemed to lift Hiram's spirits; when he returned to his quarters, he wrote a short letter to his father that was "a burlesque on the happiness I enjoyed when first going into my tent." Shortly thereafter he greatly enjoyed playing "Gillicrankie" for an old acquaintance who dropped by to visit with him.[31]

When Hiram arose the next morning, he did not feel well. Nonetheless, he walked down to the wharf to see a detachment of regulars embark on board a steamboat, "a vessel I had never placed my hand on before." In order to satisfy his curiosity, Hiram had disobeyed orders to report to the parade ground; even though he arrived quite late, he did not suffer any punishment. By noon he felt so ill that he went to Captain Cross's quarters at Mrs. Fay's and "obtained a dose of pikery which seemed to revive my drooping spirits a good deal." A long chat with Mrs. Fay, a longtime friend of the Harwood family, also helped improve Hiram's attitude a bit.[32]

That afternoon Captain Cross informed Hiram and Nehemiah Russell that militia regulations allowed him to have only a single fifer, and so he had drawn a musket for one of them. When asked whether he would rather carry a gun or a fife, Hiram responded that he preferred the fife. The captain then requested that Hiram and Nathaniel discuss the matter between themselves. Contending that he knew nothing about handling a musket, Nathaniel claimed to have turned out as a fifer. Since this was not the case with Hiram, he willingly acquiesced when Captain Cross decided that he should carry a weapon. The company then drilled until after nightfall.[33]

Hiram's spirits had not improved much by the next day. He wrote a letter to Lydia that he "concluded afterwards not to send." That morning's drill on the parade ground consisted of "facing and wheeling at which we were pretty awkward." In the midst of drill, Captain Cross called his men to attention so that an elderly man could address them. Stating that his father had been the first man to drive a team into Vermont, the speaker then described all the hardships such early pioneers had endured to bring the state of Vermont into existence. The speaker himself claimed to have witnessed many of these trying scenes and exhorted the troops gathered before him "to behave like men, and preserve the character of Vermonters." The man's story may have brought images of Peter to Hiram's mind. In any event, this presentation affected him deeply; it "came so near the tender and sympathetic feelings of the heart that I could not refrain from tears."[34]

After Captain Cross dismissed his company from drill, Hiram asked if he could be absent from camp until late the following night. The captain consented, and Hiram immediately set out for Williston to visit Uncle Ebenezer and his family. He managed to get a ride on a wagon for more than half of the five miles and arrived at his uncle's house by early evening. Aunt Eunice, who "expressed great surprise at my being a soldier and leaving so good a home as I possessed," wondered aloud how "my mother could consent to it." She firmly "believed if one of her sons should be torn from her in that manner that she should certainly run crazy." As far as she was concerned, she simply "could not bear with the principle of war — it was altogether wrong and unnecessary [and she] hoped the whole nation would be cowards."[35]

Hiram's aunt was not the only person to express such views. Her son Socrates lay ill, and the doctor attending him "let loose all his federal artillery against the war." To his mind three hundred thousand men would not be sufficient to take Canada, and "every man who crossed the line would certainly be killed." Beyond that, if something was not done about the Madison administration, "Monarchy would soon be in the place of our Constitution." Hiram did not respond: "my mind was in such a situation then that I did not feel disposed to dispute much on politics." Instead, taking a dish of bread and milk and drinking a steaming hot cup of tea, he settled into the family circle, which "in a great measure removed that camp gloom which had been preying on my mind for several days." Following supper, Hiram played several of his favorite pieces on the flute that managed to calm even the doctor's virulent Federalism. As a cold rain pelted down that night, Hiram, snug and warm, pitied his poor comrades who were obliged to spend the night in their damp and drafty tents.[36]

Hiram passed the next day quite comfortably with his relatives, but that night found him back in his tent suffering from the cold. He awoke to a frost-covered landscape. After the regiment performed "wheeling and other maneuvers," Hiram spent most of the day at Mrs. Fay's, reading *A Tablet of Memory* and visiting with his cousin Hiram and other men from the Eleventh Regiment. Over the next several days, however, military life once again began to depress him severely. He wrote a letter to Lydia, "which I would never forward to her." Then the next day Hiram and his company had the military regulations of the U.S. Army read to them on the parade ground. "On hearing these I felt a keen itching to return to my citizenship." Even though he considered the nation's cause to be "just," Hiram "concluded I possessed a bad genius for the Military — and knowing it to be possible to obtain a substitute I thought I would gladly return to my 'Vine & fig tree,' never again, unless imperious necessity should call, abandon them, to live the most honorable soldier's life that was ever lived."[37]

By the next day, Hiram experienced "great uneasiness of mind with respect to the business in which I was engaged" and wrote a letter to his father asking him to obtain a substitute to take his place in the ranks. When Ellis Doty, an old family friend who was driving baggage wagons for the militia, stopped by to ask how he was doing, Hiram answered "without reserve in the negative." He then "enlarged on the subject considerable [and] requested him as he was going directly to my father's to use his endeavor to make known my case to him." Doty spoke very kindly and offered to lend Hiram ten dollars if that would help to ease his situation. Nonetheless, before ending the conversation, Doty — an old Federalist — asked with a laugh: "Ain't you a Democrat?" "Did you not volunteer?" Joining in the laughter, Hiram admitted that he was in fact a Democrat and he had indeed volunteered; nevertheless, "as my mind stood affected then, I cared very little for what might be said provided I could return home once more."[38]

Two days later Hiram, wrestling with his own sense of manhood, reflected upon what he had told Doty and what he had written to his parents. Considering it "a total departure from that dignified station which a faithful and true soldier ever preserves, be the circumstances under which he is placed ever so disagreeable and perplexing," Hiram "looked upon myself as a degraded being in the estimation of all my friends." Even so, he still did not have the "patience to submit cheerfully to a soldier's fortune."[39]

Since his company did not have parade that day, Hiram visited a local bookstore, where he passed the time reading Thomas Ashe's *Travels in America*. While at the bookstore, he envied the "pleasure whom kind fortune placed by their books instead [of] throwing into the military ranks as she [did] me and many others." The fact that he had volunteered made it all the worse. Although it was a "satisfaction to me, even in my present unsettled state of mind, to be in the B.store, [I] could not help thinking how much greater my pleasure had been when I had visited such places in smoother times — with cheerful and inviting prospects — when instead of occupying the great State of Bustle and Confusion, I was an obscure and calm spectator."[40]

The weather, which began to deteriorate rapidly, did not enhance Hiram's mood. Rainy, cold conditions, "which occasioned me to be in lower spirits than usual," set in, and the air became "chill and searching." During such times Hiram spent his free time writing letters for his fellow soldiers to their families and friends. He also lent a rather curious attention to the regimental chaplain, who delivered prayers for the troops each day. One morning, following his devotional, the chaplain gave a short "exhortation" dealing with the "character of our officers and the subordination due from the privates to them."[41]

Following the chaplain's address, the men performed a number of "wheelings and facings" that Hiram enjoyed with "the same pleasure that a lazy ox does driven before the plow." Shortly thereafter he ran into an old friend from home who was visiting Burlington and shared with him "among other things that I did not much like my business." "Well," the man responded good-naturedly, "don't volunteer next time." Then, in a more sober vein, he observed that six months was such a short time that Hiram should "stick to it and not give back."[42]

After morning prayers the next day, Captain Cross dismissed his men until two o'clock that afternoon. Hiram proceeded immediately to the post office but, to his immense disappointment, received no letters. He left the post office desirous of writing in his journal. Hoping to escape the snow that had begun to fall that morning, Hiram thought there would be "no harm in going into the officers barracks and asking the privilege of a seat there." He quickly discovered that a "poor private would have done better not [to] have presumed so much and kept where his company was more desired." As a result, he walked to Mrs. Fay's, where he not only found a warm spot to write but dined with her as well. By three o'clock that afternoon, he was drilling on the parade ground with his comrades in a biting cold wind.[43]

The next morning Hiram, suffering from severe fatigue, felt "unwell." He was becoming increasingly depressed and disillusioned with military service. The following day, after "freely communicat[ing] the state of my mind to my friend Locke," Hiram went to the hospital in hope of finding some relief for his physical distress. While there he visited a number of Captain Cross's men who were sick with the measles. After that he walked to the printing office, where he spent several hours writing in his journal.[44]

By this time most of Hiram's fellow soldiers were also showing signs of restlessness. Under the mistaken impression that they were to receive their pay monthly, many started to agitate to draw their pay.[45] Others began to speculate on the regiment's ultimate destination: some favored Swanton, others Plattsburgh; most, however, cared little about where they might be sent so long as they had "wood enough and plenty of provisions." This made good sense to Hiram, since the weather had become increasingly cold and the mountains to the northeast had become covered with snow.[46]

On October 9 Colonel Martindale's regiment received orders to break camp. In order to ready himself, Hiram paid a shoemaker fifty cents, the last bit of money he had, to repair a pair of shoes for him. The next day official orders came for the regiment to proceed across Lake Champlain to Plattsburgh, New York, on Monday, October 12, to join the American forces under General Henry Dearborn in an attack upon Montreal. Upon learning that same day that Lieutenant Lacy had been ordered to go to Bennington to bring up more recruits, Hiram gave him a letter to take to Elijah Bullard, a relative of a messmate, who resided in the northwest part of that town. In this letter he requested Bullard "to go to my father and make a bargain with him about taking my place." Fearful that something might befall him before Bullard arrived, Hiram told his messmates that he considered the letter he had just written to be his "death warrant."[47]

By the next day Hiram, troubled over his unmanly behavior, began to have second thoughts about sending off his "death warrant." After reflecting seriously on the matter, he decided, "rather than back out of the business in such a manner, to endeavor to console myself as well as I could, and, although placed in a situation highly disagreeable, to hold out to the end." Consequently, he lost no time in writing a long "penitential" letter to his Uncle Ira, "in which I requested my father not to procure me a substitute." He carried this letter to the post office through a cold, heavy rain. At the post office he received letters from Lydia and Ruth Harwood, which he took with him to Mrs. Fay's to read. They were filled with such praise for his courage and fortitude that he was certain he never would have signed his "death warrant" had he read them earlier. In the meantime the weather became so dark, rainy, and muddy that Hiram lodged with Mrs. Fay that night.[48]

On Monday, October 12 — the day designated for the First Regiment to embark for Plattsburgh — the wind blew out of the northwest with such force that no crossing could be made. As the men began to strike their tents the next day, a violent snow squall struck, once again preventing any ships from sailing on Lake Champlain. Most of those who had already taken down their tents found shelter in the barracks; Hiram slept at Mrs. Fay's.

Finally, on October 14, the men of the First Regiment received orders to board the steamboat and the sloop *Champlain*. The wind was still blowing so fiercely, however, that the two ships could not tie up at the wharf. The troops had to be ferried from the wharf to the ships in bateaux. Hiram and most of his company boarded the *Champlain.* As soon as the sloop set sail for Plattsburgh, it began to pitch and roll in the violent winds and choppy water. Hiram believed that "never in my short career had I experienced sensations like those caused in this most unpleasant situation — Half the men on board were puking at the same time." In an attempt to quiet his own stomach, Hiram left his knapsack on the quarterdeck and went into a cabin to lie down on a berth. Very soon, however, he, too, began retching violently.[49]

When the sloop reached Plattsburgh Bay, the storm had become so violent that those in command judged it too dangerous to disembark. Hiram and a good many others descended into the hold, where they arranged themselves as comfortably as possible on piles of tents, chests, and other equipment. There, "amidst singing, hallooing, groaning, dog-barking and cock-crowing," Hiram "curled up in a very uneasy posture on one side of the hold." Throughout the night he "reflect[ed] on the means by which it appeared to me I was bro't there." The simple act of volunteering "I conceived to be the reason of My being abroad in a manner so disagreeable to me — when perhaps if I had left the matter to chance some other poor devil would have been drawn out instead of me." Knowing full well that "there is nothing like patriotism in this," Hiram felt certain that "other people placed as I was dreampt the same noble dream." Hiram realized that as a "Vermont Volunteer" he should not have allowed himself to "dwell on topics so unprofitable"; instead he "ought to have gloried in his sufferings and hardships which should he survive would load him with immortal honors." Unfortunately, "military pride was not enough in me to inspire my mind with such elevated sentiments."[50]

When Hiram arose the next morning, he had one more "grand article" to add to his "catalogue of military achievements" — the previous evening he had left his belongings on the quarterdeck when he followed his companions into the hold for the night. Now, no matter how diligently he searched, he could not find his knapsack, and with it all his clothing, his flute, and the *Fifer's Companion.* The loss, which he estimated at sixteen dollars, was "mortifying"; he had no recourse except to do without or write home for more clothing. Realizing that he must do the latter, he felt humiliated.[51]

Even though the lake remained quite rough, the troops disembarked into bateaux that took them to shore. Once the regiment had reformed,

Colonel Martindale led his men to a site nearly a mile south of the Plattsburgh courthouse. Although partially cleared, the area remained heavily forested, and the men had to spend several days clearing away trees and underbrush to make a permanent encampment. While his companions prepared a campsite, Hiram's "health was so much impaired by our late voyage that I neither assisted in fatigue parties nor marched down to the Regular Encampment to watch the execution of an unfortunate culprit." From the time he landed ashore, he "became low-spirited and dull from being much out of health & [from] a great dislike of the business — nothing went right." He became so dispirited that he was unable to keep his journal with anything like the order and precision that characterized his entries before disembarking at Plattsburgh.[52] "Discouraged and uneasy," he swallowed whatever modicum of personal pride remained and "solicit[ed] my father a second time to send on a substitute."[53]

The appearance of Joseph Day Jr., hired by Luther Smith of Bennington to serve in his stead, did nothing to improve Hiram's state of mind. Since Day had money — "and on that account only" — he gained admittance to Hiram's mess. The fact that he was financially able to contribute to the creature comforts of the tent certainly counted in his favor. However, this had to be weighed against the man's personality; it seemed to Hiram that "a more rough, savage, ill-bred Devil never existed in an enlightened country" than Joseph Day.[54]

Shortly after Day's arrival, Lieutenant Lacy returned with several other substitutes from Bennington. These included John Crawford, who had agreed to serve in the place of his son. Hiram and the old man became good friends, and Crawford did manage to "say some good things to cheer my drooping spirits." Such encouragement was certainly necessary, since Lieutenant Lacy had delivered Hiram a letter from friends at home indicating that, before the arrival of his letter countermanding his request for a substitute, Elijah Bullard had in fact agreed with Benjamin to serve in Hiram's place for twenty dollars. Hiram "was now sorry that he had not come on with Lacy as was his intention if the letter alluded to had not prevented him, for, at that period, I made but a Ghostly appearance in camp."[55]

To Hiram's great joy, Uncle Jonas arrived during the first week in November. Not only was he happy to see a familiar face, but in addition Jonas brought Hiram a pair of boots, a pair of socks, and a shirt from his parents. That night Hiram, Jonas, and Nathaniel Locke spent the evening at a tavern in Plattsburgh, "very agreeably talking of domestic affairs." They all slept on the kitchen floor by the fire and the next day walked to the "Grand Parade" to view the encampment of the regulars. They watched the changing guard discharge their weapons, viewed the heavy artillery, and looked over the horses of the flying artillery. Hiram was not impressed: "The scene which some people delight so much to be spectators of, and even in which so many like to be actors, at this place excited no pleasant sensations in me." "I should have been vastly better pleased in viewing a well cultivated farm, or fine well regulated and flourishing garden." Perhaps even a "Church-yard would have raised my spirits to as high a pitch as all the military grandeur which I saw displayed at this camp."[56]

The next day Jonas was anxious to be on his way to his home in Hopkinton, New York. Before he left, however, he "condescended to write . . . a short letter to my father, stating his opinion to be that it would be best to send on a substitute for me." Whether Jonas was embarrassed by Hiram's lack of fortitude or frustrated with his nephew's seeming inability to act like a man, "the tone which [he] gave to this epistle caused some disgraceful consequences to ensue in regard to myself."[57]

Hiram "enjoyed very few agreeable hours" while in camp, but he did make many friends within Captain Cross's company, "in whose society I enjoyed many happy moments." Such moments generally took place in the evening alongside a large pine tree that had been uprooted near the company's tents. Each night the men built a giant fire beside this tree and sat around sharing stories and singing songs, which lifted Hiram's spirits a bit. However, even at these times, Hiram "could not forget where I was and how easily I could have avoided being there."[58] Whenever he could, Hiram also enjoyed visiting the printing office, where he read newspapers and perused whatever books lay about. He particularly enjoyed looking through Isaiah Thomas's *History of Printing in America.*

With the passage of time, a good many others in the regiment began to share Hiram's uneasiness. When ordered to supply large detachments to guard the boats and to march several miles north of Plattsburgh daily to stand picket duty, men in the various militia regiments protested so vigorously to the latter that their officers took the issue up with their superiors. As a result, the militia retained responsibility only for guarding the boats. Pay was another cause of concern among the men. "As the time drew near when our two months wages became due not the softest threats were uttered by the soldiery in case it

were not punctually paid." Despite such grumbling, only two deser-
tions occurred in Hiram's regiment while encamped at Plattsburgh.
Nonetheless, "much irregularity in camp prevailed at this time." In
direct opposition to orders not to discharge their weapons without
orders, gunshots erupted thirty to forty times a day in every section of
the camp.[59]

Hiram believed this disdain for authority to be directed toward Colonel Martindale, who had begun "to show great indifference toward his
men." They, in turn, "imbibed a very unpopular opinion of him," and
many officers and men throughout the regiment began to speak out
against him. Feeling that he had displayed "unmilitary conduct" since
arriving in Plattsburgh, the men became incensed when he "betray[ed]
a mean speculating disposition." With the onset of cold weather, Martindale had purchased a large number of blankets, which he began to
sell to his men. The sale of these blankets did not offend the men nearly
so much as the fact that Martindale had cut the blankets in half before
selling them in order to double his profits.[60]

With each passing day, the cold weather increased the discomfort of
the men. Certain that they were going to be held in service through the
winter, several privates went to their officers and suggested that two
men be detached from each company to return home and procure
warmer clothing for their respective companies. Colonel Martindale
adopted the proposal, but before he could put it into execution, the
regiment received orders to proceed to the town of Champlain on the
Canadian border.

In the second week of November, Colonel Martindale's regiment
left Plattsburgh in bateaux bound for the mouth of the Big Chazy River
in Champlain Township. Rowing against a strong headwind, Hiram
and his comrades managed only to reach Point Rush, eight miles by
land from Plattsburgh, by nightfall. During the day they had become
separated from their provision boats and suffered from fatigue and
hunger by the time they came ashore. A boatload of militiamen from
another company beached their boats alongside those of Hiram's company. In their hunger, several men from that company broke into a
barrel of pork meant for the entire regiment and helped themselves.
After apprehending these "beasts," the officers present placed them
under guard. Ironically, the sergeant of the guard had himself been
implicated in the theft and, perhaps with tongue in cheek, employed
the word "Pork" as the guard's countersign.[61]

While camped at Point Rush, Hiram and several of his comrades found shelter in a poor man's cottage, where they slept on the floor in front of a large fire. That night Hiram experienced a "little piece of ill-luck" that he felt illustrated "the stamp of my character as a soldier." He also considered it "no flattering omen as to my being a man of business." Before lying down, Hiram had taken the precaution of placing his fife on a shelf so that it would not be broken if he were to roll over on it in his sleep. He was several miles down the path to the lake the following morning before he realized that he had left the instrument in the cottage where he spent the night. The fife had cost him $1.50, and he had been offered that sum plus another fife in exchange for it while in Burlington. At that time he still hoped he might be reinstated as the company's fifer and refused the bargain. Now he fully realized his mistake.[62]

When Hiram and his companions pushed off from shore early that morning, they faced a bitter cold wind and a storm-tossed lake. After rowing about three miles into a strong headwind, they hauled up on the western shore of a small island, made fast their boats, and walked up to a private house to refresh themselves. Upon entering the house, they discovered a group of militiamen from another regiment who had just finished their breakfast. "Without a cent of money and without knowing of whom I could borrow," Hiram sat down at the table, where "a more delicious meal I never ate," even though he occupied the "2nd table." Fortunately, one of his comrades loaned Hiram ten cents, the cost of the meal.[63]

After breakfast the men once again boarded their boats and pushed off for the Big Chazy. Rowing against a freshening headwind and choppy waves soon exhausted the men, but they had no choice but to continue. As far as Hiram was concerned, "the business of rowing was new and far from being agreeable to a plowman like me." Then, in a classic understatement, he observed that when one considered the threatening weather and the stormy condition of the lake, "it will not appear strange that a person like me, unskilled in navigation of any kind and inexperienced in the difficulties and dangers which attend a sailor, or soldier's life, should entertain now and then a gloomy thought."[64]

Near sunset Hiram's boat arrived at the mouth of the Big Chazy, where he and his mates landed on the north side of the river and pitched their tents amid a grove of trees a few rods from the water's edge. Unfortunately, Hiram's duties as a sailor had not come to an end; he and his company spent the next several days boating provisions from ships moored in the lake to the town of Champlain, a round trip of some ten miles.

While encamped on the Big Chazy, the men did their best to make their quarters comfortable in the biting cold weather. Most of the messes built chimneys onto their tents. A mason from another company agreed to build a fireplace for Hiram's mess and, after Hiram assisted him with the task, refused to take any payment when he completed the job. Even though the fireplace made the tent much more comfortable, Hiram "found myself obliged to quit it on account of the disgust I had imbibed against Mr. Day." The man's "manners and behavior were so rough as not to be any longer tolerable with me." As a result, Hiram, who simply could not stand Day's drinking and swearing, moved out of his mess's warm tent into the sergeant's unheated one. There he found "much greater satisfaction than in my former one — except in the article of fire which I sought in log and brush heaps abroad." Hiram would rather endure the freezing cold than suffer Day's boorish behavior.[65]

Several days after moving away from Joseph Day, Hiram had the satisfaction of seeing the man receive a bit of justice. This resulted from a case of gross insubordination on Day's part. When ordered to take his place on guard duty, Day, amid a torrent of oaths, absolutely refused to serve. Lieutenant Lacy placed him under guard. However, "finding this to be neither an inconvenience nor a mortification to the wretch," he ordered Day to sit on a tree stump near the bank of the river some five or six rods away from the fire around which the camp guard stood. In addition, Day could not move more than one pace from the stump without permission from the officer of the guard. So as not to overburden the camp guard, Lieutenant Lacy requested volunteers to form a separate guard over Day. Hiram must not have been alone in his opinion of Day, because many men immediately presented themselves and "gladly seized this opportunity to humble the audacity of the refractory prisoner." Throughout the freezing cold night, Day, wrapped in his blanket, walked or ran around the stump for an hour or two at a time. Allowed to visit the fire only three or four times during the night, the prisoner screamed at the guard with all his might, swore at the lieutenant, and sang verses of bawdy songs at the top of his lungs.[66]

Since Hiram had drawn camp guard duty that night, he was able to observe Day throughout this entire "odd and humiliating scene." The immediate effect of this punishment on Day seemed to Hiram to be beneficial; the man appeared to become more "pliable and obedient." Unfortunately, this did not last. In a matter of days, Day returned to his old form: "It was so natural to him to act out his satanical disposition that he could not govern himself, but must permit it to boil out on all occasions." Once again the man had offended Hiram's sense of decorum and self-restraint.[67]

Joseph Day was not the only man who angered the men of Hiram's company. At the time his regiment left Plattsburgh, Colonel Martindale abandoned his men and returned to Burlington on private business. Major Elihu Cross of Shaftsbury took over command and quickly gained the trust and admiration of the men. Martindale's own son served as sergeant major for the regiment and was "generally respected." His father, however, "had heavy curses laid on him by many of his men, who hoped never to see him in the command again."[68]

Within several days after landing at the Big Chazy, Hiram's regiment received orders to proceed to Champlain. Landing near that village, the men scrambled ashore and carried their equipment for nearly a mile to a location near the village, where they set up their tents once more. The first thing that caught Hiram's attention after helping to set up camp was that the entire village of Champlain seemed to be filled with regulars and militiamen "with every appearance of being bound to a more northerly clime [Canada]." However, even when General Dearborn arrived with nearly three thousand more men, Hiram did not take a propitious view of the proceedings. Indeed, "not a very flattering picture was this to [even] an eye so unmilitary as mine."[69]

Much to Hiram's relief, his substitute arrived shortly after the regiment established itself at Champlain. Hiram immediately left for Bennington. Following a brief, unsuccessful invasion of Canada, General Dearborn pulled his army back to Plattsburgh, where he dismissed most of the militia, including the First Regiment of detached militia. Ironically, had Hiram remained with his regiment for another week, he could have returned home a proud veteran with Nathaniel Locke and his other comrades; instead he journeyed in ignominious solitude toward Bennington, where he faced disgrace and humiliation.

CANADA

Champlain

Plattsburgh
Point Rush

Lake
Champlain

Burlington

Shelburne

Charlotte

VERMONT

Vergennes

Middlebury

Cornwall

Sudbury

NEW
YORK

Hubbardton

Castleton

Granville

Pawlet

Dorset

Manchester

Shaftsbury

Bennington

This map, drawn by Bill Nelson, traces the route taken by Hiram Harwood and
his detached regiment on their way to Champlain, New York, during the War
of 1812.

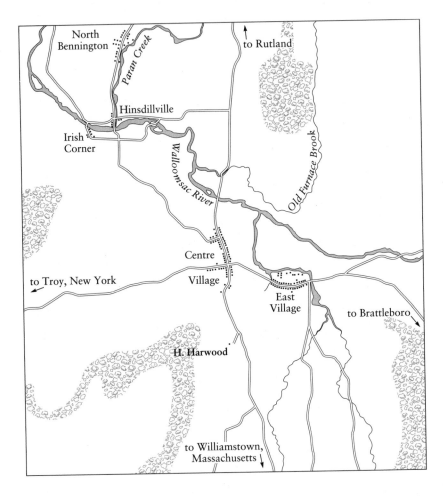

Bennington Township, showing the location of the Harwood farm. *An adaptation of the Joseph Hinsdill map by Bill Nelson.*

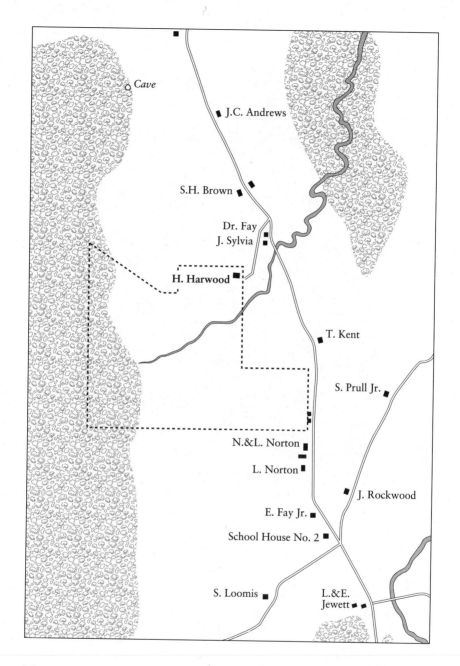

Cave

J.C. Andrews

S.H. Brown

Dr. Fay
J. Sylvia

H. Harwood

T. Kent

S. Prull Jr.

N.&L. Norton

L. Norton

J. Rockwood

E. Fay Jr.

School House No. 2

S. Loomis

L.&E.
Jewett

This section of Joseph Hinsdill's 1835 map of Bennington Township (adapted by Bill Nelson) provides detail of the Harwoods' Tanbrook neighborhood. The outline of the Harwood farm has been determined by the author using school district boundaries, land records, and road surveys. *From a facsimile of the Hinsdill map in the author's possession.*

This portrait of Benjamin Harwood, executed on a small block of wood by an unidentified artist, may have been painted by Alpheus Chapin, a Vermont native known to have done a good deal of work in Bennington. Hiram mentions Chapin in his diary on several occasions but never indicates whether he painted this picture of his father. Hiram died before the advent of photography and, for reasons of frugality, never sat for a portrait. Inferences from Hiram's diary indicate a remarkable resemblance between father and son. Thus, this small portrait is the only clue we have to Hiram's physical appearance. *Courtesy Bennington Museum.*

The Harwood houses — the old slab house erected in 1762 and the larger frame house built in 1769 — as they appeared sometime before 1870, when an addition was attached to the larger house. This drawing was rendered by Pam Bradford from a photograph that appeared in the sketch of historical buildings in Old Bennington published by Richard S. Bayhan in 1930. The list of houses along the streets of Bennington that Hiram compiled in 1837 formed the genesis of this publication. The photograph was provided by the American Antiquarian Society.

This is the view Hiram would have encountered when returning to Bennington from his innumerable trips to Troy and other towns in New York. Entering the town from the west, the Hicks Tavern appears on the left, Old First Church in the center, and a district schoolhouse on the right. *Courtesy American Antiquarian Society.*

Originally called the Dewey Tavern, then the Hicks Tavern, and finally the Walloomsac Inn, this is the tavern where Hiram attended so many dances to listen to the music played in the second-story ballroom. *Courtesy Bennington Museum.*

View of Old Bennington Village, by Daniel Folger Bigelow (c. 1870) captures a perspective of the town looking to the northeast. When traveling into Bennington, Hiram and his family would have entered via the road from the south that passed between Old First Church and the Hicks Tavern. From the perspective of this picture, they would have been moving from right to left. *Courtesy Bennington Museum.*

4

A Compact of Such Vital Importance

My being called from home on the 10th inst occasions a blank in this Volume of about three months which I shall never take the pains to fill up nor have I any desire to see it done, for previous to that period nothing in these pages had occurred but that I had as lief exhibit to the eye of some reader who might accidentally take them into his hand, — (as to any stigma or reproach they would cast upon me) as not.[1]

Upon his return to Bennington, Hiram felt totally humiliated. In a culture that equated courage with manhood, he could only view his lack of courage while in the service of his country as a failure of his own manhood.[2] The fact that his disgrace was common knowledge among the townspeople of Bennington heightened Hiram's pain considerably. As a consequence, for several years following his return, Hiram struggled to regain sufficient self-assurance to mingle freely once again among old friends and acquaintances. During this time he faced again the issue that had caused him such anxiety — marriage.

When he first returned, Hiram did not wish to leave the farm: the prospect of suffering the most extreme personal mortification plagued him constantly. He could not, however, remain in seclusion. No matter how much he might fear meeting "my friends in town this day . . . I knew [this] must take place if I would perform the duty of a independent citizen." So, regardless of how "disagreeable the task might be, I drove into town with a heavy heart and manfully stept forward and added to the number one vote for the Democratic ticket." After casting his ballot, Hiram quickly hurried home: "Not very pleasing sensations passed thro my noddle at this junction."[3]

Two days later, while on a sleigh ride into town with his father and Thomas Parsons, the same unpleasant feelings coursed through Hiram's mind. "So much did I dread meeting my former friends and acquaintances that I avoided stepping into any public or private house or store." His anxiety became so intense that he walked home rather than remain and run the risk of encountering someone who might recognize him.[4]

Close friends and relatives did all they could to comfort him. On his first visit with the Nortons, Clarissa "very cordially shook me by the hand, heartily glad, no doubt to set her eyes once more on a disgraced and humbled Democrat who had for a long time been an object of merriment with her and her colleagues." Claiming that all men were "made for society," Perez Harwood extended a cordial invitation to Hiram to come to his home and pay his family a visit. When Captain Samuel Blackmer stopped by, Hiram, who always enjoyed the man's company, walked partway home with him. During this time Blackmer "laid his hand lightly on that wound which I received in my late tour to the N. — a wound which can never be healed."[5]

Despite the best efforts of friends and family, Hiram could not shake his feelings of despondency. His journal became unusually cryptic; entries such as "during the period under consideration I really felt a great disrelish for manual operations, occasioned by dullness and depression of spirits" sufficed for four- and five-day periods of time.[6] When invited to a ball at House's assembly room, the site of so many happy gatherings prior to his service in the detached militia, Hiram refused. The following day, "dark and almost impervious were the clouds of melancholy which hung over my heathenish soul this rainy unpleasant day." In an attempt to cheer his "drooping spirits" through conversation, Hiram visited the Montagues, but he found little consolation there. Upon returning home he "took up a musical instrument hoping thereby to charm away the hateful phantom, but this only seemed to make bad worse for it carried back my thoughts to a time in which I had enjoyed as much felicity as this world (in my opinion) can ever afford," a time when "my mind was free from such unhappy reflections as now crowded themselves into it."[7]

Like a cancer, Hiram's belief in his own cowardice ate away at his sense of self. He constantly belittled himself in comparison with others: his friend Nathaniel Locke, who had served a full term in the detached militia, became in Hiram's words "that gallant and patriotic soul"; Zechariah Harwood Jr., who died at Plattsburgh while serving in the army, assumed the reputation of "a fair and spotless character," "an undeviating patriotic Republican." It was with bitter irony, then, that Hiram described a visit that Lydia and her "brave brother" made to the Montague home.[8]

Hiram's sense of guilt became so intense that he began to behave in self-deprecating ways. After agreeing to accompany Lydia and others to Perez Harwood's home for a visit, Hiram rendered the occasion "quite unpleasant" through his "dilatory manner" in getting ready to go. Ultimately realizing that he simply could not avoid making the trip, Hiram hurried to get ready. However, instead of putting on his best clothes, as he normally would have done upon such an occasion, he "refused putting off a part of my every day dress — retaining my over-alls and coarse boots which could not be removed from me by the most earnest entreaties of all who were present." Hiram had always been embarrassed to appear in public unless properly dressed, but now he was determined to go forth wearing rough work clothes. Convinced "that my humble fame was not in the least marred in so doing," he apparently believed that he did not deserve to be seen in anything except the most "humble" apparel.[9]

Just as Hiram felt compelled to debase himself before his relatives, he behaved in what he considered an appropriate manner during one of his infrequent visits to church. Following four days in which he de-scribed himself as being "dull and melancholy," Hiram attended Sun-day services with his father. When his head became cold, he covered it with a handkerchief, which "perhaps made an odd appearance." Such behavior would certainly have seemed "odd" if performed by most men, but Hiram may have deemed it entirely appropriate for an indi-vidual whose manliness had been seriously compromised.[10]

Although Hiram was hard on himself regarding his militia service, he had no intention of courting criticism from others. One day he ap-proached Frederick Jewett and Loan Dewey, two of the town's leading Federalists, as he drove his cutter along the road. He acknowledged Jewett "but had no intention of stopping, knowing that he had a large fund of blackguardism which without favor or affection he would pour upon me concerning a late event in my life." When Dewey rushed out, "thinking as I supposed to get hold of me . . . in order to make me a prisoner so as to enjoy the sport of hearing Mr. J's oration," Hiram urged his horse on. Just as he was "laughing heartily to think what a blessing I had escaped from the old man," Dewey overtook Hiram and rode home with him. Claiming that all he wanted was a ride, Dewey heartily enjoyed hearing Hiram relate why he wished to avoid Jewett. Several months later, however, Dewey "did not let slip that opportunity to give me a few hearty rubs on former transactions of which, the blessed remembrance of which always give me no small mortification."[11]

Even without the "rubs" of men like Dewey, Hiram's humiliation continued to haunt him. Four months after his return from Plattsburgh, he remained deeply despondent. "Reflected much on the past, but to what did it amount? — did it clothe folly in a more comely garb — did it blunt the edge of keen remorse or any other unpleasant feeling occasioned in the same way — did it do away anything that had been done?" His reply was, of course, a resounding "no." Unable to desist, he continued this dialogue with himself: "Where is the profit in meditations of this cast?" His answer: "There is none." Still unsatisfied, he asked "then why deal in them so much?" His response: "Why sir, do you not know that whatsoever we undertake and perform honorably and faithfully, although many serious difficulties are at the same time to be overcome, do you not know that when the task is ended it gives pleasure to the mind to review the scene. And Vice Versa if badly executed is it not ever a gnawing canker to the poor soul that shall have so conducted."[12]

~ Whatever solace Hiram found in the first years that he was home came from reading and music. Following his old habit, he read much history. His special favorite, however, was Sydney Owenson Morgan's novel *The Wild Irish Girl*. He took it everywhere but most particularly carried it with him to the Parsons household, where he read it to various members of the family. He and the Parsonses called it "preaching." If preaching it was, it was "preaching too that we all liked — many of the sentimental expressions with which it abounds made some more novel and pleasant impressions on me — too refined for me to think of describing."[13]

At first music, which had always been a source of comfort to Hiram, even during his service in the military — his messmates had dubbed him the "solitary fifer" — did not provide him with any pleasure upon his return from Plattsburgh. Playing the flute only seemed to make "bad worse" by carrying his thoughts back to a happier time.[14] Gradually, however, he began playing the flute in company. As always, this became a means by which he could be present at neighborhood gatherings without being obliged to participate fully in activities that might jeopardize his fragile sense of self-confidence.

He did not, however, turn to the flute in private times as he so often did before his ill-fated service in the detached militia. Instead, several months after his return, he borrowed Judge Fay's violin — an instrument not associated with feelings of previous happiness — and began to teach himself to play. Within two months he managed to learn "enough of drawing the bow to groan out the balance of a tune." By this time "fiddling" and "writing music" had become a pastime he preferred "to any other amusement."[15]

By this time, too, Hiram played the violin rather than the flute to ease his troubled mind. He often "vainly attempted to fiddle away dull cares" or "took down old fiddle at night which I thought might have administered great satisfaction to my mind." Such times were important to him; even though he began to play in public, he said, "I always fiddle best in solitude."[16]

It was Hiram's flute, however, that led to a most rewarding public exhibition of his musical talents. On Wednesday, April 6, 1814, Hiram walked to Paran Creek Village to join a group of musicians invited to play at the Polemic Society's exhibition, which was being held in Shaftsbury. He dined with the musicians — four clarinetists, two flutists, and two violinists — at the house of the president of the society and then practiced for a short time before joining a procession to the meetinghouse. Hiram took his place with the other musicians in the gallery opposite the stage and joined them as they played before the opening of the exhibition and at intervals throughout the evening. At nearly ten o'clock, following the final performance of various short plays and orations, Hiram and his fellow musicians "were told that they [the spectators] were highly pleased with our performance." The other musicians accepted payment for their services, but Hiram would take nothing. He did, however, accept his good friend Hiland Hall's invitation to join him in his home, where they "partook of cake, cheese and excellent cider and went to bed." Hiram did not arrive home until after ten the following morning. Even though "very dull and unsociable all day" because of his late night, he could take pride in his activities on the previous day.[17] Although he was a failure as a soldier and always made to feel uncertain of his abilities as a farmer, Hiram had been accepted and honored as a musician.

～ Music and books served to distract Hiram's mind, but these could never entirely displace the issues that most distressed him: his past cowardly behavior and his present status as a "disgraced and humbled Democrat." These ate at him constantly, and yet he had no choice except to go on with his life as best he could. Regardless of his unfortunate military experience, Hiram remained fiercely loyal to his republican principles and his duties as an "independent citizen." Consequently, he had forced himself to cast his ballot within several days of his ignominious return to Bennington.

Following that election, Hiram, suffering from long periods of melancholy, stayed as close to home as possible. By late February 1813, however, he had to go out in public. Not only that, he had to face the men of Captain Samuel Cross's company who were gathered at Cushman's Hall in Bennington to receive their pay for service in the detached militia. Since Hiram had volunteered and did not provide a substitute until well into the campaign, he remained on the muster roll and was eligible for the same pay as the others. Not willing to forfeit $19.74, he proceeded to Cushman's and with mixed feelings mingled with his old comrades.[18]

Having received the salary due him from the federal government, Hiram was also interested in garnering whatever pay the state of Vermont owed him for his service in the detached militia. Therefore, he and Nathaniel Locke sought out Lieutenant Samuel Lacy, who informed them of the proper procedure to follow. Soon thereafter Hiram wrote an order on the state auditor of accounts and asked him to forward the pay for him and Locke by mail. Within a month Hiram received a draft for $16.48 — $8.24 for each man.[19]

Since service in the detached militia did not relieve Hiram from his obligation to remain active in Captain Samuel Blackmer's local militia company, he rejoined his old comrades whenever they turned out for training. Given the urgency of wartime, Colonel Jonathan E. Robinson, a Democrat in command of the militia regiment that included Hiram's company, mustered his command for regular training quite often. Captain Samuel Blackmer, a Federalist, did not always comply.

On those occasions, when Benjamin and others went off to observe regimental training, Hiram, no longer attracted to such events, stayed home and played the violin.[20]

Although he was never enthusiastic about participating in militia drills, Hiram became particularly upset during a training session in June 1814. Having "very badly attempted to perform the fifer's duty," he "nevertheless lived out the day," only to have Captain Samuel Blackmer announce his resignation and call the company together to elect a new captain. Even though his old friend and captain was a Federalist, Hiram had always been very fond of him. Now, Samuel's brother Wilber, whom Hiram detested, stood for election. Only after the man promised to serve for only one year would Hiram vote for him. Elections followed for many positions, and as a result the competing candidates made many stump speeches. All were Federalists, but the election of his close friend John Norton Jr. and others like him did not offend Hiram. What did upset him was the election of Moses D. Robinson, son of the wealthiest merchant in Bennington and the town's leading Federalist. Robinson won his place only after making a "handsome, short speech." Miffed, Hiram petulantly observed, "and why couldn't he do *that*, when everybody knows he had been to college where all sorts of speeches are learned."[21]

This was not Hiram's only encounter with Moses D. Robinson. Following another militia training, he and Robinson "had a few words . . . on politics." This occurred after Robinson saw Hiram reading a copy of Thomas Jefferson's *Notes on the State of Virginia* and accused Jefferson of articulating "principles in that book differing widely from those which had actuated him while in the Presidency." Having his political idol charged with hypocrisy was more than Hiram could bear. A heated conversation ensued, in which each man "tenaciously adhered to his own *side*, as Politicians, or those calling themselves so, generally do, without any kind of profit."[22]

By the time he became involved with Moses D. Robinson, Hiram had once again become fully engaged in politics and political dialogue. Concerned over Federalist activities in opposition to the war throughout the nation, but particularly within Bennington, Hiram began to lend a hand to Jonas (who had returned to live with the family following his wife's death) in his efforts to achieve Democratic control of Bennington's next town meeting and all its offices. After Jonas canvassed the neighborhood, Hiram prepared a list of Tanbrook men who were prepared to vote for Democrats at the March meeting. Jonas took the list to the Democratic vigilance committee, whose members tabulated it along with many other such compilations. When Jonas returned home late that night, he confided to Hiram that if the "Republicans would be at their posts" at the coming town meeting, they should carry the elections by a majority of twenty votes. In response to an order from the Democratic vigilance committee, Hiram spent much time over the next several days writing out Democratic ballots to be handed to voters at the town meeting. His Federalist counterparts were equally busy preparing their own ballots. During this time Jonas displayed "some uneasiness in his behavior," which Hiram believed "must be accounted for by its being so near March meeting."[23]

Jonas's anxiety was well founded; the town meeting turned out to be "one of the most extraordinary ever held in this town." The parties were so evenly matched that it took three ballots before Isaac Tichenor, the town's leading Federalist, prevailed as moderator. After that things went from bad to worse for the Democrats: "the authority of the Town (all the select-men being F'l) . . . manifested no small partiality in the business." When it appeared that the Democrats might carry the election for town clerk, Tichenor managed to have the meeting adjourned until the following Monday. On that day, too, "matters were conducted in not the most honorable fair manner by the Moderator and his adherents." Democratic voters found themselves "rejected on some frivolous plea or other, while those of the fed'l party who according to their own rules had no right to vote were freely admitted."[24] Once again, to Hiram's considerable chagrin, Federalists captured every town office.

Hiram's mood brightened considerably by early August. Busy in their hayfield, he and his family heard the firing of cannons in town. Assuming that this "announced good tidings from some quarter — we supposed from the Lake," they felt as if "every discharge armed us with fresh vigor to get our work completed so as to go & hear the joy-inspiring news." When they finally got to town, they rejoiced upon hearing of a stunning American victory at Fort Erie. Unfortunately, ten days later, when Hiram visited town late in the evening, he heard the "mortifying intelligence that Washington City was captured on the 24th inst." He could not help but join in the "Great hue & cry [that] ensued throughout the land."[25]

In the face of such news, Hiram redoubled his efforts to support the Republican cause in Bennington by writing even more Democratic ballots for the September freemen's meeting. On September 6 he "quitted the plow 2 P.M.—visited the poll—voted Democratic throughout," and then retired to the office of Jonathan E. Robinson, where he pored over books in the man's library. Soon he heard shouts of "Noadiah Swift," "Swift," "Swift," "Noadiah Swift, is the man." To his chagrin, Dr. Noadiah Swift—the Harwood family's neighbor, close friend, physician, and political opponent—had been elected to the general assembly. Even more galling, "after the Constable had declared the box turned, four Democrats presented their ballots, which were rejected, it being urged, contrary to ancient usage, that the box once turned, no ballot can be accepted."[26] Had those ballots been accepted, the election would have resulted in a tie. It was small consolation to Hiram that Jonas Galusha defeated Martin Chittenden by four votes in Bennington; once again, however, the legislature selected Chittenden to serve as governor.[27]

A little over a week after enduring these disappointing election results, Hiram heard the sound of cannons once again in town. This time the news was uplifting: Thomas Macdonough and his fleet on Lake Champlain had won a tremendous victory over the British. Hiram hurried into town to join the celebration, "in which party feeling was almost suppressed."[28]

By mid-October Hiram had begun following the peace negotiations taking place between the United States and Great Britain. As he read the dispatches emanating from Ghent, he wondered who could want "more proof of British arrogance, meanness and pride?" To his mind no one could survey this evidence and "pretend to doubt their close connection with the Indians for more than 20 years past, by every art instigating them to fall on our back settlements in all previous wars which have happened within that period of time." Then, with an ironic twist, he announced that "there is certainly much grandeur in the character of Gt. Britain when coupled with so Hellish a race as the inhuman, blood-thirsty, Savages of the wilds of N. America." At last he exclaimed: "Great God, can the World any longer respect such a nation? The catalogue of bloody crimes of which that nation is the author hath swelled into volumes."[29]

Although British actions upset Hiram, the "cursed scheme" (the secession of the New England states from the Union) of Federalists gathered at Hartford, Connecticut, angered him even more. Any thought of "a separation of the States" drove him to distraction. When he discussed the actions of the Hartford Convention with a neighbor, he became somewhat calmer. The man "altogether condemned" a division of the Union and exclaimed that "he would fight against it sooner than almost anything." Much relieved, Hiram declared that the man's "republicanism was good."[30] The preservation of republicanism meant everything to him.

ᑐᓴ Hiram, like most other young men in Bennington, had always limited his political participation to voting in the various local, state, and national elections held throughout the year. He lent what assistance he could to Jonas's efforts on behalf of the Democratic vigilance committee, but he left the organization and administration of that committee to elders of the party—Jonathan E. Robinson, David Robinson Jr., O. C. Merrill, David Fay, Anthony Haswell, and Samuel Young. These were the individuals to whom Hiram and other young Jeffersonian Republicans (Democrats) had always deferred in all matters regarding local partisan activities.

In the early fall of 1813, though, when the war appeared to be reaching crisis proportions, many of Bennington's ardent young Republicans searched for some special means by which to show support for the Madison administration and to demonstrate their devotion to the principles of republicanism. In response to a request from organizations in Berkshire County, Massachusetts, that called themselves Sons of Liberty, a small group of young men gathered at the State Arms Tavern on September 5, 1813, and "as a band of Brothers," voted to form an association in support of the war.[31] Six days later a much larger contingent met again at the State Arms to discuss a constitution for their association. Once a draft had been read, the young men asked advice from Samuel Young, who attended the meeting as a spectator. He commended the young men for their efforts and advised against "secret, midnight, dark and intriguing proceedings"; instead, everything should be "transacted in a truly Republican manner." Captain David Robinson Jr., another visitor, then offered his opinion, "which went to inculcate nothing but genuine Republican principles."[32] Once these gentlemen withdrew, the young men discussed the constitution for some time and then turned it over to a committee for revision.[33]

Upon reconvening ten days later, the young Republicans named their association the Sons of Liberty in the town of Bennington and adopted a constitution. Under its provisions all members must be of good moral character, and no individual over thirty or under sixteen years of age was eligible to join the association. Every brother must subscribe to a personal declaration to support the U.S. Constitution, a

republican form of government in the state of Vermont, and the constitution and bylaws of the Sons of Liberty. In addition, members pledged
themselves to celebrate the Fourth of July, to "relieve a brother Son of
Liberty in distress" whenever it was within their power, and to form a
procession similar to that of their Masonic elders at the funeral of any
deceased brother. The constitution required no membership fees; instead, members made voluntary contributions. In a burst of youthful
enthusiasm and idealism, the members set out the rules governing their
meetings: whenever speaking on any subject, members must address
themselves to the president; they must be allowed to speak without
interruption; and no one could speak more than twice on the same
subject without the permission of the president. Perhaps most important, no refreshment except water was to be admitted in any of the
meetings without a special vote of those present.[34]

Hiram occupied a position on the furthest periphery of power and
influence in Bennington politics, but this was definitely not the case
within the Sons of Liberty. He was among the twenty-eight charter
members of that association, and his brothers selected him a trustee at
the initial election of officers. He participated enthusiastically in the
association's meetings and zealously supported the constitution's ring-
ing pronouncement that the association had "the right to discuss all
religious, political, and moral subjects."[35]

Eager to show their support for the war effort, the Sons of Liberty
voted to take up a subscription among the women of Bennington to
knit socks and mittens for Vermont troops in the field.[36] Knowing
Hiram to be well read and a diligent writer (Hiram's journal was common knowledge among most townspeople), the brothers selected him
to serve on a committee to draft an address to the ladies of Bennington
requesting their support in preparing woolen items for the troops.[37]
Whatever his contribution to its preparation was, the address employed
language strikingly similar to that found in Hiram's journal—itself a
reflection of the literature he read so avidly. Because the group was
aware of the "tender feelings of our mothers and sisters," the address
expressed confidence that the "valiant soldier on his wintry midnight
march watch" would be sensible of the benevolence of these "delicate
creatures" as he resolved "to guard their charms, and shield their dwell-
ings with his life . . . until ruthless enemies shall no longer dare threaten
their repose, or seek to shed the blood of virtuous mothers and inoffensive innocents, on the shores of insulted and abused America."[38]

Hiram assumed a major role when the association fulfilled one of its primary duties—to celebrate the Fourth of July. He chaired the committee on arrangements and also served on a committee charged with preparing public toasts to be presented at the State Arms Tavern.

At noon on July 4, members of the association gathered at the State Arms Tavern and chose I. J. Hendryx to be their marshall pro tem. Hendryx joined Colonel Jonathan E. Robinson at the head of a procession arranged in precise order—martial music, eighteen members of the association, the membership in general of the association, the officers of the association, standard bearers, the president and vice president of the association, the clergy, and finally the Democratic citizens of Bennington—that advanced to the meetinghouse. Rev. Daniel Marsh opened the ceremonies with a prayer, and William Haswell, president of the association, read the Declaration of Independence. After singing an ode composed for the occasion by Anthony Haswell, the assemblage listened to a stirring sermon delivered by Rev. Elon Galusha of Shaftsbury. After that the participants marched back to the State Arms Tavern, where members of the association dined while their fellow citizens retired to Cushman's Tavern to eat.[39]

After dinner all the celebrants gathered once again at the State Arms Tavern to drink toasts in honor of the occasion. The toasts, prepared by Hiram and his fellow committee members, repeated sentiments typical of Democratic celebrations in Bennington. These included salutes to independence, the Union, James Madison, George Washington, Thomas Jefferson, and the American character. There were additional toasts that reflected not only Hiram's characteristic mode of expression but also sentiments peculiar to him and his young colleagues. Typical of these was an attack upon Elijah Parish—a Congregational minister from Essex County, Massachusetts, who, with a number of like-minded clergy, distributed printed versions of sermons violently opposing the war—for selling "the gospels under par" and giving "a premium for the science of sedition." Another reproached the "minority Governor and late Council of Censors,"[40] and another honored "the enlightened will of the freemen—sovereign, and the people—united—Here is the secret of our strength, the rock of our safety; our power to rule in the midst of our enemies." The young men also toasted "The Fair—Smiles for *friends, frowns* for *enemies.*" Mingled with such toasts were poems attacking Federalist efforts to mingle church and state.[41]

The toasts offered by the Sons of Liberty, though not entirely new, revealed Hiram's devotion to traditional American republicanism: a

staunch antagonism to any union between church and state, a deep
feeling for the common man, and a symbolic recognition of American
womanhood. They also illustrated his penchant for poetry. For some
time Hiram had copied long poems found in books and newspapers
into his journal. Now he had the opportunity to contribute to crafting
similar pieces. More importantly, since these poems appeared as anon-
ymous public toasts, Hiram avoided any possible risk to his fragile ego.

Although Hiram regained a sense of respect among his peers through
his participation in the Sons of Libertyhe, it did little to bolster his own
self-confidence. When, for example, William Haswell nominated him
to deliver an address to the association, the brothers unanimously supported the motion. Hiram, however, quickly "arose and informed the
Ass'n that they had made choice of a most unfit person to perform the
duty assigned him, and earnestly begged to be excused." His friend
Nathaniel Locke, intimately aware of Hiram's unease, made a motion to
that effect, but it suffered a nearly unanimous defeat.[42]

The knowledge that he must deliver a personal address to his colleagues weighed heavily on Hiram's mind. He made a number of "dry
attempts" to draw up a speech, but when the dreaded moment arrived,
Hiram stood before his brothers and informed them that he had not
prepared an address, "nor never should such an one as would suit
himself and was sure it could not be so to them." He went on to state
"his great inability to perform the task, and requested to be excused
from the prosecution of it." Several brothers spoke out against releas-
ing Hiram from his elected duty, but others expressed their unwilling-
ness to press a man to do that which he felt unable to accomplish,
though they doubted Hiram's inability to be so extensive as he claimed.
President Haswell then asked what the pleasure of the members might
be. After a short pause, Hiram moved that he be excused from the duty
to which he had been called. The motion failed. Then, "after hearing
some persuasive language from the Chair," Hiram "cheerfully acquiesced in the decis'n — determined to let them know the worst if they
would not rest easy without."[43]

During the next two weeks Hiram "made some progress on my
Address." Finally, two days before his scheduled presentation, he "finished the Great Address." However, on the day he was to deliver it, he
fell ill and was unable to attend the meeting. The following day, although "indolent," he "amended a paragraph of the Wonderful Address." A week later Hiram attended a meeting of the Sons of Liberty,
whose primary business was to hear his speech. He delivered it, hurried

home, and "the paper containing that simple thing (under) named, an
address, was consigned, by me, to the flames." Nowhere in his journal
did Hiram mention the subject of his speech, much less its contents.[44]
Although eager to copy with the utmost care the writing of others,
Hiram was too self-conscious and insecure to record even his own
public words in his diary.

Hiram's brothers must have thought more highly of his performance
than he, for just a month after his address, they elected him secretary of
the association. Since the newly elected officers each contributed forty
cents to treat the members following this election, Hiram fretted that
elections every six months (as called for by the constitution) might
prove expensive for him. When his six-month term came to an end and
it was time for Hiram to turn the records of the association over to his
successor, he still had a painful sense of inferiority. Consequently, when
he returned the records to the new secretary, Hiram asked the man "to
excuse my inaccuracies." These, as well as what he viewed as enormous
blunders on his part, seriously troubled Hiram. He was convinced that
whereas "when they chose me secretary I was well aware how piteously
they mistook me, now to their mortification it may be they saw it."[45]

Along with his sense of shame that the brothers would discover his
shortcomings once they perused his records, Hiram felt an immense
sense of relief to be excused from a position of such stature and responsibility. "If ever I was sincere, it would be in acknowledging the pleasure
it gave me to see this place filled by another far more capable person
than myself. In snug obscurity I delight to dwell—It ill accorded with
such a feeling to see, now & then, in great capitals, in the G.M.F'r—
'Hiram Harwood, Secretary.' "[46] Regardless of how he viewed himself and his abilities, Hiram had gained the respect of his brothers.
He moved easily among individuals like Demos, Uel M., and Safford
Robinson; Hiland Hall; William Haswell; and Darius Clark—men
with every prospect of becoming Bennington's next generation of town
leaders.

⌒ Just as Hiram became increasingly comfortable in the company of
his brothers in the Sons of Liberty, he also began to mix more freely in
the social activities of young people in his own neighborhood. With
Nathaniel Locke as his constant companion, Hiram gradually participated in more and more sleigh rides, paring bees, and local dances. His
sister Lydia and Sophia Waters nearly always accompanied them, but
Hiram also began to see Theodosia Montague, Nancy Watson, and

Sally Stone quite often. Both Sally and Nancy had moved into the neighborhood during Hiram's service in the detached militia. Nancy lived with her family less than a mile north of the Harwood farm; Sally, who was the younger sister of Thomas Parsons' wife, came to live with the Parsonses. Shortly thereafter, much to Hiram's relief, Rebecca Cutler left Bennington to live with her sister in New York.

Although Hiram gradually became more sociable, he retained the extreme sensitivity regarding social status that had long troubled him. The nearly obsessive alertness to any social slight that might be directed at him or his family still plagued him. When he and Lydia attended Lucretia Norton's wedding, Hiram noted that "most of the youth who were collected on this occasion — belonged to what has always been understood to be the first company." Happily, he was able to observe that he "saw nothing that was beyond the reach of any comp'y in their behavior, which to be sure was decorous enough, but not in my opinion any more refined than that of companies which are taken to be of a lower grade." Hiram also gleaned much satisfaction from the marriage of his friend Columbus Bowditch to Miss Ruth Smith. Since the bride's family had long held the groom in contempt for being so much below them, it pleased Hiram no end "to see pride mortified."[47]

A wedding celebration at the Nortons' did nothing to disturb Hiram's delicate feelings. He and the women he escorted to the ceremony "were politely ushered in," and "sprightliness, gaiety, & good natured vivacity inspired the whole company." From Hiram's perspective "nothing occurred to mar the pleasures of the evening, & everything was conducted in a correct & handsome manner." The same could not be said of a dinner Hiram shared with a group of the "first company" at Judge Fay's home. Several of these young people "broke out into fits of laughter which I rather suspected were caused by some odd movement they fancied to discover, in me." Although he had no idea whether "they had been educated in this way," Hiram did not appreciate their behavior. Similarly, when Captain Barnum Whipple of Albany arrived with his lady to visit the Harwoods, Hiram was highly offended by their rich attire and supercilious manners. His mind "underwent some unpleasant disquietude during the course of the day." Upset as he was, he calmly reminded himself that "splendid equipage ought never to terrify us so as to forget to whom it is attached." In any event, such behavior grossly offended Hiram's visceral sense of republicanism.[48]

The "disquietude" that Hiram suffered may have resulted from causes other than the visit by the Whipples. Five days earlier Ira and his entire family had left for Attica, New York, where he had purchased a farm. Ira's departure deeply affected Hiram. When he observed others helping Ira and his family prepare for their trip, he became "lost in a gloomy reverie, from which I could get relief only by flight." On the following day, when men gathered around Ira's sleigh to stow away all his earthly possessions, Hiram "could liken it to nothing but a funeral." On the day of Ira's departure, Hiram and a number of others drove out in sleighs to accompany the family as far as Hoosick, New York. "At the moment of parting tears were copiously shed by the ladies, but on the part of the gentlemen they kept above it." Hiram noted with admiration that Ira "assumed a manly gaiety at this juncture, highly praiseworthy — In parting with his aged father & friends at *home*, at *this* place, & through the whole transactions of the day, he behaved with firmness, steadiness & propriety." Hiram's final journal entry relative to Ira — "God bless him" — never appeared in reference to another person.[49]

C✺ Hiram missed Ira terribly. His uncle had been an anchor during the difficult period immediately following his abortive military experience. Then, when Hiram began seeing women socially — never an easy thing for him to do — Ira had assumed the role of trusted adviser. Hiram very much needed such a person, because it was not long before the old issue of marriage emerged again with renewed force. Benjamin and Peter, believing not only that marriage should help make a responsible farmer out of Hiram but also that it would ensure the perpetuation of the Harwood farm, had begun to exert heavy pressure on him to take a wife.

Hiram's father and grandfather were not alone in their pointed references to the fact that Hiram was a twenty-four-year-old bachelor; friends, neighbors, relatives, and even casual acquaintances repeatedly raised the same issue with Hiram. Once, during a gathering at the Nortons', Hiram's close friend Elisha Smith, "in a very friendly and familiar manner discoursed aside with me on celibacy and matrimony." Upon departing the house one day, a peddler with whom the Harwoods traded regularly gave Hiram "many ingenious rubs about remaining yet a bachelor." Claiming that "time was short" and that Hiram "should soon get to be an old man," he invited Hiram to visit him in Massachusetts, where he would "select me a partner." Hiram's friend Lydia House even raised the subject of "old bachelors and old maids" one evening when Hiram escorted her home.[50]

The prospect of marriage began to weigh heavily on Hiram's mind, and once again his matrimonial condition became a matter of public concern. During a conference held at Ira's old house, "a subject nearly touching my personal interest" became the central issue of discussion between Hiram, Lydia, and his cousin Ruth. When he lodged with John Norton Jr., Hiram "had a long conversation with him on matrimonial concerns." Later he passed an agreeable evening with Lydia reading history, "besides talking in a manner very frank and friendly on affairs touching domestic concerns." Another night Hiram walked to town to visit William Haswell; after supper the two men "talked a long time alone in his office on matrimonial concerns."[51]

In the face of such constant talk of marriage, Hiram did his best to retain a sense of humor. When a relative living in New York suggested that Hiram should visit his neighborhood to find a wife, Hiram responded that "it was my intention to make trial among them here *first*; if I failed, mount my horse & go farther, and if ill luck attended me still would continue my route until I reached *their* country—where I intended making a Bold Stand." However, "if at last [I] should get liened, [I] would turn short on my heel—den up and suck the claws of an icy old Bachelor." Immediately following this seemingly light-hearted observation, Hiram confided to his diary that his "spirits [were] rather low."[52]

Hiram's anxiety regarding marriage did not result from finding women unattractive; this was far from the case. He had a keen eye for beauty and regularly took special note of women he considered particularly striking in appearance and demeanor. Upon meeting one of John Norton's visiting nieces, Hiram opined that "the young lady's figure and countenance accorded well with my notions of good looks." On another occasion, while visiting friends at Paran Creek Village, he noted that his acquaintances "were visited by several handsome young ladies of the village . . . who appeared to very good advantage." Another time, while on his way home from a trip to a neighboring town, Hiram and his companion stopped at a tavern to warm themselves. "What diverted *us* & others a good deal, was the appearance of three young ladies, who came out, it appeared, with their gallants, for a sleigh ride." These women "were *mellow enough*—Nothing seemed to trouble, nor disconcert them—perfectly happy—reeling & talking in the most familiar manner."[53]

Physical beauty, sophistication, and a slightly adventurous or independent countenance all excited Hiram. Whether he would ever dare to approach a woman embodying any or all of these characteristics was, however, quite another matter. Instead he sought out Sally Stone, Theodosia Montague, and Nancy Watson—young women who became part of his circle of neighborhood friends. Of the three, Theodosia and Nancy aroused the most excitement in Hiram. He considered Theodosia a "vivifying little animal," and on at least one occasion when he gave his arm to Nancy, "a kind of ecstatic tremor seized me, from which I did not recover in several moments."[54] Sally Stone's attraction for Hiram was quite different. She resided with the Parsonses, whose household was like a second home for Hiram, and became close friends not only with Nathaniel Locke, who also lived with the Parsonses, but also with Hiram's own sister Lydia. For all these reasons, Hiram, comfortable within this familiar social network, may have been much more at ease around Sally than either Theodosia or Nancy.

Of all the young ladies in the neighborhood, though, it was John Norton's daughters Laura and Clarissa who were the most attractive to Hiram. And yet he viewed them as he did the characters Glorvina in *The Wild Irish Rose* and Lucilla Stanley in *Coelebs in Search of a Wife*— ideal types about which he might fantasize but which his own insecurities would never allow him actually to consider as a mate.

On those occasions, which were frequent, when Hiram mentioned either Laura or Clarissa in his diary, he never commented on their physical appearance; instead he dwelt upon their composure, their sophistication, and their wonderful education—their gentility. Always he belittled himself in comparison with their accomplishments. When he wrote to Laura regarding her position as a schoolteacher, he exclaimed that he considered the "education of youth the Bulwark of Republicanism, that Liberty could not flourish in a country dark'd with clouds of Ignorance." No sooner had he written these lines, however, than he "conceived that I had handled this subject so badly, that I begged her to excuse me for my temerity in dipping into things with which I was so little acquainted."[55]

Whenever Hiram described his encounters with Clarissa or Laura, he employed the same stilted terms that characterized the literature he read so ardently. Once, however, when describing a visit Laura made to the Harwood farm, he momentarily lapsed into a much less formal language that may even have disclosed, if only for an instant, his own repressed desires. When Hiram returned to work, Laura "walked with me, arm in arm, just as I *was*, shirtsleeves rolled up above my elbows other parts of my dress equally bearish—beauish." No sooner had he mentioned the word "beauish" than he quickly exclaimed: "But why speak of *that*, ladies are, many times glad to receive addresses from gentlemen in far worse plight, although they would never confess it for fear of encouraging negligence in our sex & betraying too much attachment in their own." After the briefest of slips, the language and attitudes of *Coelebs* returned to provide a safe shield for Hiram's feelings about Laura.[56]

If Laura Norton upset Hiram's emotional equilibrium by taking his arm in such a familiar manner, her sister Clarissa challenged him in a far more subtle, yet fundamental manner. Even though they lived within easy walking distance of one another, Clarissa, anxious to discuss a variety of issues in some depth, initiated a correspondence with Hiram during the summer of 1814 that lasted for over nine months. During the course of this exchange, Clarissa clearly epitomized the image of the ideal woman — sophisticated, generous, well-educated, sensitive — that Hiram gleaned from the literature he read with such fondness.

Hiram constantly denigrated his own abilities in comparison with Clarissa's. At the very outset of their correspondence, he lamented that her "refined answers would be, comparatively, like throwing pearls before swine." Thus, when Clarissa suggested "friendship" as a subject for their correspondence, Hiram felt himself "entrapped." "I *knew* & she *knew*, I could not handle 'Friendship' with anything like dexterity." Nonetheless, fearful that Clarissa might cease writing if he did not respond, Hiram struggled for an entire afternoon to compose his thoughts on the suggested subject. Since this took place on a fair day in August, "Father viewed me in a criminal light to spend time thus in haying [season]." Even though Hiram "suppose[d] it was doing wrong," he refused to stop; he continued writing, correcting, and rewriting his composition until he felt reasonably comfortable in sending it off. Nonetheless, most uncertain of his own ability to compose original thoughts, Hiram did not record his own observations on friendship in his journal.[57]

Clarissa's response thrilled him, and, anxious to make her words his own, he carefully copied her letter into his diary. When she exclaimed that "the man who has a friend whose soul is congenial with his own — who will participate in his feelings, not only in prosperity, but when sinking under the weight of adversity; is possessed of a treasure which can never be fully estimated," she articulated the very essence of the ideal relationships Hiram so admired in the books he read. For her to

ask what pleasures could "be compared to those derived from friendship, where the sentiments and affections are so sweetly united" was to
phrase the issue perfectly. Upon declaring that "a person may be on
terms of sociability with all his acquaintances but unless he is united
with someone by the cord of friendship, must, in his gloomy moments,
feel himself alone, though surrounded by thousands," she penetrated
directly to Hiram's deepest feelings. But when Clarissa exclaimed,
"how wretched must be the life of that man, whose unsocial, suspicious
temper will not permit him to divulge his sentiments & ideas to another; he can never know the celestial joys which the votaries friendship
only can experience," she truly rose to the exquisite level of Lucilla
Stanley herself.[58] She seemed to epitomize the romantic self—that
authentic inner self concealed from the oppressive social conventions
of the outer world—found in *Coelebs* and *The Wild Irish Girl*.[59]

Hiram was absolutely enchanted with Clarissa. In many ways their
exchange of letters represented a "romantic readership."[60] It allowed
Hiram to reveal his innermost thoughts and feelings—to discuss personal sensibilities entirely foreign to his close friends and family—while
remaining shielded from intimate personal contact. Consequently,
whatever erotic tension might have been present was safely diffused.

By the middle of February 1815, Clarissa asked Hiram to divulge his
thoughts on the subject of marriage. She wanted to know his feelings
about the "matrimonial stir" then taking place in Bennington and inquired whether he should be included "in that number who are preparing to launch into the boundless Ocean of Matrimony." As for herself,
Clarissa bemoaned that "in spite of all my exertions to the contrary,
I shall soon be *compelled* to take up my residence for life on the Isle
inhabited by old Maids. *This* place it has been the study of my life
to avoid."[61]

Clarissa's letter came at a critical time for Hiram. Theodosia Montague and Nancy Watson had left Bennington the previous year, and
he was seeing only Sally Stone. Marriage was in fact being seriously
discussed in the Harwood and Parsons families. Now to have the individual who represented all that he idealized in women lament the prospect of becoming an old maid must have elicited mixed feelings within
Hiram. His response to her query about the matrimonial "stir" in Bennington revealed as much. Declaring that the stir "indicated a disposition in people to choose the least of two evils," Hiram's advice for such
people was not to be "too sanguine, lest disappointment should follow."
He added that "by carefully examining the affairs of those who had

preceded us in that way, we might derive much beneficial instruction."
Then, "as to *my* being of the number ready to launch — wrote that it
would probably take place ere long, but was waiting for a calmer sea,
saying — people who were prudent, or those who wished to be thought
so, desired to *embark* with a fair prospect at *least.*" Regarding the "Old
Maid's Island," Hiram exhorted Clarissa "not to despair, for some generous spirit stood ready to save her."[62]

This "generous spirit" would not be Hiram. Well before he and
Clarissa entered into a discussion of marriages in Bennington, Hiram
had been keeping steady company with Sally Stone. Quite unlike Clarissa, Sally was a plain, poorly educated working girl in her sister's
household. In many ways Sally closely resembled Hiram's own mother;
she was an independent, plainspoken, hardworking woman who knew
her own mind and was not afraid to speak it.

Hiram first met Sally when he returned from Plattsburgh. Several
months later he began escorting her to neighborhood gatherings at
Ira's. Soon thereafter he started spending much time at the Parsonses',
and yet Sally was not always receptive of his visits. He recalled spending
"a short time in the evening" with her, "but from actions and ap-
pearances, concluded I was rather intruding upon her peace and qui-
etude and therefore withdrew." Puzzled, Hiram lamented that "somehow the ladies never discover any great partiality for persons of my cast,
let our behavior be ever so decorous — what the difficulty may be, I
cannot determine."[63]

Their relationship continued in this manner for some time. Once,
when Hiram asked her to come to Ira's to meet an old friend of his, "she
concluded she cared nothing about seeing him or anybody else abroad
that evening." Hiram "returned home and after making myself quite
sick of drawing the bow," retired to bed. Finally, after a number of
repeated rejections, Hiram again "invited Miss Stone up, but she refused the invitation, which she may not have opportunities to repeat."
Within a matter of weeks, though, Hiram walked to the Parsonses',
where he enjoyed "a vivacious dialogue" with Sally and several other
women. Shortly after that "Miss S. Stone had the honor of cutting my
hair in which she acquitted herself in a masterly style." When Hiram
paid a visit to the Parsonses several days later, he found Sally and her
sister "in a mood for lively conversation, which they were not backward
in pursuing."[64]

Still, Hiram could never be certain of Sally's mood. When he stopped
by the Parsonses' to invite her to come to his house to visit friends, "she

answered in the negative." "I insisted on her coming." She did not. The following day Hiram again walked to the Parsons home, where he chatted with Sally and "cleared up some difficulties — not difficulties, but doubts." He then "again invited Miss S. up — she still refused." Four hours later he returned and once more asked Sally "to attend at our house — without saying one word in compliance, she set about getting ready — and soon came with me to this jovial convention."[65]

It was not long after this "jovial" evening that Hiram began plotting ways to be alone with Sally. One evening in January, carrying his copy of *The Wild Irish Girl*, a dictionary, and a newspaper, he started out for the Parsonses'. Upon arriving there he heard the voices of Nathaniel Locke and Jonathan Waters, so he "stepped back & took my stand in the shop near a window where I could observe them when they should come out." After a few moments he "had the pleasure of seeing them move off" and "pushed for the house where I found the old people gone." Alone at last, the two sat down by "a good light & perused our Irish Novel with spirit & activity." Hiram's "passions were sometimes seized & wrought up to a most enthusiastic pitch — other part of the book appeared but ordinary." The following evening, too, Hiram "passed an entertaining evg" with Sally and *The Wild Irish Girl*. Several weeks later he spent yet another evening reading the novel at the Parsonses', this time with the entire family.[66]

Hiram may have experienced a certain ambivalence while reading *The Wild Irish Girl* with Sally. He had begun to read the novel at the suggestion of Clarissa Norton and had exchanged opinions with her about the book during the very time he shared it with Sally. It was, nonetheless, Sally who rode alone with Hiram on the day he and others accompanied Ira's family to Hoosick to see them off to their new home in New York. While riding to and from Hoosick, Hiram noted with pleasure that "each gentleman enjoyed the peculiar felicity of discoursing freely & frankly with his partner during the airing."[67]

〰 However much Benjamin and Peter may have desired him to marry, and however much Hiram may even have begun to consider that possibility himself, one great obstacle confronted all the men: Hiram's mother, Diadama. Far more possessive and controlling of Hiram than either Benjamin or Peter, Diadama, unlike either man, cultivated an adolescent, dependent relationship with her son. This was particularly true whenever the issue of marriage arose. On one such occasion, when Hiram jokingly mentioned that he meant to "be married [at] the first opportunity," he received "a harsh, dry admonition from my mother whose mind was ever filled with the most hedious apprehensions in meditating upon the character of her only son, whom she hates and loves at one and the same time." His mother took whatever opportunity she could to press home her conviction that Hiram was not ready for marriage.[68]

Ironically, it was Peter who temporarily served Diadama's purpose. While hard at work one day, he fell and injured himself so badly that he required the family's care around the clock. His constant demand for attention not only threw the entire Harwood household into chaos; it caused Hiram to postpone any thoughts of marriage. Well aware of Diadama's possessive attitude toward her son, Hiram's friends enjoyed teasing him about the decision to delay his marriage. One evening Nathaniel Locke, Sally Stone, Sophia Waters, and Lydia "joked me smartly about a particular scheme which had been in agitation, but which at this time had to be abandoned till circumstances should be more favorable." They delighted in dancing about him chanting: "Oh dear — he can't — he can't — he can't — his mother won't let him."[69]

The next several days were difficult ones for all members of the Harwood family. With Peter "groaning almost constantly under his infirmities," their house "presented a melancholy spectacle." "Confusion & gloominess, impenetrable — were the order of the day at this unhappy dwelling." Whether taking his turn watching his grandfather through the night or tending to work about the farm, Hiram fell deep into thought: "The bad side of the Human character & constitution were constantly present to my mind a great part of the day — Much unhappy foreboding resulted from it." As a result, "an extensive map of futurity lay before me, which I critically examined — it gave birth to a train of thoughts quite unwelcome & which I believe to be the parent of a great many evils. It destroys patience, confidence in friends of ourselves, & that cheerfulness which is so necessary to the welfare of all those with whom we are associated."[70]

Sent to Dr. Swift's office the next day, Hiram fell into conversation with one of the doctor's associates regarding the "common pursuits of men." In response to the statement that men "derived their chief happiness from objects of sense, and making favorable comparison between their *own* & their neighbor's *circumstances*," Hiram declared that "there was no real Felicity in this Life, but, such as we found it, we must go on & make it as agreeable as we could." This conversation must have been critical to the issues occupying Hiram's mind; the very next evening he proceeded to the Parsonses', "sat down & wrote a few lines which I handed to a lady for her benefit & abruptly left the house."[71]

◡ Although Hiram never divulged the contents of the letter he left with Sally, it might have been a declaration of his firm intention to marry her. The first mention Hiram actually made of marriage in his diary came nearly a month later, when he noted that a seamstress came down "to make my wedding coat and vest." That same day, as he sat with his father to help with his accounts, "others thought it was something relating to the *wedding*, but it was not so; time enough could be had for *that business* without spending the whole evening in conclave." The "others" surely included Hiram's mother, who remained constantly alert to any discussion of marriage. Five months earlier she had raised quite a "jar" over a set of silver teaspoons mentioned as a possible wedding gift should Hiram ever marry. Unlike his wife, Benjamin was always much more receptive to discussions of marriage. In fact, Hiram recalled holding "a private interview with father in the garden" that "afforded me much satisfaction" a month previous to the "jar" with his mother. In any event, the Harwoods and the Parsonses agreed that the marriage between Sally and Hiram would take place Sunday evening, March 19, 1815.[72]

Several days before the wedding, Hiram took half a calfskin to Mr. Parsons to be made into "thin shoes." When Thomas jokingly asked him "what *I wanted* them for," Hiram in the same vein responded: "to wear in the *mud.*" While waiting for Mr. Parsons to make his shoes, Hiram went inside to discuss the "projected undertaking" with Mrs. Parsons. This was the first time he had ever raised the subject with her, "which made it hard for me to begin, or indeed when begun to proceed." He thought for a moment of "asking her opinion of the match but esteemed it needless — her opinion could make no difference with the affair, & if it were unfavorable, it was not likely she would give it me in full." Therefore, Hiram "said a word of two — then paused — began again, but something so strongly affected me that a dead silence of several seconds was necessary to give me time to get above it — looking steadily into the fire, having the tongs in one hand poking among the coals, all the while." For Hiram "the matter of *discourse* was not so grave as that of *thought*"; his mind remained focused on the gravity of marriage, while his conversation dealt only with arrangements for the wedding ceremony itself. Finally he and Mrs. Parsons "agreed very well."[73]

The day before the wedding, Lydia went about the house singing a song "strongly alluding to the business in view," Sophia Waters came down to "assist in various sorts of cake manufacture," and Jonas carried a "publishment to the town clerk & a verbal message to Col. J.E. Robinson, Esq. to have him perform a certain ceremony at a given hour in Tanbrook, Sunday Eve." That evening Hiram "sat awhile at Mr. Parsons' — all given to taciturnity — deep in thought."[74]

The first thing Hiram did on the morning of his wedding day was to write a response to Clarissa Norton's last letter, which he considered "the best I had ever received from *her*, or any other person." In that letter Clarissa bemoaned the fact that she was "gliding gently on the Ocean of Celibacy," while the companions of her youth were "passing rapidly by me in pursuit of the Sea of Matrimony." Even though "no kind being offers to conduct *me*, I will endeavor to keep as nigh the Isle of Hope as possible, to prevent my little *Bark* from wrecking on the rocks of *Despair*." Then, "when the sea appears sufficiently calm, for you to venture to sail, permit me to wish you a most delightful voyage. May no rude storms of Adversity obstruct your way — may contentment, the sweetness of life, be your constant companion — may you never be lashed by the waves of indifference, but wafted along pleasantly by affection, & at last reach in safety the Haven of Eternal Happiness."[75]

In his answer Hiram assured Clarissa that she would "arrive at the Haven of Happiness," if only she "very compliantly met her fate." He also expressed the hope that "we might either of us realize those happy wishes she gave me on my future voyage." Then, as he signed the letter "a fit of sobriety seized me that put on a little of the solemn for the mom't, not because I repented the arrival of the day — but because I thought it would be improper longer to correspond with a lady in her situation." Upon signing the letter, "my *last*," Hiram "could not but give such feelings as I have attempted to describe."[76]

With this letter Hiram ended his relationship with Clarissa Norton. Whatever romantic feelings he may have had, whatever personal sensibilities he may have revealed, were subordinated to the more practical matters of the family and the farm. By choosing to marry Sally, Hiram remained loyal to the traditional principles of reciprocal marriage.[77] The present and future welfare of the Harwood farm dictated that Hiram marry a practical, hardworking woman capable of assuming her fair share of the labor required about the farm. The Harwood household required a helpmeet far more than a soul mate.

After sending off his final letter to Clarissa, Hiram "followed my

usual employment — coarsely dressed — till 3 P.M." Then, "all things
ready," he proceeded to the Parsonses' accompanied by his father,
Uncle Jonas, sisters Lydia and Diadama, cousin Ruth, and Sophia Waters. His mother did not attend the wedding. Shortly after Hiram arrived, "the Bride, neatly dressed soon appeared — and after some few
moments of chequered deliberation, Col. Jonathan E. Robinson, Esq.
arrived." The colonel's cousins, Samuel and Safford Robinson, followed, accompanied by Samuel Robinson Jr. and five other individuals
"of whom neither, the Justice, excepted, were invited, nor was their
company desirable, with an exception of the three first who came with
Col. R."[78]

At ten minutes until seven "we were invited from the *dining room*
into the *parlour,* took the Bride by the hand, walked in, and took
seats . . . in the very place in which almost 29 years before my father &
mother were pronounced 'one,' by Govr. Robinson Esqr. April 18th
1786." When Colonel Robinson bid Hiram and Sally arise and join
hands, Hiram's heart began to beat so rapidly that it caused "a tremendous concussion throughout the entire system that rendered it almost
insupportable." He did not attribute this to "mere diffidence in appear-
ing before an attentive & in some respects a criticizing audience, but to
the solemn impression made on my mind by entering into a compact of
such vital importance to me & my fair partner." Even though Robinson
kept the ceremony short, Hiram grew "more and more the subject of
quaking fear." When the colonel finally concluded, Hiram "was very
happy, once again, to sink into my seat." For her part, Sally did not
appear at all disconcerted but rather "passed through the scene with
great composure . . . her fears had visited, & departed from her during the preceding week." Finally, "after taking seats, all was calm for a
time — the Col. took occasion to put some questions to our young lady
concerning her age, nativity &, but *this* was interrupted by Dr. W. who
introduced the kissing ceremony." At this point "a piece of rusticity
escaped me quite unawares — [I] omitted to rise when the ladies came
up to salute the Bridegroom." After that the "usual amusem's closed the
scene."[79]

That night Hiram spent at the Parsonses'. After breakfasting with
them, he returned home to write lists of Federalist and Republican
voters in the southeast district of Bennington. All this time "the girls
were diligently employed in arranging matters to receive comp'y in the
P.M." At two that afternoon, Hiram "brought up my lady, who was
kindly & courteously received," and the "remainder of the day sat in the

parlour among the ladies, none but our *own*, present — played on the violin & flute — felt tolerably composed."[80]

That evening the Harwood house became the site of the second-day wedding, a common practice among the old settlers of Bennington.[81] At this time "high relish was given by the good things of this World, which we meant to serve around liberally." The cake, "being made by our good friend Sophia [Waters] was most delicious; and this lady assisted materially in procuring salvers, glasses, etc. for the occasion." Sophia's help was essential, since Hiram's mother contributed nothing to the preparations. In light of this, Hiram was much relieved that at the end of the day he could write, "with this evenings entertainment we were altogether satisfied, nothing fell out to spoil it."[82]

On the following morning, the "breakfast table being removed, Mr. Parsons took sister Lydia by the hand, Dr. Jonas in like manner with Miss Sophia Waters, had a lively dance which they called closing the Wedding." During the day "work moved moderately," and "nobody dined here but the family including its new member." That evening Hiram walked with Sally and the Parsonses to their home, where Sally spent the night. Hiram returned home to sleep. He spent the entire next day at home and slept that night with his grandfather, who was still in bad health. He awoke the following morning to a "profound *reverie* several hours, concerning my future destiny — it amounted to no more than all such fits do — evaporated in thin air."[83]

Whether this "reverie" resulted from the fatalistic Calvinist worldview that characterized so much of his thought, Hiram never made clear. It might have had quite a different cause — his deeper insecurities and uncertainties about marriage. Sexually inexperienced and personally insecure, Hiram may have suffered anxiety about his own untested sexual adequacy; sexual intimacy may have terrified him. In any event, five days after his marriage, Hiram revealed his innermost feelings. Sitting alone with Mr. Parsons, who was "in low spirits," Hiram described himself as being "not far from the horrors."[84] Whether Sally and he had consummated their marriage he never made clear; what was clear was Hiram's feeling of terror at the prospect. Once again he had to face a new set of circumstances — circumstances that tested his ability to overcome his persistent self-doubts.

ᶜ∾ 5

Husband, Father, Neighbor

In the evening father desired me & Sally to go into our grand-fathers apartment — we readily obeyed & enjoyed a pleasant hour.[1]

When Benjamin encouraged Hiram and his wife to enjoy some time to themselves, Sally had been living in his home only a short while. Just five days earlier Hiram had announced that the "lady to whom I was wedded Mar 19th came here to live this day." Before that Sally had remained with the Parsonses, whose home had become the center of the couple's social activity since their marriage. Nearly every evening Hiram would walk over to the Parsonses' with a book and his flute. Some evenings Uncle Jonas would accompany him. Once there, the company enjoyed dancing and card playing. Hiram took great pleasure in playing the flute while Sally and the others danced; cards were, however, quite a different matter. On one occasion he complained that he "could not read conveniently, cards were so plenty." Another time he joined Sally at the card table, "but being monstrously ignorant of those things, no chances were *there* for me — quitted it in disgust — went to playing the flute."[2] Hiram could easily quit a game that made him feel incompetent, but such was certainly not the case with more important responsibilities looming before him as a married man. He must face these squarely and deal with them to the best of his abilities — abilities that would be stretched beyond anything he might have thought possible at the time of his marriage.

⟪ One of the first responsibilities Hiram had to assume — with others of the family — was the care of his grandfather. Eighty-year-old Peter still lay quite ill, and family members kept watch by his bedside day and night. The Harwood women assumed this task collectively during the day; the men alternated remaining alone by the old man's bed throughout the night. Sensitive to Hiram's recent marriage, family members and friends did what they could to allow him as much time as possible with Sally. Occasionally Jonathan Rogers — an apprentice to Thomas Parsons — and Jonas would take Hiram's turn, watching by Peter's bedside for an entire night. Often the women moved Peter's bed into the kitchen during the day so they could continue with their chores while watching over him. It was during one such time that Benjamin urged Hiram and Sally to spend some moments alone in Peter's quarters.

With the help of his father, his close friend Jonathan Rogers, and his Uncle Jonas, the uneasiness Hiram experienced immediately following his marriage began to dissipate. Gradually, Hiram started to feel less anxious about his relationship with Sally. Even with this support, he missed Ira. More like a brother than an uncle, Ira had been his lifelong confidant, his support in times of uncertainty and anxiety. Now, when the family received a letter from Ira, Hiram considered it "a cheering thing" and responded not only by commending Ira for his "honesty & integrity" but also by exclaiming how much he had "endeared" himself to the family by "possessing a character so just & upright." Nonetheless, though he lacked Ira's companionship, Hiram managed to feel increasingly comfortable around Sally. One evening he recalled with pleasure that "a certain lady & I had a chit-chat by ourselves that gave me much delight — by her assistance I put my violin in tune, she being so good as to manufacture some silken treble." Another time Sally and Hiram "spent a few pleas't moments in the spinning room at Ira's old house — *she* spinning and *I* sounding the Violin." The following evening Hiram again played the violin in the spinning room of Ira's old home. Upon returning to his own house, however, he received tragic news: Ira had died of cholera at his home in Attica, New York.[3]

Ira's death deeply troubled Hiram. He had lost the dearest "companion of my youth." In his mind, "the many days I have toiled with him . . . up to the day of our separation, can never, while a spark of reason remains, be forgotten by me." When Hiram attempted to write a letter to Ira's widow, Theodosia, he experienced feelings of being "sensibly moved — *not* because I had used any nice pathetic expressions — but to contrast this occasion with former brilliant, exhilarating times. . . produced sensations in me more easily conceived than described."[4]

The Sunday after learning of Ira's death, Hiram accompanied his father and Jonas to church. He neither napped nor read throughout both the morning and the afternoon services; instead, he listened intently to Rev. Daniel Marsh's preaching from Revelation and his discussion of "the Divinity of the Savior." If Hiram attended church services to find peace, he was unsuccessful; Ira's death continued to plague him. Throughout the ensuing months, he "thought much when alone respecting my departed friend." Early one May evening, "there being a bright moon, the recollection of past rural & happy scenes, which I had enjoyed with my departed friend & uncle, *especially during Autumn,* was brought fresh to my mind." For Hiram, "there is scarcely an inch of the farm but that some way or other causes me to think of him."[5]

Gradually, though, Sally became Hiram's greatest source of comfort. He "retired with Sally into the N. room at the other house [and] enjoyed her company with some coarse music on the Violin," "enjoyed a fine walk with Sally, to visit the flock at the south end of the farm," "gathered up some papers of a private nature over which Sally looked with pleasure," "had a lively dialogue with Sally concerning past events," "finely enjoyed the day, reading, writing & walking in the fields with my lady," "retired to our chamber to discourse apart — our interview was pleasing & agreeable." Late one afternoon as Hiram returned home alone from a visit to town, he experienced a feeling of profound melancholy: upon "viewing those objects which had been familiar to me from childhood, the many happy days I had passed in school were rapidly passed in review." Near sunset that evening, however, when he "walked with Sally to get some good apples in the young orchard."[6] Hiram felt much more at ease.

This contentment emanated in large part from the growing sense of comfort Hiram and Sally felt in each other's company. There was, however, a deeper empathy between them, an empathy resulting from the fact that Sally, too, suffered from grief and anxiety. Her father had died earlier in the year, and she worried about the fate of her mother. Thus, one day Hiram found Sally in "low spirits from which I exerted to rally her, & had the pleasure of partially succeeding." After Sally's spirits revived, the couple "enjoyed that kind of happiness which can result only from mutual esteem & confidence, in our retreat this evening."[7]

Whatever peace of mind Hiram began to gain with Sally suffered considerably from the deteriorating condition of his grandfather. Taking his regular turn at watching, Hiram often "felt dull on account of laying in grandfather's room the night preceeding." One night, "to avoid the noise of grd father while watching," Hiram lay down in the kitchen. His attempt at a good night's sleep came to nothing when Peter "followed me — had no fire in his room by accident." When Benjamin left for Attica in mid-June to settle Ira's estate, Hiram assumed his father's turn at watching Peter; consequently, he experienced yet "another night deprived of usual rest, which with other circumstances rendered me dull, sleepy & melancholy."[8]

By the middle of July, Benjamin arrived home from Attica. His return helped Hiram and Jonas immeasurably with the crush of summer work about the farm. In addition, he could once again take his turn at watching Peter, whose condition worsened daily. One Sunday Peter, "with difficulty, strolled up the lane on crutches a rod or two beyond the first brook and there laid himself down close by the fence, determined never to rise again." After a time Hiram drew a small wagon by hand to the spot where his grandfather lay, helped him in, and safely returned him to his bed. Recalling the incident, Hiram noted that "before I came to him and without knowing that anybody was near him, his resolution to die, failed him, he began to cry loudly for assistance." Then, evincing little sympathy, Hiram declared: "See what age brings us to."[9]

Throughout the following two weeks, Peter grew increasingly unwell. On August 12 he died. Hiram left that day completely blank in his journal. Upon resuming regular entries the following day, he made no mention of his grandfather. Unlike the heartfelt sorrow and admiration he expressed upon Ira's death, Hiram wrote nothing about Peter's character or accomplishments. He did note with appreciation the kind assistance tendered by friends, neighbors, and relatives throughout the funeral process, but his only comment on the funeral service itself consisted of a critique of the presiding minister's thick Scottish brogue and a brief statement about the man's message.[10] Years of harsh chastisement at the hands of his grandfather had taken their toll; Hiram was too honest to record a tribute he did not believe and too respectful to enter a candid appraisal of the man. Silence, then, was best.

Shortly after Peter's death, Sally and Hiram began to discuss the possibility of taking a trip to Connecticut to visit Sally's old friends and relatives in the neighborhood where she had been born and grew to maturity. Even though harvest season would soon be over, the hectic time of cider-making still lay before the Harwood men. Nonetheless, out of consideration for Sally's feelings, and with Jonas to help him with the cider press, Benjamin consented to the trip. Early in September Hiram began to make preparations for the journey: he readied the family's one-horse wagon and tack, borrowed a trunk from Luman Norton, obtained a copy of Morse's *American Geography* from Jonathan Hunt, studied the book's map of Connecticut carefully, and even insisted that Sally "assist me in finding out distances."[11]

Sally and Hiram left the Harwood farm in midmorning on September 14 to make the relatively short drive to Williamstown, where they intended to spend the night with old friends from Bennington. Hoping to reach their destination before dark, Hiram "made a vexatious blunder" by taking a wrong turn. After "mutter[ing] a few harsh expressions," he "turned sharp about & regained the main road without losing much distance or time."[12] They soon arrived in Williamstown and spent a cheerful evening fluting and dancing.

Early the next morning, Hiram visited a neighboring fulling mill and carding machine before breakfast. "Works of this nature always attracted my notice."[13] Soon thereafter he and Sally left for Barrington, where they spent the night at the home of relatives. At an early hour the next morning, the couple struck out for Litchfield, Connecticut, some forty miles away. When they stopped to refresh themselves at a tavern in Canaan, the innkeeper "appeared to affect a loftiness in his deportment, toward a stranger too forbidding, too dignified, too morose, to gain favorites, according to *my* low Democratic ideas." Nonetheless, Hiram did visit the man's anchor manufactory and "enjoyed this scene very rationally as I ever do where water is made subservient to man's use."[14] After leaving Canaan, Sally and Hiram made their way toward Litchfield, where they were to visit Sally's sister. By sunset they still had several miles to travel along "a road entirely new to me & almost forgotten by Sally, of whom I made frequent & vain enquiry how to proceed." After darkness enveloped them, the hilly road and slow progress caused Hiram to grow "impatient"; he soon became "petulant, talked roughly at Sally because she recollected the way so poorly — this sorely grieved her, [and] rendered this evening's ride very unpleasant." Upon arriving at their destination, however, "our little troubles were soon consigned to oblivion," as Sally rejoiced at being reunited with a sister she had not seen for over three years.[15]

After spending several days with Sally's sister, Hiram and Sally set out on the turnpike for New Haven. At the first gate south of Litchfield, the attendant "made us some trouble about change, which filled me with all those sensations felt by the anxious traveler when hindered." With this matter settled, the couple rode happily on. However, Hiram's anxieties returned when he concluded that they had taken the wrong route. Always fearful of embarrassment, Hiram, instead of asking for directions, "muttered along the road several miles, declaring I would persist in keeping that road till night, if I were to arrive at a place 40 miles from N.Haven." No matter how Sally might urge him to ask directions, Hiram remained convinced that it would appear "too clownish to ask anybody the way, when I was in the great 'Litchfield Turnpike.'" Fortunately, they were on the proper road and had no trouble proceeding to New Haven, where they found the home of Sally's brother Josiah Stone with surprising ease.¹⁶

The visit with the Stones began quite pleasantly. Josiah took Hiram on a tour of the town, and Jonathan Rogers, who had completed his apprenticeship with Thomas Parsons and taken a job in a shoe factory in New Haven, joined them for the evening. Shortly after Jonathan departed, however, a cry of "Fire" interrupted the family's pleasant conversation. Josiah and Hiram rushed out to join a bucket brigade that had formed in an effort to extinguish a fire in a nearby barn. Faced with a nearly total lack of cooperation, however, Josiah and Hiram soon became spectators. Although noting that a few sailors manfully fought the blaze, Hiram believed that the majority of individuals "were warmly engaged at boxing or clandestinely picking pockets . . . and it was supposed the fire was willfully set for that very purpose." Everywhere Hiram looked, he saw utter chaos: "no regularity whatever prevailed, except in the Engine Department, which acquitted itself honorably—but the body of citizens were a mere rabble without a head." Appalled, Hiram considered what he had just witnessed to be a "drama entirely novel . . . and highly disgusting to me—little did I envy those who preferred a City life to a free more expanded country residence."¹⁷

The following day brought more novel experiences for Hiram. He sat down to a breakfast of boiled lobsters, never having seen such a creature before. "Some part went smoothly—some heavily—but having eaten a lobster's tail, could get down no more." Concluding that "it was necessary to be in motion," Hiram walked about the city, bought a pair of spectacles, visited a large bookstore, and then made his way to the wharf, where he boarded several coasting vessels and admired the large ships anchored in the harbor. Still "finding my lobster to be very uneasy at my stomach," Hiram returned to the Stones', where he attempted to write in his journal. "Soon convinced that this would not do," he "posted off to the stable where my horse was kept" and prepared it for the trip to Sally's brother's home in North Branford. "Meantime the lobster greatly disturbed—some part of it at last cast up." Though feeling somewhat better, Hiram had difficulty facing, much less eating, any of the boiled lobster dinner prepared by Mrs. Stone before the couple's departure.[18]

Upon leaving for North Brandon, Hiram experienced mixed feelings. He had enjoyed meeting Sally's relatives, but he felt "confined" by the environment of New Haven. Even though the Stones lived "in a pleasant part of the town . . . out of the crowd," Hiram "preferred the sweet country air" and was happy to be on his way to the small village of North Brandon.[19] Once there, they stayed with another of Sally's brothers and his family.

While in North Brandon, Sally and Hiram often went their separate ways; she visited old friends and neighbors while he sought out local musicians. One such quest took him to the store of H. Monroe, a former resident of Bennington whom Hiram knew to be a fine flute player. Upon his arrival Hiram was disappointed not only to find Monroe absent but also to discover that the store was under the care of a slovenly clerk who had married Monroe's mother. "A short tarry here was sufficient to establish in my mind the character which this poisoned shop bore. There were a number of idle, worthless, unprincipled men hanging round who busied themselves at pitching quoits to get grog." Quickly "satiated with a scene so opposite to my feelings," Hiram left and joined Sally at a nearby neighbor's.[20]

The following day Hiram again visited Monroe's store, but finding only the clerk and "a fellow toper . . . playing their idle pranks, retreated in deep disgust." Later that day Hiram finally encountered Monroe and accompanied the man to his store while Sally went to visit a longtime friend who had recently married. Even in Monroe's presence, however, Hiram's sensibilities suffered: "The store, as I presume was customary, was filled with such characters as every moral, sober minded person must deprecate the existence of in society—their actions & conversation made a lasting & most hideous impression on my mind." Nothing could dissuade him from the certainty that "if Mr M. did not soon dismiss such a worthless gang from his shop, ruin must inevitably follow."[21]

The next day Hiram met many of Sally's relatives, visited the home where she had been born, and viewed her father's grave. That night, after supper, Hiram walked alone to a neighbor's house to enjoy several hours of music. To his surprise, he discovered the man to be "a democrat, but not on a broad scale having taken no papers nor attended Freemen's Meetings for several years." Nonetheless, it "was a great gratification to me to find a democrat in so federal a part of the Union."[22]

Over the next several days, Hiram and Sally visited with even more of her relatives, made a trip to the ocean, ate a dinner of friend oysters, and readied themselves to return to Josiah Stone's. They arrived in New Haven during the afternoon of October 2 and immediately took another tour of the town. After supper Hiram, accompanied by Josiah Stone and Jonathan Rogers, walked to the opposite end of town "to board the steam-boat Fulton — the view of which gratified me more than all that I had seen or could see besides such descriptive powers as I possess are totally inadequate to the task of even hinting at the elegance and beauty here displayed."[23] Even after such a thrill, Hiram regretted not having arrived several days earlier, when Josiah had arranged for a boat to take them on board one of the large ships moored in the harbor.

The following morning they left for Bennington. Retracing the route they had taken, and staying with the same people, Sally and Hiram arrived home late on the evening of October 5 to find the whole family, with the exception of Diadama, who suffered from a severe cold, in good health. The returning couple slipped immediately into their familiar work routines; he assisted with the cider press, and she helped with the household chores. Over the next several months, Hiram's primary responsibility beyond his regular farm duties involved the settlement of Peter's estate. At the request of his father, he opened and read Peter's will in the presence of the family on the last day of November 1815. Following that, he wrote to all of Benjamin's brothers and sisters to request that they come to Bennington to attend a final property settlement.

Responses to Hiram's letters slowly began to arrive. Uncle Asa wrote from Sempronius, New York, that he had become a Methodist, encouraged Benjamin's family to do the same, and said that he was "much in want of a horse & saddle, hinting broadley that he expected it as his share of the estate."[24] Lucy's husband, James Waterman, wrote from Brookfield, New York, to request that Benjamin keep his share of the property until he could call for it. Uncle Ebenezer's widow, Eunice, responded from Gates, New York, that she wished to have her share transmitted to her in money if possible; if not, then she wanted whatever property was hers to be sent by some trusted person.

During the second week in February, Samuel Safford and John Norton came to the Harwood home to appraise the household furniture left by Peter. They appointed Hiram their scribe and set about the work at hand. The inventory amounted to $203.12. Since Jonas and Ira had already received their shares, and Benjamin did not draw for his, this left the property to be divided into five equal portions. Once this had been accomplished, Hiram wrote each of the heirs to notify them of what had been done. This meant informing Uncle Asa that "no reserve was made in the Will favoring him more than the other heirs." It also meant writing a very difficult letter to Ira's widow, Theodosia, informing her of the disposition of the property and that Benjamin was unable to "advance any pecuniary aid at this time."[25]

Of the five individuals who were to receive property, only Asa and Clark demurred to the settlement. Clark, the eldest of Peter's children, did so in the bitterest terms. Blaming Peter and Benjamin for the fact that he had never prospered, Clark claimed that Peter had promised him forty dollars over and above his allotted portion. Employing the most insulting language, he refused to accept any of the furniture or to receive any additional information about the settlement until his demands had been met. In response, without "a word to his saucy letter," Hiram wrote Clark a friendly letter explaining the manner in which the settlement had been made.[26]

Uncle Asa responded by expounding on "the goodness of God — for God was working there in a miraculous manner, bringing sinners out of darkness into light by scores and hundreds." It appeared to him that "the Glorious Day was at hand," and he wanted "his brothers and sisters to seek an interest in Christ ere it was too late." He also claimed that years before Peter had sent him word that he "might have a horse." Months later, after getting no satisfaction, Asa declared that he would settle for thirty-five dollars cash, since he had no way of receiving any furniture.[27]

During the same period that Hiram dealt with his relatives over the property settlement, Sally began to spend increasing amounts of time at the Parsonses'. In the first months of pregnancy, she sought advice and comfort from her sister rather than her mother-in-law, who was still not entirely well and none too sympathetic to Sally under the best of circumstances.

Hiram reacted with characteristic uncertainty and insecurity in the face of circumstances that might call for more understanding and strength than he felt he possessed. Nonetheless, for all his eccentricities, Hiram was usually sympathetic and gentle with Sally. Caring deeply about her comfort and concerned for her condition, he brought a feather-erbed for her from the Parsonses and took her on easy sleigh rides about town. When the weather became warmer, the couple spent time together walking in the fields or gathering "sweet briar root to make tea for supper — mother being in a rage for it."[28] Occasionally they would walk out together to pick corn or simply to view the crops.

During the day of September 28, 1816, Hiram worked steadily gathering corn and threshing wheat. Then, "about 3 P.M. another kind of business fell to my lot." He left right away in search of Dr. Noadiah Swift, whom he found on his farm directing a number of workers digging stone for a wall. Upon learning of Sally's condition, the doctor said he wanted to get a large stone out before he left. Hiram immediately threw off his coat and set to work. Fifteen minutes later he and the doctor were on their way. At nine o'clock that night, "a fine healthy daughter was announced." Hiram had been "anxious that it had been a son, but would not *murmur* as it was."[29]

Sally and the baby did quite well following the birth. Then a month later, Sally developed a painful, festering breast. Hiram brought Dr. Swift to see her, and he lanced the breast. After that, Hiram went to town to get a "breast pipe," which "answered a good end." Five days later he returned to town to exchange the pipe for a larger one, "which answered a better purpose."[30]

Although extremely solicitous of Sally, Hiram was anxious and uncertain about his relationship with the baby; his characteristic lack of self-confidence in unfamiliar circumstances gripped him. He did not know how to respond to the child. Three days after the arrival of his daughter, Hiram visited a woman in town who had just given birth to a son. He kissed the baby, "which was more than I had done with my own child." Two months later, when Hiram wrote a letter to his cousin Ruth and mentioned "Sally's babe, & its name," he had yet to write the child's name in his own journal. Instead, he referred to "Sally's babe" or noted a visit made by "Sally with her child." His first mention of his daughter's name came on March 28, 1817: "Adeline six months old this day."[31]

With the passage of time, as Hiram began to gain confidence in himself as a father, his relationship with Adeline became increasingly warm and sympathetic. One evening, when Hiram came in from work, a friend "held the child and dandled it while I played to it on the fife." Shortly thereafter Hiram anxiously noted that "Adeline was restless with a bad cold." A month later, "our little Adeline" suffered severely from the colic, and Hiram went out at midnight to call for the doctor. After several days he thought "our darling" was doing better. Then three days later the condition of "my little daughter" caused Hiram "much anxiety." Her recovery brought him much peace of mind.[32]

As Adeline's presence gradually transformed Hiram into a gentle, loving father, it also deepened his relationship with Sally. Five months after Adeline's birth, Hiram noted his "joy and real contentment and hearty satisfaction with what fortune has been pleased to give." This contentment showed through the pages of his diary in his references to Sally. During the first months after their marriage, Hiram had always referred to "my lady" or "the lady I married." These formal appellations gradually gave way to much warmer references to "my Sally." Then, when Hiram became involved in a conversation with his friend John Norton Jr. over the "contrast between celibacy and matrimony," they both "argued very clearly in our own favor."[33]

Adeline also helped to bring about a much more cordial relationship between Sally and her mother-in-law. Over time quite a warm bond formed between the two women, a bond created out of mutual responsibilities and a deep mutual concern for Adeline's welfare. Whenever Adeline showed the slightest signs of illness, Diadama hurried to help Sally tend her. Consequently, the very day that Adeline began to develop a bad cough, Diadama lost no time in proceeding to town to find a muskrat's skin "to fasten round Adeline's neck to guard against the whooping cough." When that safeguard failed — as did the application of a hornet's nest and then "skunk's cabbage" — Diadama took her turn sitting by the child during the anxious times that followed. Adeline's recovery not only warmed the hearts of the family but also brought Sally and Diadama that much closer together.[34]

As Sally and Hiram's mother gradually began to develop a new connectedness, Hiram, too, faced a new relationship. Sally's brother Rufus asked Hiram to take in his son Chauncey until the boy reached the age of sixteen. Hiram agreed, and Chauncey came to live with him and Sally in January 1817. They treated the boy as if he were their own son. Hiram not only sent Chauncey to school but worked with him at night on his spelling and reading as well. Still Hiram's personal insecurities remained. On his twenty-ninth birthday, he observed that "C. Stone lived with me, but was none of mine — a good boy, but wanting good guiding better than I had abilities to do." In spite of such reservations, Hiram expressed satisfaction with his life. Indeed, "all that appertained to me was the partner of my choice & a fine daughter little more than 10 months old."[35]

᷍᷍ Shortly after Hiram's birthday, he and his father reached an important conclusion, and "a mutual separation took place in the family." As a result of this decision, Hiram, Sally, Adeline, and Chauncey moved into separate quarters on the lower floor of the Harwood house. Just as Benjamin had been anxious to establish his own household while under his father's roof nine years earlier, Hiram and Sally wanted to have their own kitchen and living quarters.[36]

The move had important consequences. In many ways it symbolized the changing dynamics of the Harwood family. Now that Sally and her mother-in-law had separate households to maintain, the sympathetic relationship developing between them became much stronger. In addition, Hiram gained a modicum of stature within the family, but only a modicum. At a time when marriage generally marked a man's assumption of greater responsibilities — the achievement of full adult status — this was not the case with Hiram. As long as Benjamin lived, he would be the family patriarch and Hiram the obedient son.[37]

Although loyal to the Harwood tradition of patriarchy, Benjamin was anything but an overbearing tyrant; he loved his family far too much. Thus, when Hiram and Sally wished to visit her old friends and family in Connecticut once again, he was more than willing to comply. Consequently, Hiram rented a one-horse wagon, borrowed a trunk from his old friend Clarissa Norton, and early on the morning of September 8, Hiram, Sally, Adeline, and Chauncey Stone "set sail for Connecticut."[38] They took the same route and visited the same relatives as on their previous trip to Connecticut until they approached New Haven. This time they bypassed the city and proceeded directly to North Branford, where a large congregation of Sally's relatives awaited them. These included the Parsonses from Bennington, who had picked up Sally's mother en route. During their stay of more than two weeks, Sally enjoyed sharing little Adeline with her many relatives; Hiram passed the time by seeking out musicians and reading books with various ones of Sally's old friends and neighbors. He also returned Chauncey to his father, who wished to take advantage of an opportunity to apprentice his son to a local shoemaker.

In contrast to his previous trip, Hiram found little to incite his curiosity. He did, however, attend two militia gatherings: a company muster in North Branford and a regimental review in nearby Wallingford. Both events offended his growing sense of propriety. By far most of North Branford's militia "appeared to be composed in part of pretty rough characters, many of whom staid till late in the evening committing some irregularities at the tavern which I shall pass over in silence." At Wallingford it was the composition of the "immense crowd of spectators" that most interested Hiram. He firmly believed that "a great proportion of the spectators was made up of ladies many of whom I took to be not of the highest order."[39]

Several days after Hiram viewed the regimental parade at Wallingford, he and his family started for home. After stopping for a time with friends in Litchfield, they arrived at the Harwood farm and discovered that "our good father had improved every moment of each day since my absence to the best advantage."[40] Immediately upon their return, Hiram and Sally, too, set about improving each moment of the day as they resumed their accustomed routines.

The first Thanksgiving after their return from Connecticut, Sally and Hiram "sat down to our table to sup with no other company than a crying child, dog & cats." If their table that day was relatively lonely, the same could not be said of their everyday lives. Once Jonathan Rogers, who had served out his apprenticeship and returned to Bennington, set up his shop in Ira's old house, there was precious little time to be alone. Jonathan and his journeymen and apprentices lived above the shop and boarded with the Harwoods. As a result, they rarely had fewer than six or seven boarders on hand. When the census taker visited in August 1820, he recorded sixteen people living on the Harwood farm. Although this was a hardship for the Harwood women, the fact that each boarder paid one dollar per week in room and board helped the family greatly during increasingly difficult financial times.[41]

When Jonathan married and moved his wife into Ira's house, they took up housekeeping in the lower floor behind the shop. This not only eliminated one boarder from the Harwood table but also introduced a new couple into Hiram and Sally's circle of acquaintances. They enjoyed Jonathan and his new wife immensely. In many ways Hiram was like an older brother to Jonathan; he assisted the younger man with his bookkeeping and intervened on his behalf when he experienced difficulty settling accounts with uncooperative customers. But Hiram did not neglect his own little girl. Having taught her nearly all the alphabet by the time she was three, he purchased a spelling book just for her. When she was not quite five, he rode with her to the district school. Then, when school closed a year later, he proudly announced that Adeline "had learned well . . . and seemed to gain the good will of her teacher if we might judge from the frequent written expressions which she bro't from school." It was a wonderful thing to see Adeline "gain in useful knowledge."[42]

Hiram was always in quest of "useful knowledge" himself, and his intellectual curiosity led him to attend the initial sermons of Bennington's new minister, Absalom Peters. A graduate of Dartmouth College and Princeton Theological Seminary, Peters had been called to Bennington when the village gentility, led by Isaac Tichenor, forced the removal of Daniel Marsh. Although the plainspoken, democratic Marsh was an old friend of the Harwood family, Hiram did not consider him a stimulating preacher; he had never aided Hiram in his quest to gain an "established mind" regarding religion.

This quest led him to Peters, and during the spring and summer of 1820, Hiram attended a number of services led by the young minister. Initially Hiram believed that Peters "eminently displayed his talents" and "performed handsomely." Several months later he noted that Peters preached "in his usual masterly style." By the end of the summer, though, when Peters and others were holding conferences in the various neighborhoods in order to encourage a renewal of religious zeal throughout Bennington, Hiram began to cool a bit. He attended one such meeting at the district schoolhouse in which Peters "enthusiastically addressed us on this point, that if we did not *believe* we must be damned—all the morality & everything else notwithstanding." To a man who put much stock in morality and leading a good life, this was a shock. A week later he felt much better after attending the meetinghouse in Bennington to hear Lemuel Haynes, Rutland's black minister. Hiram took "great pleasure" in what the man had to say and felt that "his color ought never to be thought of." For Hiram, Haynes "painted the loveliness of faith & Christianity which tallies with my ideas of preaching better than the pictures which some delight of pain of H..ll & the damned." When Reverend Peters came to a meeting held in Tanbrook, Hiram did not appreciate it at all when the pastor "made a lash of his tongue." Thus, one day when "Mr. Peters and his lady made a short call—father attended them—my business called me to some places about the farm not often frequented."[43]

The religious "stir" brought on by Peters and others had little effect upon Hiram. He agreed with a friend that "if a person had been a poor paymaster or even worse than that in his usual dealings among men *before* his conversion, according to our experience, it was no reason why we should trust him afterwards." When Jonathan Rogers, before his marriage, had visited his sweetheart rather than attend a scheduled meeting with Hiram to go over his books, Hiram easily forgave him. "Who, that has a just view of the human system, could blame him—who can assume all that self denial so much talked of by ministers & philosophers—at once—never tell it—let us enjoy a few fleeting moments of happiness when they come in our way without disturbing our heads about the hidden consequences that may follow." Hiram displayed this same tolerance for the religious views of others. When a neighbor "related, in every particular, a wonderful religious experience that had occurred to him," Hiram "was rather surprised" but "said very little—considered him a happy man." The man's happiness was far more important to Hiram than any religious doctrine that he might espouse. Hiram simply could not surrender the idea that leading a moral life was essential to the happiness of all men. It was also his hope that such a moral life might be sufficient to gain salvation.[44]

Although his mind may not have been entirely "established" with regard to religion, Hiram was relatively content with his life. On his thirty-third birthday, he wrote: "so old, and yet very young in understanding . . . enjoyed great satisfaction by being surrounded by my nearest relatives who all enjoyed comfortable health. My father, altho' near 60 lived yet with all his family under one roof—this is worth noticing." Hiram's satisfaction increased appreciably on April 1, 1822, when Sally gave birth to Hiram Hopkins, "a fine healthy character & hopeful youth." Having been a father now for over five years, he was quite comfortable with the new baby and immediately wrote about the behavior of "our young heir" and "our babe."[45]

The birth of Hopkins, like that of Adeline, changed the dynamics of the Harwood household considerably. Diadama helped Sally with Hopkins all she could, and the relationship between the two women grew stronger each day. They stood by each other more and more often, as Hiram recalled when one "noon we held a spirited dialogue on the Poor or Rag Society—father & I opposed, the ladies approved the plan." It was the bond between Hiram and Adeline, however, that strengthened most appreciably. With her mother busy tending Hopkins, Adeline spent more and more time with her father. She accompanied him when he went searching for missing cows, sowed plaster in the fields, mended fences with his father, and salted the colts and the sheep. It was Adeline's progress in school that most pleased her father. He could barely contain his pride in Adeline the night her teacher closed the district school for the season: "My daughter Adeline received a certificate which stated that she had been at the head of her class 30 times and this night was one of them."[46]

∿ Hiram displayed a similar feeling of contentment in his approach to music and reading, which had long been sources of gratification for him. In his earlier years, playing the flute had been a solitary enjoyment — a means to find solace during troubled times. Throughout his first year of marriage, Hiram still turned to the fife in anxious moments. Often during the evening hours, he would take "one of my heedless walks" and fife to himself along the way.[47] With the passage of time, however, music became something Hiram shared with others; it brought mutual enjoyment rather than lonely solace.

Increasingly, Hiram played with and for others. When Sally and he took a cutter ride to visit friends in nearby Arlington, he gave them a performance of "Gillicrankie." In return one of them sang "The Tidy One" and "The Hornet & Peacock." When they attended Cousin Samuel Robinson's second-day wedding, Hiram supplied the music for the celebration. As it was for so many other rural New Englanders, music was central to the lives of the Harwoods.[48] Hiram particularly enjoyed playing with others at his home or wherever a group of friends might gather. On one such occasion, he brought out his flute and played while friends and family danced. Hiram enjoyed himself immensely, "but nothing gave greater entertainment than the lively pranks of little Adeline who was so transported with the music that it was impossible to keep her off the floor — she danced in her fashion like a puppet, though she had seen but little short of 15 months."[49]

Hiram was usually the only musician present at these impromptu festivities. He would report that "we were full of music this evening," had "a little dance here for which I played," "a little apple-paring drew together our young friends here, for whom I played for them to dance," "in the evening we had one of our old fashioned little dances at the other house in spinning apartment . . . myself [the] coarse musician," or "a small ball was had here this evening." Although Hiram gained immense pleasure from playing for friends and family at such gatherings, he found the most satisfaction in using his flute or violin to soothe or please his children. Not uncommonly he recalled that he "fluted to Adeline at night" or noted, "late P.M. to please the babe [Hopkins] played the violin a few moments coarsely."[50]

No longer was Hiram the lonely fifer. Music, which had for so long separated him from friends and family, now became a means of drawing him out, of joining him with others. As he gained self-confidence, music took on a different role in his life; it linked him in joyful communion with others rather than isolating him in lonely solitude. Now when he took up the flute or the violin, it was to share his feelings with others rather than to withdraw into himself in an effort to escape from anxious situations that he felt incompetent to deal with.

Much the same was true of Hiram's manner of reading. Books, like the violin or the flute, had long been a means by which Hiram maintained his fragile emotional stability in times of personal uncertainty or insecurity. They had been a way to escape, a conduit into a private world of safety. Now, as he grew more self-assured, Hiram's attachment to books also became a link with others rather than a retreat into solitude. Reading became as much a communal as a solitary activity for him. He read a wide variety of books, including a borrowed volume of Shakespeare, to the various members of the household. He and his father shared many happy moments reading from a book or a newspaper or discussing a topic of mutual interest. Both men gained huge satisfaction from Hiram's reading the orations of Dr. Joseph Warren and John Hancock on the occasion of the Boston Massacre from "Webster's old Third Part." Hiram was particularly fond of this "old book, which I hold in great reverence on account of its being a celebrated school book in my youthful days." When Hiram obtained a copy of Frances Wright's *Views of Society and Manners in America*, it "pleased me to the life." He even grudgingly admitted that "her remarks are more suited to the profoundest searcher of history & the statesman than to a person of her sex." When he "read my English woman an hour or two to Father — we enjoyed it well." Both considered this "a fine work — sentimental — sympathetic — truly republican."[51]

Hiram's love of books as well as his intellectual curiosity led him well beyond his own household. Although careful "to avoid exposing intellectual poverty" by speaking out too much, he joined the Social Society — a debating group that met in the village and engaged prominent members of the community in conversations about books.[52] Hiram and fellow members of the Social Society were very much participants in the "Village Enlightenment" spreading across New England at the time; they eagerly exchanged ideas drawn from books that they read in order to discover more about the rapidly changing world in which they lived.[53] By no means, however, did Hiram limit his literary curiosity to meetings of the society. He began to spend increasing amounts of time in the office of his old compatriot in the Sons of Liberty, Hiland Hall, who was rapidly becoming one of the town's most prominent attorneys. From time to time, Hiram recalled having spent "a few sweet moments reading the big books at Hall's office."[54] Over time he borrowed many books from his friend.

Often, when Hiram wandered from the house on Sundays, it was to visit with his friend Luman Norton. The two had a special relationship and greatly enjoyed reading to one another. One Sunday afternoon, as they shared a volume of David Hume, Hiram admitted that "for my part I never enjoyed myself more happily — it might be said I was arrogant in engrossing all the reading to myself — this was not what I wished to do — presented the book to him several times, but he said he had rather hear me." To hear such words from a man of Luman's social stature caused Hiram to exult that "reading was never more easy to me."[55]

Whether alone or with others, Hiram was a prolific reader. Although his eclectic tastes took in a wide range of printed works — atlases, almanacs, medical texts, law books — Hiram always had a work of history in progress, particularly one dealing with the American Revolution. His interest in the Revolution was not restricted to books, however. Whenever he could, he engaged veterans of that war in conversations to learn details of their experiences. Thus, when a neighbor came by to purchase rye, Hiram listened eagerly as the man "stated several particulars respecting his revolutionary services — was in Bunker Hill Battle — lay at Valley Forge in 1777." On another occasion, when Benjamin and Hiram had business to attend to in the neighborhood, Hiram was fortunate enough to encounter another veteran, who was "sociable indeed about White Plains battle & a great many things relative to the war of '75." One year, when there was no Republican celebration of the Fourth of July, Hiram and Benjamin "rode down to the ground on which Bennington battle was fought." They had no one to guide them about the battlefield, but Hiram drew on his close reading in a number of histories to determine the location of the British and American forces.

Bennington was not the only battle that Hiram recognized in his journal. As the almanacs that he read recorded dates, he noted the anniversaries of all the major battles, not only of the Revolution, but of the War of 1812 as well.[56]

Hiram's fascination with the past went beyond the Revolution; he enjoyed learning as much as he could about the early settlement of Bennington, the Tanbrook neighborhood, and his own family ancestry. Whenever he had the chance, he engaged prominent members of the Bennington community in conversations about the town's history. Thus, one day, when General David Robinson stopped in to warm himself by the Harwood fire, "the conversation first began about the situation of the lines between lots & Rights in this neighbr'd and from that to the first settlement of the town."[57] On other occasions he enjoyed talking with relatives about his ancestry on his mother's side of the family. Consequently, he was especially pleased one day when he went to clean flaxseed at Eldad Dewey's. Finding himself weatherbound, Hiram "entered into a very entertaining discourse with Mr D. respecting my forefathers on the side of the Dewey's, wherein he gave much pleasing information." Several years later, following conversations with other maternal relatives, Hiram compiled a brief record of his Dewey ancestry. He also looked forward to conversations with his Aunt Sarah, who had married into the Robinson family, for she, too, was quite interested in family genealogy. Perhaps Hiram's most fortuitous discovery came one day while poring over papers left by his grandfather Peter. He came across an account of all the families that had lived on the "south-west quarter of Right No. 20 (containing 90 acres) since the first settlement of the Town of Bennington." The record, compiled by Peter Harwood and Jonas Fay, had been recorded by Heman A. Fay on December 6, 1801. After discovering the document, Hiram attempted to bring the record of the Tanbrook neighborhood up to date from memory.[58]

In addition to being a lover of history and somewhat of an amateur historian himself, Hiram paid careful attention to the current events of the day. Fond of newspapers, he read with care the two papers — the *New York Columbian* and the *Vermont Gazette* — to which he subscribed and whatever others he could obtain. Very little escaped his attention. A confirmed republican, he followed the course of Napoleon with rapt attention; considered the compensation bill "a degenerate thing"; pored over every presidential message; opposed the admission of Missouri into the Union, observing with disgust that "the Missouri questions had been over given by the folly of our northern members"; approved of the efforts of those who would occupy the Columbia River; and supported all tariff measures.[59]

In order to be able to refer to his newspapers whenever needed, Hiram carefully arranged them in exact chronological order and had them bound by a printer in town. He meant to have ready access to this historical source. It was a very disappointing when "through motives of economy," Hiram was forced to drop his subscription to the *Columbian*. So that he would have access to news beyond that offered by the local *Gazette*, Hiram began to borrow the *New York Spectator* from Dr. Noadiah Swift.[60]

Hiram's intellectual curiosity was not restricted to books and newspapers. Whenever the opportunity arose, he attended local lectures, plays, musical performances, and even exhibitions of exotic animals. One cold March night, Hiram joined "a numerous audience" at the courthouse to attend a lecture on chemistry given by a local teacher. The man also executed a number of experiments, "all which he performed according to my judgement in a masterly style — the science being new to me, I say no more of it." Chemistry may have been new to Hiram, but he meant to learn all he could about it. The day after the lecture, he began to read a series of essays in *Spafford's Magazine* on the subject, and by time of the man's last lecture, several weeks later, Hiram was engaging Colonel O. C. Merrill, U. M. Robinson, and others on the subject.[61]

When Captain Moses Robinson sponsored the exhibition of an elephant at his new barn, east of the meetinghouse, people from Bennington and the surrounding towns flocked to view it. Hiram and his family waited until the animal was "suffered to bathe in Safford's Mill Pond" and then observed it without cost. "It was a female — she very adroitly performed many rational actions such as persons unacquainted with this noble animal would not suppose it capable of doing."[62]

In the single month of September 1822, Hiram and his family enjoyed a wealth of entertainment: a traveling theater company performed at the courthouse; an exhibition of wild animals appeared at Ballard's Tavern; and horse races took place in the East Village. On the first day of the theatrical performances, Hiram stood outside the courthouse to enjoy the music, which he considered "fine." The following evening he did the same, only to discover this night that "they played so little that it was but a vexation to be there." The next day, he not only visited the wild animal show and the horse races but also attended the

theater in the evening. He thoroughly enjoyed the music, and the "acting suited me well, but the choice of pieces was bad in my way of
thinking—too many clownish notions and immodest cants for so enlightened an audience, as I fancied was present, to relish." Two days
later he returned again to the theater, where "there was a full house
which was handsomely entertained." So effective was the performance
of "The Stranger" that "very few were there among the hearers who
had command enough of themselves to resist the gush of tears which
several parts of it naturally drew forth." Hiram could not have been
more pleased; to enjoy such a variety of entertainment uplifted him. In
addition, it linked him and his family to a growing network of sociability that brought together families scattered throughout Bennington township.[63]

Although Hiram and many other townspeople thoroughly enjoyed
the theater, the animal exhibit, and the horse races, there were others in
town who did not. This was particularly true of young Reverend Peters,
who brought not only sophistication to First Church but a zealous
moralistic fervor as well. Peters had been out of town when all these
events took place, but on the first Sunday after his return, he "took the
occasion to make very pointed remarks on what had transpired the past
week—condemning without reserve the races, Theatre, wild-beasts
show & all." The *Gazette* the following day carried an editorial that
pointedly criticized Peters' sermon. When Hiram, who rarely took
sides in disputes among townspeople, heard the editorial read to a
group in Fassett's Tavern, he observed that it dealt "hard" with the
minister, "tho' not perhaps without just provocation." Hiram saw nothing wrong in such harmless entertainment; indeed, he thrived upon
it. From his perspective Peters' attack upon such activities represented a needless interference in the private lives of the townspeople of
Bennington.[64]

൭ If Hiram valued his own leisure time, he was equally concerned
about his communal responsibilities. To shirk such duties would be
unthinkable in the Harwood family. Hiram paid the strictest attention
to fulfilling the demands made by the township upon him and his
family; primary among these was the maintenance of roads and a common school within their local district.

Ever since the family first settled in Bennington, all the Harwood
men were accustomed to working with their neighbors to improve
that portion of the main road running from Bennington village to the

Pownal town line that lay within their district. This meant turning out with rakes and shovels to remove large stones, level uneven spots, and fill in badly eroded portions of the road, under the supervision of whichever neighbor had been appointed surveyor of the highway that year by the town selectmen. When circumstances warranted, those families with oxen would contribute their animals to the effort. Benjamin never objected to this, so long as others in the district contributed whatever they could. One year, however, when Dr. Swift and the Harwoods brought their oxen to the task, Benjamin noted how few hands had turned out to help. By late afternoon, feeling that too many "borough-mites were receiving the benefit of others labor," he "ordered us away."[65] When Hiram received his commission as district surveyor of the highway in May 1821, he, too, expected all residents of the district to display the same sense of public duty that animated the men of the Harwood family.

Although all male members of the Harwood household regularly turned out for work on district roads, Hiram became the family's representative at local school meetings. His interest in learning made him a natural choice, and he took this responsibility seriously. Unlike many of his neighbors, Hiram made it a point to attend school meetings whenever they convened. Much of the time, the primary reason such gatherings took place involved hiring a teacher and settling with that individual on both a salary and a manner of payment. Since teachers tended to be transient or easily called to another post, such meetings were generally annual or even semiannual affairs. Male teachers often demanded payment of $11.00 per month, regardless of the number of scholars in attendance. The district inhabitants preferred, however, to pay $1.25 per scholar per quarter, so difficult negotiations often resulted. For this reason, Hiram and the others favored hiring female teachers. After Clarissa Norton had taught for several years, "a fond hope was entertained that we would have a full, cheap and well taught school this present season." Unfortunately, this was not to be; Clarissa married and left the school in order to prepare to move away with her husband. Judge Fay immediately contracted with Eunice Jewett to teach the school at one dollar per student, to begin the next day. He even "suggested that if this old maid should be taken off by marriage, we would immediately employ another of the fraternity in her stead and in like manner proceed by rotation through the whole neighborhood."[66]

Hiram was duty-bound to fulfill his responsibilities to the township, but his deepest loyalties lay with Tanbrook. He felt a bond of kinship with neighbors that carried no official sanction. From his perspective, neighbor supported neighbor in whatever way possible within a supportive web of mutual obligations. One assumed reciprocity from those capable of responding in kind, but one gave freely to those who could not.

Like his father and grandfather before him, Hiram remained staunchly loyal to the traditions of localism that bound neighborhoods together. He spent long nights "watching" with men who lay ill (women watched with women, men with men) and faithfully honored the practice of "watching" with the dead. When Jonathan Rogers married, Hiram and Sally held the second-day wedding at their house. When neighbors needed help in raising a building, moving a barn or shed, or hauling stones for construction purposes, Hiram either contributed his own labor or freely lent the Harwood oxen.

Whenever problems arose within the neighborhood, Hiram firmly believed that those involved should settle the matter between themselves as amicably as possible. He was even elliptical in his own journal when dealing with disagreements that arose with neighbors. On one such occasion, he wrote only that "an explanation on certain points took place between two neighbors, but it was not so full as could have been wished — Nothing however was retained in malice — where peace is the object a settlement is easily made." Another time, when a neighbor's oxen broke through a fence and consumed a good deal of the Harwoods' spring wheat and corn, the man, being a "very kind & obliging neighbor," not only repaired the fence but also "viewed the damage and said he'd leave it altogether to us to say what the amount was, which he was willing to reimburse." When another neighbor's cattle broke into the Harwoods' spring wheat, Hiram wrote only that "some of the cattle were rogues — the fence bad — to make good neighbors it should be made good."[67]

If dealing with men he respected, Hiram went out of his way to be cordial and fair. Once, when William Haswell complained of the quality of the wheat Hiram had sold him, "I informed him that we did not mean to deceive him and would make it up to him as much as he should say." Believing that one of their yearlings had mixed in with Captain Norton's herd, Hiram and his father went to talk with him about the matter. When they "found one which nearly answered the description of that for which we were enquiring, but could not exactly ascertain the mark — and Capt. N. not fully satisfied, tho' he would not claim it if marked, his having none — we postponed it till another time." Rather than returning home upset, Hiram "got very interestingly engaged talking with friend Luman about Earthquakes & the causes thereof."[68]

Hiram was not uncritical in his attitudes toward even his closest acquaintances if they behaved badly. On one occasion Thomas Parsons searched for a lost cow; Hiram could not conceal his disappointment and disapproval when Parsons, "in a low and most ungenerous, unbecoming, disobliging way, took a neighbor's [Benjamin Harwood's] lame colt, without asking, or in any manner obtaining his consent, which had been denied before, and rode it several miles, not having even the plea of necessity in his favor for so doing."[69]

Neighbors simply did not treat neighbors in this way. They were expected to behave in a friendly and considerate manner toward one another. When Hiram left his acquaintances in Tanbrook or Bennington village, however, he behaved quite differently. Asked by Captain Norton to pick up some boards at a sawmill in Pownal, Hiram, "after much chasing," ran into "a number of the rough unmannerly Hardscrabblers who made no scruples in saying very familiarly 'How do you do' though I had never seen them since I was born." Such easy familiarity among neighbors was one thing; from total strangers, quite another. Worse, such behavior offended Hiram's emerging sense of propriety.[70]

Whether dealing with neighbors, close acquaintances, or "hardscrabblers," Hiram remained firmly convinced that individuals must settle their own differences without outside interference. Above all, they must never call on the legal profession. Hailed into court as a witness when two neighbors feuded over land titles, Hiram left the proceedings with one thought firmly in mind: "Deliver me from Lawyer craft." Two days later, he had these feelings confirmed when he sat through another disputed land case, which "ended in expence & botheration to the parties." In his mind this was simply another "instance of the folly of going to law." Warming to the subject, he exclaimed: "Let it be a warning to those in cool blood to beware of asking advice of, or in any way meddling with lawyers—what mischief ensues from their intricate shufflings—let them alone & keep about our business & we shall do well enough."[71]

As Hiram surveyed his neighborhood, he had reason to question whether, even in the absence of lawyers, his neighbors were doing "well enough." Tanbrook was changing. Many of the families that originally settled in the area were gone; the founders were dead and their children departed. Each year, as men of means like Noadiah Swift and John

Norton purchased the farms of these people in order to rent them out, the composition of the Tanbrook neighborhood changed considerably; more and more of the Harwoods' neighbors were tenants rather than independent landowners. Nonetheless, whenever "our new neighbors began to solicit favors," the Harwoods responded charitably. Observing that it was "very hard times for the poor," Hiram and the rest of the family tried whenever possible to accommodate their less fortunate neighbors.[72]

As "times" grew increasingly difficult for all residents in Bennington Township, it was not unusual for Hiram to make such comments as "Dr. Worthy Waters had contracted debts to amount of about $2,000 and absconded to parts unknown." Later, "Asher Wilcox cleared out for Ohio" late one Saturday night, owing more than four hundred dollars in debts to various townspeople, including the Harwoods. Wilcox's family was to follow the next day, but before they could get out of town, all their property had been attached by the town authorities. What made this case so heinous for Hiram — "what completely caps the climax" — was the fact that Wilcox "left totally dependent his aged and decrepit parents to the mercy of their neighbors or the public." In Hiram's eyes the man had sinned twice: first he deserted his aged parents; second he broke the bond that linked neighbors together in mutual trust and support.[73]

Hiram's reactions to the changes taking place around him varied immensely. Upon encountering a "wretched poor family from Berkshire county bound to Brandon, Vt.," he could only exclaim, "Peace be with them." When he witnessed "a portable building containing a family, stove and furniture moving to the West, drawn by 3 yoke of oxen," he hopefully dubbed it "The Ark." However, Hiram felt quite differently about the bankruptcy of a local merchant. The man's fall "exemplified the folly of inordinate thirst after gain and boundless anticipation of means," and he believed the affair should stand as "a sufficient warning to all new beginners." But it was the marriage and imminent departure of Clarissa Norton that caused Hiram the most concern. "The marriage of our old playmates ought I think to demand more than ordinary attention, because in many instances it breaks off all former connexions — removing persons to a great distance from each other." For Hiram, "domestic society is of all others the sweetest where anything like unity prevails."[74]

The sense of loss — the disintegration of the "unity" of his childhood — led Hiram to dwell upon the changes taking place all about him.

"At no later period in life than that to which I am now advanced, on looking around I find my youthful friends are some of them in eternity, while others have removed to distant places." When he compiled a list of twenty-seven friends born and raised in Tanbrook, he discovered that well over half of these people no longer resided in the neighborhood.[75]

Hiram may have lost many of his old friends and neighbors, but he never lost his sense of obligation to residents of Tanbrook, regardless of how recently they may have arrived or what their circumstances were. If a poor widowed woman needed wood cut, Hiram did it willingly; when an aged black man who had long lived in the neighborhood as a hired man fell ill with consumption and became a ward of the town, Hiram, his father, and other neighbors visited him regularly; when the man died of consumption, these same men devoted a morning to "laying him out." When the town authorities met to "vendue the poor," Hiram worried over the fate of several families in his neighborhood. Happily, "Mrs Stiles & her children were excepted from being included among the paupers put up at auction." Unfortunately, when "Mrs. Rugg desired a like indulgence respecting her daughter," this did not happen.[76]

Although sympathetic with the plight of less-fortunate neighbors, Hiram had very little patience with those whom he felt to be largely responsible for their own troubled circumstances. Thus, when "Old Blazedell & his wife quarraled so violently that they were heard all over the neighborhood" and several neighbors were called upon to quiet them, Hiram would have nothing to do with the matter. "The affair was not new, nor was the cause latent. Rum and the great disparity of years between the couple was the sole cause — the old man being about 60 & his wife a little past 30 occasioned in him great jealousy, which on all these occasions he breathed forth unreservedly." On the next day a justice of the peace "went to neighbor Blazedell's to settle the hash." The man "made them take each other by the hand and solemnly promise to forget the past and be friends and live peaceably for the future, but it was supposed he had not gone out of hearing before the fracas was renewed."[77]

Several weeks later Hiram could no longer ignore this problem. Just as he was settling in to read newspapers after a long hard day, Mrs. Blazedell's little girls appeared at his door and told him that their stepfather had thrown their mother and all her clothes out of the house and forbidden her ever to return. Knowing full well that such "quarrels were common, especially in rum times," Hiram hesitated a bit. Finally, though, he and Benjamin left with the girls to see what they could do about the situation. "Thinking it best suited the occasion," Hiram took out his flute and played the "Rogues March" as they walked toward the Blazedells'. Upon nearing the house, they "found the lady crying—sitting by the wayside." Accompanied by the tearful woman, they "marched slowly up to the house," where they "rapped & halloed at every door." Receiving no answer, Hiram "serenaded him awhile, then growing impatient—made some heavy thumps against his south door and talked roughly, which had the desired effect—he advanced to the window above us and began a conversation." Then, "after hearing mutual accusations, denials and threats we prevailed on neighbor B. to let in his wife & her children & then came home."[78]

As the difficulties between the Blazedells continued, Hiram became increasingly annoyed. "Suffice it to say that by intemperance they were made instruments in the hands of the devil to mutually torment each other unceasingly." The feelings that Hiram vented toward this unfortunate man sprang from attitudes about work, social responsibilities, and personal behavior that were taking shape in his mind as he struggled to become a mature citizen and head of a family. It was upon the death of close friends and neighbors, however, that Hiram revealed the values he most highly esteemed. In numerous brief obituaries that appeared throughout his diary, he gave free expression to the personal characteristics he valued and those that he disparaged. After the funeral of one longtime neighbor Hiram observed that the man "had lived a retired and rather eccentric life, yet by his attention to business & good management, he had honestly acquired a considerable fortune." The man "possessed a good heart, never oppressed the poor, & left the world with the character of an honest man." The death of another old acquaintance elicited quite a different response: "An inordinate thirst for gain was the chief rule of action with her—no opportunity to gratify this was lost—means and measures, however *hard* and *oppressive*, were pursued with avidity, if lucre was the object. To the poor she was unkind, but to the rich & those in good circumstances, she was neighborly & accommodating."[79]

Although all deaths caused Hiram anxiety, he expressed the most shock and dismay over the suicides that took place in Bennington. When Gustavus Walbridge hung himself in his father's attic, Hiram supposed "he committed this awful deed in a fit of insanity." When news arrived that Smith Crawford, a man of Hiram's age, had "in a fit of insanity," cut his own throat "in a most shocking manner," Hiram was very upset. The "most shocking & melancholy instance of suicide," however, was that of Saxton Pickett, who "in a fit of despair, which grew out of a course of intemperance that he had been *in* a few years past . . . cut his throat with a razor from ear to ear & died instantly."[80]

Pickett's death involved not only a suicide but also intemperance. If a single theme pervaded the obituaries Hiram mentioned — as well as the entire diary — it was Hiram's strong feelings against intemperance. Frequently he entered variations of a single phrase: "died of wanton intemperance," "poor man finished his life of dreadful intemperance"; "his death being caused by intemperate drinking"; "death without doubt was occasioned by intemperance"; "a very intemperate character . . . was lost a few days and found frozen to death in the snow." The most painful of such death notices was that of Samuel B. Young, a prominent attorney and leader of the Republican Party in Bennington, who had been supportive of Hiram over the years. Sadly, Hiram noted that Young at one time "had the reputation of an intelligent, active, & vigilant attorney — possessed good talents, but closed his life as many do — in folly [drunkenness]."[81]

Charity — a sympathetic feeling for those less fortunate — had long been practiced by the Harwoods, and Hiram inherited this sense of responsibility for those in need. "Kindness to the poor" was one of the traits that Hiram honored most highly in his discussions of friends and acquaintances; he and his family practiced this ideal in their everyday lives. Time and again his journal related that "an elderly gentleman," whose "appearance bespoke age and indigence . . . solicited and received a dram, likewise victuals"; "A struggling elderly poor woman of Pownall stayed all night"; "Father found a traveller on horseback who appeared to be poor & destitute — invited him home with him"; "Ishmael Titus, a man of color from Pownal, appeared with a bull in lieu of a horse to carry his baggage which consisted of such things as people had charitably bestowed on him . . . spent the night."[82]

Hiram was happy to help truly needy individuals, but he deeply resented being gulled by those who had the means to pay for whatever assistance had been rendered or were fully capable of working to sustain themselves. Once, when "a nasty, ugly, beggarly impudent boy & girl" left after spending the night with the Harwoods, Hiram "was opposed to bestowing more charity upon them than their food & lodging because they were apparently in good health & could earn their living as well as anybody." Not only that; he was certain that if the

children received additional charity, "it would encourage them to per-
severe in their vagrant, dissolute course of life." Similarly, after spending the night with the Harwoods, a poor Irish widow asked if they
would take in her twelve-year-old son Michael. They agreed to take the
boy on trial for a period of time and to treat him as one of their own. To
be one of their own, however, meant that he must contribute to the
welfare of the household. Things went well for two months, and then
Hiram noted that "Michael disobeyed orders"; "Michael behaved ill at
harrowing"; "Michael very lazy"; and "Michael worked lazily." After
this last entry, the Harwoods sent Michael back to his mother. To allow
him to stay would have been to provide charity to an individual capable
of earning his own keep; this they would not do.[83]

As citizens of Bennington, the Harwoods extended their charity
beyond the confines of their neighborhood to the larger community.
This generally took the form of signing subscriptions brought around
by various townspeople. Mrs. French came by with a subscription for a
new stove for the meetinghouse, which Diadama signed in the amount
of $.75. When lightning burned Edward Savage's house to the ground,
Buckley Squires brought a subscription paper by for the relief of the
poor man and his family. Considering Savage "an industrious, good
citizen — a correct house joiner and carpenter — generally esteemed
and respected wherever known," Hiram signed in the amount of $5 to
be paid in produce. A month later he was happy to see that Mr. Savage,
"that industrious, persevering, and curious genius," was hard at work
keeping the running gears working at a local fulling mill. When S. H.
Blackmer brought down a subscription paper for the purpose of purchasing Governor Isaac Tichenor's encyclopedia at $5 per share, Ben-
jamin signed on for one share. He did this because Tichenor promised
to supply the meetinghouse with a fine brass bell with the proceeds of
the sale. And that summer the Harwoods paid $2 as their part of a
subscription to paint the meetinghouse. The following year Hiram
drove his mother to Captain David Robinson's so that she could drop
off three pairs of socks and $.50 in cash to the widow Catherine Robin-
son, who was the agent for the Female Juvenile Society. When the
widow of Moses D. Robinson came to the Harwoods "to solicit alms for
poor children," she "received a favorable reception."[84]

Two community issues — Absalom Peters' salary and the construction of a new academy in Bennington — caused the Harwoods, like
many other townspeople, much anxiety. As always, they willingly signed
a subscription paper calling for them to support First Church's newly

settled minister. A short time later, however, Hiram and Benjamin attended a meeting of the church and congregation only to discover that they had totally misunderstood the paper they had signed and stood to pay more than they anticipated. Others found themselves in the same situation, and "a long gingle ensued on this head without coming to a clear decision." In the end the Harwoods were obligated to pay more than they intended to support Peters, which did not enhance their enthusiasm for the young man.[85]

Shortly after this meeting, another issue arose that exacerbated the bad feelings caused by the manner in which the minister's salary was to be paid. Peters and the leading Federalists in Bennington attempted to take control of how a new academy being constructed in town would be administered. They intended it to become an elite academy rather than simply another common school. The town's leading Democrats took offense at this, and a dispute arose that divided the town into feuding factions.

Although the Harwoods did all in their power to remain "aloof," the struggle between the contending factions in town grew worse. The two parties became "extremely jealous of each other" and "accused one another of many vile intentions & actions." All this led Hiram to conclude, "I think myself that colleges & academies are nurseries of monarchy & aristocracy — that the money laid out for education there might do much greater service to the public to be put into a vast fund for the support of our common schools — I would not throw them *all* away, however, I would take care not to increase their numbers."[86]

Such an attitude on Hiram's part evinced the maturity he had achieved as a result of his marriage, the birth of his children, and the responsibilities that he shouldered as a member of the Tanbrook community. Such maturity would be sorely needed in an even more important undertaking — the future success of the Harwood farm.

6

Entrepreneur

Visited a young dairy lady this m'g in the neighborhood, who had been highly recommended by Mr P's family and conditionally engaged her to make cheese for us during the present season at 7/0 Y'k per week.[1]

Shortly after making these arrangements, Hiram, accompanied by his Uncle Clark, who was visiting the family for a time, set out for Williamsburg to call upon Clark's daughter, Margaret, who worked for a family living several miles south of that village. While visiting with Margaret and her employer, Hiram became fascinated with the man's cheese press and had Clark take down its precise measurements. Soon after returning to Tanbrook, Clark, aided by the Harwoods' neighbor and close friend Thomas Kent, set to work constructing a press according to the plans he had sketched out. Four days later the two men completed their task and moved the press into the kitchen of Ira's old home, which Hiram had prepared to serve as the family's dairy house.

To hire a "dairy lady," construct a large new cheese press, and create a special dairy house marked an important departure for the Harwoods. They had long been accustomed to making cheese and butter, but the products of their labor had always been consumed by the family or traded locally to neighbors or shopkeepers in town in return for needed goods and services. Now, with the changes they had just instituted, the Harwood family intended to enter into the larger commercial market that was beginning to open up throughout western Vermont and eastern New York.[2] The success or failure of this new venture — a venture upon which the entire future of the Harwood farm depended — rested primarily upon Hiram's shoulders. There was much at stake, not only for the farm and the Harwood family; Hiram's own perception of himself as a man became intimately intertwined with this new entrepreneurial endeavor. Now, more than ever, he faced challenges that tested his ability to become the man Benjamin expected him to be.

Even before setting out on this new course, Hiram had begun to assume much more responsibility for the well-being of the farm. With the departure of Jonas for his own farm in New York in May 1816, Hiram took on his uncle's primary duties. Most important of these was marketing the farm's crops — the Harwoods' primary source of income — in Troy, New York. Not only must he transport the grain; Hiram then had to negotiate with agents in Troy for the best price. After that it was up to him to bargain with various merchants in order to gain acceptable prices for goods required by the family to maintain the farm. Making four to five such trips a year, usually during the winter months, Hiram gradually became a thoroughly seasoned trader. With each succeeding trip to Troy, Hiram displayed more of the disciplined work ethic so characteristic of his father. It was not unusual for him to drive all night in order not to be trapped in Troy for lack of snow to bear his sleigh. Once, "having completed my business, tho't it prudent to make the best of my way for home, as the sleighing was every moment wasting away." Consequently, "letting my horses travel at a slow rate, arrived here, having suffered much from cold & want of rest, at 5 in the morning."[3] Another time, again to save his horses from the strain of poor sledding, Hiram left Troy after four o'clock in the afternoon and, after driving throughout the night without rest, arrived home at three the following morning.

Hiram applied this same discipline and intensity to work on the farm. "Business being urgent," he spent most of Vermont's annual fast day in 1818 sowing plaster on a wheat field. Several months later he and his father "rallied at three in the morning to secure hay against a threatened thunder storm." Fortunately, "the moon gave us considerable light which enabled us to proceed with dispatch in the business." During one of the hottest days of the summer the following year, "father left field early on account of ill health," and Hiram stayed the entire day with two other hands. A week later, under similarly intense heat, several hands gave out, but Hiram remained steadily beside his father in the field. In order to be on hand at all times, Hiram managed to get excused from militia training. When he noted on his thirtieth birthday that "time is consuming us fast—how important it is that we improve it well," he articulated the work ethic by which he was now living; for him time had become money.[4]

As Hiram became increasingly diligent around the farm, he assumed a much more serious tone in his diary. He often commented that "it was a pretty good day for business" or "business went so badly that it caused low spirits." Concern for "business" also caused him to take careful note of market prices in Troy. Thus, when the family moved into the hard winter of 1820–21, he despondently reported that he "heard that pork had fallen from 5 to 4 1/2 at Troy—wheat 75—everything on the same scale which is raised by the farmer."[5]

By this time Hiram had become quite familiar with the family's financial affairs; on August 5, 1818, Benjamin gave him full responsibility for keeping all the family accounts. Thereafter, he entered into his daily journal the amount of every business transaction, the parties involved, and how payment had been made. If it entailed either long- or short-term credit, he also made note of the interest and the term for which the credit had been extended. In addition, he kept detailed records of everything produced on the farm. He knew precisely how many acres were planted in wheat, corn, barley, oats, and flax as well as the number of sheaves, bushels, or pounds that each crop produced. He also kept a close record of the livestock held on the farm and how much cheese and butter were produced annually and a detailed account of the operation of the cider mill. From these records it was apparent that cheese and butter accounted for roughly one-fourth of the family's annual income, the cider mill another fourth, and wheat another fourth; the rest of their income came from the sale of livestock, the marketing of beef and pork, and the sale of wool and flaxseed.[6] In addition to such accounts, Hiram kept careful records of the family's yearly income, their yearly expenses, and the annual total of the "great debt" (notes held by various individuals against the Harwoods). Averaged over a six-year period (1818–23), Hiram's records revealed an annual income of $462.20 and annual expenses of $321.66; this left $140.54 to service the debt, which stood at $356.76.[7]

Full knowledge of the family's financial transactions brought little solace for Hiram. The existence of such a large perpetual debt troubled him deeply. He often experienced "a rank fit of the hypo which lasted most of the day" or admitted that he "felt very downhearted in contemplating expenses." The "peculiar pressure of the times—gave full scope to the hypo" and led him to conclude "that the way in which we were going must lead to destruction." Upon noting that a member of a longtime Bennington family went bankrupt, he observed that "instances of this kind were now daily multiplying." Two months later he saw a great deal of traffic on the road running in front of the Harwood farm — "Pownal people coming to see friends confined to the jail limits in Bennington, and Bennington lawyers, justices, sheriffs, etc. going to Pownal to kidnap more of their poor debtors." Such matters bothered Hiram considerably, especially when he noted that "paying up old arrearages & meeting present wants took off money as fast as rec'd."[8]

Perpetual debt plagued Hiram mercilessly. According to his best calculations, the family's income stood at $246.55 on August 5, 1819; their current debts amounted to $318.53. Hiram made up the difference of $71.98 by "hiring cash" from a friend. By May 1819 the great debt stood at $504.61. Of this amount the family owed S. Brown $242.28. Two years later, having been able only to service the interest on this debt, they still owed the Brown estate $242.28. A year later they had worked the principal down to $94.00; the following year it stood at zero. However, their debt to Noadiah Swift, which had previously amounted to $80.00, jumped to $177.79 during the same period. In order to pay off the Brown estate, they had extended their note with Dr. Swift. Although one creditor was owed less, they remained as deeply in debt as ever.[9]

Hiram became increasingly anxious. Constantly in need of money to settle his accounts, he had to dun those who owed him in order to pay those to whom he was indebted. When he borrowed $10.00 from his neighbor and good friend Luman Norton, he found himself only able to repay him $5.00. So he "called on Col M.[errill] for $5 to pay the residue which must be paid between this time & Tuesday m'g next — but the good man could not muster a cent & could but faintly promise me the sum required by Monday in the course of the day." Feeling quite heartsick, Hiram returned home. There he found Noadiah Swift, "who assured me that I might have it of him." This was a godsend for Hiram, who considered that "the times were the most distressing for money ever known."[10]

This was not the last time Dr. Swift would help Hiram. A year later Hiram again found that "being put to my trumps so much to collect money gave me melancholy ideas — my spirits were low — the frailty of human nature stared me full in the face." He visited town in an attempt to borrow money from several merchants with whom he regularly traded; they all refused him. He then "marched back to Dr. Swift's," who "without hesitation lent me the money." Hiram thanked his good fortune for "having a rich good man in the neighborhood."[11] He may have been the town's most prominent Federalist, but Noadiah Swift always came to the Harwood house, no matter what hour of the night, to tend to the sick, and he never turned Hiram away when he needed a loan. By this point in his life, Hiram was forming a reasonably clear opinion of which of his acquaintances were loyal men and good neighbors.

$\backsim$ Noadiah Swift's willingness to extend the Harwoods' note year after year enabled Hiram to begin to involve the farm and the family more and more with the needs and operation of the dairy. Even with the increasing emphasis upon the dairy, however, the work routine of the Harwoods did not change appreciably. Sally, aided by her sister-in-law Lydia and Patience Barber, the young woman hired by Hiram, took charge of the day-to-day production of cheese and butter. At the same time she and the other women, like so many of their sisters throughout rural America, remained as responsible as ever for keeping house, cooking, spinning, weaving, and tending the children.[12] Benjamin and Hiram, with the help of Justin Martindale and Henry DeBarr—two neighbor boys living with the Harwoods—milked the cows, helped turn the heavy cheeses, cultivated the crops, tended the sheep, did the butchering, and assumed responsibility for gathering apples and making cider. Little wonder, then, that when Sally's Connecticut relatives visited Tanbrook at the height of harvest season, Hiram left them "to amuse themselves as best they could without my company—indeed business was so great that I could not without injury to our interest oblige them with it."[13]

Harvesttime caused Hiram distress, but it involved tensions he had experienced many times before. Marketing the dairy, however, was an entirely new undertaking—one filled with the perils of any number of unknown economic pitfalls.[14] Thus, when Austin Harmon Jr., owner of the largest dairy in the county, offered to allow Hiram to include his cheese in an agreement Harmon had struck with a cheese agent from Adams, Massachusetts, Hiram readily agreed. Although Harmon's intervention eased Hiram's mind somewhat—he would not have to negotiate the disposal of his dairy himself—other issues raced through his head. What if the agent did not like his dairy? What if there were only enough casks to ship Harmon's cheese? What then? How would Hiram get his dairy to market?

These questions remained unanswered even after Mr. Cheesebro and his son arrived on the appointed day at Harmon's, where Hiram had been waiting nervously for several hours. As the agent and his son set about packing up Harmon's dairy, Hiram remained "anxious to know what course to take." Cheesebro had supplied seventy-seven casks: would there be enough? Was he to have what was left over? If not, would he have to travel to Adams to obtain more? Finally, Hiram's other duties forced him to leave with these questions still unanswered. Mr. Cheesebro did assure him that he would visit Tanbrook the next day, view the dairy, and report on the matter of the casks.[15]

Much to Hiram's relief, Mr. Cheesebro and his son did arrive at Tanbrook the following day, "inspected our cheese which they pronounced good," and "informed us in some measure how the business was to be executed." Hiram was to transport the cheese to Troy, where Mr. Cheesebro would assume responsiblity for marketing it in New York City for the highest price possible. He speculated that Hiram could expect to receive six and one-half cents a pound, less the agent's commission of fifty cents per hundred pounds. Before leaving, the agent informed Hiram of even more welcome news; there were spare casks at Harmon's sufficient for Hiram's needs.[16]

As soon as the cheese agents departed, Hiram hurried to Harmon's with a wagon to retrieve the casks he so coveted. Two days later he had, with the assistance of Thomas Kent, packed and weighed the cheese meant for shipment to Troy. In addition, the two men weighed other cheese on hand in order to reach some final calculation of the year's production. In a little over four months, the dairy, consisting of sixteen cows, had produced more than 2,100 pounds of cheese. This included 1,428 pounds that went to Cheesebro, 611 pounds sold to merchants in Bennington, and more than 100 pounds saved for the use of the family and neighbors. Filled with a sense of satisfaction, Hiram declared that "all things considered we think we have done tolerably well."[17]

Such an uncharacteristic flush of optimism lasted through Hiram's trip to Troy, where he took a receipt from Mr. Cheesebro for seven casks of cheese, made necessary purchases for the family, viewed the canal boats, and happily played the fife with a young joiner who had previously worked in Bennington. But when days of waiting to receive some word from Cheesebro turned into weeks, and then into months,

Hiram's sanguine attitude dissipated entirely. Two months after he returned from Troy, he had to endure questions from townspeople who "sarcastically enquired if I had heard anything from our cheese?" He could only reply weakly that "we had plenty of company." To make matters worse, Hiram heard reports in March that Cheesebro "had cleared out of the country." Then, when Dr. Noadiah Swift — the Harwoods' most trusted source of financial advice — "seemed to give some credit to the story of Cheesebro's running away," Hiram became distraught. Finally, after seven agonizing months, word came on May 1 that Cheesebro had sold their cheese for five and one-half cents per pound. After subtracting his commission, freight charges, casks, and storage, the agent forwarded to the Harwoods $67.59 in cash.[18]

Upon receipt of this money, Hiram was able to determine the family's income over the past year. By his calculations the local sale of grain, cider, and butter came to just over $350.00. Cheese sold to townspeople accounted for another $12.00. At nearly the same time, he made a precise accounting of the family's outstanding debts, which amounted annually to over $300.00.[19] Fortunately, Dr. Noadiah Swift carried the bulk of this debt. Each year he allowed Hiram, after paying the annual interest charge, to renew his note for another year. In addition, he continued to loan Hiram small sums of money throughout the year on short-term credit that helped the family meet day-to-day expenses.

Given the Harwoods' financial situation, Hiram saw no alternative but to continue the commercial dairy venture. For all its anguish and relatively meager return, the dairy appeared to him to be the means by which the Harwoods might eventually prosper. He was committed to the endeavor and meant to make it work. Therefore, even before receiving Cheesebro's payment, Hiram had begun making arrangements for the ensuing season. When Justin Martindale went to live with a local carpenter to learn that trade, and Henry DeBarr left to clerk for a merchant in Troy, Hiram hired Sylvanus Daniels, a local neighbor boy, to work for seven months at five dollars per month. He also made a tentative agreement with a woman he met in town to work for the Harwoods beginning in early June. However, "on enquiry respecting my lady found her reputation bad — had a bad habit of taking more [than] was her own sometimes." Hiram terminated the bargain immediately.[20]

Several weeks later Hiram hired Betsey Pope, who resided with her parents in Pownal, to live with the Harwoods, beginning in the first week of June, "to spin wool, assist daily about milking & occasionally to do housework at 4/0 pr week." When he arrived home with this news, "some part of my transactions [occasional rather than regular housework] underwent severe animadversion from the ladies, which caused me to feel some ruffled." Nonetheless, shortly thereafter Sally "prepared her office for making cheese," and two days later "Mrs. S. Harw'd began making cheese this day."[21]

By the time Sally closed her "office" late in October, she had made more than two thousand pounds of cheese from the milk of seventeen cows. Although this output did not exceed the total for the previous year, Hiram managed to sell it for a larger profit. He did this by arranging for a merchant in Troy, who had recently begun to market cheese in New York City on commission, to assume responsibility for selling the dairy. From his years of trading in Troy, Hiram had become quite familiar with this individual and consequently trusted him much more than his previous agent. Hiram's faith seemed well placed when he received payment for the dairy less than a month after he had delivered it to Troy. From the sale of cheese and butter, the Harwoods earned just over $150.00.[22]

Each year for the next several years, Hiram and Sally managed to produce more cheese and to increase the amount of money they earned as a result. Regardless of this fact, Benjamin was certain that the expanded dairy operation contributed mightily to the family's financial problems. To increase dairy production, Hiram had to secure additional cows each season, and additional land must be devoted to pasture in order to feed the enlarged herd. This in turn necessitated purchasing more plaster to enhance the annual hay crop. At a time when the family's outstanding debts still hovered around $300 annually, Hiram calculated the cost of plaster and other necessities purchased from merchants in Troy, Bennington, and Hoosick, New York, at more than $200. As a consequence, anxiety over the family's economic straits created tension between Benjamin and Hiram during the 1826 season. Lack of hay in April made their prospects "seem very gloomy" at the very outset of the dairy year. By the end of the month, Benjamin "was in great trouble respecting his business." By October, when the frenetic pace of harvesttime coincided with the marketing of the dairy, Benjamin experienced "a most unreasonable turn of hypo." No matter what Hiram might say to calm him, Benjamin adamantly maintained "that nothing pertaining to the business of the farm moved a peg or a morsel without his making the greatest & first exertion." It is not surprising, then, that one day when father and son worked together at

the cider mill, the "business made us in a small degree a little snarly —
ended in a few words."[23]

Given such circumstances, Hiram and Sally were under intense
pressure to have a successful dairy season. In addition to his regular
duties about the farm, Hiram helped Sally and Cousin Margaret maintain the cheese. This became particularly difficult when an unusual
period of extreme heat settled over Bennington in August. If not carefully "overhauled," precious cheeses would melt down. During this
same time, Hiram spent a good many late-evening hours absorbed in
reading about dairying in the Abraham Rees *Cyclopedia* borrowed from
Dr. Swift. When Sally "closed the business of making cheese" on October 14, she had made more than forty-two hundred pounds of cheese
from the milk of twenty cows.[24] It was now up to Hiram to turn a profit.

Rather than negotiating with his contact in Troy, Hiram decided to
bargain with E. Carpenter, an agent in Pownal who would buy the dairy
outright rather than sell it on commission. After some negotiation, the
man agreed to pay Hiram six cents a pound, payable on delivery in
Troy. After striking this bargain, Hiram had a neighbor make casks for
him and agreed to pay another to help him transport his cheese to Troy.
On the day he was to leave for Troy, Hiram "felt the keenest kind of
sensibility to any thing that had the slightest relation to my present
undertaking — never endured more misery in the same length of time
on a similar occasion." Anxious to receive his pay, Hiram sought out
Carpenter, who at first "amused himself a little at my expense, [by]
saying he supposed I expected to receive money of him, but that he was
unable through disappointment to meet me." Carpenter continued
talking in this vein "until I began to be wrought upon in some degree."
Finally, realizing that he had upset Hiram, Carpenter admitted his joke
and exclaimed that if Hiram would treat him to a beer, he would pay
him. Greatly relieved, Hiram stood the treat.[25]

When Hiram returned home with Carpenter's money, he had every
reason to feel contented. It had been a good year for the farm. Hiram
calculated the income from the dairy for the year, and it stood at
$312.00. This was twice what had been earned from the sale of grain
and three times the value of the cider production.[26] The dairy venture — in which Hiram had invested so much psychological as well as
physical energy — appeared to be taking hold; he might yet fulfill his
father's lifelong expectations for him and prove himself worthy of assuming the mantle of the family patriarch.

Although Hiram's bargain with Mr. Carpenter gave him a modicum of self-satisfaction, it was not accompanied by financial peace of mind. The following year the family's indebtedness to Noadiah Swift alone remained at more than three hundred dollars. It seemed to Hiram that he was constantly "contriving how to accomplish money engagements coming up against us."[27]

Debt was not all that occupied Hiram's mind. Each year he had to accomplish certain tasks vital to the success of the farm. These included purchasing additional cows, finding and employing a satisfactory dairy girl, and hiring farm hands to help him and his father maintain the dairy, tend the hay and grain crops, harvest the apples, and operate the cider mill. Each of these involved not only careful accounting but also a good deal of time, effort, and stress. In order to have a sufficient number of cows giving milk by late April or early May, for example, Hiram had to search throughout the county for animals with newborn calves or those soon to give birth. It was not unusual for him to spend one hundred to two hundred dollars in a single season in order to maintain a productive herd. The fact that such expenditures rested entirely on his own personal evaluation of the future milking capacities of these animals, as well as his ability to bargain over the purchase price, created many anxious moments for Hiram. His personal insecurities often surfaced with a rush during such negotiations. On one occasion, believing himself "very easily stuffed and gulled out of about $5," Hiram felt "ashamed of having acted a part so contrary to the rules of prudence & judgment." Another time he castigated himself for "exhibit[ing] that softness and want of penetration & knowledge of mankind which is found only in the green young man who has never ventured abroad into the wide world." But he had to persevere.[28]

With every passing year, Hiram became more and more frustrated in his search for a suitable dairy girl. This resulted more from their increasing scarcity than from whatever negotiations were necessary to convince a girl to come and live with the Harwoods for the season. Invariably, Hiram would arrive in towns as far from Bennington as Petersburg, New York, or Williamstown, Massachusetts, only to find that "nearly all working girls were employed in manufacturing establishments," "all girls had gone to factories," or the prize he sought was "off to some factory." Whenever he managed to find a family that would discuss hiring out one of its daughters, Hiram did his best to provide assurances that the Harwoods, "in true Democratic style considered our girls, if their characters were fair, as good as ourselves," described "the Republican relation in which we hold such ladies," explained to them "my republican notions respecting hired girls," or explained "the respect in which we always held girls of proper character at our house." After "preliminaries were settled in favor of democracy," Hiram generally settled on a payment of from seventy-five cents to one dollar a week. Whenever he completed a successful search, Hiram invariably considered himself "as having been very lucky" and thereby "could go home with flying colors."[29]

Although Hiram had a difficult time finding suitable dairy girls, he was extremely fortunate in his choice of hired hands. In October 1829 George P. Harwood, the only son of Hiram's Uncle Jonas, came to live with the family and worked for $10 per month. By the time Sylvanus Daniels completed his indenture in January 1831, George Harwood had become Hiram's most trusted and loyal hand. Each year thereafter Hiram and his cousin agreed on an annual salary as well as the conditions under which George would work. In 1833, for instance, they agreed that George was to reserve four days to himself during the months of January, February, March, and December. He "wanted days off in these months so that when weather became severe he could enjoy books or papers at his option." The following year George had the "option to judge severity of weather this present season — option whether to work abroad on those days." Each year Hiram signed a note for George's annual salary of $110 to $120 and paid him whatever interest had accrued on the previous year's note. Consequently, by October 1836, Hiram owed his cousin nearly $500.[30] Such an arrangement served the best interests of both men quite well: Hiram gained a loyal, dependable, and hardworking hand for little outlay of cash; George, happy to be a part of the Harwood family, treated his salary as a solid, interest-bearing investment.

By the time George came to live at Tanbrook, the farm was undergoing significant changes. The year before he arrived, the Harwoods milked 22 cows and produced a little more than 5,000 pounds of cheese. By 1830, in order to accommodate a larger dairy herd, they gave up keeping sheep. With this decision, they committed themselves fully to expanding their dairy operation. By 1834 the results were apparent; in that year they made more than 16,000 pounds of cheese from 34 cows.

Responsibility for the dairy itself rested primarily with Sally. With the help of Lydia and whatever dairy girl could be hired, Sally took complete charge of making the cheese. Indeed, she would brook no interference from Hiram. When Hiram returned from visiting another dairy with a novel set of written instructions on how to prepare the rennet (contents of the stomach of an unweaned calf used to curdle milk) so essential to making cheese, Sally told him in no uncertain terms that "it was best not to attempt the practice—as it might in new hands be productive of more evil than good." Another time, when he dissented with her decision to set milk in pans overnight, Sally simply ignored him. So Hiram, aided by George and seasonal hands, milked the cows, lifted the heavy cheeses on and off the presses, and then helped turn and rub them as they seasoned. As in most other rural dairies, the actual production of cheese remained entirely in the hands of the farmer's wife.[31]

With each passing year, the dairy became more important to the Harwoods' financial well-being. When Benjamin dismantled the cider mill for the last time in the fall of 1835, cheese and butter became the sole source of income for the family. Hiram often sent Sylvanus or George to Troy with a load of butter when the demand seemed particularly promising, but most of the Harwoods' excess butter still went to merchants and tavern keepers in Bennington. These same individuals continued to purchase cheese on a regular basis. It was the market controlled by commercial cheese agents, however, that was central to the Harwoods' success. The continued existence of the farm had come to depend on that market.

This fact was not lost on Hiram, and the pressure he exerted on himself to succeed increased each year. Occasionally this pressure led to flare-ups with members of the family. One Sunday evening, while turning cheeses with Sally, a particularly large cheese "showed itself to great disadvantage," which "occasioned a harrowing up of all my bad feelings which had vent in no very handsome language." During an unusually hot September, "some very earnest conversation respecting the situation of some cheeses passed between my fair one and myself—not of the most pleasant kind." The very next day, Hiram "spent some time in the dairy with my lady—some few hard words were exchanged in allusion to the bad condition of a few cheeses." Even Adeline, who helped out by painting identification marks on the Harwoods' cheese casks before they went to market, had to endure Hiram's occasional wrath. Once, when she and an acquaintance, "in a kind of frolic," accidentally tore a document Hiram considered very important, he "let out on the poor girl [Adeline] for so doing, considering her the principal aggressor." Fortunately, "the storm soon blew over—damage but trifling and of but little importance."[32]

Hiram's relationship with his father was more complex. For all intents and purposes, Hiram had taken over management of the farm. Still, Benjamin remained the patriarch — the titular head of the farm — and Hiram had to be careful about the changes he instituted in the farm's operations. Having read intensively in the Rees *Cyclopedia* regarding how to feed cattle, sow plaster, and maintain proper conditions in the dairy room, Hiram attempted to put these innovations into practice. He usually accomplished such changes over Benjamin's vigorous objections. Benjamin still considered the farm to be his and stormed about whenever prospects appeared bleak. The scarcity of hay facing the Harwoods in the early spring of 1835 "almost made my father run mad — his chief spleen was leveled at me." As a result, "father suffered severely in his mind on account of lack of hay — his prospects were gloomy in the extreme — and he hotly poured out his wrath on my head and shoulders as the author of his troubles."[33]

Benjamin simply could not relinquish responsibility for the farm. Even though receipts to the Harwoods by 1832 were made out to "B Harwood and Son," Benjamin demanded that he be treated as the head of the operation. When he fell ill in the spring of 1835 and had to remain in bed, Hiram, ever the dutiful son, "at the conclusion of the day made a regular verbal Report to my father of the business of the day." Nonetheless, even as Hiram honored his father as the head of the household, he knew that he had complete accountability for the farm. Its future rested in his hands.[34]

Of all the responsibilities shouldered by Hiram, the most weighty always involved the marketing of the dairy. Each year he sought out a cheese agent, bargained with him over the price he was to receive for his dairy, and then spent weeks, sometimes even months, driven nearly to distraction with worry over whether the agent would make good on the bargain. Over the years Hiram became increasingly obsessed with the fear that he would be cheated out of an entire year's profits by an unscrupulous cheese agent. One year, this obsession nearly cost Hiram his life.

On October 1, 1835, an unfamiliar agent, Dr. Emerson Hull of Berlin, New York, visited Tanbrook and offered Hiram eight and one-quarter cents per pound for his dairy. In addition he would pay fifty cents for each cask — all to be delivered in Troy with no deduction of interest. After carefully checking with trusted friends about Dr. Hull's character, Hiram agreed to the bargain. When the time came for Hull to pick up the cheese, the doctor's son informed Hiram that his father's firm would not be able to pay for the cheese on the day of delivery. The firm would, however, pay interest to Hiram until the full amount could be delivered. Hiram "consented to all very contentedly—feeling no alarm whatever until after their departure—when we began talking about it—raising one scare-crow after another." By the end of a family conference, Hiram was beside himself with anxiety. He determined to go to Berlin to get the matter settled once and for all. If Dr. Hull could not pay on time, he must provide firm security for the future payment. With this in mind, Hiram set out in his wagon well after dark. While driving along under good starlight, Hiram picked up a passenger who resided near Berlin. Then, anxious to get his problem settled, Hiram whipped his mare up and took a corner much too sharply. The wagon tipped abruptly to the side, and Hiram fell out, got his legs entangled in the reins, and was dragged for some distance with his head bouncing off rocks in the road before his passenger could get the mare under control. Dazed, but feeling as if he were unhurt, Hiram got to his feet and, after a short respite, continued his journey.[35]

When he arrived at Dr. Hull's at two o'clock in the morning, he unharnessed and stabled his mare, entered the house without knocking, and "necessarily made some noise" that awakened the frightened doctor. When the poor man got his wits about him, Hiram informed him that the dairy would go to another agent if the contract could not be met. The doctor assured him that all was well, and Hiram left for home satisfied.[36]

Two days later, when no money had arrived, Hiram "grew some uneasy—was previously well satisfied and calm—now became not a little disturbed in my mind." Finally, around four o'clock that afternoon, Hull's partner arrived and paid nearly $900 for the first part of the dairy. By the end of their transaction in late November, the firm of Hull and Boon had paid Hiram more than $1,000. By the first of the year, then, Hiram confided to his journal that "as to pecuniary circumstances without descending to particulars—might safely say that all demands against the establishment on the first instant could have been fully met and perhaps a small sum and it would have been small, might have remained in the locker." At year's end, when Hiram made a final summary of the family's account, he showed receipts of $2,259.74 and payments of $2,091.65. The Harwoods were not only solvent but had money left over. It seemed that Hiram had finally lived up to his father's expectations.[37]

At the same time, whether consciously aware of it or not, Hiram was emulating a masculine persona that was beginning to emerge throughout much of the nation. Above all, this perception of manliness stressed the determination and skill with which men managed their economic environment. It demanded a personal efficacy in business: a man must deal successfully with changing markets, conceive and implement his own building plans, and be shrewd in all land transactions. Whereas his father had striven to attain a competency—a small measure of economic independence that would feed, clothe, and house his family— Hiram worked to develop and manage the farm not only to maintain such a competency but to improve the economic and social standing of his family.[38] More than anything else, Hiram wanted to achieve respectability for himself and the Harwood family.[39] Like so many others born to his generation, Hiram could shape his life in ways that people of previous generations could not. If Bennington had been a society with markets for his father, it was rapidly becoming a market society—an enterprising, commercial, capitalist society—for Hiram and his generation. Within such a society, a man born to a simple competency could, through calculation, hard work, self-control, and self-interested striving, achieve respectability for himself and his family.[40]

For Hiram, unlike many others, the desire for respectability—which not only demanded social and economic advancement but also insisted upon temperance, moderation in all personal behavior, sociability, and a strong emphasis upon education—did not take him away from the farm and his family. Nor did it involve a new style of family life; home and workplace remained one and the same, and the father figure continued to be dominant in the Harwood household. The patriarchal tradition of the Harwoods remained firmly in place.[41]

༄ The Harwoods' loyalty to the ideal of patriarchy, however, was definitely an altered version of this traditional belief. Although Benjamin remained the titular head of the family, Hiram had eclipsed him in every other way. It was Hiram who made the fundamental economic decisions. It was his ability to contend with the market mechanisms of an increasingly commercial world that determined the family's social and economic stature. At the same time, with Sally's support and his successful transition into a confident, loving father, Hiram had matured considerably. He felt more secure, even expansive at times. And as Bennington changed in ways that made the community more accommodating to someone with Hiram's interests and ambitions, he appeared far less eccentric. No longer Benjamin's fatuous son, Hiram, with the passage of each year, achieved increased respectability within the larger Bennington community.

Concurrently, many changes took place in the lives of the Harwoods. Some alterations became immediately apparent; others were more subtle and less easily detected. The most obvious of these resulted from the decision to concentrate solely on dairy production. First, having turned their fields exclusively to the production of hay to support the dairy herd, the Harwoods had to purchase whatever rye and corn was necessary to supplement the herd's diet. Next, they quit raising sheep and hogs in order to give their full attention to the dairy. This meant they had to purchase whatever wool or pork the family required. And finally, once they decided to shut down their cider mill permanently, they had to depend on others to press their apples.

As the herd grew and the production of cheese and butter increased, Hiram and the family also began to question whether they should enlarge their operation. When Hiram consulted with John Norton to see whether they might cooperate in the purchase of the old Fay farm, Norton declined the offer, but he suggested that Hiram buy the entire farm himself. Ever cautious, Hiram "did not think it prudent, viewing the whole ground, to take such a violent leap into Debt." Hiram did eventually offer to pay $700 for the western half of the property. When the owner held out for $750, the Harwoods, after holding "a kind of family conference," decided against the purchase. They were all in agreement that "whenever we attempt to buy we should have the means to pay." So ended the family's brief flirtation with buying up some of the property that was constantly coming onto the market as small farmers failed all around them. For years the purchase of such farms had been the sole province of the Nortons and the Swifts.[42]

During the summer of 1833, Hiram did persuade the family to invest in a major building project. Having studied the pages allotted to dairying in the Rees *Cyclopedia*, as well as the many plates picturing the proper sorts of buildings necessary for an efficient dairy, Hiram employed Hiram Waters and his workers to construct a large new barn. The building, a double-sided structure measuring thirty-six feet by forty feet and costing more than four hundred dollars, was a source of great pride to Hiram. It presented a particularly "imposing appearance"; he loved to describe its "double boarded" walls and its large doors "made from boards free from splits." Its cavernous spaces for storing hay filled him with a sense of accomplishment. It was his barn; it stood as a symbol of his efforts to take charge of the farm, to turn it into a profitable commercial venture.[43]

However, the barn drew criticism from others. When Dr. William Bigelow asked Hiram to sign a subscription paper to construct a sounding board in the meetinghouse, Hiram claimed that the Harwoods "felt too poor to assist in this business." Bigelow immediately "remarked on our extravagance in building such a barn" and "supposed from my habit of staying at home so much on the Sabbath, that I cared very little for preaching & that my motto of course was 'Eat, drink & be merry,' calculating on many days yet to come." Responding that "as to a long life, there was vast uncertainty in that case — and it was not my way to indulge in such revery," Hiram, not willing to have his accomplishment maligned, exclaimed that "property like the barn if I should not live to enjoy its use, might be serviceable to some one, if not to my heirs." Such a structure, like his father's stone walls, would stand as a useful monument to hard work and practical effort for years to come.[44]

The barn and its contents led Hiram to undertake precautions that had never previously entered his mind. No sooner was it constructed than he had representatives of the Vermont Mutual Fire Insurance Company come out to take its measurements in order to issue an insurance policy. Shortly thereafter he signed a note in the amount of $97.88 to insure his barn and its contents against destruction by fire.[45]

Hiram's increasingly intense concentration on the dairy led him gradually to alter his behavior in other ways as well. By the summer of 1836, with the dairy producing more than ever before, he casually observed that he was "not personally employed on road, but father, G.P., E. Wright and Hopkins were." A year later he noted that "our highway rates not having been fully worked out — all hands except myself went down and spent forenoon on the road."[46]

Never an ardent militia participant, Hiram had nonetheless always turned out dutifully for local musters. As he began to consider his time more valuable, however, such activities became increasingly onerous to him. When the various Bennington companies were ordered to spend several days at a brigade muster in Manchester, Hiram went to Colonel Jonathan Robinson to ask if he might be excused. Claiming to have been swamped with similar requests, Robinson would only promise to "do for me all he could." As luck would have it, Robinson was unable to have Hiram excused, and he had to endure several days of arduous training away from home.[47]

Two years later, following a particularly strenuous training session in Bennington, Hiram declared himself "too far advanced in life & too much debilitated to endure this military business." He was determined to "get rid of it if possible." Instead of taking his case to his militia officers, Hiram went to town officials—with a good deal more success. Indeed, "Mr. Safford hinted that I might without difficulty get rid of military duty." As a result, the next time Hiram received a call to attend a local muster, he responded that he "would be absent and risk the consequences."[48] There were none. Hiram never attended another drill. In subsequent years he even paid a man fifty cents to take G. P. Harwood's place at local musters. After that he regularly loaned his military equipment to a neighbor in return for a day's work.

Trips to Troy to sell grain, deliver cheese, and buy plaster had long been a part of Hiram's regular fall regimen. Some Octobers he had made as many as six trips to that town. With the passage of time and the increased attention given to the dairy, this routine gradually changed. Hiram began to hire neighbors to deliver his cheese to Troy and to purchase his plaster. In a characteristic bargain, Hiram agreed to pay Nathan Robinson $.25 a hundred to transport plaster from Troy. This was payable in apple brandy at $.46 a gallon. If Robinson ever used one of the Harwoods' horses for this trip, he agreed to pay them $1.00. After a number of years, Hiram instructed the person who transported his plaster not to buy from merchants with whom he had regularly traded, "because they cheated me last year." The following year he told S. W. Daniels to return three casks to the merchant where he purchased his plaster. If the man refused, "after telling them I was a customer using annually 3 tons plaster," Sylvanus was "to quit them entirely, if they should set so small a value on such a man's trade."[49]

Hiram displayed a similar sense of confidence when dealing personally with tradesmen in Troy and Bennington. Once while in Troy, Hiram "talked some with clerk about opening a trade with them on credit if they should sell cheaper than I could buy at home and no dearer than their brethren" in Troy. "He promised favorably." Another time he "did not much like a very sleek headed clerk who waited upon me at this establishment—discovered nothing very pernicious about him neither, but thought him too reluctant in showing me a better quality of goods than he at first exhibited—seemed anxious to turn me off with mere trash—a trick too common among our little gentlemen of the counter."[50]

As the dairy thrived and Hiram had more money at his disposal, whatever deference he may have previously displayed toward shopkeepers disappeared entirely. When a local merchant "had the impudence to request something by way of a fee for his trouble" in handling a debt Hiram owed to another party, he replied that he "did not think I ought to allow anything as I had paid promptly before the expiration of the time and besides he would find delinquents enough out of whom he could obtain his profits." Another time, when he entered a factory store, Hiram "took great pains to get them to set their goods at as low prices as they could—told them it was our determination to pay down for everything bought of merchants—he that would sell most reasonably would get our money." A year later, when he and Sally returned to the same establishment, the "clerks appeared very careless and indifferent—so after looking a bit we bought nothing and came away" to Lyman Patchin's store. There, after Hiram "paid cash on the nail," Patchin "very pleasantly treated [Hiram] with excellent wine." Acceptance of this libation greatly "displeased my better half." Shortly after this Hiram visited P. L. Robinson's store to "let them know their neighboring store [Patchins] had undersold him—must be careful to make bills to me as low as he could afford—he protested that was his aim and offered to pay back the difference of 6 cents—refused it but warned him against going too high in the future." In Hiram's mind, merchants "all need watching."[51]

Hiram's growing sense of self-confidence and the family's increasing prosperity manifested themselves in a variety of additional ways. Hiram made trips by steamboat to New York City in the fall of 1833, 1834, and 1836.[52] His purpose in making these excursions was, more than anything else, "to see and be seen." The highlight of his second visit to the city was an evening at the Bowery Theatre, where he enjoyed performances of *Tom Cringle, Beulah Spa,* and *The Last Nail,* or *The Drunkard's Doom.* To him, "the novelty of being in a N.Y. Theatre was perhaps the best argument that could be adduced in favor of my being there—otherwise the little imitations I had seen in Bennington afforded more real satisfaction than the Original *itself*—if I may so express it." Nonetheless, it was his "humble opinion" that "there were a number of good performances belonging to that Company."[53]

On his third visit to New York, Hiram combined a bit of business with a large amount of pleasure. Ever suspicious of his dealings with local cheese agents, Hiram visited with large cheese dealers in the city to check on the profits being made by these men. When he discovered that they were treating him quite fairly, Hiram, not wanting "to be thought meanly of in skulking about the City trying covertly to get up a rival customer in [the] Market," asked these merchants not to reveal his inquiries whenever they might be in contact with Hiram's cheese dealers in Troy.[54]

Hiram devoted much of his remaining time in the city to visiting the National Institute's exhibition at Niblo's Garden, a center of respectable family entertainment, where he saw "displayed some of the noblest specimens of the inventive and mechanical powers of our countrymen to be met with in any place in the U. States." Machines driven by steam particularly fascinated him. When he entered the Grand Saloon, however, "enchantment itself reigned." There he viewed "an immensity of cutlery, porcelain, cut glass ware," and much more than could possibly "fall under my observation." What impressed Hiram the most was the fact that "in every Branch of Mechanism or manufacture — all was American — nothing foreign."[55]

On the day he was to take passage for home, Hiram visited the offices of the *New York Commercial & Spectator*, where he saw the presses turning out two thousand copies per hour. The man in charge of the press made Hiram a present of a copy of the newspaper. Then, before leaving for the wharf, Hiram "enquired for [a] hair dresser" and a "little Frenchman — real dwarf — soon parted me from my beard." Only now did Hiram feel himself appropriately prepared to make the journey home.[56]

Hiram did not restrict his expenditures to personal pleasure trips. He intended his children to be well educated and took whatever steps he could to achieve this for them. Rather than have Adeline taught by an inferior schoolmaster in his own district, Hiram sent her to the school in East Bennington, where she could learn from a more skilled master. For the convenience of all, Adeline boarded, at a cost of $.75 a week, with Jonathan Rogers and his family, who had recently set up shop in East Bennington. Several years later, when Hiram decided to send Adeline and Hopkins to the Brick Academy in Bennington, he made certain that his daughter had a new "frock" and "other new things to accommodate her in attending the Academy." He gladly paid the extra $1.00 necessary for her to attend lectures involving the use of special chemical apparatus. When the academy principal presented Hiram with a bill for $7.04 and an additional $1.00 for "Blake's Philosophy," he sent the full amount to the academy the following day. After attending the public examinations held at the academy, he declared them "evidence of the industry & faithful care of the Principal & assistant and of the intellectual improvement of the pupils." When friends praised the performance of Hopkins, Hiram felt that he "ought to be pleased that it was so, but not exclusively because he is my son."[57]

Because Adeline proved to be a serious student, Hiram allowed her to live in town during the week with her Aunt Diadama, who had married Hiram Waters. He made certain that she had appropriate clothing, so that she would not be embarrassed when going to the homes of her "mates." Hiram himself even went to a tailor in town to be fitted for a new suit. Upon returning home, he commented without the least self-consciousness that he had viewed some "very handsome pictures of fashionable dandies" during his time at the tailor's shop.[58]

Although he often favored Adeline, Hiram did not intend to short-change either of his children in educational opportunities. Consequently, when an itinerant writing master offered lessons in penmanship, Hiram enrolled Hopkins, who "seemed to like it very well." After Hopkins received ten lessons of the agreed-upon twelve, Hiram nonetheless paid the man the arranged fee of $1.50. Hopkins made out the receipt, "which served as a specimen of his skill in the art," which was in Hiram's opinion "pretty fair, but not superior to what is often done by clerks in mercantile houses & other situations of the kind."[59] Even though it was common to train young men in penmanship in order to further their careers in business, the Harwoods had no intention that Hopkins would leave the farm. He was to carry on the family's patriarchal tradition. When a business acquaintance of Hiram's in Troy wrote that he had located a position for Hopkins in an apothecary's shop in that city, Hiram responded that "we did not design him for anything more than agricultural business & could not spare him."[60]

When Adeline began to express an interest in learning French, Hiram wrote a letter to a schoolmaster who had previously boarded with the Harwoods to determine what books would be needed to study the language and where he might find them. One day, though, when Hiram stopped by to visit with his sister Damia, Adeline showed him a copy of a French dictionary, to which he "said something by way of doubting the utility of the study of that language." Apparently this did not "suit" Adeline, for she immediately left to visit a neighbor. Sufficiently chastened, Hiram, before his own departure, "left word with her aunt to buy said book if she pleased" and then spent some time talking earnestly with his sister on the subject of female education.[61]

As Adeline's interest in studying French intensified, Hiram agreed to do what he could to help. He consulted with an acquaintance about obtaining information about Castleton Seminary for women. He then wrote the principal of that school and "made strict inquiry into the expenses of supporting a female student there during winter term provided her studies were merely English." He also wanted to know the cost including French. Bluntly, he "requested to know the whole & the worst without disguise." Shortly thereafter the principal replied that the charge for a winter term would be thirty-five dollars with everything included. "So of course it was resolved that Adeline would be a member of that institution for that length of time."[62]

With the decision made, "much [was] done fixing off Adeline for Castleton." When the morning arrived, Hiram and his nineteen-year-old daughter settled into their sleigh and started off for the seminary. Once they arrived, Hiram met the principal, who appeared to be a pleasant fellow, and immediately "took him aside — solicited his good offices in selecting a good room mate for our daughter." This done, he brought Adeline's trunk up from the sleigh and set it in her room. He then went to a local tavern to change a five-dollar bill into ones, which, with a dollar in specie, he left with Adeline. Shortly after that he departed and spent the night with friends in West Poultney. While there he noticed a new book in the hands of one of the children that he found "quite amusing & entertaining — calculated for catching money — like almost everything that is passed upon the credulous public — whether moral, Religious or Literary — whether Colleges, Academies or District Schools — all may be summed up in a word — To Make Money."[63] Nevertheless, Hiram never begrudged spending money on Adeline's education. She was his cherished daughter, and he wanted the best for her.

During Adeline's five-week stay at Castleton, the Harwood family lived for her letters. This was especially true of Hiram. A warm bond had been formed between father and daughter, and he missed her. Finally, on February 12, he returned by sleigh to Castleton to retrieve his daughter and gladly paid the principal for her quarter's study. During this time she had studied natural and intellectual philosophy as well as French. After bidding the principal and his wife good-bye, Hiram drove to the front of the seminary, where Adeline "received parting kisses from many of her female associates standing under grand piazza." With "all compliments & kisses cleverly pocketed," the two "came off in good spirits — my daughter being most favorably impressed towards Principal & lady & all with whom she had become acquainted with one or two solitary exceptions — left no broils, nor had any to settle — all harmonious or at any rate apparently so."[64]

Education was not the only endeavor that Hiram supported for his children. His increased willingness to spend money on activities and material goods that would have been unthinkable a few years earlier became increasingly apparent in the pages of his journal. Among other things, he repeatedly noted subscriptions to singing and dancing schools, not for himself and Sally, but for Adeline and Hopkins.[65]

While grooming their children for a social world quite different from their own, Hiram and Sally also began to make improvements about the house. In 1832, at a cost of nearly a hundred dollars, Hiram had lead pipes laid from the spring into the house, so that the family could enjoy running water. He also "bargained for 8 common parlour chairs including rockers to be fitted to one" at the chair factory of B. Squires. A few years later, while visiting a furniture manufactory in Troy, he ordered "a good cherry table provided with castors," to be delivered within three weeks. Three months later he purchased a "settee" from a local chair-maker, which he considered not only "well made" but also "not inelegantly painted & ornamented." Shortly after that he and Sally had their bedroom wallpapered with material purchased from local merchants. Whether aware of it or not, Hiram and Sally had become active participants in a transformation taking place throughout New England: the increasing refinement of both rural and urban culture.[66]

By this time, too, an aggregate of social values, practices, and attitudes had become firmly entrenched in the lives of Hiram and members of his family. Hard work, self-discipline, temperance, honesty and integrity in all personal relationships, a proper sense of responsibility about business, a high value placed upon education and individual improvement, and a careful attention to personal appearance and hygiene formed the essential core of this frame of mind.[67] These attitudes, which had long been entrenched in Hiram's mind, represented a composite of beliefs and customs drawn largely from traditional Harwood family values, the Bible, Noah Webster's blue-backed speller, and the various almanacs the Harwoods had followed diligently for years.[68] Taken together, they preached honesty in all personal relationships, prudence in business affairs, and a careful regard for personal appearance. The *Vermont Register*, the only almanac to which Hiram actually subscribed, combined the latter two by advising that "if a man depend on raising and selling butter and cheese, he is sure to meet a quick market, if he is known to be neat and clean about his husbandry."[69]

Another important change took place in Hiram's life — a change so gradual, so imperceptible, that even Hiram likely remained unaware of its influence. This involved his relationship with Dr. Noadiah Swift. Long the Harwoods' trusted family doctor and the source of much-needed loans, Swift gradually became much more. An avid newspaper reader, Hiram had always depended on members of the local gentry to loan him copies of national newspapers to which they subscribed. With the death of Judge Fay, Dr. Swift became Hiram's sole source of national news. Swift, a staunch Federalist, had never subscribed to either the *Philadelphia Aurora* or the *National Intelligencer*; his paper of choice was the *New York Spectator*. And so it became for Hiram, who constantly dropped by the doctor's home to gather up "bundles" of the *Spectator* that had been saved specifically for him.[70]

Sharing the *Spectator* rather naturally led to long conversations about politics between Hiram and Noadiah Swift. Their political differences had been so marked in the past that this had never previously been possible. Now they were much more cordial, as were social relations between the families. When Noadiah's brother Heman, one of Bennington's wealthiest individuals as well as a physician who had often treated the Harwoods, made a professional call one evening, he brought his wife with him, "who although bred and born in Bennington had never been at this house before."[71]

The growing bond of friendship and trust developing between Hiram and Noadiah Swift became evident after Dr. Swift became president of the newly formed Bank of Bennington. Whenever accosted to purchase shares in the new bank, Hiram had always resisted by "signifying the extreme want of means to do so as well as my determination to have nothing to do with it." Nonetheless, whatever his attitude about banks in principle, Hiram responded out of friendship whenever Noadiah Swift called on him to assist with bank business. For example, when Swift asked Hiram to transport him and a large amount of bank money to Troy, he graciously acquiesced. On the appointed day, Hiram drove his wagon up to the bank and helped the directors "carry downstairs bags of specie in a basket," which they "stowed" in Hiram's "big calico trunk." Next they "brought down a keg (10 gallon) full of half dollars — $3,600." Last, Noadiah Swift had "his traveling trunk put aboard in which he had great deal of specie on other banks." With that the two men set out for Troy carrying $8,945 in specie and more than $21,000 in paper to be deposited by Swift in a Troy bank. When they arrived in Troy, "Swift went off to bargain away his cash to highest bidder," while Hiram stayed with the wagon and team. After Swift struck a bargain with the Farmer's Bank, Hiram drove the money there, where "a Paddy assisted in unloading." On a different occasion Hiram "conveyed a packet of money—$5,000 to Cashier of Farmer's Bank, Troy for Dr. Swift, Pres. of Bennington Bank." Another time he "assisted at the Bank in loading into the Eastern Stage, M.L. Selden driver, two boxes very heavy which I supposed contained specie."[72]

As president of the bank, Swift did all he could to help Hiram financially. Once, when the bank could not discount any notes, Swift signed a letter to merchants in Troy "pledging his responsibility to them for the payment of $100 which I wished to obtain at Troy Bank." A year later, with the bank still not discounting notes, Swift again wrote a letter to a merchant in Hoosick, "signifying that he would become responsible for whatever sum I might hire of him." At other times, when the bank was being extremely careful of the individuals to whom it would discount notes, Swift saw to it that the cashier accommodated Hiram's needs. Once he had done this, the cashier was careful to ask Hiram "not to let any man know where I got it—as they refused every applicant for money." In addition, Swift often made personal loans to Hiram or allowed his notes to "run one month longer without renewal."[73]

As the Harwoods' income from the dairy steadily increased, Noadiah became a trusted financial adviser to Hiram. When the time came that Hiram actually had sufficient money to lend out at interest, Swift agreed to help him choose a reputable individual in need of a loan. Finally, after lengthy consultations with Swift, Hiram loaned two hundred dollars to Isaac Doolittle, manager of the Bennington Iron Works.

Unaccustomed as he was to this new role of moneylender, Hiram immediately suffered second thoughts about the wisdom of engaging in such a transaction. He shared these apprehensions with Swift, who promptly assured him of the "good standing" of Doolittle. Nonetheless, Hiram could not shake his misapprehensions. These became particularly acute during a conversation he had with H. Fassett and General Henry Robinson—two members of the old Republican gentry. These men spoke about "the changes of manners among the people of Bennington within 15–20 years—from social to selfish, reckless almost—every one taking care of himself, forgetting his neighbors." Both men imputed this to the townspeople's "being much more absorbed at present in a variety of businesses" rather than caring about the community as they had in the past. Shortly after this conversation,

Hiram spoke with another respected member of the community; their "chief topic was manners of dealing among men, the late failures, & necessity of economy, prudence, and honesty" in a time when all the traditional values that had held communities together in the past seemed to be vanishing in the vortex of the present shaky times.[74]

Within two weeks of loaning the money to Doolittle, Hiram's mind "was considerably harrowed up on account of many things which I had lately had a hand in . . . that rendered me unhappy for the moment." The very next day, he "supped in a vast sight of melancholy during this day—found myself guilty of many foolish calculations within the last six months." It was in this frame of mind that Hiram had a conversation with T. C. Parsons, which "threw me into a violent fit of hypo" at the mention of Doolittle's name in connection with "the extreme uncertainty of obtaining my $200 when due" and "showing in high colors the shallowness of my letting that money." Consequently, two weeks before the loan came due, Hiram visited Doolittle but "could obtain no positive promise it could be paid by March 1." It was little consolation to Hiram for his debtor to tell him "not to lose sleep over it." Finally, nearly a week past the due date for the loan, Doolittle paid the debt with interest.[75]

After this experience, Hiram was hesitant to loan money; even the thought of it made him nervous. As a result, when a friend asked for a loan of twenty-five dollars for only four or five days, Hiram "felt afraid—didn't know what the end might be—knew my money came from & must return to the Bank again," and refused to part with his money. Given this cautious frame of mind, he responded in an entirely businesslike manner—a manner that would have been utterly foreign to him a decade previously—when his cousin Nathan Robinson asked him to cosign a loan from Noadiah Swift. Before signing the note, Hiram had his cousin give him a promissory note and a mortgage on his father's farm—signed by his father—as security for his signature.[76]

Whatever success the Harwoods had managed to achieve over the course of time rested uneasily upon Hiram's shoulders. Once during negotiations with an individual over a debt, Hiram informed this person that he was "as destitute of money as other people." When the man replied that "he did not know who *should* have money if I didn't," Hiram was utterly taken aback. Nor did he know how to respond when another acquaintance called him "a money making man—kept a dairy—fatted pork—cared for nobody but myself—no accommodation [tolerance] about me." Totally at a loss, Hiram "laughed and joked him mildly." Hiram simply could not view himself as anything other than a plain, republican farmer.[77]

Even if Hiram was not fully aware of his changed status in the community, others definitely were. This included Judge Luman Norton, who informed Hiram "that it was in contemplation [in the state assembly] to bestow on me the all important appointment of J.P. [justice of the peace]." That same year, as well as the following one, voters at the annual town meeting elected Hiram to be a petit juror.[78]

Hiram entered upon his experience as a juror with two basic preconceptions: first, he firmly believed in the traditional concepts of equity and fairness that had always held true in Tanbrook; second, he considered "interest" to be "the great bond of union among men — take from a person the prospect of future gain & you throw a most powerful damper upon his attachment." Above all, he never hesitated to give his "opinion pretty freely of the farcical nature of our courts of law — my great hatred of the glorious uncertainty of the law."[79]

Hiram's actual service on juries elicited quite a different set of attitudes — attitudes that may have emanated quite unconsciously from his changed circumstances. In a case involving a partnership between a man of known integrity and good character and an individual given to drink and profligate ways, Hiram and his fellow jurors "fancied there was iniquity in the transaction [between the two partners], but so completely did we find him [the man of integrity] held down by written contract that we could not help him." Indeed, "every one of us felt for him — but according to evidence & law there was no getting away from it." Forced to decide the case according to the terms of the contract drawn between the two partners, they had to find against the man of integrity. On another occasion, when Hiram served as foreman of a different jury, he helped find against a man on the grounds that he had "failed to prove the contract." To Hiram, the commercial dairyman, contracts had become sacred.[80]

Before this trial, the Vermont General Assembly did name Hiram to be one of the thirty-two justices of the peace for Bennington County. In a manner that had become inbred in him over the years, Hiram claimed that the legislature "must be a set of silly fellows to make such improper selections." Nonetheless, his friend Judge Luman Norton swore him in, and Hiram assumed this position of local prestige and authority — a position he took quite seriously.[81]

Simultaneously with his growing respectability within the larger community, Hiram might have taken pride in the manner in which he was meeting his father's expectations of him. It was almost as if he had taken the humiliating observations his father had obliged him to record on his twenty-first birthday as a blueprint in his effort to become a responsible adult. Having advanced well beyond "the rule of three," he had assumed full responsibility for keeping all the family's accounts. If not acquainted with all the "little arts . . . necessary for the quick dispatch of many sorts of work," Hiram had certainly become a tireless worker, and through his efforts he had made the farm into a prosperous commercial enterprise. Always eager to please his father, Hiram had striven mightily to assume the role expected of him. While struggling to become the kind of man Benjamin wanted him to be, however, Hiram was actually fashioning an understanding of masculinity quite different from his father's. Hard work and a sense of duty to family and neighbors certainly remained important to Hiram, but so, too, were sensibility, gentility, and new forms of sociability. His love of literature, letter-writing, keeping a commonplace book, and shared discussions of books, the theater, and musical performances involved a sensitivity quite foreign to Benjamin. In many ways, Hiram was constructing an image of manhood that more closely resembled Coelebs than it did his own father.

At the same time, though, Hiram and Benjamin were undergoing a transformation in their political beliefs that made them far more alike than different. Facing the partisan turmoil that increasingly enveloped Bennington following the War of 1812, both men had cause to question their old political allegiances.

～ 7

Birth of a Whig

Mr. Rich came to work in our service. We knew him to be a Republican &
wished to keep him sober that he might act clearly & understandingly on the day of
Election; and not be cheated by the opposite party as he had been.[1]

The Harwoods reaped their reward the following day when "Mr.
Rich rode up with us & behaved well the whole time — returned with us
sober." The election for representative to the state assembly had been
so hard fought, however, that another of the Harwoods' close friends,
"beset by his friends on both sides, had so much equivocation and
irresolution that he positively refused voting at all."[2] Such indecision
was difficult for Hiram to understand. Bred within a family traditionally devoted to republican social and political principles, he was fiercely
committed to the Jeffersonian-Republican Party as the ultimate means
of supporting such ideals in America. All the Harwoods had been loyal
Jeffersonians since the partisan divisions of the 1790s. So, too, had
the bulk of Bennington freemen; the town had voted solidly Republican since the party came into being. The War of 1812, however,
changed all this; Federalists began to carry town elections regularly.
With the end of the war, Bennington entered a time of political change
and uncertainty.

So long as partisan confrontations in Bennington followed old party
lines, Hiram felt perfectly at ease; his inbred republicanism and loyalty
to Jeffersonian Republicanism united him with the town's traditional
Republican leadership. With the passage of time, however, he became

increasingly troubled as partisan alliances in Bennington began to shift in unexpected ways. With only his old republican values to guide him, he found himself forced to chart his own course through increasingly uncertain political waters.

~~ Like so many of his fellow Republicans, Hiram considered recent Federalist victories as merely temporary aberrations — the result of the unpopularity of the War of 1812 among most Vermonters. Bennington had always been a Republican town and would be again as soon as passions elicited by the war passed. So when Hiram attended the annual town meeting in March 1815, he experienced "a degree of indifference respecting the result of the proceedings of the day." Even after Federalist candidates won most of the contests, Hiram presumed that "if my brother Republicans had not, too many of them, imitated my sluggish conduct, . . . their party would have won the prize." Having it on good authority that "the Democratic party were really a majority of 15 or 20," he confidently concluded that it was simply "want of attention & perseverance that prevented their triumph this day."[3]

His belief in the security of his party remained unshaken. Consequently, when Colonel O. C. Merrill and William Haswell, two of the town's leading Republicans, talked to Hiram "with great earnestness respecting the coming elections," they had little impact: "I considered that they labored in a field where they looked for a good harvest while I expected or wished nothing." Hiram did, however, agree to canvass his neighborhood in order to ascertain the party allegiance of various newcomers and to establish whether they had lived in Bennington long enough to vote. Then he joined the "Grand Committee of Vigilance" at Cushman's Tavern to help work out strategy for the September freemen's meeting. Even though the room was oppressively hot, those present "could admit no air lest spies might intrude." Finally, "after summing up & casting off doubtful characters it was determined, as near as we could then get to it, that the Democrats were in this town 16 majority."[4]

Such reckoning proved to be wishful thinking. At the subsequent town meeting, Hiram experienced only disillusionment. The gathering quickly turned into "a disgraceful fight — making the meeting a perfect mob." Such "heat was generated by equality of numbers in the parties and a spirit of intrigue and overbearing ambition which pervaded federal ranks, that day, which called forth all the energy of the democrats to repel." Unfortunately, there were neither enough Democrats nor enough energy for the purpose. Once the Federalists elected Noadiah Swift moderator and Aaron Robinson clerk, they were able to control the outcome of the meeting. To Hiram's chagrin, the Federalists, "not even having republicanism enough left to consent to the question's being tried," overwhelmed a Democrat's desperate call for adjournment. The Federalists, in their exultation, soon initiated "the most disorderly and savage bellowing & huzzaing, ever witnessed in a deliberative assembly." At this point Hiram and his fellow Democrats walked out of the meeting. Convinced that "the federalists stooped to the exercise of means the most foul to carry the elections, the most powerful of which was the '*drum Dram,*' [alcohol] often and faithfully administered." From Hiram's perspective, "one thing is certain, they attempted to browbeat their opponents." All Hiram could say of his good friend Noadiah Swift was that the business of being moderator "came left-handed to him" and that he was a "much greater physician than Moderator."5

Even though a Republican defeated Aaron Robinson that September to become the town's representative to the state assembly, Hiram drew little pleasure from the result. Given the intensity of partisan feelings in Bennington, Hiram and his Republican colleagues redoubled their efforts. He attended a party caucus at Cushman's Tavern in late August to assign to various individuals the number of ballots they were to write and to give notice to their neighbors to attend a caucus on the night before the September freemen's meeting. When Hiram left this meeting, he walked past McEowen's Tavern, where he "observed a bustle which indicated that the caucus which the other party had held there had likewise broke up—was obliged to quicken my pace to keep from falling in company with two members who turned aside at Dr. Swifts."6

When the next Republican caucus convened, men such as Judge Jonathan Robinson, General David Robinson, and Judge David Fay "exhort[ed] their brethren to sacrifice private opinion and unite." Hiram did just that. Although acknowledging the private worth of Joseph Hinsdill, he questioned the man's ability to be a good legislator. Nonetheless, "to conform to a few who appeared determined to be suited with no other than Hinsdill, it was thought best to do as we did." Then, before adjourning, the "whole meeting resolved itself into a committee of Vigilance to use every reasonable exertion to bring on their friends to the poll." The following day, however, Hiram saw all his efforts fail: the Democrats lost the election. Sadly, he noted that "ever since our elections terminated federally, our democrats held up the idea that a majority in this town were democratic, but owing to inertness, want of spirit and organization, it could not be brought into action." Nevertheless, with this election, Hiram "gave it up that the town was federal."[7]

Within a short time, Hiram became even more disillusioned by political activity in Bennington. During the freemen's meeting in September 1819, "great warmth was betrayed by many, especially among the democrats, where some serious jars arose which a long lapse of time may not ally." It seemed to him that such "feuds & bickerings are no credit to the good citizens of Bennington — their attention ought to be directed to higher and more important objects than office-seeking." Such was not to be. During the freemen's meeting of 1821, "great exertion was used by both parties — every kind of appetite was tampered with among the mean characters to carry the day — liquor, pork & meal & all the good things of this world were said to be plentifully distributed by the great movers among the federalists." Finally, at the annual town meeting held in March 1822, Hiram became completely disenchanted. After observing that "foul play was used on both sides" during the election of town officers, he expressed his ultimate dismay: "giving drams & gifts, I do abhor it, & always *shall* — indeed I always till now boasted of the correct principles of my party — but alas they are departed from the good old rules which governed our ancestors who laid the broad foundation of our liberties, they are gone astray & unless a reform takes place, we are a ruined people."[8]

The following year brought even more disappointment. O. C. Merrill, who, with Darius Clark, edited the *Vermont Gazette*, the state's leading Republican newspaper, had long been the figurehead for that party in Bennington. For this reason Hiram became particularly upset when Moses Robinson Jr. defeated Merrill for a seat in the Vermont Assembly at the annual freemen's meeting in September 1823. Firmly convinced that "a strong Church party backed up by the real old federalists along with other causes prevailed against our friend Merrill," Hiram considered this "a bad defeat to him."[9]

When Hiram mentioned a "strong Church party," he alluded to the staunch followers of Rev. Absalom Peters — individuals bent upon the moral reformation of Bennington. They, in alliance with the traditional Federalist leadership, meant to impose strict Sabbatarian measures upon the town, eliminate theater productions and dancing schools, prohibit horse racing on the Sabbath, and impose total abstinence upon the townspeople. In addition, they intended to shape the newly constructed academy into an elitist institution emphasizing moral as well as academic discipline.

The measures promoted by the "church party" infuriated Republican leaders. Peters' attempt to shape the new academy in an elitist manner elicited vitriolic responses from Darius Clark in the pages of the *Gazette*. The feud that developed between Clark and Peters quickly spilled over into the larger community and disrupted local politics for years. The town's Democratic leadership, traditionally referred to as the "uphill" party, now became known as "Old Line" supporters; Federalists, long recognized as "downhill" leaders, assumed the title of "Pioneers."[10] As a result, local issues—particularly the matter of the academy—led to intense disagreements.

Hiram did his best to avoid becoming entangled in such issues. He was far happier when attending "a meeting of the principal inhabitants of this & the town's adjacent to draw up resolutions to forward to Congress on the depressed state of the Farming & Manufacturing interests of the country." When the convention named a twenty-man committee to draft resolutions, it included not only David Robinson Jr. and O. C. Merrill but also leading Pioneers such as Moses Robinson Jr. and Stephen Hinsdill.[11]

Perfect unanimity characterized this committee's deliberations; its findings, delivered at an adjourned meeting a week later, expressed a consensus not only within the committee but among all participants at the convention as well. Hiram believed that "the committee made an able Report."[12] The report itself, which demanded that Congress pass higher tariffs in order to protect home manufacturing, rested on the conviction that agriculture and manufacturing shared inseparable interests. In the opinion of committee members, the time had arrived "when placing 'the manufacturer beside the agriculturist' " had become the "great moral and political desideratum" of the age. The resulting memorial to Congress stoutly maintained that "the union of manufactures and agriculture, had invariably increased commerce, and been the fountain of national prosperity, wealth, knowledge and distinction." Only a stronger tariff policy could guarantee the future of such a union. Realizing this, "the *cultivators of the soil* require the measure."[13]

The cooperation between Old Line and Pioneer leaders proved to be short-lived; local issues immediately replaced the tariff and brought about renewed bitterness between the town's opposing leaders. Since decisions made at the state level might affect the disposition of local matters, the annual freemen's meeting to elect a representative to the state assembly assumed vital importance. Both groups held caucuses to decide upon candidates to be put forth at the September elections. Although happy to join with Pioneers in support of a higher tariff, Hiram could not associate with old Federalists in town elections. He therefore consulted only with individuals such as O. C. Merrill, David Robinson Jr., and Darius Clark on these matters. Local issues were so hotly contested at the freemen's meeting of September 1824 that no decision could be reached even after taking several votes. Unfortunately, from Hiram's perspective, "bad means were used on both sides—many were heavily laden with strong drink." He would, however, "Say no more."[14]

By early the next year, national politics attracted Hiram's attention. On February 19, 1825, he recorded that the family "learned the pleasing intelligence that J.Q. Adams was elected President of the U.S." This marked the first time since he began keeping the diary that Hiram had taken note of a presidential election. Then on March 4 he observed that "J.Q. Adams takes the Presidential chair today." Two weeks later he "read to father Mr. Adams' Inaugural Address, which we highly esteemed." Although having a New Englander in the White House provided Hiram much satisfaction, he was not entirely provincial in his outlook; he also followed the pronouncements of the Kentuckian Henry Clay with great interest.[15]

Hiram's enthusiasm for Adams had no effect whatsoever on his local loyalties; Merrill, David Robinson Jr., William Haswell, and Darius Clark remained his most trusted political confidants. He also began to spend a good deal of time in the law office of Hiland Hall, one of his closest friends since the two had been enthusiastic members of the Sons of Liberty. It was still Merrill, though, for whom Hiram felt the greatest respect. Consequently, when Merrill gained election to the state council in September 1825, Hiram expressed his "thanks to the God of elections [that] Mr. M., although poor, obtains his seat at the Council board this year, in spite of every effort of his enemies who assailed with all the weapons they could invent of the low & meaner kind." He then exclaimed, "Let not the glare of riches and the popularity usually attached thereto always triumph, but let the men of worth when in low circumstances, *sometimes* have his place."[16]

Similar convictions shaped Hiram's perspective when Hiland Hall lost the election to the state assembly to Charles Hammond, proprietor of the Bennington Furnace Company. Hiram objected to Hammond's election because "it looked too much like paying adoration to property." For weeks it had been "urged that because this man belonged to a company that had located itself here & was annually expending large sums among us, upon a principle of gratitude we were bound to give him office." In Hiram's opinion, "so many persons were in one way or another in the company's employment or otherwise interested that it was no wonder that he obtained the election."[17]

Hiram remained so upset by this election that a week later, while in Troy on business, he felt obligated to respond to several individuals who expressed their pleasure at the outcome of Bennington's election. Delivering his sentiments "in a plain coarse manner," Hiram argued that "3/4 of those who voted for Hammond did so not because they considered him the best qualified, but because they supposed it would in some way or other favor their own individual interests." He emphatically maintained that "with property any man having ambition could rule the town of Bennington at will — only throw out the bait & fishes enough would be taken."[18]

To Hiram's way of thinking, Hammond's election raised the specter of the old Federalist Party. He became even more uneasy when he read letters in the *Gazette* from members of Vermont's congressional delegation regarding O. C. Merrill's candidacy for that body. He thought these "avoided the principle of real old Republicanism." Then, upon paying a visit to his friend William Haswell a short while later, Hiram's fear of Federalism received added support. Haswell, who was busy writing a letter to an associate about the upcoming congressional elections, "feared Col. Merrill would not succeed — thought Federalism was rising — many appointments made lately by the Pres. particularly favored that party."[19]

Hiram received additional support in his concern regarding Hammond and Federalism with the approach of the September 1827 freemen's meeting. A week before that day, he talked with David Robinson Jr. about the coming election. "We agreed against Hammond & Factory influence generally." Then on the morning of the election, David Robinson Sr. stopped by the Harwood farm and "argued against Mr. Hammond." Such arguments were superfluous, since Benjamin and Hiram "disapproved of him [Hammond] enough before — we were against supporting these great capitalists for office."[20]

The results that afternoon could not have pleased Hiram more: Hiland Hall won the election. The day was not entirely satisfying for Hiram, however; it seemed to him that "the old parties were strangely worked up in this instance, in fact principle was not the governing question — it was merely confined to men — the minds of the people of this town were highly wrought upon about this time."[21]

The reason so many townspeople were "highly wrought upon" bore little relation to the contest between Hiland Hall and Henry Hammond; rather it sprang from the presidential contest emerging between John Quincy Adams and Andrew Jackson. Several months before the annual freemen's meeting, Hall had openly "avowed his sentiments to be in accordance with [the] National Administration." It was at nearly this same time that Hiram had begun to borrow the *New York Spectator* — a strongly pro-administration newspaper — from either Luman Norton or Noadiah Swift. Whenever he read anything in this paper about Andrew Jackson, he "could find nothing inviting in the character ascribed to him." After reading an address by Henry Clay, Hiram believed it "proved Gen. Jackson to be a person possessed of a vindictive revengeful spirit, nowise comporting with the character of a gentleman qualified to preside over 24 Great States." Upon borrowing several issues of the *Spectator* from Noadiah Swift that contained a virulently anti-Jackson tirade from the Virginia Assembly, Hiram noted that the doctor "liked it very much." Hiram's father also "liked it to excess" when he heard the address read at home.[22]

Hiram received what he considered to be personal validation of such views when he encountered a clerk in Troy who had lived in Tennessee. The man "expressed surprise & wonder at the infatuation so prevalent at this juncture among our northern people in supporting the Jackson interest." Having lived within ten miles of the Hero of New Orleans, he claimed that Jackson's "personal and private character was bad & none of his friends in that quarter pretended to defend it." In his opinion, "all this tumult and noise was got up by designing men & echoed by the inconsiderate multitude who knew or cared very little for the man apart from other views." Hiram could not have agreed more heartily. The clerk, "like myself tho't the gen. entitled to all his military fame but as a candidate for the Presidency considered him a most exception[al] character." Then he exclaimed, "Keep off the Joabs & Cromwells we want none of them for President of these Free & Independent States."[23]

By the time of the freemen's meeting the following year, emotions still ran high, but no clarity of thought regarding issues before the public had yet evolved. When a friend asked Hiram his opinion of the opposing candidates for the state assembly (Hiland Hall and Noadiah Swift), he replied that he "much esteemed both of them" but that he "was sorry that Dr S. had suffered himself to be set up because I felt a difficulty in going against him." Since he had voted for Hall the previous year, Hiram, "not knowing any weighty fault committed by him in the Legislature, considered myself bound to vote for him this year." A week later, Colonel Jonathan Robinson stopped by the Harwood farm, "excus[ing] his errand or his visit by saying that he came to buy cheese & eggs — but in reality it was for another purpose — to electioneer for Dr S." The colonel quickly got to the essence of the matter. "After delivering a long discourse against the Administration of the U.S. Gov't, and in favor of gen'l Jackson, and giving his opinion against H. Hall and talking warmly for Dr S. — retired as light as he came." By strongly supporting a principal leader of the town's old Federalist Party, Robinson, long a prominent member of the Jeffersonian party, mirrored perfectly the anomalous nature of political thought emerging in Bennington. Similarly, that evening a lively debate took place between Hiram, his mother, and a neighbor regarding the pending election of a town representative to the state assembly. Diadama lustily advocated her old friend Noadiah Swift; Hiram, with equal vigor, supported his young friend Hiland Hall. Both candidates were strong supporters of the Adams administration. Five days later, after a "warm Election," Swift carried the day with a majority of just fifty-some votes.[24]

With the presidential election looming in another month, partisanship in Bennington did not slacken after September's freemen's meeting. Hiram tried to remain as calm and reasonable as possible. Indeed, when he encountered Judge Stephen Robinson and O. C. Merrill talking politics in town one day, "they seemed to wonder a little at the lack of interest that I manifest in regard to those concerns." The same had been true previously, when Hiram attended a meeting called to discuss academy affairs, where he attempted to keep an open mind on issues pitting Noadiah Swift against Merrill and other leading Republicans. "There were those who considered me almost beside myself because I did not go into all the warmth of their feelings on the subject — particularly my old friends Saff'd R. [Safford Robinson] & O.C.M. [O. C. Merrill] — but in reality they would have found on examination that I had not departed from good principles, but they themselves were a little too much wrought upon by present excitement." Several months later, when Hiram found Merrill composing an editorial for the *Gazette* in support of Jackson's candidacy, the colonel "mourned the dreadful degeneracy of the times — was afraid of Aristocracy." Hiram responded that "whichever of the candidates for the Presidency obtained the election, he and his friends could not carry us quite off—there certainly was but little danger from the present Administration—a majority of both houses of Cong. being against it—& withal it was very closely watched etc."[25]

As tension grew between supporters of Adams and Jackson, Hiram's position became increasingly sensitive; even though most of his old political friends and associates supported Jackson, he could not bring himself to vote for the man. Nonetheless, when a new administration paper, the *Journal of the Times*, recently founded in Bennington under the editorship of William Lloyd Garrison, became involved in a vicious exchange with Darius Clark and his *Gazette*, Hiram remained loyal to his old friend. To his mind, the *Journal* "began the war unprovokedly."[26]

On the day of the election, Hiram and Benjamin attended the polls, where the Adams ticket triumphed by a large majority. Hiram could not help but notice that it was "gloomy to witness the distraction of the Democratic Party in this town." He was "almost afraid to enquire of my old friends which ticket they supported." The following day Hiram encountered Stephen Dewey and Colonel Merrill involved in a heated discussion in which the two men "got greatly at variance—the former [Dewey] swore eternal hatred to Jackson and his party—No Jackson man should ever go to the Assembly, if he could prevent it, from this town."[27] Hiram tried mightily to keep aloof from such quarrels; he attempted to maintain neutrality at a time when the political world around him appeared to be in constant flux.

The results of the presidential election revealed that Adams had carried Bennington County and the state of Vermont but had lost the national election to Jackson. Although naturally disappointed in this outcome, Hiram still displayed no increased interest in politics. This was particularly true of local affairs. When the tension between advocates of the Pioneer and the Old Line factions became so intense that a separate seminary had to be constructed, Hiram attended the raising of this building even though his closest political associates snubbed the affair. Hiram believed that he had "nothing to gain or lose in these quarrels respecting churches & academies among the great ones."[28]

Later that same summer, when Merrill invited Hiram to attend a meeting to make arrangements for a partisan celebration of August 16 and to form a caucus to nominate a representative to the General Assembly, Hiram chose to "decline & turned a short corner for home." The following year Hiram again received an invitation to attend a "Jackson meeting," but he "declined both for want of inclination &

time." As to the partisan battles beginning to appear in the newspapers, Hiram "felt a disposition to laugh at the praises & faultfinding
of either party—all of but little worth to a person of a retired & peaceful habit."[29]

Hiram's habit was neither so "retired" nor so "peaceful" that he
ignored national news. He followed such events with as much interest
as ever. The certitude that characterized his reaction to national events
in an earlier era was, however, missing; in its place ambiguity and
uncertainty troubled his mind. The same was true for many of the
leaders of the old Jeffersonian party in Bennington. They simply could
not discern with any immediate clarity how to react to the presidency of
Andrew Jackson. Such uncertainty did not characterize the stance of O.
C. Merrill, who "rejoiced in the cause of Jackson." Indeed, he "anticipated something superlative in the Pres. Message at the beginning of
the pres't session of Congress." Following the delivery of that message,
Merrill pronounced it "superior to anything of its kind."[30]

Unable to interpret the national scene with anything like Merrill's
confidence, Hiram fell back on old republican principles as his only
means to make sense of what he read in the newspapers. Unfortunately,
as politicians in Washington increasingly made full rhetorical use of
these same themes, little clarity resulted. Thus, when "the papers of the
day were filled with the speeches of Webster, Hayne & others on the
Public Lands," Hiram could only see them all "calling up Old Embargo, War and Hartford Convention times." Although he disapproved
of Robert Hayne's stance on tariffs and internal improvements, Hiram
considered the South Carolina senator's response to Daniel Webster
"ably performed—too much truth in it for old Federalism, [which it]
went hard against." Two weeks later, though, he read Daniel Webster's
"last and very able speech" in response to Hayne. The very next night a
friend read Webster's speech aloud to the Harwoods "in fine style."
Jackson's use of republican rhetoric in his veto of the Maysville Road
had much the same effect upon Hiram. After reading the president's
message, he "could not see but that he reasoned fairly & correctly."
Even in the face of such language, though, Hiram's visceral mistrust of
the president would not be still. Believing that "no small deceit" was
often "played off in matters of great solemnity & Importance," and
considering himself to be "a mere bungler in politicks," he concluded
that he could "hardly tell chaff from wheat."[31]

Upon visiting with David Robinson Jr. about the matter, Hiram
discovered that the captain "viewed the leading measures of the Jackson

Administration to be right, so much so as even to immortalize his fame & name to all posterity in the single instance of his withholding his signature to the Maysville Road Bill." However, "as to his Removals he did not esteem that part to be judicious." Nonetheless, Robinson "considered in the main — the present Administration must be supported."[32]

Having long respected Robinson's political leadership, Hiram kept the captain's advice well in mind when he attended that September's freemen's meeting. He cast his votes in support of "the Jackson Cong. & State tickets — as to the last felt pretty indifferently — never could have great personal regard for the hero, but considering his Administration as about as good as we can get concluded there would be no harm in giving it a moderate suport." Such was certainly not the case with Isaac Tichenor, whom Hiram encountered shortly after all votes had been cast. Beside himself with rage against the president, Tichenor, for years the preeminent Federalist in the state, denounced Jackson "as an assassin, duelist, horse racer and anything but a statesman." Still, the pull of traditional personal and party loyalties remained strong with Hiram. When Jedediah Dewey, longtime Federalist leader in Bennington, and O. C. Merrill vied for election to the state assembly at the next freemen's meeting, Merrill received Hiram's vote, "because his age & experience in Legislation seemed to point him out as the most proper person for that place."[33]

Hiram's ambivalence regarding national politics continued unabated. When he examined the "doings" of a "National Convention" in New York, he "liked them well."[34] Shortly thereafter he heard Colonel Merrill "talking of the justice & fairness of the Jackson administration." Barely a week after that, he "heard President's message read through by O.C. Merrill" and "did not see why it was not a very good one." Upon reading the speeches of Daniel Webster and others in opposition to the appointment of Martin Van Buren as minister to Great Britain, Hiram approved of that action. He considered Van Buren's rejection by the Senate "a just act" and thought it best to "keep our party quarrel at home." When he read Henry Clay's "last great speech in support of the American System," Hiram and his family "all thought [it] very fair and reasonable." However, when the matter of the National Bank arose, Hiram "liked well the remarks of R.M. Johnson of Kentucky," one of Jackson's staunchest supporters. Perhaps because of his ambivalence, Hiram did not attend the meeting of either party when each held a caucus in town to nominate candidates for Congress.[35]

Early in June 1832, Hiram made an agreement with Luman Norton to pay half of a subscription to the *New York Spectator,* "he to have 1st reading & I to preserve them." As a result of this bargain, Hiram and his family now read the *Vermont Gazette,* which had become the leading Jacksonian paper in the state, and the *Spectator,* a virulently anti-Jackson paper. When John S. Robinson defeated John Norton Jr. for the state assembly, at the freemen's meeting in September 1832, Hiram's ambivalence became readily apparent. Both men were good friends of Hiram, but since Norton "was not Jackson, [he] received my vote, but on other accounts esteemed the successful candidate [Robinson] as [a] most proper person — particularly in regard to legislation."[36]

When Andrew Jackson vetoed legislation to renew the charter of the Bank of the United States, the *Gazette* and the *Spectator* filled their pages with opposing viewpoints. Hiram did his best to absorb the material from both papers. By October, he was beginning to form a definite opinion regarding the matter. When he read Daniel Webster's speech of July 11 in opposition to the veto, he considered it "very able, and much to the point." Indeed, he believed it "left the Message [Jackson's veto] in a mangled state — we must support the U.S.B.[United States Bank] & the Constitution" Nonetheless, Hiram remained suspicious of leaders in both national parties. His view was that "both the great political parties of our country love flattery [and] will greedily swallow the most glaring misstatments respecting their opponents."[37]

With the passage of time, Hiram began to draw his political opinions almost exclusively from material published in the *Spectator.* He particularly liked a series of essays, "The Conduct of the Administration," printed in that paper which attacked the Jackson administration in detail on nearly every issue before the public.[38] Hiram said that in these essays "the Hero and his followers are in my opinion very truly portrayed." There he also found that most of the "charges respecting Bank corruptions were refuted." When he read Daniel Webster's speech against the Jackson administration, delivered at Worcester before the Massachusetts convention of National Republicans, he considered it "good and full of truth in my humble opinion." By this time when Hiram visited his old friends, neighbors, and longtime Federalists, they "talked about Masonry, Anti-Masonry, Jacksonianism, etc. — in which we perfectly agreed." And when Noadiah Swift visited and "gave his opinion freely on politics," Hiram confirmed that "in that we of course coincided." This was simply no longer true of his old Democratic associates.[39]

Given his political beliefs, Hiram viewed the November 1832 elections with mixed feelings. Jackson's reelection disappointed him, but the fact that Hiland Hall won a seat in Congress pleased him no end. Not only had a like-minded individual been sent to Congress, but also Hiram could now carry on a regular correspondence with his old friend that would enable him to gain personal insights into a process that had always seemed distant and a bit mysterious.

Nullification—the first issue to occupy Hiram's mind following the presidential election—elicited mixed reactions from him. Upon first glancing at the proceedings of the South Carolina nullification convention, Hiram "became highly incensed against them." He felt that "if their case is bad, the remedy is violent & uncalled for, but of a piece with Southern Impudence & folly." Then, emphatically in support of the president, he declared: "Let Jackson put them down if he can." The next day, however, after carefully reading the South Carolina convention report, he believed there "appeared to be much good reasoning—but not enough to bear them out in all their doings." Here again, the presence of old republican principles—the tyranny of power and its threat to liberty, state rights, fear of coercive central power—appealed to Hiram. This was particularly true for him when he noted the many references made to Thomas Jefferson as the "fair authority for the support of Nullification." Nonetheless, Hiram's visceral belief in the Union conflicted with his traditional republican beliefs. Consequently, when considering the threat South Carolinians posed to the Union, he "viewed Mr. Calhoun & his friends to be altogether lost in unprofitable theories—[their] brains turned"; and yet when he read Calhoun's defense of nullification, "though on the wrong side—yet it would entertain—many parts were grand & sublime."[40]

The whole issue of the South and nullification "warmly engaged our attention." Hiram and others spent endless hours talking about the South—the "natural production of the country, habits & manners of the people." The matter of nullification also caused Hiram to take a different view of Andrew Jackson. Upon reading Jackson's proclamation against nullification, Hiram observed that "contrary to the doctrine taught in the Bank Veto Message, the Supreme Court [now] appeared to be properly recognized." He considered the entire message a "very able document." Then, as "Southern politics" continued to engage the citizens of Bennington, Hiram finally exclaimed: "Let the President's Proclamation be supported at all events—The South is wrong." Still, the pull of old republican ideas remained strong. Upon reading Governor George McDuffie's inaugural address to the South

Carolina legislature, Hiram believed "there were many weighty truths in it" but that these ideas were still "too much mixed with Nullification Doctrine for our approbation." Again, Hiram's intense belief in the Union conflicted with his deep attachment to the traditional republican ideals so long enshrined by his family.[41]

If the dispute over nullification elicited strong feelings from Hiram, the issue that gave rise to that controversy — tariff duties — touched an equally sensitive nerve. Long accustomed to equating the interests of agriculture and manufacturing, Hiram considered tariff protection to be absolutely vital to "the interests of the North." While on a trip to North Adams, Massachusetts, he came across a local newspaper editorial that he claimed perfectly articulated his thoughts on the matter.[42] Written in opposition to nullification, this essay extolled the impressive progress made in New England since the passage of the Tariff of 1816: trade had increased, the population had doubled, the "farmer has found a home market and received just compensation for his produce," the "hardy sons" of New England "have pushed West where Savages previously held undisputed sway," and "the war whoop has been replaced by the noise and bustle of civilized life — birch canoes replaced by mighty steamboats." European nations viewed with "the greatest chagrin and envy the encouragement afforded by that government to the ingenuity and industry of its citizens," considering it second only to the establishment of a republican form of government. It was "under this benign protection [that] the genius of Internal improvement unfurled its banner." As a result, "Roads, Railroads and canals arose as by the touch of magic." In addition, "manufacturing has appeared everywhere — scarcely a neighborhood north of the Potomac has not been touched — nearly all boast its Factory — all reveals the touch of the hand of American protection and industry." A few years more of such protection and American products would rival those of Great Britain. To reduce duties now would imperil the fantastic prosperity and happiness that had resulted from tariff protection. Reductions would satisfy "only the envy, hatred and jealousy of the South." Here the editorial made its final and telling point: "The industry of the North, which mortifies the South — has carried its possession to wealth, happiness and fame while slavery hangs like a millstone to the neck of our prosperity."[43]

Hiram found further confirmation of such ideas in the pages of the *Spectator*. Upon reading there the speeches of senators opposed to nullification, he believed that these men "lead us back to first principles."[44] In these debates he saw "southern members lead toward Nullification," while "Northern & Eastern on other hand contending manfully for the Constitution as it naturally reads — wishing to use all proper means to enforce obedience to the laws made under it." To his mind, "the plain truth is that these Modern State Rights Men are using arguments which they will one day repent of — reasoning which would lead to the dissolution of this happy Union — in which we are all equally interested."[45]

Although supportive of Jackson's stance toward South Carolina, Hiram could not bring himself to look favorably on the Old Hero's administration. When Thomas Parsons expressed admiration for Martin Van Buren as vice president, Hiram sarcastically commented, "so much from an admirer of the Great Magician — as Mr. Van Buren is sometimes styled." He continued, "in conclusion I would give my opinion that all great seekers of Political distinction are whiffling inconsistent beings — riding on a whirlwind of Party Strife."[46]

Local politics were, however, quite another matter. When he received an "electioneering visit" from a neighbor in support of Jedediah Dewey in the upcoming election for the state legislature, Hiram let him know that he supported John S. Robinson, an Old Line Democrat. Dewey, a prominent Federalist, was now running as an Antimason. After the election — won by Robinson — Hiram, torn between his own instinctive egalitarianism and his loyalty to traditional Democratic associates, admitted that "I hate Masonry, but am not yet a Political Anti-Mason."[47]

Local issues could not hold Hiram's full attention for long. Instead, with the papers "full of Bank-Bank-Bank," Hiram, like so many of his fellow citizens, became intently involved in trying to come to grips with the issues of the Bank War.[48] In this effort, however, he found that the "great Bank Documents were so monstrously prolix" that he had difficulty reading through them. Consequently, he wrote Hiland Hall and asked him to discuss the matter "compressed in as few words as possible." Hiram also took this occasion to request that Hall send him a "description of leaders of parties — likewise of those who were most modest, unassuming, pleas't companions — not disposed to stir the waters of strife."[49]

From this time on Hiram depended on correspondence with Hall and the speeches of members of Congress published in the *Spectator* to shape his feelings on the bank. Here again his belief in old republican principles deeply affected his perceptions. He admired the speeches of men such as George McDuffie in the House and John C. Calhoun in the Senate, even though both men were ardent nullifiers. He considered McDuffie's observations regarding Jackson and the removal of bank deposits to be "very powerful."[50] He firmly believed that Jackson had unconstitutionally usurped far too much power to the executive branch. Likewise, he was enthralled when McDuffie warned that Jackson's removal of deposits from the bank and subsequent placing of this money with selected state banks would lead to "the sacrifice of the honest and the industrious, to make princes of brokers, speculators, and stock-jobbers." By creating a system of state banks tied to the federal government and associated with the political purposes of that government, "no human power can rescue us from the hand that wields the whole. The man who controls a bank, controls all who are indebted to that bank; and thus by sanctioning the meretricious union of money with power, you deliver up your country into chains which nothing but a Divine interposition can ever break or dissolve."[51]

When he read Calhoun's speech regarding the bank deposits, Hiram believed the South Carolinian "used up Taney & Dr. Jackson." Calhoun's observations so impressed Hiram that he "considered him able, even beautiful."[52] In his speech Calhoun had warned that the country was "in the midst of a revolution." The very existence of free government rested on the proper distribution of power. "To destroy this distribution and thereby concentrate power is to effect a revolution."[53]

Observations made by Henry Clay, Daniel Webster, William J. Duane, and other prominent political figures elicited Hiram's ardent approbation as well. They, too, warned against executive usurpation and decried the economic ruin that would befall the nation as a result of Jackson's actions.[54] It was, perhaps, the letters of Major Jack Downing that most appealed to Hiram and his family.[55] When the family read Downing's letter on the bank, "we all nearly died laughing during its perusal." Downing's common-sense approach and humorous satire on the political situation struck a chord with Hiram. Andrew Jackson's actions most decidedly did not. When Jackson defended himself against his political opponents, Hiram delivered his most telling critique: the president's arguments were "far enough from being Republican."[56]

For information regarding the actions of various members of the House and the Senate, Hiram depended on his friend Hiland Hall.[57] From his perspective, Hall believed that the most difficult issues he faced in his first sessions of Congress related to Andrew Jackson's attack on the bank, his insistence upon a specie currency, and his disdain for those who lived on credit. Skeptical of Jacksonian rhetoric on these matters, Hall was particularly disturbed by terms such as "Monied

Aristocracy," "Monster," and "monopolies." He took a practical stance toward the Bank of the United States and banking in general. Confessing that his "notions about a National bank do not arise from any love towards institutions without souls, but from the fear of a general derangement & apathy of business without one," Hall declared that he feared that it would be easier for people swayed by Jackson's emotional language to pull down an institution accused of "dangerous powers" than to get along without it.[58] Consequently, he inquired of one of his Democratic constituents: "If we fight down the bank, what show of business are we to keep up in our village, except a few days in court time?"[59]

Loyal to these beliefs, Hall rose in the House of Representatives on May 5, 1834, to present a memorial from his constituents opposing President Jackson's war on the Bank of the United States as well as his criticism of paper money and credit. Hall specifically defended a resolution to the effect that "the declaration of the President, that 'any man ought to break who trades on borrowed capital,' is a foolish and wicked assertion." Like his memorialists, Hall believed that "borrowed capital" rested entirely upon good credit established only by "the industry and integrity of the borrower." He then characterized Jackson's position as an "insult to honest enterprise."[60]

Warming to his subject, Hall defended the citizens of Vermont for being "as purely republican in their habits and notions" as any people in the country. In their minds, as well as his own, a reliance upon credit was clearly "in accordance with their republican principles." It was credit that "enabled the poor but enterprising citizen, who has established a character for integrity and skill, to commence life with some prospect of raising himself to the level of his neighbor who derives his capital from the gains of his ancestor." Credit placed "worth on something like an equality with wealth, and enables honest poverty to outstrip and conquer riches on the fair field of honorable competition."[61]

Hall had nothing but disdain for the remedy that Jackson recommended for the nation's economic troubles: hard money. For him and his constituents, specie currency was a "humbug." They believed that a "well-regulated paper medium, founded on a species basis," was more fitting for the transaction of business in an "improved state of society." According to Hall, "Congress might as well undertake to carry the people of this country back from the canal to the forest horse-path, from the steamboat to the scow with its setting poles, from the railroad car to the handbarrow, as to expect to legislate them back to a 'hard-money system.' "[62] Instead of the backward economy fostered by Andrew Jackson, Hall championed a progressive, democratic form of capitalism in which government — local, state, and national — fostered economic opportunity for all citizens by supporting institutions such as banks and factories.

Hall could not have expressed Hiram's views with more precision. By articulating the demands of his constituents, he provided meaning and coherence to Hiram's inchoate political beliefs. The Harwoods had long relied on credit; without it they could not maintain their commercial dairy operation. The family's very existence, as Hiram saw it, depended on his own personal character and integrity; without these he could not gain the credit necessary to maintain the farm and the family's independence. Nothing could be more republican. At the same time, Hiram shared Hall's vision of progress. Bennington should not remain a sleepy village with business linked only to court days; instead, it should become a dynamic and prosperous town where all men were free to prosper through hard work. Hall's words resonated perfectly with Hiram's views on life and politics; they melded his devotion to republican independence with his desire for commercial success.

At the freemen's meeting in September 1834, Hiram had the opportunity to support his principles: his old friend John Norton had been nominated by the "Nationals" as a candidate for the state assembly; Hiland Hall stood as the congressional candidate for the same party. Hiram and his father cast ballots for their friends, both of whom won easily. The day did not pass entirely to Hiram's liking, however; he became very upset by the presence at the polls of "an unusual number of drunken fellows."[63]

Public drunkenness — man's inability to control his base instincts, to moderate his behavior — had long troubled the Harwood family. Several months before that September's freemen's meeting, Hiram had eagerly signed a petition to the town authority "against reconsidering the vote to not grant licenses to merchants to sell ardent spirits by small measure." He attended temperance lectures whenever possible, subscribed with George P. Harwood to the *Temperance Advocate*, and even traveled to Arlington to attend a countywide temperance convention. When John Norton told him of the "excellent regulation under which he was going to run his distillery — not a drop to be retailed to drunkards on any acc't, none to be drank there by those who rec'd bandy in paym't for cider," Hiram "approved much of his scheme."[64]

For some time temperance had been a divisive issue among the

townspeople of Bennington. Ministers of Old First Church, in cooperation with Stephen Hinsdill, and other leading Pioneers insisted upon
imposing strict abstinence upon the townspeople. Their zealous advo-
cacy of such a policy contributed mightily to the angry divisions between Pioneers and Old Line supporters that so troubled the town.
Moderate in all things, Hiram never supported efforts to promote total
abstinence. Instead, he "manifested sentiments favorable to the cause,
but would not go so far at first — believing a gradual change preferable
to a radical one." While distancing himself from the moral authoritarianism characteristic of prominent Pioneers — men who also con-
stituted the early leadership of the National Party in Bennington —
Hiram did adhere to their conception of society as a progressive,
organic whole. Once, upon encountering a "hearty looking mountain-
eer" loudly exclaiming that men surrendered their individual rights
upon joining temperance societies, Hiram "replied as faithfully as he
could in their favor — telling him that such men as himself, it was not
expected could be reclaimed, must be left to destroy themselves — that it
was the rising generation who would derive benefit from these societies." Hiland Hall could not have said it better.[65]

If Hiram felt alienated by the moral zealotry of so many prominent
local Nationals, he was equally offended by the stance being adopted by
his old Democratic friends; they had abandoned issues that Hiram
considered vital to the economic well-being of Bennington and the nation. Before Jackson's election they had unanimously supported banking, internal improvements, manufactures, high tariffs, and even the
American System as essential for the growth and prosperity of their
community.[66] Now that such issues had become the stock and trade of
the Whigs — the party label assumed by National Republicans in the
1830s — Bennington's Democrats were left with little more than rhetorical issues stemming from their emotional attachment to the Jacksonian attack on aristocracy. This was not enough for Hiram; he did not
want to abandon the economic measures once deemed so essential to
Bennington's Democratic leaders. For years he had consistently supported measures that might enhance the economic well-being of his
community.[67] Thus, upon reading a presidential message in December 1834, Hiram felt that Jackson's "bitterness [toward the Bank of
the United States] is without bounds." Even if the bank had done
wrong, "the Corporation as men have rights — let them be heard in
their own defense — & not crush them at once, as it appears he would if
he had power."[68]

Gradually Hiram began to give "my view pretty freely on the conduct of the old Hero." These feelings had grown so strong by the time of the September 1835 freemen's meeting that his political beliefs overwhelmed his old loyalties entirely. Hiram's longtime friend and Democratic leader John S. Robinson stood as the Jacksonian candidate for the state assembly; Jedediah Dewey, a lifelong Federalist, opposed him. "The former as a *man* was my favorite, but being of a very different political faith from me — conceived it not proper to vote for him." Prior to casting their votes, Hiram and his father were accosted by many of their old friends and political associates in an effort to convince them to vote for Robinson, "but it was of no avail. We stuck to *our* party just as *they* ever have done to theirs." It pained Hiram "to be obliged by an imperious sense of duty to vote in opposition to so fine a man as John S. [Robinson]. There was nothing of ill will, nothing personal in this." Although Hiram and his father "*loved* & *respected*" Robinson, they could not support him in this election. "In voting we must be independent of all little personal impartialities — these should all give way to what we may conceive to be most for the Public Good." Hiram and his father had become dedicated Whigs.[69]

Having voted for a party rather than a candidate, Hiram still harbored no illusions about the political process. Often when a conversation turned to politics, Hiram gave his "opinion pretty fully that there was a great game of deception constantly played off by both parties — & most adroitly & successfully by *that* in power." After reading a newspaper account of affairs in Washington, he exclaimed that "the whole facts were plainly & energetically told — Corruption stares us full in the face — but the devotees won't see it — all will go well while deception & cupidity shall rule." Several days later, referring to yet another newspaper article regarding congressional legislation, Hiram commented "Smoothly done — but facts are stubborn things and they are out — no getting them back." He could not help noticing that candidates of both parties in Bennington claimed that their actions were "all for the 'People' — that unwieldy many-headed monster to whom so many feeling & unanswerable appeals are made." And yet, "giving certain men office of places of profit — little would they care for the 'People.'" Still, when accosted by an acquaintance, Hiram responded positively to the individual's query as to whether he and his father would be "wide awake respecting the Presidential Election." On the day of the election, Hiram noted, "of course we voted the Whig ticket."[70]

After the Whig loss in the presidential election, Hiram displayed even less patience with the egalitarian rhetoric of Bennington Democrats. He immediately reprimanded his old friend John C. Haswell, editor of the *Vermont Gazette*, for his imprecations that all old Federalists were now Whigs. He asked Haswell what percentage of his readers were Whigs. When the editor responded that about one-third of his readers belonged to that party, Hiram "then inquired why he abused them so by calling them exclusively Federalist when it was notorious that there were so many of that old party in the Jackson Van Buren Ranks." Haswell "excused the matter by saying the elections were passed — the offense could of course cease."[71]

This did not end Hiram's frustrations. When an old Democratic acquaintance, who often "let off loudly & hotly against the wealthy," pronounced "terrible imprecations against banking & all engaged therein without distinction — wishing the destruction of every institution of the kind in the U S," Hiram could only respond: "Poor man — I suspect he little tho't of the consequences that would follow the consummation of a wish so full of mischief." In a far more critical tone, he observed that if the man "spared some of his breath, spent thus, & applied himself heretofore more closely to business in his shop he would have seen less occasion for belching forth such inflated bombast." Then, when another old Democrat suggested removing all tariffs because it "would be a great favor to the poor," Hiram responded that "there was a great deal of whining hypocrisy played off in Washington — respecting that class in the community."[72]

What upset Hiram and so many fellow Whigs the most following the November elections was the effort made by the Democratic majority in Congress to expunge the resolution censuring Andrew Jackson for his removal of the bank deposits.[73] For Hiram, such an action was "beneath the dignity of that august body & is a severe commentary of our boasted Republican Institutions." Not only that; it also demonstrated "the tyranny of party — whose dictation is as irresistible as that of the greatest despots in existence." From this point on, the expunging resolution became, in the view of Hiram and his father, "that black revengeful deed."[74]

Hiram was so infuriated by the passage of the expunging resolution that he considered giving up his subscription to the *Vermont Gazette*, the paper to which he and his family had been loyal for nearly four decades. The *Gazette*, as the foremost Democratic organ in the state, had, of course, come out strongly in favor of the resolution. The fact that Haswell had printed the names of the senators who had voted to censure Jackson surrounded by a dark black border exasperated Hiram. From his perspective, "the spirit manifested by the present majority in the U.S. Senate is as overbearing & full of political persecution as that of the Federalists in the hottest times of 1798, 1799." Then, when Haswell printed "a most scurrilous piece against banking," Hiram considered it "not gentlemanly at all."[75] Worst of all, with the passage of time, Haswell's attacks upon Whigs became increasingly shrill. He declared in unequivocal terms that Whigs in Vermont must be voted out of office because they "have shingled the State over with BANKS AND CORPORATIONS, which like putrid canker sores, are gnawing upon the vitals of the body politic — consuming the wages of Labor, eating up the profits of Industry, and making THE RICH RICHER AND THE POOR POORER."[76]

Hiram would have none of this. Instead, he looked to the speeches and letters of Hiland Hall for a true understanding of the issues inflaming Congress. Hall invariably emphasized traditional republican values as the primary means of fostering honest government and a democratic society. In America the people were sovereign, but only through "intelligence & vigilance" could they retain "the privileges & preeminence of free men."[77] He lauded the "purely republican" habits of Vermonters and the way they judged governmental actions in "accordance with their republican principles." It was just such principles as these that led the people of Vermont to oppose measures that promoted "the aristocratical accumulation and transmission of wealth in particular families."[78]

Hall believed that Andrew Jackson and his supporters, by assaulting the Bank of the United States "under color of attacking 'aristocratical monopolies,'" were actually "waging a destructive war upon the labor and business of the country." Because of Jackson's war on the national bank, ordinary citizens — farmers, mechanics, and laborers — saw their fortunes declining. Unless stopped, Jackson's actions would "transfer a large share of the property of the country into the hands of capitalists, and leave in poverty and want a great portion of that class of society which is below them in wealth." Placing himself in that "lower class," Hall entered a solemn protest against the war on "aristocrats" that the president was inviting him to join. To him it was perfectly obvious that at the end of Jackson's war, "the 'aristocrats' will bear off the 'spoils' and the 'glory,' and 'all the blows will fall upon us.'"[79]

Hiram had great admiration for Hall, who had been born into a poor farm family in North Bennington. The two men respected hard work, and each maintained a pragmatic view of progress and reform within their society. For this reason, their association with the preeminent Whig leaders in Bennington made both men more than a little uneasy. The moral authoritarianism and latent elitism displayed by Isaac Tichenor, Stephen Hinsdill, James Ballard, Aaron Robinson, Moses Robinson Jr., and Elijah Dewey offended their basic egalitarian and progressive outlook.

By March 1837, however, the political leadership of the Whig Party in Bennington had undergone a striking transformation. In February of that year, Stephen Hinsdill, the richest man in Bennington, had gone bankrupt. His mills and the mill village named after him shut down. Hiram viewed Hinsdill's failure "in a very serious light — but could not sympathize with him as I should with one who appeared to be guided in business transactions by the plain rules of common sense." He exclaimed: "Away of your ambition of setting up Seminaries — Instituting, organizing & establishing new Religious Societies & Churches, building meeting houses, etc. etc, as everybody knows this gentleman has been doing a few years past."[80] Hiram simply had no patience for such activities; neither did he agree with Hinsdill's zealous support of complete abstinence, the formation of Bible societies, support for foreign missionaries, and the immediate abolition of slavery. The man's moralistic fervor and his coercive manner of promoting reform offended Hiram, who favored a far more moderate approach to such matters.

Hinsdill abandoned Bennington shortly after the failure of his business; James Ballard, principal of Bennington Seminary and moral zealot, left with the Hinsdill family. William Lloyd Garrison had departed shortly after the presidential election of 1828. With the deaths of Elijah Dewey, Aaron Robinson, Moses Robinson Jr., and Isaac Tichenor, leadership of the Whig Party in Bennington underwent a major transformation.[81] The pragmatic capitalism of Hiland Hall replaced the moral authoritarianism and elitism of Hinsdill and his associates. As a result Hiram felt much more comfortable with his new political associates. These individuals had prospered as a result of their own honest, disciplined labor. Like Hiram, they melded a continued devotion to old republican principles with modern business practices.[82]

Shortly after Hinsdill's departure from Bennington, a large "Union Meeting" took place "at which almost every citizen of the Centre V[illage] was present." At this meeting, characterized by harmony and consensus, the participants easily agreed upon making necessary repairs to the meetinghouse and the courthouse, building a new stone jail, and establishing a female seminary in the building just vacated by James Ballard's Bennington Seminary. Speeches delivered by David Robinson Jr. and Noadiah Swift helped to bring about such results and led Hiram to extol "Union" as "the order of the day—No Old Line nor Pioneer—No up Hill nor down Hill hereafter." Such actions, "if followed up closely," would usher in " 'The era of good feeling' as was said once, I believe, during the Administration of President Monroe."[83]

Hiram had high hopes for the peace and harmony of his own community, but he remained deeply concerned about the well-being of the nation as a whole. His visceral sense of the American Union never left him. Even though he had little fondness for the South and Southerners, he did not want the pressing issues of the day to exacerbate tensions that might threaten the Union. For that reason he favored a moderate alteration in the tariff that would placate the South without doing harm to Northern interests.

It was abolitionism that caused Hiram the most anguish. He referred to supporters of the movement as "crazy, foolish, & demented fanatics." Abolitionism, he thought, aroused the people of the South and needlessly threatened the Union. Consequently, he feared that politicians throughout the North might follow the example of Benjamin Swift, senator from Vermont, who, in Hiram's opinion, supported the "Great Puff of Abolition—calculating to ride this hobby to keep himself in office, like hundreds of others equally hollow as himself."[84] For this reason Hiram had mixed feelings about Governor George McDuffie's address to the South Carolina legislature.[85] Although Hiram presumed "the spirit of it to be pretty pure Nullification—some of it was really good—more especially in regard to Texas." McDuffie advised the nation "to let them, the Texans, alone." Fearing that the annexation of Texas would raise the issue of slavery and divide the nation, Hiram responded, "Amen to *that.*" For quite similar reasons, he and others in the Harwood family "liked the sentiments & language" of Martin Van Buren's inaugural address. This was particularly true of his opposition to abolition. They were unanimous in their sentiment that he "treated abolition right." Hiram was happy that Van Buren "came out so clearly & fully on that." For this reason, too, Hiram supported President Van Buren's statement that he "should not like to go to war for Texas." As for Texans themselves, Hiram admitted that he "cared but little for them."[86]

Of all the issues facing the country, the matter of economic depression worried Hiram the most; he considered the "failure & stoppage

of Business in all parts of the country" to be "tremendously appalling."
It appeared to him to be the "most extraordinary time ever seen in
our country—failures & stoppages or suspensions occurring daily,"
combined with "numerous instances of manufacturers standing still,
operative[s] consequently thrown out of employment."[87] Although
bemused by the manner in which leaders of each party blamed the
other for the nation's economic woes, Hiram remained acutely aware of
the hard times that pressed in upon him and his Tanbrook neighbors.
Such conditions, combined with the religious revivalism that was building throughout Bennington, affected Hiram powerfully as he solidified
his position both within the Harwood household and throughout the
larger community.

8

H. Harwood

2 o'clock P.M. according to previous notice a religious meeting was held at this house for the purpose of admitting my mother into the church — several members of that body being present — Mr. Peters presided — went through all the exercises, ordinances and ceremonies usually performed on such occasions — Preached a good sermon from a text selected from Paul to Titus, 2d Chapter, 11th, 12th, & 13th verses. Made an appropriate address at the Lord's Supper. Old Mrs. Gleason by recommend from the Church at Rowe, Ms., was admitted a candidate for the membership — standing propounded till next communion day. Cousin Amanda Maria Robinson was baptized.[1]

From the time of her admittance into the church, Diadama took it upon herself to bring others of her family to salvation. It was not unusual for her to "read tracts and sing hymns until a late hour in the evening" or to "very attentively read a religious book on which she very amply dealt out comments now and then." This often led to intense discussions in which family members became "much divided on religious points."[2] These discussions caused Hiram, "divided" in his own mind about religious matters, much anxiety. Religious revivalism, in combination with the political unrest of the time and the unrelenting nature of the dairy business, left Hiram seeking some solace, some solidity and certainty in his life. For this he turned increasingly to his love of history, his fascination with Tanbrook and the larger Benninton community, and his diary. At the same time, his family provided him with immeasurable comfort and satisfaction. This was especially true as his position within the Harwood household changed with the passage of time.

For the Harwoods and other townspeople, Absalom Peters' announcement in November 1825 that he intended to leave Bennington in order to become corresponding secretary of the United Domestic Missionary Society initiated a time of uncertainty regarding the fate of Old First Church. Loyal to the end, Benjamin attended Peters' farewell sermon several weeks later. For the next four months he supported an interim minister and asked Hiram to sign a subscription paper to pay the man for his services. Then, when Major Luman Norton presented a subscription supporting Daniel Clark to be the newly settled minister, Benjamin "ordered [Hiram] to put his name down against $6.00 — this was done."[3]

Clark, a graduate of Andover Theological Seminary, approached moral issues with an even more zealous and intolerant attitude than his predecessor. No sooner had he assumed his position than he began to hold prayer meetings in people's homes throughout the township. As the religious fervor stirred by these gatherings spread, Benjamin attended many of those held in the neighborhood, and Adeline began to go to Sunday school at the meetinghouse in town. Soon Benjamin and other members of the family were attending evening meetings regularly at the schoolhouse near the Harwoods. Still uncertain of his own beliefs, Hiram rarely accompanied them. When Hiram visited with Darius Clark and O. C. Merrill at the latter's office, the colonel "joked me lightly on the religious nature of the subject in hand — hoped it might prove beneficial to me." Hiram could only reply that "at present my mind was so agitated with worldly concerns that the consideration of serious affairs could not now be expected to take place."[4]

Nevertheless, Hiram could not help but note that "some stir respecting religion was said to prevail at this period within our borders." Benjamin and Adeline often went to church together and attended many local meetings. Finally, perhaps at Diadama's urging, the Harwoods hosted a religious gathering in their own home. Reverend Clark "handsomely invited us to be Christians — Said we need not have anything to do with the Doctrine of Election — God would choose from among the wicked whom he would — any or all might come in if they would — God's desire was to save everyone." After this Clark "particularly invited my father to come over to the Faith — bade him come in — for a terrible storm was coming on soon — wished him to shun the danger in season." After closing the meeting with a prayer, Clark, expressing surprise and disappointment at the poor turnout, mentioned that his meetings in other parts of town were fully attended.[5]

Several weeks later, Hiram, Sally, Benjamin, and Lydia attended a religious gathering at the home of Hiram Waters. After Reverend Clark appeared, the folks began to pray and sing. Then Clark addressed them on the "subject of depravity and the various ways in which the sinner evades and opposes Christian religion." After an exhortation by Deacon Safford, Clark extolled the virtues of a great awakening taking place in Hinsdillville. "After going some time with this he mentioned what he conceived to be a great barrier to the work now begun on the Street, meaning I suppose the neighborhood of the courthouse, which barrier must be done away with." Although no one had ever "made it a topic of public discussion before, every man, woman, and child ought to unite against it — he meant the Dancing School." Clark then warned all present of the "dreadful danger" emanating from such an institution.[6]

Reverend Clark did not restrict his criticism of the dancing school to private meetings; he delivered powerful attacks from the pulpit upon the dancing master, his students, and particularly parents who would allow their children to attend such lessons. He also criticized Darius Clark, the editor of the *Vermont Gazette*, for opposing such a stance. When Hiram entered the editor's office one afternoon, he found David Robinson Jr., Anthony Haswell, and Colonel O. C. Merrill firmly convinced that Reverend Clark would very much like to "rule" the *Gazette*. "At any rate, they hinted that they presumed he would like to stir up contention." Colonel Merrill expressed the opinion that religion would not suffer from slight attacks from the pages of a newspaper. He thought "the better way was to let them be devout that wanted to be so — to let them dance who wished to."[7]

Although thoroughly in agreement with his old Democratic friends, Hiram did occasionally attend religious meetings with other members of the family. Throughout the months of February and March 1827, he attended weekly meetings at the home of a neighbor. After hymn singing and much fervent prayer, Reverend Clark or a deacon of the church would exhort those present to come to the Lord. Clark "made it clear that there was no neutral ground." One was either a sinner or among the saved. The tension began to build within these meetings. Truman Hendryx, the tailor who had done so much work over the years for the Harwoods, "first spoke in public as a Christian Professor — had struggled with the Spirit 15 years." Then, when a neighbor's eleven-year-old son, who had not had the saving experience, died a terrible death, the loss was "particularly cutting to the parents — most especially to his mother whose anxiety for his future welfare was very great."[8]

Hiram faced particular uneasiness whenever Reverend Clark visited the family. On one such occasion, the "scene [became] rather solemn and impressive—most, if not *all* the ladies were in tears." Finally, Reverend Clark's "questions were directed to a pretty interesting point [Hiram], my replies were dilatory and evasive." Clark's "answers or remarks went to show the great danger of unbelief—peculiarly calculated to excite alarm and inquiry in the mind." Finally, after examining every other individual in the room, Clark "closed with a prayer on his knees."[9]

Over time, Clark became increasingly unpopular among the Democratic leadership in Bennington as well as with a growing number of others. Try as he might to avoid the confrontations springing up between his longtime associates—David Robinson Jr., O. C. Merrill, Darius Clark, Uel M. Robinson—and Reverend Clark and his supporters, Hiram could not help but form a disagreeable opinion of the pastor. This was particularly true after Reverend Clark, "having appointed a meeting here in late p.m. came down to officiate, but found that the people did not attend—made some remarks on their backwardness, asked a few questions of individuals, made some pretty frightful comments and rode off." Finally, when Clark thundered out against the theater that was to open in the courthouse, Hiram had had enough. He had no intention of staying away. Indeed, Adeline and other young folk living with the Harwoods attended a number of performances. Hiram himself eagerly purchased a ticket to see a performance of *Othello*. He enjoyed himself thoroughly and declared emphatically that "it could not be said that anything indecent or immodest appeared on Stage this evening."[10]

Benjamin continued to attend Reverend Clark's sermons at First Church despite his son's growing distaste for the pastor. It was not unusual, however, for him to report that Clark "particularly and emphatically" appeared to be the "chief fault-finder" as he continued his moralistic crusade against singing, dancing, horse racing, drinking, and the theater. Earlier, when a close friend of the Harwoods died, Clark had done much the same thing; to the chagrin of those present, he performed the funeral ceremony in such a manner that "many thought they discovered a harshness in his remarks the force of which was intended more particularly to apply against those who were employed in teaching music and dancing." Then when Captain John Norton, the Harwoods' close friend and neighbor, died, Reverend Clark behaved in a particularly repugnant manner. Hiram had always had a lot of respect for Norton; he was "not a professor of Christianity—yet no one could find fault with his general course of life—always of a friendly, frank, manly, and noble disposition." Hiram believed his friend's mind to be "too enlarged for him to stoop to commit any act of meanness in any circumstance whatsoever—fair and perfectly honorable in all his dealings—in short he was a good man in every sense of the word except that being a 'Christian.'" When Reverend Clark preached a powerful sermon at Norton's funeral, however, "he made some rather harsh remarks on the religious principles of the deceased" that did not set well with Hiram and his neighbors.[11]

When Melissa Street, one of Hiram's dearest childhood friends, fell seriously ill, Hiram had even more reason to question Clark's critical attitude. On her deathbed Melissa "manifested great concern for the future welfare of her soul." Clark "spent some time with her in religious exercise, but after was said not to be satisfied that her case was safe—was afraid that her repentance was insufficient to satisfy the demands of a just and Holy God." Hiram observed, "be this as it may, we must support her as having supported a fair reputation, having led a life of honesty, respectability and usefulness up to the hour of her decease."[12]

Hiram had doubts about Reverend Clark for theological reasons, but many townspeople attacked him on cultural grounds. David Robinson Jr., Hiland Hall, and others simply could not abide the man's moral authoritarianism. These individuals managed to gain a majority in the Congregational Society and brought the issue of Clark's dismissal before the church. Hiram attended nearly every session of the society that discussed this issue. By this time even Benjamin had abandoned Clark and was attending church in the East Village. Only Lydia remained loyal to Old First Church. Finally, during the second week of October 1830, a council of clergymen and deacons from neighboring towns met and unanimously agreed that Clark must be dismissed. To his great relief, Hiram exclaimed that Clark's "tyrannical career" had at last come to an end.[13]

After Clark's departure, First Church had visiting ministers, and various deacons read sermons on those Sundays when no visitor could preside. Many people—including Sally, Hopkins, and Adeline—began to frequent the Methodist meetings held on the Sabbath in the district schoolhouse near the Harwood farm. By the summer of 1831, though, most folks in Bennington became caught up in a protracted meeting on the Hill led by Rev. R. W. Gridley of Williamstown and ministers from the surrounding area. Employing the "new measures" of Charles Grandison Finney, Gridley and the other pastors held prayer meetings extending until dawn, fostered intense family devotionals, public prayer by women in mixed audiences, neighbor-to-neighbor canvassing by the faithful, praying for individuals by name, and the open humiliation of sinners driven to the anxious seat by the intense pressure of the moment.[14] Such practices brought sinners into intimate public contact with ardently professing Christians. Most important, they transformed prayer and the conversion experience from a private to a distinctly public affair.

Hiram attended several such sessions as well as prayers and exhortations held by Methodist and Baptist ministers in the area. After one such performance, Hiram exclaimed that the man "made a most pompous, bombastical, would-be oratorical prayer." Although he "knew not the feelings of others, I esteemed the performance a most ridiculous one." During one of the sessions at the protracted meeting held in Bennington in June, he witnessed that "many persons were anxious inquirers after Eternal Salvation — some obtained hope while others were left in the blackest despair." In his opinion Reverend Gridley's "discourse [was] very good and well suited to the state of mind in which many of his auditors were situated — inviting sinners unconditionally to submit to the will of God." As for Hiram, "the church music I liked well — after sermon I came away — did not stay to hear the anxious ones questioned."[15]

The effects of the protracted meeting lingered for some time in Bennington. That July 4 there was "no celebration here — people had their minds raised to higher objects." In mid-August 110 converts stood propounded as new members of First Church. In late August another protracted meeting began that lasted into the first week of September. Hiram attended one of the late-afternoon sessions, in which he "heard a plain elderly man preach from some remarkable passages in Job which went to show that God did not dispense his favors according to character in this life." Afterward he talked with Loan Dewey on the subject of religion and found that he "did not see and believe" as the old preacher did. Dewey "had perused his Bible pretty thoroughly too."[16] Hiram remained uncertain in his own mind about the manner in which an individual could achieve salvation.

On January 7, 1832, Deacons Noadiah Swift and Stephen Hinsdill called on the Harwoods to solicit a subscription for the settlement of Rev. Edward H. Hooker as pastor of First Church. Hiram signed for six dollars, even though the deacons requested a larger amount. Hiram felt "that was enough, all things considered." His experience with Peters and Clark had made him hesitant to subscribe more. When the Harwoods attended Hooker's installation several weeks later, Hiram judged the man's sermon to be "a fair one," considered "our music was fine," and concluded that "all went off elegantly."[17]

Hooker became the first settled pastor of First Church to face direct competition from other churches. By the time he came to the pulpit, Baptist, Methodist, Universalist, and Episcopalian churches had been formed in Bennington. Indeed, shortly after Hooker became its pastor, First Church itself split when Deacon Stephen Hinsdill formed a Presbyterian church in his factory village and took away many parishioners. The townspeople of Bennington simply could not avoid the religious currents surging throughout the region that fed revivals, splintered churches, and created thousands of zealous new converts.[18]

Within a year after his installation, Hooker took steps in response to the religious fervor sweeping through Bennington. He reinvigorated the Friday meetings that had long been a tradition at First Church. Then in December 1833, he joined with the renowned revivalist Horatio Foote in beginning a protracted meeting in Bennington.

Hiram accompanied the rest of the Harwoods to the initial meetings of the revival. He heard Foote attempt to "persuade his hearers to decide whether they would be followers of Baal or the Lord." In Hiram's opinion, Foote "handled" the subject "very spiritedly and eloquently." After hearing Foote close on the second night "by fervent prayer during which professors only were previously requested to hear standing," Hiram did not return. Other members of the family, however, continued to attend. After several days Hiram "was informed that among the hopeful converts now coming forward under preaching of Mr. Foote was Miss A.M. [Adeline] Harwood." When Cousin Henry Duncan visited the Harwoods, he "fervently and feelingly put up a petition to the Throne of Grace for the conversion of sinners, particularly in our family." Following this pointed message, Hiram attended Foote's address to the new converts at the meetinghouse. He "very attentitively listened to an able discourse in which was embodied excellent advice." Mixed "among many good things he recommended was honesty and fairness in dealing which suited my notions well—agreeing with me that no man could be a Christian without this virtue."[19]

Following the revival, Adeline, George P., and Hopkins continued to attend evening meetings held at the Brick Academy. Hiram remained ambivalent regarding revivalistic techniques. In this regard he had an interesting conversation with old Mr. J. Hunt, who "disapproved of these protracted meetings, none of which did he deem it his duty to attend." To him regeneration of the heart meant a feeling of "Universal Benevolence to all men." Hunt believed that "Heaven began on earth and without which there could be no Heaven—and said he thought he possessed that feeling."[20] To a man like Hiram—caught between his family's strict Congregational beliefs and his own more liberal inclinations—such ideas seemed to make perfect sense.

Regardless of Hiram's opinions about evangelistic behavior, February 2, 1834, proved to be a "proud day for Christians of the Congregational Church of Bennington": forty-seven of the converts brought to the Lord by Foote's preaching joined the church. Hooker, not willing to let such fervor subside, began to make house-to-house visits throughout the parish. When he called on the Harwoods, he "said a few words to me in particular on Religion."[21] Relentless in his pursuit of lost souls, Hooker returned repeatedly to the Harwoods to pray with Benjamin and Diadama. As a result Benjamin became a regular member of the Friday night meetings. In addition, he often attended the nightly meetings being held at Dr. Noadiah Swift's home.

On January 3, 1836, Hiram attended a "small religious meeting" held at Judge Luman Norton's. Reverend Hooker presided. When he returned home later that evening, Hiram carefully recorded in his diary that Hooker had delivered a "grave & impressive Discourse from the words of St. Paul," in which he "pointed out to such persons as Abraham, David & Paul as true examples of piety though they possessed very great faults in their several characters." What most impressed Hiram was Hooker's "inference that all unconverted persons, by use of proper means could, in a measure, become as St. Paul was."[22] This possibility—that unconverted men could "by use of proper means" become like St. Paul—raised questions that had long troubled Hiram. What were these "proper means"? Would he ever come to know them? Could he ever be saved?

Hiram's diary entry for January 3 was actually more revealing for what it did not mention than for what it did. The express purpose of the meeting earlier that evening had been to accept Benjamin and Damia, Hiram's sister, into the church. And yet Hiram made no reference to this.[23] The possibility held out by Hooker that unconverted men might find salvation totally eclipsed the fact that his father and sister had experienced saving grace. Whether consciously or unconsciously, Hiram had shut this fact out of his mind; he could focus only on the troublesome question of his own salvation.

Theological matters had long vexed Hiram. He was particularly concerned with the relationship between saving grace, church membership, and moral behavior. When T. C. Parsons, back from a visit to Washington, D.C., observed that things were much "more peaceable there since the panic was over," Hiram immediately responded that "in politics as in religion—call a thing good & it would pass for such." A month later, when a clerk who saluted him "as a brother—so that we may presume him to be *a professed* Methodist," cheated him on a sale amounting to little more than fifty-six cents, Hiram wondered "if men trick in small things—what will they do in large ones?" To his way of thinking, "fair dealing is the jewel—'Honesty is the best policy.'" Later that same year, when Hiram read an account of "the silly followers of the iron hearted Matthias," he believed that these people "really deserved the treatment from him which they received." Hiram was certain that the Prophet Matthias was not the only rogue or charlatan parading under the cover of religious beliefs.[24]

When such people as Matthias could claim the saving experience, what was Hiram to think? In the face of such uncertainty, he nonetheless retained a reverential attitude toward revealed religion. Certain beliefs were sacred to him. Upon becoming involved in conversation with a group of leading Federalists who opposed the revivals taking place in Bennington, Hiram recalled "many lively things said which as I think the subject a serious one—we ought not to treat quite so indifferently." On another occasion, after attending a lecture on philosophy at the Masonic Hall in Bennington, he concluded that the speaker "mixed scripture passages with scientific questions too much for my notion of propriety." Still another time, as Hiram rode past a new Baptist church, he noticed a handsome clock face painted on one of its walls. Upon discovering that the clock bore "false hands," Hiram considered this "an impropriety not fully weighed by the proprietors I presume, otherwise they never would have sanctioned such flimsy, ill designed deceptions in a place so sacred & exclusively appropriate to the all important purpose of dissemminating Eternal Truth."[25]

Whenever he had the chance, Hiram took part in conversations relative to the religious beliefs of others in an attempt to come to grips with his own personal feelings. In one such conversation, he and a friend discussed "things not present—he seemed to think there was no being after death." In the midst of a discussion regarding the Calvinist principle of election, Hiram agreed wholeheartedly with Captain Pliny Dewey when the latter claimed that he could not accept the idea "that an honest, upright neighborly person should forever be miserable in a future world." Upon becoming engaged in an exchange with a friend in Troy over the matter of revivals, Hiram expressed considerable relief when the man "called himself a very wicked man, but did not know as he should ever become better."[26] To know that others suffered the same anxieties as he somehow relieved his mind, if only for the moment.

Such respites were short-lived. Troubling questions constantly reappeared to plague Hiram: Must an individual have a conversion experience to be saved? Would he ever experience such a conversion? Were conversion experiences real, or did individuals simply claim them in the heat of religious fervor? Could not a man become saved merely by being honest, moral and upright in his personal life?

It was such issues that led Hiram to dwell on Hooker's statements on the evening of January 3, 1836, at the home of Luman Norton. Consciously or unconsciously, they caused him to sublimate the fact that his father and sister had experienced saving grace and been accepted into the church. The fact that his mother, father, and youngest sister claimed to have had saving experiences profoundly affected Hiram. He knew they were not hypocrites; they must, therefore, have actually experienced saving grace. Such an occurrence must truly take place. Hiram was torn: rationally, he believed that honesty and morality in this life should be sufficient for salvation; emotionally he wanted desperately to experience grace. Too honest to claim a saving experience he had not truly undergone, he could only live with the anxiety of being a "wicked man."

❧ Hiram sought respite from such religious uncertainty in some of his old habits. First among these was reading. As always, newspapers held a particular fascination for him. A subscriber to the *Vermont Gazette* and the *New York Spectator*, he read these papers regularly, augmenting them as often as possible with the *Albany Argus*, the *New York American*, and whatever others he could borrow. Hiram was an omnivorous reader and normally paid the most attention to political news on both the national and international scene. There were, however, several events to which he paid special attention; these involved murders that troubled him profoundly — so much so that he devoted an inordinate amount of space to them in his journal. Like many other New Englanders at this time, these murders, and the subsequent trials, held a particular fascination for Hiram.[27]

When members of the family returned from church on May 20, 1827, Hiram first learned that his cousin John Whipple of Albany had been murdered.[28] The next day Noadiah Swift "read an article respecting the murder of John Whipple of Albany—nothing very authentic." By the following day, however, Hiram had obtained several other newspaper accounts that caused him to "reflect much on the late murder in Albany."[29] These reports indicated that John Whipple's wife Elsie had conspired with Jesse Strang, the family's hired man, to kill her husband; worse, by all accounts Strang was Elsie's paramour.

John Whipple's murder deeply affected Hiram. Whipple's father, Ezra, lived in nearby Sunderland and had been a close friend of the Harwoods for years. Decades earlier, when forced by hard times to put his children out to sympathetic families, Ezra sent his daughter Lucinda to live with Hiram's maternal grandparents. Since that time she had continued to be like a sister to Hiram's mother, Diadama. Beyond that, Hiram was well aware of John's attempts to purchase a new farm for his father in order to "transfer him to a more comfortable situation." Hiram thought it was a particularly "fine trait in his [John's] character that he seemed endeavoring for the convenience & good of his aged father, brethren & sisters."[30]

The fact that John Whipple had been working to care for his aged father was very significant to Hiram. Such concern for a parent comprised the very essence of the Harwoods' patriarchal tradition. The supportive web of family was central to Hiram's life. He cherished the ideal of family continuity within a fixed community. Amid the flux and uncertainty that gripped Tanbrook, Bennington, and the nation at large, he considered the family—his own as well as the families of others—to be the surest anchor of stability. Consequently, any threat to the family—death, intemperance, economic instability—created the greatest anxiety for him. But to have a wife destroy a family upset Hiram nearly beyond measure; this struck at the core of the patriarchal tradition so central to his very existence. Although patriarchy for the Harwoods had always meant subordination of all family members—men, women, and children—to the patriarch, it particularly stressed loyalty to the words of the Apostle Paul: "Wives, submit yourselves unto your own husbands, as it is fit in the Lord" (Colossians 3:18). Of all individuals, then, it was unthinkable that the wife, traditionally meant to be the family's most subordinate member, should ever be responsible for its destruction. For Elsie Whipple to take a lover and then to conspire with that man to kill her husband threatened the very principles of family life that were so vital to Hiram's personal sense of stability and security.

Impelled by such strong feelings, Hiram followed the trials of Jesse Strang and Elsie Whipple with rapt attention. He perceived both individuals to be "imps [devils, fiendish spirits] in human shape."[31] As the trials progressed, he spent many evenings reading the testimony of each case with particular care.

When an Albany jury found Strang guilty and sentenced him to hang, many "everyday kind of remarks were made respecting Strang" by Hiram's friends and associates. He was particularly struck by Darius Clark's observation that "it was an easy way to die to be hanged by the neck." The hanging itself promised to be an event that would draw people from far and wide. In fact Hiram loaned a neighbor a dollar as expense money on the road to Albany, where he "calculated on going with many others to witness the execution of the unfortunate & never to be forgotten Jesse Strang." Hiram "counted the hours allotted for the unhappy Strang." On the day of the execution, Hiram "never thought more on anything than of this awful character — my mind has been more or less haunted with the circumstances attending the black deed from the moment I first became acquainted therewith." Nonetheless, Hiram had no desire to view the execution. The day following the execution, Hiram visited with a friend from Pownal whose brother had "returned with a wonderful account of the vast concourse of people assembled there" for the hanging. Five days later, Hiram himself "sat up late reading the confession of J. Strang — Deadly Deed — Deadly Deed." He could not help but feel it a great "pity that those imps could not have been detected ere it was too late."[32]

Although he reflected at length on Strang's "Deadly Deed," Hiram made no further mention of Elsie Whipple. A strange silence came over his journal on this point; no diary entry recorded the fact that an Albany jury released the woman. The betrayal of her husband may have been so unspeakable in Hiram's mind that he could not bring himself to enter the woman's name again in his diary.

Six years later the murders of two women, Mary Hamilton and Sarah Cornell, drew Hiram's careful attention. The two cases elicited quite dissimilar responses from him, however. Mary Hamilton, described as a lovely young widow — "chaste, beautiful, urbane, and lively, and as pure as the unclouded sky" — living respectfully in her mother's boardinghouse, had continually rebuffed the romantic advances of Joel Clough.[33] Clough, vowing that if he could not have her, she would never marry another man, brutally murdered her within sight of her mother and several boarders. All accounts of the murder and sub-

sequent trial emphasized the warm, peaceful qualities of the boardinghouse, the loving relationship between Mary Hamilton and her
mother, and the victim's own spotless character.[34] When Hiram read
that Clough's trial had just been completed and that the man had received a verdict of guilty, he remarked, "and very justly too." For a
man with Hiram's sensitivities regarding families and family life, Mary
Hamilton's murder "was a most cold blooded deed—shocking to hu-
manity." He could only consider Clough himself to be "a most heinous,
outrageous, bloody murderer." Worse, "how wretched must forever be
Mrs. Longstreth the good mother of Mrs Hamilton. Let any parent
bring home the case to himself & it would awaken every feeling of the
sympathetic kind of which the human heart is susceptible." Clough's
attack on Mary Hamilton had been an attack upon the sanctity of the
family itself. So profoundly did it affect Hiram that "the history of the
last [Clough's murderous act] I wish I could never have known, for my
mind has been almost constantly haunted with it ever since seeing the
fiendish act in print."[35]

   At the very time that Clough's murderous act caused him such distress, Hiram was following another murder trial as well. A young mill
worker, Sarah Cornell, had been found hanged near the town of Fall
River, Massachusetts. At first authorities considered her death a suicide. Soon, however, evidence surfaced implicating Ephraim Avery, a
Methodist minister, and the case sparked heated exchanges between
Methodist supporters of Avery and mill workers vigorously calling for
his prosecution.[36] Hiram, reading the reports of the trial with rapt attention, had no strong feelings about either Methodist ministers or mill
girls; he was much more familiar with the latter. He knew and respected
many women working in Bennington's cotton and woolen factories.
But when he read the testimony of witnesses attesting to Cornell's
"lewdness,"—her repeated sightings in compromising situations with
young men and the fact that a doctor had treated her for a "foul disease"—Hiram had difficulty disagreeing with the defense attorney's
statement that young Sarah Cornell was "abandoned and profligate."[37]
In light of such testimony, Hiram declared that he "should pronounce
S. M. Cornell to have been what we call a real___ —no matter what."
This led him to question the validity of her statements regarding her
intimate relationship with Rev. Avery prior to her death. Such utter-
ances "might have been altogether false." That night, gripped by such
testimony, Hiram stayed "up late reading the trial of Avery."[38]

   The following day Hiram read a tract containing the closing statement of Avery's defense attorney. The man seemed to give voice to Hiram's innermost feelings when he exclaimed that there was a "charm, a refinement, a delicacy in the female sex, superior to man, [that] no civilized community has ever doubted. It is female character, when pure and unstained, which contributes to the embellishment and refinement of society in the highest degree." However, "in the same proportion as woman, when chaste and pure, excels the other sex, by just so much, when profligate, does she sink below them; and if you were to seek for some of the *vilest monsters* in wickedness and depravity, you would find them in *female* form."[39] For Hiram the defense attorney's words proved irresistible. After reading them, he concluded that "it would appear that the character of S.M. Cornell was bad, which considerably did away the feeling I at first entertained respecting the prisoner." Although Hiram "still must think him the author of the deed," he concluded that it was "without intent to kill."[40] When Hiram read of Avery's acquittal, he offered no critical comment at all.

The attorney had articulated perfectly the feelings that the Clough and Avery cases aroused in Hiram. Enclosed in the warmth and support of a family setting, the chaste and pure Mary Hamilton truly represented the virtuous woman of Proverbs whose price was "far above rubies." When mill girls retained their close association with families — just as Sophia Waters had with the Harwoods — they, too, represented this same ideal. The fallen woman, however, was a threat to all such social stability and harmony.

Such feelings may explain Hiram's reaction to the murder of Helen Jewett — the cause célèbre of the early nineteenth century.[41] On June 19, 1836, Hiram wrote that he "commenced late in the day reading Trial of Rich'd P. Robinson for murder of Helen Jewett — City N.Y" but made no further mention of the case. He was busy with the dairy and serving as foreman of a jury, but the reason for Hiram's silence more than likely emanated from the fact that the case did not threaten his feelings about women and the family. Helen Jewett was a known prostitute with no ties to a family whatsoever. The individual accused of the murder was a young man who had left a respectable family to clerk in New York City. No matter what the trial might reveal about the facts of the case, both individuals had been corrupted by the city; neither represented a threat to the values Hiram ascribed to the home.

Throughout the years stretching from the trial of Jesse Strang to that of Richard Robinson, Hiram became more and more intensely involved with the dairy. During this time he attempted to maintain the reading routine he had established over the previous years. That is, he read steadily in a major work, while sporadically reading shorter works or snatches of larger books. By the summer of 1833, however, Hiram was fighting a losing battle. "This keeping so many cows is a terrible damper to the reading spirit — but necessity goads on — can see no way very clearly to avoid it." Several months later he complained that "my head was wrong for much reading."[42]

Hiram had no alternative but to succumb to the "necessity" that goaded him on; he finally had to alter his reading routine to fit an increasingly demanding work schedule. Though never abandoning newspapers, he did give up large tomes. In their place he substituted articles in encyclopedias and magazines such as the *North American Review* and the *Penny Magazine*. It was the stories in *Waldies Literary Omnibus*, however, that most attracted him. He claimed that many of these stories were "too verbose to suit my taste," but he stuck with them. His favorites included "The Confessions of an Elderly Gentleman," "The Rambler in Mexico," and "Rosamond's Narrative of Female Capers in Life," which he described as "of a low disgraceful order — yet entertaining." He did not enjoy works such as the *Journal of Moral Reform*, "a new publication in the McDowal style — not approved much by me."[43] Instead of McDowell, Hiram turned to the likes of *The Ladies Own Book*, a work far more in keeping with his increasingly conventional tastes. He considered it a "very proper thing, many excellent articles in it." In addition, he "found many fine things laid down by way of advice" regarding proper social behavior.[44]

One author that Hiram could not abandon during this time was Thomas Paine. Quite often he would pick up Paine's political works and read *The Crisis* or *Common Sense* or peruse portions of *The Rights of Man*. Hiram considered these "all very fine Republican works which ought to be read by every friend of freedom in this & in all enlightened countries."[45]

Hiram's attraction to Paine resulted as much from his ties to the American Revolution as from his republicanism — the two remained inseparably joined in Hiram's mind. Consequently, when Hiram heard that the Marquis de LaFayette had landed in New York City and planned to tour New England, he was ecstatic: LaFayette was not only a link to the Revolutionary past that Hiram so revered but also one of the heroes of the war itself. When told that a number of Bennington's most prominent men had actually met and talked with LaFayette during his stop in Albany, Hiram was pleased to learn that his hero was "of very easy & unassuming manners, perfectly accessible to persons of all ranks." For a time Hiram "had flattered myself a little with the prospect of seeing this justly celebrated personage, but must now give it up as something too good for me": the general was being escorted by "the great worthies of Vermont."[46]

In addition to LaFayette, Hiram always remained deeply attached to Vermont's own Revolutionary War figures. Upon encountering Judge Fay one day, the two men "talked about old E[than] Allen, Tho's Chittenden and other revolutionary worthies who are now no more." Several months earlier Hiram had borrowed the *Vermont State Papers*, by Slade, and spent two nights reading portions of this work aloud to his father. Both men "found great entertainment concerning the N.Y'k controversy etc."[47] Another time he visited with a neighbor about "the shortness of time of the reputation of gen E. Allen of Green Mountain Boy memory, for courage which had been disputed, but which our friend could not give up." Neither could Hiram relinquish his own admiration for Allen and the Green Mountain Boys. The following year he again borrowed the *Vermont State Papers* and spent most of one evening "reading Correspondence between Governor Tryon of N.Y. and the real old Green Mountain Boys whose answers and statements were unvarnished, fearless, energetic and powerful" — quite unlike the political rhetoric Hiram constantly witnessed all about him.[48] He believed that Ethan Allen and the others who created the republic of Vermont stood as true and faithful advocates of the American Revolution. These men towered above the politicians of Hiram's day; they represented a time of honest values and true principles, a time that Hiram longed to regain, if only through his love of history.

Hiram's historical awareness included his own family as well. When a neighboring family visited the farm one day, Hiram sat with that family's matriarch, "the daughter of Nathaniel Harwood, the eldest of my grand-father's uncles." He was able to glean from the old woman that "her father died about 64 years ago at the age of 60 — supposing his father to have been at his, Nathaniel's, birth 25 years old, it would fix the time of his own birth at about 1675 — his christian name was Peter, resided in Concord, Mass., was lame and followed the butchering business for a livelihood." As far as Hiram could ascertain, "this is as far back as, I am informed, the Harwood's can trace their ancestry."[49]

When Sally and Hiram visited Sally's mother in New York, Hiram carefully recorded "the family register of Osborn, and Lydia Stone which I found entered in the old lady's bible." It was, however, Hiram's

Aunt Sally Robinson who was of the most assistance in his search for his
family's roots. Intent upon writing a genealogy of the leading families
of Bennington, Sally happily shared her "collections of Family Records" with Hiram. Then, when Hiram's cousin Nathaniel Robinson
returned from a trip to Amherst, Massachusetts, he recounted a visit
to "the farm on which our great-grandfather resided at the time of
his death which happened, if I am rightly informed, in 17 — His name
was Benjamin Harwood, followed the business of weaving, dying and
Pressing cloth etc." Perhaps the incident Hiram most delighted in
recording was that of his grandfather's participation in the battle of
Bennington. It was this story that forged a personal link for Hiram with
the Revolutionary past he so revered. It also contributed to the idea
of family continuity within a fixed community that Hiram so firmly
wished to maintain.[50]

   In addition to his own, Hiram remained deeply interested in the
history of other Bennington families. He never missed an opportunity
to talk with longtime residents about their experiences during the early
years of the town's existence. When he visited with M. L. Selden "about
the old fathers of this town," he noted that "some particulars I would
be happy to give if time permitted." On another occasion, while waiting
to get his horses shod, Hiram had chatted with old Governor Isaac
Tichenor, who "related many anecdotes respecting the Revolutionary
patriots of his time." Well aware of Hiram's interest in Bennington's
past, Aunt Sally sent Hiram a list of the first organized militia company
in the town, written in the hand of Colonel Samuel Robinson, dated
October 24, 1764. As if to recapture the moment for himself, Hiram
copied this entire roster into his diary. Then, when Uncle Samuel and
Aunt Sally Robinson visited the Harwoods several years later, Hiram
carefully recorded their account of "bygone days respecting the first
settlers of Bennington — how they behaved to the Yorkers when they
were trying to confiscate their lands after having endured great priva-
tions in bringing them to — having in many instances already paid the
original grantees therefor."[51]

   Artifacts and old buildings also intrigued Hiram; they, too, consti-
tuted a link in that chain joining past and present that Hiram wished so
ardently to forge. Once, while conversing with Hiram, Captain David
Robinson Jr. showed Hiram a "piece of timber that formed a part of the
old Military Store built late in the year 1777." In recording this incident, Hiram carefully traced the lineage of the building — the object of
the British foray that led to the battle of Bennington — from Revolu-

tionary times to the very day of his conversation with Captain Robinson. He then noted with approval that Captain Robinson intended to "preserve a block of said timber as a memorial of those important times."[52]

The destruction of a house in Tanbrook also commanded Hiram's attention. Here, too, he attempted to reconstruct the building's lineage in an effort to recapture its history in the pages of his diary. This particular house held special memories for Hiram. His parents had been married in its east room. He had courted Rebecca Cutler and then Sally Stone in that same room. On March 19, 1815, he had wed Sally in that very same east room. Now the building and all its previous occupants had disappeared from Tanbrook; of the families linked to that house, only the Harwoods remained. Through his persistent interest in buildings, Hiram had quite unself-consciously managed to capture both the changes and the continuities so important to his own life.

Hiram's careful attention to various structures in and around Bennington actually represented a broader desire of his: to write history. As early as July 1827, when he copied the list of names of Bennington's first militia company into his journal, he confessed that not only did he take pride in recording their names, but also, were he "possessed of materials & the requisite ability for the task," he "would cheerfully devote a portion of my time to drawing up a regular history of the early settlement of this town." This was not an isolated admission; similar statements coursed throughout his diary. Following a discussion of the deaths of several longtime friends, Hiram wrote that if he had "the necessary talents & qualifications," he very much would like to write "full Biographical Sketches of my old friends & neighbors as they are taken off the state." Unfortunately, he felt that his "failures [were] very great in every respect—especially in time." Four years later, a similar refrain appeared in reference to the entrance of the first six families into Bennington, June 18, 1761: "If I am spared long enough [I] mean to enter some particulars respecting those patriarchs of Bennington." Similarly, after relating his grandfather's experience at the battle of Bennington, he noted that "perhaps I may on a future day undertake more of this." On the anniversary of the arrival of the first six families in the township, Hiram noted that "at some future time with assistance of my father I will enter their respective names & endeavor to give some particulars touching that interesting epoch of the History of this town." Finally, one evening in June 1836, as Benjamin gave a running account of the adventures of the first settlers in Bennington, Hiram mused that "an accurate account of that event & circumstances connected with it, well drawn up, would be far more useful & entertaining than anything I have entered on record in all my life."[53]

Hiram longed to write a history of Bennington. To this end he collected information on houses and families along the main street of Bennington. By February 1837 he had "completed Family Register to a certain extent" and "made out list of houses in Town Street to which annex'd dates so far as could be ascertained." This was all he was ever able to accomplish; the "failure of time" prevented any further work on the project. As a man of business, he had to abandon it.[54]

Devotion to the increasing demands of the dairy destroyed whatever hope Hiram had of writing history. The crush of business became such that Hiram went so far as to claim that he was no longer fond of spending so much time with his diary. He even claimed that "if my life should be spared I may wholly lay it aside as it excludes from my enjoyment many pleasant hours of reading which it is likely would be or might be more useful to me." The following year he complained that the "business of journalizing hung heavily on me — executed it as hastily as I could."[55] And yet, at the very time he made such statements, Hiram's journal became increasingly voluminous. His journals for the years 1833 through 1836 were half again as large as those of previous years.

Rather than illustrating how "heavily" "journalizing" hung upon him, these volumes revealed a man absorbed with his inner life, his inner desires. Though forced by the crush of business to give up many pursuits that meant so much to him throughout his life, Hiram quite unself-consciously could not abandon his love of the aesthetic. He had always noted the first "peeping" of frogs, the welcome sounds of "Bob O' Lincolns," and the appearance of sun dogs. He had he recorded many climbs up Mount Anthony with friends and family members. Now, however, his descriptions became much more expansive, much more lyrical. He noted "a most singular and curious kind of mackeral sky — beautiful beyond description." In describing a "grand eclipse of the sun which this day occurred," he wrote that "at first we began to observe it before any clouds passed over to dull the sharpness of the rays. Soon however, there were light thin clouds intervening — so curiously transparent that all that could be viewed by the naked eye was most majestically & nobly shown up while we were slowly proceeding from a point near Mapleton meeting house to the line hill — halting at short intervals to take a view of a sight so rare & imposing."[56]

Sunsets transfixed Hiram, and in his own halting way, he recognized his own appreciation of such phenomena. Viewing a particularly impressive sunset at the end of a cloudy day, he carefully noted that "it shone out just before going down — so as to give that beautiful pale crimson hue to the E. mountain which I have so often in the course of my life — with pleasure observed." Although "I am no poet, no scholar, no nothing, *but as it is*, am generally, when in tolerable health a clumsy observer of some of the more striking features of nature."[57]

Once, while on a trip to Pownal, he passed by a millpond, "principally indebted to nature for form & existence — Indeed a Novelist or Poet would be very forcibly impressed with views of this little expanse of water and the surrounding scenery. I have rarely if ever witnessed anything of the kind in my very stinted travels that would at all compare with it. Let those who dispute what is here stated go & see for themselves." Still another time Hiram recorded viewing the "most extraordinary N. Lights — displayed all evening — showing up a crimson red very much in appearance like clouds reflecting rays of the sun — either rising or setting — Its beauty & sublime grandeur no one can possibly portray."[58]

He was neither a "Novelist" nor a "Poet," but Hiram possessed similar desires and passions — repressed, perhaps, but nonetheless present. Unconsciously he lived these desires through his diary; he could never have given it up. It was the life he had long desired for himself but had to suppress in order to take charge of the family farm. In many ways, then, Hiram's outer life bore a striking resemblance to Benjamin's. His inner life, so utterly different from his father's, persisted only within the solitary confines of his diary. There alone could he express the aesthetic sensibilities — the protoromantic longings — that were such an important part of his life.

༄ Hiram's journal remained a constant in his life — a source of solace and contentment — and so did his family. Long attracted to an ideal perception of family continuity, stability, and harmony, Hiram became increasingly aware of the centrality of his own family to his sense of peace and security. Almost from the time they were married, Hiram and Sally kept their own kitchen. Consequently, whether butchering beef or salting pork and packing it into separate casks, there had always been "one for each branch of the family." However, as Benjamin and Diadama grew older and began to suffer the infirmities of age, Hiram noted with increasing frequency that "father and mother took seats at our table."[59] Gradually, Hiram was becoming the actual, if not the titular, head of the Harwood household. As a result familial relations assumed more importance for him.

Since childhood Hiram had revered his father and mother. And yet he had a very different relationship with each of them. He observed all of his father's birthdays in his journal and took pride in referring to him as "the first living white child born in Bennington"—an oft-repeated refrain. Hiram also boasted that even at the age of sixty-nine, Benjamin "performed as much labor the past year as many of the young bucks who work by the month." Several years later he described his father as in "good health, high spirits for a person of his years—sight some impaired, hearing very much so, hair extremely thin & grey—shoulders something round, but withal his step was firm & he could perform as much labor in a day as any man in these parts of same age."[60]

Hiram rarely revealed as much emotion in his diary as the day his father fell into a horse stall and suffered "many heavy dreadful blows." When George P., who was nearby, managed to drag Benjamin to safety, Hiram recalled that "to all appearance he was a lifeless corpse—at any rate such was my impression, and my feeling at that critical moment I shall not attempt to describe." For several hours it appeared to Hiram that his father was dying. Dr. Heman Swift arrived very quickly and "for awhile felt seriously alarmed" and prayed with the family while administering brandy to his patient. "During most of this period of intense watchfulness & heart rending anxiety," Hiram noted that "the members of the family generally preserved great calmness & resignation—to this remark my own feeling & behavior formed a reprehensible exception." Happily, Benjamin emerged from this experience with only severe cuts and bruises about his head and several broken ribs that prevented him from lying down without suffering terrible pain. When he retired at the end of the day, even though his father was out of danger, Hiram "could get no rest during great part of the night."[61]

No such heartfelt anxieties appeared in the diary with respect to his mother; Hiram never mentioned her birthday, nor did he ever give the sort of tender physical descriptions of her that characterized his portrayals of his father. Such lapses might stand as mute testimony to the depth of Hiram's patriarchal beliefs—another link with an idealized past. Nonetheless, though often noting, "mother very ill—greatly distressed for breath." Hiram never expressed much concern. When, for example, Dr. Swift came down early one evening to give Diadama a puke, he left shortly thereafter. By 2:00 A.M. she was still suffering great distress, and Hiram went for the doctor again. "He came without hesitation & his measures produced almost immediate relief." Hiram then concluded the incident by writing only that "much praise is due this faithful physician for his promptitude & kindness on this occasion in particular as well as many others."[62]

Hiram's notations relating to his mother generally involved arguments. On one occasion he "disputed with mother on the question of acquiring riches — for which I was an advocate." Another time, when Hiram "got home a little after dark . . . a warm debate took place between Mr S.[outhworth], myself and our good mother, respecting the pending election of representative for the town of Bennington." Hiram intended to vote for Hiland Hall, in opposition to Dr. Noadiah Swift, whom Diadama supported without reservation.[63]

Another time, when Diadama, "showing her great respect for the memory of my late paternal grandfather," declared Peter to be " 'a likelier man than any son he ever left behind him,' " Hiram, unwilling to accept such criticism of his father, claimed this to be "more than I am willing to allow, however highly I revere his [Peter's] good name." However, out of respect for his mother and the memory of his dead grandfather, Hiram was unwilling to detail his own opinion on the matter. Rather than vent his true feelings about Peter, Hiram closed the incident with the simple declaration: "More I say not."[64]

Hiram's journal observations about Sally, although much warmer and certainly more intimate than those relating to his mother, contained something of the same ambivalence or irony that characterized his notations about Diadama. He quite often mentioned that "with my dear & my daughter rode to Hinsdill's" or that "I with Mrs. Harwood took a moon light walk." Although always taking note of Sally's birthday, he usually inserted an observation to the effect that "my fair partner arrived this day at age 34 healthy & able to perform business about house." Wedding anniversaries, too, received dutiful notice: "Nine years since my wedding"; "my wedding day was on the 19th March, 1815, not sick of that bargain yet — though it should be pronounced [by most] a poor one — I never considered it so"; "being anniversary of my wedding day — 1815 — many pleasant allusions were uttered by my lady & self bearing on the doings of that period — not sick of the bargain yet, calculating to hold on at least another year." Sally, "the partner with whom I was united in March 1815 is as near being what she ought as any other female the world could produce, taking into consideration all my oddities, faults & circumstances in life — in a word she leaves me nothing to wish on that score."[65]

There never was any doubt that Sally did indeed know full well how to deal with all Hiram's "faults" and "oddities." She rarely if ever gave in to his demands. On one occasion, while en route to Hoosick, Hiram recalled "a curious kind of dispute that happened on this occasion between me & my dear who refused doing as I desired her." Another time, "past noon — returned to house with idea of going to town — in shaving cut up a scab that made me bleed — felt vexed at being hindered by so trivial an affair." Worse, when he "called for a clean shirt — a close rummaging ensued — all because my better half was absent at Mrs. Kent's — the right one was not found — made it do with a wrong one." When "the real woman appeared & offered to correct the matter," Hiram, "being under no moderate excitement, refused her interference." He then "tried to reason on the subject to show up how contemptible a man must needs appear thus hampered when taking leave in haste — but she laughed at me & promised no reform." Still another time Hiram wrote that he "shall relate an instance of heedlessness on my part — left wallet in very exposed position, had bank notes of $35." Finally, "my worthy companion after many hours found it — secured to herself $10.00 & having caused me some anxious inquiries, safely placed the remainder of the treasure in my hands with a word of caution against doing the like again."[66]

Time after time Hiram opposed Sally's wishes; time after time she got her way. Much like his father's, Hiram's sway stopped well short of the domestic hearth. One mid-September day, for example, Hiram declared it to be too early in the season to set up the stove. The following morning the "stove was brought from other house & set up in this house this morning." All Hiram could say was that he "was not over condescending in this thing." That same day the "bedstead set up & restored in its place — here again, I refused to act — thinking it might be put over to more convenient time." Sally simply had one of the hired men serve as "chief engineer." Once, when a friend stopped by who "solicited & got leave from me to have a drink of cider — the ladies would not agree to it in any shape — having learned that he was already full enough — no room for more." The man left without receiving any cider from the Harwoods.[67]

He was occasionally at odds with Sally, but Hiram nonetheless relied on her companionship and good judgment. A friend once confessed to

Hiram that whenever he made a "bad business bargain he [kept] it totally from his wife" and "entrust[ed] very few secrets to his wife that touch[ed] on his affairs." Such behavior was entirely foreign to Hiram. He responded that "when I had got into a twist of that nature, my weakness caused me to disclose it for the sake of getting help to bear up under my troubles."[68]

Just as Sally was, most of the time, a source of comfort and support to Hiram, so, too, were his children. A special bond had existed between Hiram and Adeline since shortly after her birth. He took her with him into the fields and on short trips. During the brief time she attended Castleton Academy, Hiram anxiously visited the post office in hopes of receiving a letter from her. He himself sat up late at night to write to her. When Adeline wrote saying how "eagerly my [Hiram's] letters were sought after by her friends," Adeline "supposed George would say she was soaping me here." In any event, Hiram sat up late to answer her letter and made it a point to write "encouragingly & sympathetically." His correspondence with Adeline meant the world to him.[69]

Hiram had a similar relationship with Hopkins. He loved the boy dearly and worried about him while he was an infant. Typically, he observed that "my little boy suffered greatly from a bad cold — very cross" or "our little boy was quite unwell." Then, after "our little Hopkins was rigged out in boys' clothes," Hiram swelled with pride when Dr. Swift "saw him & gave him a compliment." Neither could he resist noting that when Sally was absent for a time, "H. Hopkins was very good." Often, when Hiram took the horse and wagon on a short trip, "my little boy went with me." When "young Hiram Hopkins for the first time in his life" attended school, Hiram was happy to note the "he could read & spell his abbs." When Hiram read to him from Shakespeare's *Richard III*, "Hopkins seemed to be pleased with the old Bard."[70]

When his son turned twelve, Hiram described Hopkins as "thoughtless, full of play, fine enough yet." Still, Hiram existed in relation to Hopkins in much the same manner that Benjamin had toward him years earlier. Hopkins, too, was an only son and would inherit the farm one day. Like Benjamin before him, Hiram had to ready his son to assume the role of patriarch. Hiram was therefore a bit disturbed when "Hopkins gave himself up to playthings far below his years, nor could I get a book into his hands except by the most positive command, and then it was soon laid aside." Although Hopkins inherited his father's love of music, this did not entirely please Hiram. Despite his father's disapproval, Hopkins continually "amused himself in low songs, such as 'Long tail blue' 'Black Rose' & some light buffoonery in the evening caught up at caravans & elsewhere."[71]

Despite whatever setbacks he suffered in his efforts to guide his son's musical preferences, Hiram felt a constant obligation to discipline Hopkins in other more important ways. When Benjamin requested that Hopkins accompany him to the East Village, "Hopkins hated to go in the very worst way — but on my telling him there was no retreating, no backing out — he went with rather bad grace." Hiram "insisted more upon this thing because I wanted to gratify father in his wish — meant to have my son see it in that light also." It was important to Hiram that Hopkins show the proper respect for his elders — a tradition much revered by the Harwoods through past generations. Consequently, upon observing Benjamin piling wood under a nearby shed, Hiram was "sorry to say that Hopkins was with him, but stood aloof, offering or giving *now* & *then* very feeble assistance." For such "unkind, undutiful, & disobedient behavior [Hopkins] received a Lecture from his father in plain terms." Another time Hopkins "worked much at cleaning & oiling harness." When "his task became so galling in the evening as to produce tears," Hiram "endeavored to allay his grief — without much apparent effect." Nonetheless, like his father before him, Hiram could not give in; he must prepare his son to follow in the patriarchal tradition of the Harwoods. This meant, above all else, hard work and self-discipline.[72]

During the infancy of Adeline and Hopkins, Sally and Hiram received much help and support from Hiram's sisters Lydia and Damia. Lydia, who never married, became Sally's best help around the dairy and the house. She also assumed the major burden of caring for her mother, who suffered from chronic respiratory problems that often incapacitated her for days on end. When free of such responsibilities, Lydia loved to take part in social gatherings with Sally and Hiram or simply to take long walks with them around the farm. She became like a sister to Sally and was always a loving aunt to Adeline and Hopkins.

By the time Hiram and Sally became involved in their commercial dairy operation, Damia had become a seamstress. Even though actively involved with the dairy, Hiram always found time to procure needed materials for his sister and to help her keep her accounts.[73] In the summer of 1829, Hiram happily reported that a local dentist "performed an operation in his line on the jaws and teeth of our sister D. insetting a row of artificials in front — improving her looks & speech greatly." It was a little over a year after this operation that Damia and Hiram Waters had their marriage banns posted at the Baptist meeting-house in the East Village. On February 1, 1831, Elder Teasdell of the Baptist church married them in the "North Room" of the Harwood home. Since no civil authorities were involved and only close friends and relatives attended the ceremony, there was no second-day wedding. Instead, "cake and wine were pretty liberally distributed" to all, and "the comp'y afterwards tho' small indulged themselves in kissing & running round the chimney at no moderate rate." Hiram could not have been happier; the entire event "turned out to be just such a wedding as we wished it to be."[74]

After the wedding, Damia and her husband lived with the Harwoods for several months. During this time Damia went to Troy to purchase furniture with the money she had earned as a seamstress. When the couple moved into Hiram Waters' house in the village, their home became a gathering place for the Harwoods, who had always been close with the Waters family; the Harwoods had employed Hiram and his father as carpenters for years. Upon their marriage, then, Damia and Hiram Waters became an integral part of an extended family. Often, when Hiram stopped by to visit his brother-in-law's carpentry shop, he found Lydia and Adeline there helping Damia in her new home. Long accustomed to the warmth of Damia's company, Adeline visited her aunt whenever she felt "lonesomeness"; much to her joy, she lived with the Waterses while she attended the Brick Academy. Hiram, too, felt comfortable in the Waterses' home. Once, upon being asked to share a bit about his youth, Hiram "gave a little sketch of my life — calling myself a bad boy when young — deserving and getting many floggings from my mother." Then, in the confidential atmosphere of the Waters home, he confessed to having "enjoyed life best and most happily from 15 to 20 etc." — the years before assuming larger responsibilities about the farm.[75]

In March of 1834, Hiram Waters lost his shop and tools to a fire that damaged his house to such an extent that it was uninhabitable. Hiram immediately invited the unfortunate couple to come live with his family, loaned his friend Waters $54, and subscribed an additional $20 when Noadiah Swfit circulated a subscription paper to help the Waters family. Finally, in November, Damia and her husband moved back into the portion of their house that was not destroyed by fire.

The Harwoods extended the same hospitality to Hiram's Uncle Clark when he came to live with them in March 1825. He stayed for over three years, working at odd jobs of carpentry, tinkering with the perpetual motion machine that he hoped to invent, and drinking. Finally, by December 1828, it was "judged to be most prudent, as he owed some small sums, to load up and be off." Although Hiram was "for having everyone pay his honest debts if he be able — This was not the case with our uncle." Hiram "was anxious to get him off without being beset by constables and sheriffs — If his creditors must lose it would be no worse for them than for me — I presume I could find a balance in my favor against him of not much short of $20. — perhaps considerably higher than that." In any event, Hiram loaded his Uncle Clark with most of his carpenter's tools into a two-horse wagon and set out on a night darker than any Hiram could remember. After several days' driving through cold, stormy weather, Hiram left Clark at Silas Harwood's home in Rupert, Vermont.[76]

This was not the last time Hiram heard from his uncle. Within a matter of months, Clark once again began to make claims on the estate of his father, Peter. Benjamin left it entirely to Hiram to handle this business. Hiram dealt with the problem by consulting with a local attorney, who assured him that Uncle Clark "had not the shadow of a claim on the estate of the late Peter Harwood." Two years later Hiram received a letter from one of Clark's sons claiming that his father was doing badly and that he had expended much of his own property to help him. He then stated his belief that his father had not received a proper share of Peter's estate and asked that ten dollars be sent immediately and "perhaps more later, until he could get money for his work." Hiram immediately replied that Clark had received everything and more of his portion of the estate and that he "possessed not the shadow of a claim." Further, "if his children are unable to do more for him, the town of R.[utland] must take him in hand. He has no claim here equitably or lawfully, therefore his solicitations will avail him nothing." Before mailing this letter, Hiram was careful to make a copy, which he saw "safely preserved" with an "acquittance" that Uncle Clark had signed at Castleton, Vermont, October 1816 and renewed June 4, 1823, "acknowledging that he, Clark Harwood, the father of my cousin, had rec'd his full share of his father Peter Harwood's real & personal estate." Hiram's letter "was a plain piece of blunt composition — flatly denying the validity of my good uncle's pretended claim upon this estate — went pretty warmly through the whole — Shall say no more than to refer to the copy and to said Acquittance, the last being lodged with the old Will in the large desk."[77]

Four years after this incident, Hiram received a letter from Clark's neighbors in West Rutland claiming that he was sick and unable to work. He had been deserted by his son and kept from being a charge on the town only by the liberal charity of his neighbors. The letter "prayed in respectful terms assistance from his brother." The letter also stated in a postscript that Clark "had entirely left off habit of drinking ardent spirits." Upset about his uncle's condition, Hiram conferred with his cousin Nathan Robinson about the matter. After viewing the letter, Nathan "pronounced the begging part very handsome" and informed Hiram that an acquaintance had told him that a friend of Clark's had offered to take the old man in for a period of two years but that Clark had refused to go with him. With that the two men let the matter rest. Two months later Clark died.[78]

Through his experiences with the Waters family and his Uncle Clark, Hiram became increasingly aware of the responsibilities shouldered by the head of a household. When Albert Harwood, Ira's only son, came to visit the Harwoods, he was particularly interested in viewing the dairy house, where his parents had lived when he was born. After showing his cousin through the old house, Hiram hunted up letters written by Ira and Jonas to their father. Albert "request[ed] me to present them to him—but for sound reasons refused to." Hiram meant to protect the estate in any way he could—no matter how tenuous the threat.[79]

By this time Hiram had assumed full responsibility for the care of the farm. Further, he had been elected highway surveyor, petit juror, and justice of the peace for the town of Bennington. Most significantly, when Joseph Hinsdill published a minutely detailed map of the township of Bennington—a map so detailed that every building in the town appeared with the name of its proprietor's beside it—he placed the name "H. Harwood" beside the symbol representing the Harwood farm. Clearly, the townspeople of Bennington recognized Hiram as head of the Harwood household. To their minds at least, Hiram had finally achieved the position demanded of him by Harwood family tradition. But at what cost?

⌣ 9

A Miserable Man

About midday while at work accidentally dropp'd my hat in the brook — left it to dry in the sun — continuing busy all the while, raking hay — being sensible every few moments that the rays of the noon day sun played powerfully upon my bear head which was but poorly defended by the thin crop of hair it bore — rendered still worse by late shearing. Lost no time in getting the hat & placing it on my head — came to watering trough without experiencing any uncommon feeling — Washed and made for the house — began to have queer sensations, which by the time I entered the kitchen door amounted nearly to fainting — Marched through S. room to the front door — seated myself on threshold — drank camphorated spirits & water — had the same plentifully applied externally to the cranium & got over it. The ladies managed, for which they receive my acknowledgments. From the manner in which this fainting was brought on — must own I was once alarmed.[1]

Although he was terribly shaken by his fainting spell, this was not the first time that Hiram had suffered physical distress. Ever since the night two years earlier when he experienced a life-threatening mishap during his frenzied drive to Berlin, New York, he had been plagued with pain. Several weeks after that mishap, he "was seized with violent pain in the eyeballs." Suffering from constant headaches as well, he visited Dr. Noadiah Swift, who listened attentively, felt his pulse, and gave him some pills. By the first of April, Hiram was still "plagued with sore head"; he had been suffering "so more or less for some time past." Finally, in early May, Dr. Heman Swift explained to Hiram the cause of his discomfort: he suffered from a damaged nerve resulting from the accident he experienced while driving to Berlin, New York, the previous year.[2]

Learning Swift's diagnosis did nothing to remove Hiram's discomfort. One evening, having endured headaches for some time, he "vomited like a horse" while suffering "great pain in eyeballs." Another time, after taking heavy cheeses down from the shelves in the dairy house, he lamented that "the exertion I made very sensibly affected me afterward." In addition, two entries in his journal indicated that Hiram was aging prematurely. The first came when he encountered several young strangers on the road who "remarked that I walked smart for an old gentleman." Upon hearing this, Hiram asked them how old they believed him to be. When they said they thought he was sixty, he replied that "I knew my look would warrant that but I was just a bit over 48." The following year, a visiting peddler persisted in addressing Hiram as "Uncle" and, "when inquiring for me of family said where's 'The Old Man.'"[3]

There was nothing Hiram and his family could do about his aged appearance — which continued to confound them — but they did employ a number of remedies to ease the pain resulting from his physical ailments. To counteract "a sort of trouble that had been felt many weeks," Hiram had his head "bathed in camphor & brandy." When he suffered from an aching jaw, Sally "applied scorched tow, cider brandy & ginger bound on with silk handkerchief," which Hiram considered "instantly efficacious." Another time, when Hiram suffered "ague in left under jaw," he spent an entire morning heating his feet by the stove.[4]

In Hiram's opinion, this last course of action was not simply a home remedy. His wide reading, which included any and every medical book he could obtain, led him to Benjamin Rush's work on the mind, from which he inferred that it was possible to ease pain in the upper parts of the body by heating the lower extremities. In his discussion of remedies for hypochondriasis, Rush had in fact mentioned the "excitement of pain." Here he maintained that once the pain of gout had been "fixed" in the hands or feet, the "hypochondriac gout which floated in [the] nerves and brain" disappeared. So, too, did blisters on the skin create "a centrifugal direction of the fluids" that relived the distress caused by hypochondriasis.[5]

Although particularly fascinated with Rush's book, Hiram had an insatiable appetite for medical literature. It was not unusual for him to browse through medical books whenever he visited Heman or Noadiah

Swift's office. So interested was he in current medical knowledge that he subscribed to the *Journal of Health*, a magazine dispensing medical advice on a wide range of problems.[6] He was also familiar with *The Botanical Thomsonian Advocate*, a newspaper printed in nearby Troy, which acquainted him with Samuel Thomson and his various cures. A good many of his friends practiced Thomsonian methods, and Hiram made an effort to remain current with their practices and beliefs.[7] Whatever the source, Hiram remained ever alert to new medical advice that he might apply to his own circumstances.

More than all the other medical problems that interested him, Hiram developed a marked preoccupation with material dealing with hypochondriasis.[8] He often "found steady employment in the perusal of Dr. Johnson on Hypochondrias & Dyspepsy" and spent hours poring over the Rees *Cyclopedia* entry for "hypochondriasis."[9] Mention of the "hypo" had appeared throughout his journal for years. Once, when an acquaintance was "said to be under great concern of mind," Hiram and his friends presumed the malady "originated from a hypochrondical affection." When another friend "unburdened his mind to us," Hiram "strongly recommended to him the practice of temperance & industry as a wholesome remedy for the hypo." It was not unusual for Hiram to record feeling "an uneasiness of mind which is much better imagined than described, by so attacked persons." In fact, "within the last 12 mo's had suffered largely in this hypochrondical way."[10]

Although Hiram had endured periods of hypo for many years and had suffered excruciating discomfort since his accident on the night of October 28, 1835, these were but preludes to what he underwent after the fainting spell he experienced while raking hay July 29, 1837. Three days after that attack, he set out with his father and Hopkins to bring hay in from their south field. Immediately, Hiram "found myself unfit for business." Upon her father's premature return to the house, Adeline rushed off to fetch a doctor. When Heman Swift arrived later in the day, he spoke encouragingly respecting Hiram's condition and left more pills for him to take.[11]

If the doctor's visit cheered Hiram's family members, their relief was short-lived. The next morning inaugurated a "day of tribulation" for Hiram. He often "felt as if my time was but short." Only "those who have been distress'd in the same manner may conceive something of an idea of the unhappy situation in which I was placed." His discomfort was not, however, constant; "intervals of calmness and composure did take place, for which I ought to be truly thankful." In addition, "the

care & attention of my help-mate as well as others of the family shall
be duly acknowledged." At no time was Hiram "reduced to feeble-
ness of body. It was more in mind—occasioned by nervous affection—
proceeding from the left part of the lower projection of the head in
the neighborhood of the neck—running down to the stomach, producing . . . frightful sensations . . . including chill & slight cramp."
Hiram felt his strength to be "quite full—could walk firmly & with
ease," and yet "in time of agitation—heart beat high & unusually quick
throwing me into a perfect tremor in spite of all the fortitude & good
sense (in both—always greatly deficient) I could rally." Panicked by the
"frightful sensations" he experienced, Hiram feared himself to be in
imminent danger and suffered from feelings of impending doom.[12]

The following day brought no relief. Unable to work, Hiram drove
into town with his sister Damia. When she went into a store in search
of calico, Hiram remained in the wagon, "uncertain whether to step in
or not—felt rather chilly—suspicious of experiencing an attack." He
chose instead to walk toward the printing office, but no sooner had he
done so than "my heart failed me." As he returned toward the store, he
met an old friend, with whom he attempted to converse, only to suffer a
disconcerting lapse in memory. He quickly faced "rightabout & cut
lively for the store," where, after "taking a few turns across the floor,"
his eyesight began to blur. Fortunately, Damia was ready to leave, and
Hiram made it home without further incident.[13]

Shortly after arriving at the farm, however, Hiram experienced "a
severe fit of *hypo* sat down & wrote Jour'l awhile—my hand unsteady
from strong excitement." In an attempt to calm himself, he "took flute
& performed many old airs which so allayed my troubled thoughts that
I felt almost like another being." He "imagined also that bathing affected parts of my head in vinegar had a most happy tendency in restoring it to its wonted condition." Later that evening Heman Swift returned and, after talking at length on the politics of the day, left some
additional medicine for Hiram before returning home.[14]

Throughout the next two weeks, Hiram continued to experience
"some depression," "high capers in hypo," and a "return of melancholy." Whenever he could, he conversed about "nervous complaints"
with supportive friends and neighbors. At the same time, though, he
made every effort to maintain his equilibrium and to lift his spirits by
continuing to maintain a close accounting of the dairy business. This
became troublesome when he began to experience difficulty in sleeping. He would often suffer "a restless night with colick pains—no dis-

position to sleep." After enjoying some relief following a "bad night with colick," Hiram "passed tolerably comfortable day, tho' at intervals highly wrought upon in imagination."[15]

Whenever he could, Hiram also attempted to work around the farm. From time to time he helped at cutting and raking hay. Unfortunately, it was common — as on the occasion that he used a scythe — for him to report that afterward he experienced a "severe attack of hypo." Nonetheless, he continued to try; at times he even seemed to gain some comfort from these efforts. One day he "came home & passed the day pretty quietly, seeing the ladies make cheese and the men & boys mow barley — even handled scythe myself a few moments." The very next day, though, Hiram "was miserably nervous & unhappy almost the livelong day." Worse, when he took a morning walk, he became "sensible of increasing weakness of limbs." Alarmed by this, he returned to the barn and asked George P. to weigh him. When he "pulled down no more than 132 lbs.," Hiram knowingly remarked: "See Jan31." On that date he weighed 151 pounds. What caused such a precipitous loss of weight in just six months puzzled him.[16]

The same day that Hiram had George weigh him, the "operation of medicine or something caused all tremor possible." He managed to "still it however at times by walking the floors — visiting the barn — visiting the mowers." All the while, he "underwent dreadful apprehensions." Later that same day, his sister Damia visited with her baby. Acutely aware of Hiram's distress, she "said much to me by way of encouragement & it did cheer me not a little." Damia simply "would not give it up but that I should surely recover." She said that Hiram "must pluck up & with lady & children visit Old Connecticut this Fall." Shortly after his sister's visit, Hiram managed to eat a full meal and encouraged himself with the thought "Let us hope for better days." Later, when Noadiah Swift, informed of Hiram's "unhappy feelings," stopped by, he said that "I had some fever, had lost much strength, my stomach greatly deranged, but fully believed he could help me." The good doctor concluded by telling Hiram that "as to the final result, [he] felt no doubt but that it would be favorable."[17]

Despite the encouraging words spoken to him by Damia and Dr. Swift, "the night which followed was a most disturbed one to me. Very little rest." As a consequence, the following morning Hiram felt "extremely reduced . . . after passing so restless a night." Indeed, "it was sometime before I could bring myself to take repose which I did about noon." Later that same afternoon, he visited with a neighbor and his wife, who was "much emaciated from complaint like mine. She knew the whole story in relation to such cases." Both agreed that they suffered from a nervous disorder.[18]

The following day Dr. Heman Swift and Hiram Waters made a "friendly call." After talking some on politics, the doctor "felt my pulse — said it was nearly regular — reasoned upon the nature of my complaint — ordered some change of medicine — gave strong assurance of recovery." That evening, with Sally's kind assistance, "an anodyne plaster [a warm, herb-filled wrap] was tried with excellent effect between the left part of the head & collar bone." As a result, Hiram "went to bed more quiet than usual."[19]

Such peace did not last. The following day, in an attempt to calm his nerves, Hiram took two walks to watch the men mow thistles. During the second trip, he suffered "a sort of affright which required all my resolution to suppress." Still, he "fancied myself, notwithstanding these little disturbances, to be doing well." The next day, however, he "gave way to a weak fit of hypo early in the evening — soon over it." The following day, too, Hiram "suffered some in mind & body too," but, in an effort to maintain some semblance of calm, he declared that "it's not worth while to write much of it."[20]

Even while suffering such distress, Hiram continued to keep a close eye on the cheese market and persevered in his attempts at physical labor about the farm. On one occasion he helped George P. and Hopkins rake hay for a brief time but "came away both on account of inefficiency & helping the ladies put cheese in press." That same day he "sawed more old rails — otherwise my behaviour was disgraceful. Very unhappy." The next day, too, "was gloomy to me — felt very uneasy — had a tightness about the lungs — a sort of sly tickling in that region which kept me continually dissatisfied with myself." Struggling still to keep up his flagging spirits in the face of physical decline, he observed, "No matter, no matter let it pass." Then, in a desperate effort to exert the power of mind over matter, he declared: "Conceit can cure — Conceit can kill." Nonetheless, it was "late in the evening before I was quiet."[21]

The next day Hiram sawed wood for a brief time and helped cut oats. As a result he "felt very weak in the morning — ate meals regularly — grew better." Later that same day, however, when his father, George, and Hopkins became agitated over their inability to find the family's horses, Hiram "grew very uneasy." When his distress worsened, family members summoned Heman Swift, who arrived and ordered a different set of pills. Despite the doctor's efforts, the following morning Hiram "was in the usual restless discouraging way." Worse, he was "saying and doing all manner of foolish things." Greatly alarmed by this, family members did all in their power to calm him: "Every comfortable word that could be thought of was said to me — without doing any good." After dinner Hiram "experienced a very unhappy train of thought, occasioned by nervous sensibility." Sally applied another anodyne plaster, which allayed his distress somewhat. Consequently "the remainder of the P.M. passed very quietly — comparatively speaking." In an effort to maintain this peaceful feeling, Hiram played the flute and fleshed out the record of his visit to New York City in October 1836. Despite the relative calm of the afternoon, Hiram kept "up all hands late, I had fidgets."[22]

The following day Heman Swift visited Hiram, read to him from the *New York American*, left some different medicine, and "exhorted me to have patience, calmness & fortitude in meeting my complaint." Nonetheless, that night it was "long before sleep came to my relief." The next day, still struggling with severe uneasiness, Hiram milked two cows in the evening but could do no more. Despite such efforts to overcome his distress, Hiram began to fear the worst. One Sunday Benjamin did not attend church but instead took a walk with Hiram, whose "spirits [were] very low." During this time Hiram talked with Benjamin "on an interesting subject." His father responded that he would "fulfil my request if the event I anticipated should take place." Apprehensive that he did not have long to live, Hiram had asked Benjamin to care for Sally, Adeline, and Hopkins after his death. Perhaps fearful that to write the word itself would be to acknowledge the finality of the condition against which he struggled so desperately, "death" became "an interesting subject" in Hiram's journal.[23]

As Hiram became increasingly depressed, his family and close network of friends throughout the community did all that was in their power to support and encourage him. On the day he walked with his father, "all the family spoke encouragingly to me." Dr. Heman Swift also "came down & spoke very confident of my case." The following day Hiram visited Diadama, "who spoke cheerily." That same day he also encountered William Haswell, "who exhorted me to throw aside all bad impressions — be not discouraged & I should get well." After completing a sale to Hiram at his store, N. L. Robinson "came out and encouraged me." Hoping that Hiram's old love of music might help bring him out of his depression, Hiram Waters borrowed a violin and brought it to Hiram. "Some of the young fellows of the neighborhood came in to hear me try to make music."[24]

Such efforts proved fruitless; Hiram continued to sink deeper into depression. The day after playing the violin, he noted little more than weather conditions in his journal and then recorded that he was "not able to write more at this time."[25] For the first time since he began keeping the journal, nearly thirty years before, Hiram began to omit daily entries. He missed three days, wrote jagged cryptic comments, and then failed to make an entry for nine straight days. Alarmed by Hiram's mood, family members summoned Reverend Hooker to pay a visit and to pray with him.

Hiram believed that Hooker supplied him with "some excellent advice as to both spiritual & Temporal affairs — to be what I ought in the former & be resigned to whatever should take place in the latter." Although satisfying in some respects, Hooker's visit awakened feelings that had long concerned Hiram — feelings arising from the state of his unconverted soul. On the Sunday following Hooker's visit, Hiram made an unusual entry in his journal, one he had never previously recorded: "By the blessing of kind Providence we were enabled to make during the month of Sept. past Lbs 2628 cheese as weighted from the press — whole weight pres't season amounted to Lbs 15124 — Exceeding last year by 24 lbs up to same date." He had never before related the "blessing of kind Providence" to the family's dairy business, and he had most assuredly never stated anything like his final observation of the day: "This entry [made on the Sabbath] of worldly concerns has taken place inadvertently — beg it may [be] pardoned by the Same Great & Good Being who preserves our lives from day to day tho' we can see no reason why it should be so."[26]

Spiritual thoughts remained very much on Hiram's mind the following day when a young acquaintance from Troy passed away. Observing that "she died calmly & resigned in the firm belief that she should go to a world of Happiness & rest," Hiram had no doubt such would come to pass because she "was a professor of Christianity & left good evidence that she was a Possessor [of God's saving grace]."[27] The fact that he had never experienced such grace and was not a "possessor" himself troubled Hiram.

Although the state of his soul never left Hiram's mind, his other troubles remained omnipresent as well. "These are most discouraging times. No offers for dairy. No good prospects in regard to health. As these records prove my abilities — Where gone?" Upon tallying the total earned by the dairy the previous year, Hiram noted that it exceeded thirteen hundred dollars. Unfortunately, there was "no prospect like it now." Not only did Hiram believe the dairy to be in serious trouble; he also considered his "actual situation to be most dangerous." But Hiram's parents did not believe his condition to be precarious; whenever he spoke of his condition as life-threatening, "my folks differ from me." To them it was all "hypo."[28]

Then early in October, Hiram concluded a journal entry with a cry of "O' my right leg." The next day, "besides wailing & lamenting about sore leg," he perused the Bible. Struggling desperately to lift his own spirits, Hiram also reviewed entries made in his diary throughout the previous year — all of which "reminds me of better days." And yet he mournfully concluded: "Of what use to write that my decayed constitution stuck close by me. Perhaps might have once more got up the hill, if, if, if it had not been for the leg." Then, observing that he "ought to be resigned to my fate," Hiram admitted that he "can't toast so much." Fearing death to be eminent, Hiram's unconverted soul continued to haunt him.[29]

Tortured by his spiritual state of mind, Hiram was certain that "my condition & prospects [were] no better." His leg continued to plague him. One night he "retired about the usual hour — exercised with excruciating torments in the right leg above the knee." His mother "& all the rest of the family were fully satisfied it was more than half hypo." For his part, Hiram lamented: "I wish they had been right." At the same time, always "religiously resigned to the will of Providence," his father spoke seriously to Hiram on the subject of religion. Nonetheless, Hiram "wore out the folks making my moans — and of what use was it. The fates were against me."[30]

Suffering increased physical pain and sinking into an ever more troubled state of mind, Hiram became convinced that not only the fates, but the times, too, conspired against him. As the mental and physical strain he suffered intensified, so, too, did the suspicions he had long harbored about the cheese agents with whom he had dealt over the years. Finally he gave way to his worst fears. Declaring the "times very uncertain," Hiram exclaimed that "the merchants of capital now have a grand chance of getting the farmers so deeply indebted to them as to sweep their farms from under them, soon or later."[31] Not only did Hiram's physical condition plague him; he now imagined that the farm itself — the Harwood family's very reason for being and the means

whereby Hiram had struggled so long to establish his own manhood—
was in danger of being lost.

He was helpless to prevent this, and his mental condition worsened.
He "saw no enlivening prospects—saw very bad night." And still the
rest of the family "think it mostly hypo on my part." Wistfully, he
wrote: "I think I am correct—hope I am not." Still, he experienced only
personal distress. "The state of my health may be gathered from appearance of hand writing—which pain & inquietude can never improve."[32] Then, to a man dreadfully fearful of falling prey to hypochondriasis, the worst of all possible events occurred; Hopkins accidentally
struck him in the stomach while vigorously swinging a jacket about.
Hiram concluded that he could "expect nothing but pain & misery
from this."[33]

While friends and family continued to talk to him about "hypo,"
Hiram grew progressively worse; he gradually slipped into a state of
hopeless despondency. On the day before his forty-ninth birthday, he
and his father walked together over the southwest part of the farm.
This "worried my right knee & ankle most terribly" and "deprived [me]
of almost night's rest." In the face of his suffering, the family still
"referred all to imagination—never would hurt me." The following
day Hiram turned forty-nine. In his entry on this date—the last he ever
made in the journal—Hiram referred to himself as a "miserable man—
no peace—no contentment in any spot." He was "happily situated
too as any reasonable man could wish—But to such despair was I by
indisposition driven."[34] "Indisposition"—physical weakness—silenced
Hiram's journal. It also prevented him from fulfilling his responsibilities to the farm and to his family. Without these—the farm, his family,
and his diary had been vital to Hiram's very perception of himself as a
man—Hiram sank into a hopeless sense of despair.

᭘ Several weeks after making his final journal entry, Hiram, accompanied by several friends, traveled across the mountains to Brattleboro, where he entered the Vermont Asylum for the Insane. Upon
their return to Bennington, Hiram's friends must have been filled with
hope for his speedy recovery. The asylum, consisting of a commodious
three-story frame house surrounded by fifty acres of farm land, did
indeed resemble the "cheerful country residence" promised in the circular published throughout the state upon the opening of the institution less than a year earlier. Better still, it included a small library con-

taining a selection of newspapers and magazines.[35] Surely this would please their friend; perhaps it might even bring him that peace of mind they so wished for him.

Although the asylum's circular promised a comfortable living environment, it held out something far more important to Hiram's friends and family: the belief that "*in the first three months of insanity, the chances of recovery by proper treatment, are vastly greater than at any subsequent period.*"[36] Buoyed up by this prospect, Hiram's friends must also have drawn hope from the competency and professionalism of the asylum's superintendent—Dr. William C. Rockwell. Rockwell, a graduate of Yale Medical School, had assisted Dr. Eli Todd, one of the country's leading alienists, when Todd served as superintendent of the Hartford Retreat for the Insane. Upon Todd's disabling illness and subsequent death, Rockwell had become acting superintendent at Hartford.[37] Another of the nation's foremost alienists, Dr. Samuel Woodward, had served as Rockwell's examiner at Yale Medical School, and the two worked closely together during Rockwell's time at the Hartford Retreat and afterward when Woodward became superintendent of the Worcester State Hospital.[38]

William Rockwell's experience with Dr. Todd at the Hartford Retreat, as well as his relationship with Dr. Woodward, convinced him of the efficacy of moral treatment for the insane. It was this method of therapy, with its emphasis upon humane treatment and concern for the patient's emotional and physical needs, that Rockwell intended to implement at Brattleboro.[39] Imbued with this same belief, the trustees of the asylum declared that the system of moral treatment employed at their institution incorporated kind treatment, useful employment, and wholesome discipline.[40] Further, they announced emphatically that the moral treatment practiced within the asylum emanated from the Christian principles of benevolence and kindness to all mankind.[41] Rockwell considered the institution's discipline to be "truly parental." The superintendent, who lived in the central part of the asylum building with his wife and new baby, meant this quite literally. Just as "soon as the patients are in a proper condition, they eat at our table, are received into our parlor, join with us in our family worship, go with us to church, — in a word are members of our family."[42]

Rockwell was not alone in viewing the asylum as a large family. Woodward, too, referred to his patients as "children and kindred" and considered himself the sympathetic father of a large family.[43] Such a familial pattern was not unusual among both European and American insane asylums of the day.[44] From such a perspective, madness came to be viewed as childhood; the organizational structure of the asylum transformed the insane into minors.[45] Like children, the insane were thought to require immediate rewards and punishments in order to shape their behavior. Consequently, the superintendent became the father figure from whom the patients were to accept without question all such favors and punishments. Ironically, the family model being practiced within the asylums revived the prestige of patriarchy. The superintendent was not a modern father at all; he assumed the character of an eighteenth-century patriarch.

In addition to kind treatment, Rockwell, drawing upon his years of experience, considered useful labor to be a desirable means of restoring good health to his patients. From his perspective, inactivity on the part of his patients was counterproductive. He was convinced that the insane, if confined without some form of employment, often "become fretful and irritable, tear their clothes, become violent and filthy, and hasten to an incurable state." But given useful employment, inmates "will then be quiet and cheerful through the day, and sleep well at night." Not only that, but "their former habits and associations will be awakened, the mind and body will be invigorated, and reason will often be restored."[46] Of all forms of employment, exercise in the open air was by far the best. So Rockwell encouraged his male patients to tend the garden, work in the fields, take long walks, or ride out in the asylum carriage. Females should be involved in riding, walking, and gathering flowers. When not outdoors, they might practice needlework, knitting, or reading.[47]

Religious worship also played a central role in the moral treatment propounded by Dr. Rockwell. Each evening after tea, he and his wife held a "family worship," to which they welcomed all "quiet patients." During these sessions they read passages of Scripture, sang hymns, and joined together in prayer. On Sundays Rockwell read short sermons. He claimed that "the effect of these exercises on the patients" was "highly salutary, and has shown that they are no less a means of cure than gratification to them." At these sessions, most were "very quiet and attentive, and several have begun to exercise that self-control which has resulted in their restoration."[48] In addition to these family gatherings, Rockwell had the third floor of the mansion converted into a chapel, where "those who are in a suitable condition attend church on the Sabbath."[49] Attendance at all religious services was entirely voluntary.

Invitations to family worship and the freedom to attend Sunday services in the chapel depended on Rockwell's classification scheme, which divided patients into "noisy" and "quiet" categories according to their behavior. The granting or denial of certain privileges to individual patients depended entirely upon their demeanor. "In order to promote their self-respect, the patients are brought forward in their classification as fast as their condition will allow, and are never returned, until after trial they have shown that they cannot control their feelings so as to retain their places."[50] Thus, in "truly parental" fashion, Rockwell rewarded "quiet" patients (complacent and orderly) by admitting them to the family table and to family worship; he denied such favors to "noisy" (unruly) patients. Like a stern father, he intended to shape the behavior of his children by meting out immediate rewards and punishments in a systematic fashion.

Convinced that moral therapy within an institutional environment was absolutely essential to the treatment of insanity, Rockwell drew upon the writings of the most influential men in the field — the Frenchmen Philippe Pinel and Jean-Etienne-Dominique Esquirol and the Englishman Francis Willis — in his efforts to perfect that approach at Brattleboro. In addition, he depended heavily upon the work of another Englishman, George Man Burrows, when dealing with not only the treatment of insanity but also its causes.[51] Rockwell firmly believed that the work of these men — as well as that of his fellow countrymen — must be brought to bear upon the problem of insanity in the United States. Convinced that "one of the greatest evils of civilization and refinement" was the "introduction of insanity," he stoutly maintained that "perhaps there is no country in which it prevails to so great an extent as in these United States." He believed that "among the greatest moral causes, are disappointed hopes and mortified pride." These resulted from the fact that in America, "where all the offices of government are open to every freeman, and where the facilities for accumulating wealth are so numerous, persons, even in humble life cherish hopes which can never be realized." Consequently, "expectations high raised are the usual precursors of disappointment, and the mortified pride thereby occasioned not unfrequently precedes insanity."[52]

When dealing with the causes of insanity, Rockwell followed the findings of Burrows and Samuel Woodward. Like them, he believed that "every mental aberration is caused by some disorder of the physical system." Because he was convinced that "the mind and body act reciprocally on each other," Rockwell firmly believed that "moral remedies assist in removing physical diseases, and physical remedies in removing mental aberration."[53] Such beliefs led Rockwell to declare forcefully, "In the pathology adopted in this Asylum, it is an axiom which has a commanding influence on its practice, that insanity is, in all cases, a corporeal disease." He therefore steadfastly believed that "insanity is frequently caused by a diseased state of the body operating through sympathy on the brain, and in almost every case when it is not caused by bodily diseases, it is greatly aggravated by them." Medicine often became essential in the successful treatment of insanity: "When we restore health to the body, we have gained an important step towards restoration to reason, and frequently the manifestations of the mind immediately become sane."[54]

To restore health to the body, Dr. Rockwell would not hesitate to employ whatever medicines he had at hand in the most aggressive manner. Like Woodward, he believed in the necessity of medical treatment to control the more violent symptoms of patients and thus bring them within the range of moral treatment. As a result, both men employed strong doses of narcotics, particularly opium and morphine, to quiet their patients and to improve their physical health so that moral treatment could have a chance to work.[55]

꧁ Upon Hiram's admission to the asylum, November 17, 1837, Dr. Rockwood interviewed both him and his friends. Apparently dating Hiram's "insanity" from his "fainting spell" of July 29, his friends (most likely George P. Harwood, Samuel Robinson, and Hiram Waters), informed Rockwell that he had been "insane" for about three months.[56] Following a conversation with Hiram, the doctor declared him to be "a striking case of hypochondria." He "thinks he has some fatal disease upon him." The doctor located his new patient in the south wing and ordered that he take his meals there as well. Rockwell then entered a confirmed diagnosis of "monomania" (a single pathological preoccupation in an otherwise sound mind) caused by "hypochondria" into the official record of the asylum.[57] In doing so he conflated the classificatory systems of Esquirol (mania, lypemania, monomania, and dementia) and Burrows (delirium, mania, melancholia, hypochondriasis, demency, and idiocy). Like his colleague Samuel Woodward, Rockwell apparently felt that little benefit accrued to the treatment of insanity from precise nosological systems.[58]

During the first two days Hiram spent at the asylum, Rockwell simply observed his behavior. He noted that his new patient spent most of his time "in walking about," was apparently "fearful of a tight room," and "thinks he shall die soon." For his part, Hiram awakened on his second day at the institution convinced he "had some fever and was afraid to eat much breakfast." He informed Rockwell that "the reason why he thought he was unwell was he slept warm." The following day Hiram wrote to friends, but he expressed strong doubts to Rockwell that he would live long enough for them to receive his letter. At this point Rockwell, convinced that Hiram's "trouble is chiefly about himself," initiated a medicinal regimen directed toward curing his patient's hypochondria. Since "nothing has passed his bowels since he came," Rockwell gave Hiram a laxative pill. In addition, he prescribed two ounces of conium maculatum to be taken three times a day with sarsaparilla syrup. The doctor had addressed Hiram's constipation with a laxative pill and his "noisy hypochondria" with a powerful narcotic. The sarsaparilla had no therapeutic value and may have been employed as a placebo or as a vehicle for administering the conium maculatum.[59]

From this time on, Hiram and his doctor increasingly talked past one another. Each man represented a distinctive mode of experiencing reality. Hiram, frightened by the physical pain he endured and confused by his mental state, spoke almost exclusively of physical problems and his imminent death; Rockwell saw and heard only the classical signs and symptoms of a particular illness. Such was the power of the concept of monomania among physicians at this time that it served as an unconscious filter whenever Rockwell visited with Hiram. It shaped his mode of listening and dominated whatever inquiries he might make about his patient's problems. As a result, all he could see were signs of the classic illness monomania brought on by the equally classic condition of hypochondriasis. It was not unusual, then, at the end of a day, for Rockwell to respond to a declaration by Hiram that he "thought he should not live the day out" with the simple statement "His bowels are more regular."[60]

Rockwell kept Hiram on the initial medication he had prescribed for two weeks. During this time he noted that his patient primarily "spends his time walking about telling of his troubles." After giving Hiram another laxative pill, Rockwell wrote with some satisfaction that "his bowels are regular." Nonetheless, the doctor also had to admit that his patient "remains much the same. Full of his hypo notions."[61]

At the end of this two-week period, Rockwell concluded that Hiram "has slowly improved since he came but still is full of his hypo notions. Thinks or says he has some disease upon him that will shortly carry him off." The basis of the doctor's statement regarding Hiram's "improvement" rested entirely on the fact that his patient's "appetite is good. Bowels regular." Given the continued presence of Hiram's "hypo notions," however, Rockwell considered it necessary to take further action. Consequently, in addition to the medicine he had already prescribed, he added tincture of stramonium, another potent narcotic, and calomel to be employed as a laxative.[62]

Over the next month, Rockwell noted with some degree of optimism that his patient was "slowly improving." Hiram corresponded regularly with Sally, Adeline, and his friends in Bennington and received a box of apples from home. One day he "split and sawed wood"; another time he "rode out." In keeping with the advice found in Burrows' *Commentaries*, Rockwell did his best during this time to gain Hiram's confidence by responding to his complaints as if they were real. Thus, on one occasion, he "applied an anodyne plaster to his neck and a wash for his knee."[63] Regardless of the "improvement" being made by Hiram, Rockwell never invited him to join the "quiet" patients at dinner with the Rockwell family or to attend their evening prayer sessions. Neither was he allowed to attend church services in the chapel. Throughout his stay at the asylum, Hiram was classified with the "noisy" patients and, like a disobedient child, denied the favors of the superintendent.

For an individual who had spent most of his adolescent and adult life struggling within the parameters of a patriarchal family situation, such treatment must have been very confusing and frustrating. To thrust Hiram—a man who had seemingly overcome these demands and achieved the status of patriarch himself—back into childhood simply intensified the anxiety and bafflement he suffered. Compounding his bewilderment was the fact that at the precise moment when he felt most concerned about the state of his eternal soul, he was denied the opportunity to attend church services. Benjamin had always encouraged Hiram, even implored him, to attend church with him; now Superintendent Rockwell not only refused his company but also denied him access to the chapel.

With the coming of the new year, Dr. Rockwell reported that Hiram "has improved for the last month but is still given to hypo." His "hypo" focused "mostly upon his losing one of his legs which he has both frozen and heated." Once again, Hiram's "improvement" stemmed from that fact that "his appetite is good and bowels regular." Rockwell was still determined to overcome Hiram's "hypo notions," which he adamantly believed resulted from a seriously disturbed digestive tract. Thus, in addition to all the previously prescribed medicines, he now included a teaspoon of yellow bark as well as tincture of lyttae (an archaic term used in England for *tinctura cantharidis*), also to be administered three times daily.[64]

The day after increasing Hiram's medication, Rockwell entered a simple notation: "Improving." Then, ten days later, Rockwell found himself compelled to make a series of quite different observations: "much as usual complaining constantly of some mishap which is going to carry him off"; "expected to go off, but applied the tinct and saved him. His leg is perishing"; "says, 'No hope for me'"; "his leg is perishing. Wrote a hypo letter to his wife. Tried to bargain with me to carry him home before he died." "Does not think he should live to get home"; "thinks his heart is ossified. His digestion is stopped . . . [and he] begins to feel death chills come over him."[65]

On the same day that Hiram reported his "ossified" heart, he wrote a letter to Dr. Rockwell revealing the deep-seated fear for the fate of his unconverted soul that had long troubled him. Terrified, he exclaimed that he " 'sincerely pray[ed] that I may be prepared in a much better manner than I now am to leave this world.' " Then, alluding to another deeply felt need — the security of familial love and support — he concluded the letter by lamenting that he would " 'always regret being torn from my family and sent here.' " In response to Hiram's plaintive letter, Rockwell simply observed, "no uncommon complaint more than usual." Indeed, the following day, Dr. Rockwell claimed that his patient "has slowly improved the past month."[66]

Hiram's letter actually expressed far more than the unprepared nature of his soul and his anguished sense of separation from his family. In a desperate attempt to explain his condition to Rockwell, in the hope that the doctor might be able to ally his physical suffering, Hiram exclaimed: " 'It was the fatal fall from wagon in Petersburg, N.Y. that the foundation of my ruin was layed. To wit, injury of nerve running down from left side of my neck into stomach, highly weakening powers of digestion. I am of that opinion.' " This was precisely the diagnosis given by Dr. Heman Swift more than a year earlier. Then, in an even more revealing statement — a statement that plumbed the depths of his lifelong struggle to achieve patriarchy — he explained that this accident occurred " 'in consequence of over anxiety to save good faith and property.' "[67] With this statement Hiram revealed the tension he had endured since initiating the dairy enterprise: to his mind, the success or failure of the Harwood farm, and with it his own success or failure as a man, depended entirely upon his efforts to conclude profitable sales of the dairy each year.

The following day brought Hiram no relief; he "spit up some 'red mixture'" and claimed to be "bleeding at the lungs and could not stand it." In addition, he "scalded his foot in the sun." Two days later, "a stick struck his leg which he thought would kill him." He also believed he had a "paralysis of the throat. Says it is a 'loud call.'" The next day Hiram "complained of his 'swallow' being stopped up." Rockwell assumed all of Hiram's complaints to be "hypo" and simply ignored them. Hiram's habit of "scalding" his foot struck the doctor as particularly eccentric. Drawing upon his past reading of Rush, Hiram assumed that this action represented a perfectly rational attempt to localize and dissipate the pain that wracked his thigh and knee. In any event, Rockwell claimed his patient to be "much as usual."[68] He seemingly remained oblivious to observations made in his own inaugural address linking insanity to the precarious nature of the American business environment. Consequently, for the doctor, Hiram's reference to his "over anxiety to save good faith and property" became just another manifestation of his patient's "hypo notions."

Two days later, after writing what he considered to be his "last letter," Hiram told his doctor that he "expect[ed] to go today." The next day Rockwell "was called in very great haste"; Hiram explained to him that "mortification had taken place in his thigh." On the following day Hiram exclaimed that he was "on his last legs." The next morning Hiram told his physician that "he bled most of last night inside. Did not quite go."[69]

In response, Rockwell commented that his patient was "much as usual," "more hypo than common," and had "used up most of his excuses." His only medical reaction was to give Hiram a "laxative pill." But when Hiram expressed the fear that he "thinks or says he has been taking opium," Rockwell made no response. He did not mention that his pharmacist often mixed opium with calomel in order to achieve the proper cathartic effect without a complete purge. And three days later, Rockwell, again without comment, prescribed one *camph opii* (opium) pill to be taken three times a day.[70]

Rockwell's general analysis contended that "Mr. Harwood on the whole has slowly improved the past month but is still given to his hypo notions." Best of all, his "appetite is good." The very next day he repeated the belief that his patient was "slowly improving." Two days later, however, Rockwell observed that Hiram "appeared better in the morning but got rather hypo like towards night." Then, when Hiram "complained of sickness," the doctor "omitted the camphor pill."[71]

The same day that Hiram complained of feeling sick, he told Rockwell "that we think he has done something and we are authorized by law to put him out of the way soon." Within a week after that, Rockwell reported that Hiram "has a notion that he has putrified and smells so no one can come near him." In response to such statements, Rockwell simply observed that Hiram was "much as yesterday," "walked to the village," "about so," and "rode out." Although familiar with Burrows' analysis of "melancholia," Rockwell remained oblivious to the signs of severe depression being manifested by Hiram.[72]

Even though Hiram considered himself "on the brink of Hell" and claimed to have "received a mortal wound on his arm," Rockwell insisted that his patient "is now on the gain and appears more like getting well." Over the next several days, he claimed that Hiram was "improving" and observed with satisfaction that he "takes more exercise." By the last week in March, however, Hiram frantically reported "a 'sad accident'" he had experienced; as recorded by Rockwell, Hiram claimed to have "got some tobacco in his hat and [it] like to have killed him." Three days after that he suffered "mortification in his toe" and "about killed himself by eating bread."[73] Apparently, however, Hiram's bowels must have been regular and his appetite good, because on April 3 Dr. Rockwell discharged his patient with the notation "improved" inscribed as his "condition on discharge."[74]

❧ The actual reason for Hiram's discharge is unclear. The monthly fee of three dollars may have become burdensome for his friends and family, or they may also have responded sympathetically to Hiram's mournful letters expressing his sense of desolation at being "torn from my family and sent here." As superintendent of the asylum, Dr. Rockwell, always concerned that his annual report to the state legislature reflect success, was not eager to have another chronic case on his hands.[75] In any event, convinced that Hiram's digestive problems had been cured, Rockwell must have concluded that he had done all he possibly could for this particular patient.

Regardless of the cause of his release, Hiram returned to Tanbrook in complete despair. Although he never wrote in his journal again, the record of his last month at the asylum revealed him to be suffering from severe depression. In much worse condition than when he left home four months before, he must have wandered about the farm in a desperate attempt to calm the demons raging within him. While at the house, he likely "wore out the folks making my moans." Worse, if he had said and done "many foolish things" prior to his stay at Brattleboro, the psychotic delusions he now suffered must surely have alarmed and disconcerted his loved ones. Hiram may have been aware of the distress he caused members of his family, but he also knew that his "indisposition" rendered him physically unable to contribute to their welfare and to the well-being of the farm. He had become a useless dependent.

Existing in a state of desperate hopelessness for nearly a year after his return from the asylum, Hiram, distraught and confused by his inability to overcome his physical disabilities, left the house after breakfast Wednesday morning, March 6, 1839. This was not unusual; he often walked about the farm. However, when he did not return by dinnertime, family members became concerned and began to search for him. At three o'clock that afternoon, they found his lifeless body hanging from a rafter in the new barn — the barn that was to stand as a lasting monument to his effort to perpetuate the success and prosperity of the Harwood farm.

It was left to Hiram's longtime friend John C. Haswell, now editor of the *Vermont Gazette*, to pay public tribute to Hiram in the pages of his newspaper. Haswell declared unequivocally that Hiram "enjoyed the esteem of all who knew him — and has ever been . . . industrious and remarkably methodical and upright in all his dealings with the world."[76] Whether in his heart of hearts this was what Hiram truly desired, he had become the very man his father and his grandfather had demanded that he become since childhood — industrious, methodical, and upright. In death he had finally achieved the stature that had eluded him all his life.

Hiram's final battle with dementia served as a metaphor for the struggles that marked his entire life. Having spent a lifetime seeking control of his destiny, only to have cultural forces (particularly gender and family constructs), fate, and his own strong sense of duty deny him countless opportunities, he had seemingly become a man without choices, or with choices so narrowly circumscribed as to be terribly confining. Ironically, Hiram's life ended with loss of control of his body as well: one final, sad instance in which he was robbed of choices. As his physical ailments became material, he lost the last vestige of control he had over his life. In the end death appeared to be the only choice left him.

Epilogue

Following Hiram's burial in the family plot, adjacent to Old First Church in Bennington, Benjamin and his extended family resumed their lives on the farm. With the assistance of Hiram Hopkins, George P., and most particularly Sally and Lydia, the dairy operation continued as before. In December, after the crush of farm responsibilities subsided, Benjamin, shaken by Hiram's death and concerned for the remaining members of his family, composed his last will and testament.[1] This document not only reflected the financial success achieved by the Harwoods over the years but demonstrated Benjamin's abiding commitment to traditional patriarchal beliefs as well. He allotted to his wife Diadama the customary "widow's third" of his property during her lifetime as well as the exclusive use of whatever rooms in the house she desired. Lydia, too, was to enjoy such use of the home as long as she lived. Upon their mother's death, Lydia and her sister Damia were to receive equal one-half shares of the household furniture; at this time Hiram Hopkins was to inherit the farm in its entirety. Upon taking ownership of the farm, Hopkins had to assume important familial obligations: he must pay Lydia $60 per year for the remainder of her life; in addition he was responsible for providing his aunt Damia and his sister Adeline the sum of $500 each. And, according to the promise he made to Hiram prior to his son's commitment to the asylum, Benjamin instructed Hopkins to pay Sally $60 a year for the remainder of her life. The most important duty Benjamin mandated to Hopkins was to assume the mantle of the patriarch, to perpetuate the Harwood farm — the family's very reason for being through so many years of struggle and sacrifice. As the last living male, Hopkins was responsible for continuing the efforts made by Peter, Benjamin, and his father to establish the Harwood family as respected members of the Bennington community.

Within two years after writing his will, Benjamin, hoping to prepare his twenty-year-old grandson for the day he would assume complete responsibility for the farm, leased his property to Hopkins and George P. for a period of two years at the rate of $175 per year. According to the terms of the lease, the two men agreed to use and improve the land "in a good husbandlike manner," to keep all buildings and fences in proper repair at their own expense, and to pay all the taxes. In addition, having been granted full use of all farming tools and dairy equipment, they agreed to keep this material in serviceable condition, except for "natural wear." Upon its termination, the lease required Hopkins and George to provide Benjamin with 10 bushels of rye, 25 bushels of corn, 115 bushels of oats, 300 bushels of potatoes, and two tons of plaster—a precise inventory of the produce on hand at the time they signed the document.[2]

Significant changes took place within the Harwood family after Hopkins and George P. took over the farm. Adeline married Elias B. Burton and went to live with him in nearby Manchester. With this marriage, Hiram and Sally's efforts to prepare Adeline for a social position above their own reached fruition. Burton, too, constantly strove to enhance his family's status and influence. A graduate of Middlebury College, he enjoyed considerable prominence as an attorney at the time he married Adeline. In the years following their marriage, Adeline's husband steadily augmented his wealth and influence: he served in both the state assembly and the state senate, held the office of state's attorney, attended the Republican National Convention in Chicago as a delegate in 1860, was president of the board of Burr and Burton Seminary in Manchester, and became one of the directors of the Battenkill National Bank.[3] During this time Adeline gave birth to five daughters. She took great delight in sharing her girls with their grandmother Sally and their Aunt Lydia, both of whom doted on the children. Sally and Lydia remained close to Adeline and her family throughout their lives, and upon their deaths, both women left all their silver cutlery to Adeline's daughters.[4] Although retaining intimate ties with the Harwoods, Adeline committed herself fully to her life in Manchester. Upon her death in 1885, Elias buried Adeline in the Manchester cemetery beneath an impressive Burton family monument.

Several years afer Adeline's wedding, Hopkins married Mary Hicock, a young Connecticut woman, and the couple took up residence in the apartment formerly occupied by his parents. Tragically, within two years after the wedding, Mary died. The Harwoods buried her in their family plot in Bennington. Three years later Hopkins married Amanda Nichols, the daughter of an old and affluent Bennington family, and brought her to live on the farm. For a period of time, then, the Harwood household assumed the appearance that had characterized it for so long — a stem family consisting of three generations living under the same roof. With the death of Benjamin in 1851 and Diadama three years later, however, this was no longer the case. Only Hopkins, his wife Amanda, his mother Sally, and his aunt Lydia maintained the household; George P., either unable or unwilling to serve as executor of Benjamin's will, left Tanbrook in 1851. Then, with Sally's death in 1871 and Lydia's several years later, only Hopkins and Amanda, who never bore children, remained. For years they lived alone on the farm.

After his grandfather's death and George's departure, Hopkins assumed complete control of the farm. Whether he was responding to transformations taking place in the dairy business as cheese factories rapidly replaced home production, or attempting to emulate the new gentry emerging as a result of increased commercial activity in Bennington, he behaved in ways quite unlike his father and grandfather. In 1868 Hopkins mortgaged the farm in order to purchase two adjacent farms originally owned by the Fay family — a decision family members had pondered and rejected as improvident more than thirty years before.[5] The old farm of 100 acres now encompassed 160 acres. And yet this purchase marked just the beginning of efforts by Hopkins to buy and sell property in and around Bennington.[6] In 1874 he mortgaged the farm once again to finance these purchases.[7] Finally, on April 2, 1889, the Harwood farm passed out of the family forever; on that date Hopkins, unable to repay his debt, signed over the mortgage to an individual from Pownal.[8] After losing the farm, Hopkins and Amanda moved into a large white frame house in Bennington near his Aunt Diadama's home on the old road leading from Bennington to Pownal — the very road that Hiram had traveled so often on his trips between Tanbrook and the Hill.

Although Hopkins failed to maintain the Harwoods' patriarchal tradition linking the family to the land, he did achieve a measure of respectability and stature within the town of Bennington never enjoyed by either his father or grandfather. Well before his move into town, Hopkins had been elected a deacon in Old First Church. Known throughout the village for his deeply religious nature, Hopkins served as senior deacon of the church for many years. Upon his death in 1900, Hopkins enjoyed a reputation for being an "excellent citizen, kindly disposed, charitable, sympathetic, and thoroughly honest" — traits traditionally honored by the Harwoods.[9] And yet, no members of that family remained at the time of his death. In their absence, Amanda interred Hopkins in the Nichols family plot some distance from where Hiram and Sally lay buried.

With the death of Hopkins, the long and arduous quest begun by Peter Harwood more than a century and a half earlier to establish his family's prosperity and respectability in Bennington came to an end. Today, a small stone monument placed beside the road between Old Bennington and Pownal to commemorate Bennington's pioneer families marks the location of the Harwood farm. The last remaining vestige of that determined quest, it stands as mute testimony to the effort that cost Hiram his life.

Printed Material Referred to
in the Harwood Diaries

Whenever possible, the author has supplied the publication data for the following material. At times Hiram Harwood made only the most cryptic references to authors or titles. In these instances no such information can be provided.

An Account of All the Different Denominations in the Christian World.
Adams, J. Q. *Letters.* A pamphlet.
Adams, John, *The Flowers Of Modern Travels, Being . . . Extracts, Selected from the Works of the Most Celebrated Travellers . . . Intended Chiefly for Young People of Both Sexes.* 2 vols. Boston: John West, 1797.
Addison, Joseph. *The Spectator.* Philadelphia, 1803. Bound in 8 vols.
Address to the Youth of the Town of Shelburne, Occasioned by the Death of Miss Melinda Fisk . . . Who Died April 5, 1806. Greenfield, Mass.: John Denio, 1808.
The Adventurers. 4 vols. Philadelphia: H. Maxwell, 1813. Originally published in 140 numbers, 7 Nov. 1752 to 8 March 1754.
Advisor or Vermont Evangelical Magazine. Middlebury.
Aikin, John. *The Arts of Life: Of Providing Food, Clothes, Shelter for the Instruction of Young Persons.* Boston: Hosea Sprague, 1803.
Albany Argus.
Albany Guardian.
Alexander, Caleb. *Grammatical Elements, or A Comprehensive Theory of English Grammar, Intended for the Use of Children of Both Sexes.* Boston: I. Thomas & E. T. Andrews, 1793.

Allen, Ethan. *Reason the Only Oracle of Man, or A Compenduous System of Natural Religion.* . . . Bennington, Vt.: Haswell & Russell, 1784.

Allen, Thomas. *An Historical Sketch of the County of Berkshire, and Town of Pittsfield.* Boston: Belcher & Armstrong, 1808.

American Magazine, a Monthly Miscellany Devoted to Literature, Science, History, Biography & the Arts, Including Also State Papers & Public Documents. Albany.

American Magazine of Useful Knowledge. Boston.

American State Papers, and Correspondence between Messrs. Smith, Pinkney, Marquis Wellesley, General Armstrong. . . . London: Longman, Hurst, 1812.

Ashe, Thomas. *Travels in America, Performed in 1806.* . . . Newburyport, Mass.: E. M. Blunt, 1808.

Bancroft, Aaron. *An Essay on the Life of George Washington.* Worcester, Mass.: Thomas & Sturtevant, 1807.

Barnett, Francis. *The Hero of No Fiction; or, Memoirs of Francis Barnett, the Lefevre of "No Fiction;" and a Review of That Work.* Boston: C. Ewer and T. Bodlington, 1823.

Baynes, Edward, D. *Childe Harold in the Shades: An Infernal Romaunce.* . . . London: Thomas Hookham, 1819.

Beecher, Lyman. *Sermons on Intemperance.* New York, 1827.

Belknap, Jeremy. *American Biography; or, An Historical Account of Those Persons Who Have Been Distinguished in America.* 2 vols. Boston: Isaiah Thomas, 1798.

———. *The History of New Hampshire.* Philadelphia: Robert Aitken, 1784–92.

Bennett, James. *The American System of Practical Book-Keeping, Adapted to the Commerce of the United States . . . Designed for the Use of Schools.* New York: Abm. Paul, 1820.

Bennington News Letter.

Bennington Vermont Gazette.

Bentley's American Instructor.

Beresford, James. *The Miseries of Human Life; or, The groans of Samuel Sensitive, and Timothy Testy.* Boston: Greenough, Stebbins & Hunt, 1807.

Berquin, Arnaud. *Biography for Boys; or, Interesting Stories for Children.* New Haven, Conn.: Sidney's Press, 1812.

Bigland, John. *A Geographical and Historical View of the World.* 5 vols. Boston: Thomas B. Wait, 1811.

Bingham, Caleb. *The American Preceptor: Being a New Selection of Lessons for Reading and Speaking, Designed for the Use of Schools.* Philadelphia: Thomas & William Bradford, 1813.

Bissett, Robert. *The History of the Reign of George III, to the Termination of the Late War.* 4 vols. New York: Inskeep & Bradford, 1810–11.

Blair, Hugh. *Lectures on Rhetoric and Belles Lettres.* Philadelphia: Robert Aitken, 1784.

Blake, John L. *Conversations on Natural Philosophy in Which the Elements of That Science Are Familiarly Explained and Adapted to the Comprehension of Young Pupils.* Hartford, Conn.: G. Goodwin, 1823.

Blas, Gil. *The Comical Adventures of Gil Blas of Santillano.* Philadelphia: William Spotswood, 1790. An abridged version was published in Worcester by Isaiah Thomas in 1796.

Bolingbroke, Henry Saint-John. *Remarks on the History of England.* Many editions.

Boston New England Farmer.

Boswell, James. *The Life of Samuel Johnson, LL D.* 3 vols. Boston: W. Andrews & L. Blake, 1807.

The Botanical Thomsonian Advocate.

Bourne, George. *The History of Napoleon Bonaparte.* Baltimore: Warner & Hanna, 1806.

Bradley, Eliza. *An Authentic Narrative of the Shipwreck and Suffering of Mrs. Eliza Bradley . . . Wrecked on Barbary Coast in June, 1818.* Boston: James Walden, 1820.

Branagan, Thomas. *The Penitential Tyrant: A Juvenile Poem, in Two Cantos.* Philadelphia: Author, 1805.

British Glory Revived: Being a Compleat Collection of All the Accounts . . . Relating to the Late Glorious Action at Dettingen. London: J. Roberts, 1743.

Buck, Charles. *A Theological Dictionary.* 2 vols. Philadelphia: W. W. Woodward, 1810.

Budget of Wit and Amusement: Being a Select Collection of Anecdotes, Bon Mots, etc., of Celebrated Characters. Albany, N.Y.: Daniel Steele, 1812.

Bunn, Matthew. *A Journal of the Adventures of Matthew Bunn. . . .* Providence: Bennett Wheeler, 1796.

Butler, Frederick. *The Farmer's Manual; Being a Plain Practical Treatise on the Art of Husbandry.* Hartford, Conn.: Samuel G. Goodrich, 1819.

———. *Sketches of Universal History, Sacred and Profane, from the Creation of the World to the Year 1818.* Hartford, Conn.: Cocke & Hale, 1818.

Butler, Samuel. *Hudribras, in Three Parts; Written in the Time of the Late Wars.* Troy, N.Y., 1806.

Carey, Matthew. *American Atlas.* Philadelphia: Matthew Carey, 1795.

———. *The Olive Branch: or Faults on Both Sides, Federal and Democratic.* Philadelphia: M. Carey, 1814.

Carr, Sir John. *The Stranger in France; or, A Tour from Devonshire to Paris.* Hartford, Conn.: Oliver D. Cocke, 1804.

Casket. It bore this title from 1826 to 1830. After that it was *Graham's American Monthly Magazine of Literature, Art, and Fashion,* published in Philadelphia.

Catlin, Jacob. *The Horrors of War.* Stockbridge, Mass.: H. Willard, 1813.

Chambers, Ephraim. *Cyclopedae; or, An Universal Dictionary of Arts and Sciences. . . .* 4 vols. London: J. F. & C. Rivington, 1784–86.

Chambers, Robert. *History of the Rebellion in Scotland in 1745, 1746.* Edinburgh: Constable & Co., 1827.

Chicago Democrat.

Christian Advocate. Published in New York; contained an article by David Robinson Jr.

Christian Advocate and Journal. Organ of the Methodist Episcopal Church, 1826–.

Christian Soldier. An anti-universal newspaper published in Boston.

Christian Watchman. It bore this title 1819–48, then was called *Watchman-Examiner;* a national Baptist paper published in Worcester, Mass.

Christ's Second Appearance.

Clark, Daniel. *Proofs of the Corruption of Gen. James Wilkinson, and His Connexion with Aaron Burr.* Philadelphia: W. Hall, 1809.

Clarke, Edward D. *Travels in Various Countries of Europe, Asia, and Africa.* Philadelphia: Anthony Finley, 1811.

Cook, James. *Captain Cook's Third and Last Voyage to the Pacific Ocean, in the Years 1776, 1777, 1778, 1779, & 1789.* Philadelphia: W. Woodward, 1796. Abridged.

Cooke, George Frederick. *Memoir of the Life of George F. Cooke.* 2 vols. New York: D. Longworth, 1813.

Cooper, James Fenimore. *The Pilot, a Tale of the Seas.* New York: D. Appleton & Co., 1819.

———. *The Pioneers.* New York: Charles Wiley, 1823.

———. *Precaution, a Novel.* New York: A. T. Goodrich & Co., 1820.

———. *The Spy, a Tale of the Neutral Ground.* New York: Wiley & Halsted, 1821.

Cooper, Rev. Mr. *The History of North America.* Bennington, Vt.: Anthony Haswell, 1793.

Counting-House Almanack. Philadelphia.

Criminal Recorder; or, An Awful Beacon to the Rising Generation of Both Sexes . . . Collected from Authentic Records by a Friend of Man. Philadelphia: Matthew Carey, 1810.

Cultivator. Published by the New York state agricultural society, Albany.

Danbury (Conn.) Republican Farmer.

Davies, Samuel. *Sermons on Important Subjects.* Philadelphia: Robert Campbell, 1794.

Davis, Matthew. *Memoirs of Aaron Burr, with Miscellaneous Selections from His Correspondence.* New York: Harper & Brothers, 1836–37.

DeFoe, Daniel. *The Voyages, Travels, and Surprising Adventures of Captain Robert Singleton.* New York: Christian Brown, 1802.

Dickinson, Rodolphus. *Elements of Geography, or, An Extensive Abridgment Thereof.* Boston: Bradford & Read, 1813.

Dolphin, James. *A Narrative of the Travels of James Dolphin.* 1802. An account of a fictitious Indian captivity.

Duane, William. *Politics for American Farmers.* Washington, D.C.: R. C. Weightman, 1807. Published originally in the *Aurora.*

Eccentric Biography; or Memoirs of Remarkable Female Characters, Ancient and Modern. Worcester, Mass.: Isaiah Thomas Jr., 1805.

Edgeworth, Maria. *Castle Rackrent, an Hibernian Tale.* Boston: T. B. Wait & Sons, 1814.

Edinburgh Encyclopedia, the American Edition of the New Edinburgh Encyclopedia. Philadelphia: Edward Parker, 1812–31.

Elegant Extracts; or, The Literary Nosegay. Baltimore: Philip Mauro, 1814. Moral reflections and dictionary of literary conversation.

Eliot, John. *A Biographical Dictionary, Containing a Brief Account of the First Settlers.* Salem, Mass.: Cushing & Appleton, 1809.

Emerald. A Boston periodical work of 1807.

Essays of Howard, or Tales of the Prison. New York: C. S. Winkle, 1811.

Examination of Col. Aaron Burr before the Chief Justice of the United States. Richmond, Va.: Bellmon & Swartwout, 1807.

Family Magazine. Much like the *Penny Magazine.*

Farmer's Register. A periodical published at Conway, Mass., 1798.

Fatal Cabinet; or, The Profligate Mother. 2 vols. in 1. Boston: Isaiah Thomas Jr., Samuel Avery, 1810.

Federalist Papers.

Ferguson, Adam. *An Essay on the History of Civil Society.* Boston: Hastings, Etheridge & Bliss, 1809.

———. *The History of the Progress and Termination of the Roman Republic.* 3 vols. Philadelphia: William Poyntell & Co., 1805.

Ferguson, James. *Astronomy Explained upon Sir Isaac Newton's Principles, and Made Easy to Those Who Have Not Studied Mathematics.* Philadelphia: Matthew Carey, 1806.

Fielding, Henry. *The History of Tom Jones, a Foundling.* Many editions.

The Fifer's Companion, No. 1: Containing Instructions for Playing the Fife, and a Collection of Music, Consisting of Marches, Airs, etc., with Their Second Added. Salem, Mass.: Joshua Cumings, 1805.

Fletcher's Defense of the Bible. This is most likely John William Fletcher (1729–85), who published a great deal on religious thought and the Bible.

Foxe, John. *An Abridgment of the Book of Martyrs.* New York: Samuel Wood, 1810.

———. *The New and Complete Book of Martyrs.* New York: Willliam Durrell, 1794.

Franklin, Benjamin. *The Works of the Late Dr. Benjamin Franklin Consisting of His Life Written by Himself, Together with Essays, Humorous, Moral & Literary, Chiefly in the Manner of the Spectator.* New York: Tiebout & Obrian, 1794.

Gaya, Louis de. *Mariage Ceremonies; As Now Used in All Parts of the World.* London: J. Nott, 1704.

Gibbon, Edward. *The History of the Decline and Fall of the Roman Empire.* 8 vols. Philadelphia: William Y. Birch, 1804–5.

———. *The Life and Letters of Edward Gibbon with His History of the Crusades.* London, n.d.

Goldsmith, Oliver. *The American Speaker; A Selection of Popular, Parliamentary and Forensic Eloquence; Particularly Calculated for the Seminaries in the United States.* Philadelphia: Abraham Small, 1814.

———. *The Citizen of the World; or, Letters from a Chinese Philosopher. . . .* London: Author, 1762.

———. *Dr. Goldsmith's Roman History. Abridged by Himself. For the Use of Schools.* Philadelphia: Robert Campbell, 1795.

———. *The Grecian History, from the Earliest State to the Death of Alexander the Great.* Philadelphia: Mathew Carey, 1800.

———. *She Stoops to Conquer.*

Goodrich, Charles A. *A History of the United States of America, on a Plan Adapted to the Capacity of Youths.* Hartford, Conn.: S. G. Goodrich, 1822.

———. *Lives of the Signers of the Declaration of Independence.* New York: W. Reed & Co. 1829.

Goodrich, Samuel G. *A System of Universal Geography.* Hartford, Conn.: Cooke, 1824.

Gordon, William. *The History of the Rise, Progress, and Establishment of the Independence of the United States of America.* New York: Hodge, Allen & Campbell, 1789.

Grandpré, Louis M. *A Voyage to the Indian Ocean and to Bengal, Undertaken in the Years 1789 and 1790.* Boston: David Carlisle, 1803.

Greenbank's Periodical Library. Philadelphia.

Greenleaf, Benjamin. *Rules of Syntax, Selected from Various Authors, for the Use of Students.* Haverhill, Mass.: E. W. Reinhart, 1825.

Green Mountain Farmer. Same as *Vermont Gazette;* the name changed over the years.

Gregory, George. *A Dictionary of Arts and Sciences.* 3 vols. Philadelphia: Isaac Peirce, 1815–16.

Guide to Domestic Happiness. New Haven, Conn.: Increase Cook & Co., 1807.

Guthrie, William. *A New Geographical, Historical, and Commercial Grammar.* Philadelphia: Johnson & Warner, 1809.

———. *A New System of Modern Geography.* 2 vols. Philadelphia: Matthew Carey, 1794–95.

Hallam, Henry. *History of Europe during the Middle Ages.*

Hanger, George, Baron Colerain. *The Life, Adventures, and Opinions of Col. George Hanger.* New York: Johnson & Stryker, 1801.

Harmon, Daniel W. *A Journal of Voyages and Travels in the Interior of North America.* Andover, Mass.: Flagg & Gould, 1820.

Hedge, Levi. *Elements of Logic.* Cambridge, Mass.: Hilliard & Metcalf, 1816.

History of Gods and Godesses.

Hive; or, A Collection of Thoughts on Civil, Moral, Sentimental, and Religious Subjects. New York: Brewer & Lang, 1795. Reprinted through 1814.

Hodgson, Adam. *Letters from North America, Written during a Tour in the United States and Canada.* London: Hurst, Robinson, 1824.

Holford, George P. *The Destruction of Jerusalem an Absolute and Irresistible Proof of the Divine Origin of Christianity.* Burlington, N.J.: Joseph Sharpless, 1807.

Homer. *Iliad.*

Horrors of a Monastery; or, The Villainy of Priestcraft Exposed, in the Affecting History of Bernard and Elmira. Greenfield, Mass.: N.p., 1811.

Hubbard, William. *A Narrative of the Indian Wars in New England, from the First Planting Thereof in the Year 1607, to the Year 1677.* Boston: John Boyle, 1775.

Hume, David. *The History of England, from the Invasion of Julius Caesar to the Revolution of 1688.* 6 vols. Philadelphia: Samuel H. Smith, 1795–96.

Humphreys, David. *An Essay on the Life of the Honorable Major-General Israel Putnam.* Hartford, Conn.: Hudson & Goodwin, 1788.

Huntington, Jonathan. *The Apollo Harmony.* Northampton, Mass.: Horace Graves, 1807.

The Interesting Life, Travels, Voyages, and Daring Engagements of the Celebrated Paul Jones. Hudson, N.Y.: N. Elliot, 1809.

Irving, Washington. *The Life and Voyages of Christopher Columbus.* Boston: Aldine, n.d.

Jauden, Daniel. *A Short System of Polite Learning; Being a Concise Introduction to the Arts and Sciences. Adapted for Schools.* Litchfield, Conn.: Thomas Collier, 1797.

Jefferson, Thomas. *Notes on the State of Virginia.*

John Robins, the Sailor. New York: American Tract Society, n.d.

Johnson, Samuel. *The Lives of the Most Eminent English Poets: With Critical Observations of Their Works.* 2 vols. Philadelphia: Coale & Oliver, 1803.

Journal of Health Conducted for an Association of Physicians. Philadelphia, 1829–33.

Journal of Moral Reform. This could be the *Journal of Reform* published in Portland, Maine, 1836–37.

Journal of the Times.

Kendall, Edward A. *Travels through the Northern Parts of the United States, in the Year 1807 and 1808.* 3 vols. New York: I. Riley, 1809.

Knigge, Adolf. *Practical Philosophy of Social Life; or, The Art of Conversing with Men — 1st American Edition by P. Will.* Lansingburgh, N.Y.: Penniman & Bliss, 1805.

La Croze, Mathurin V. *A Historical Grammar; or, A Chronological Abridgment of Universal History — Revised and Enlarged by Caleb Bingham.* Boston: David Carlisle, 1802.

The Ladies' Own Book.

Lady's Monitor. A ladies' magazine published in 1801.

Lansingburgh (N.Y.) Gazette.

Las Cases, Emmanuel, Comte de. *Letters from the Cape of Good Hope.* New York: C. Wiley & Co., 1817.

Lay, Amos. *Map of the State of New York with Part of the States of Pennsylvania, New Jersey, etc., Compiled, Corrected, and Published from the Most Recent Authorities and Accurate Surveys by Amos Lay, 1817.* New York: Amos Lay, 1819.

Ledyard, *Praise of Women.*

Lempriere, John. *Bibliotheca Classica: or, A Classical Dictionary.* London: Charles Anthon, 1797.

——. *Universal Biography.* New York: E. Sergeant, 1810.

Letters on Courtship and Marriage. Boston: J. White, 1802.

Lyttelton, Thomas, Lord. *Letters of the Late Thomas Lord Lyttelton: With His Poems on Several Occasions, and a Sketch of His Lordship's Character.* Philadelphia, 1782.

The Male Coquette.

Manchester Bennington County Whig.

"Manufacturer, Merchant's Register." This may have been the Lewiston, Maine, Manufacturers and Mechanics Library Association.

Manvill, P. D. *Lucinda; or, The Mountain Mourner Being Recent Facts in a Series of Letters from Mrs. Manville of the State of New York, to Her Sister in Pennsylvania.* Erie, Pa.: Rufus Clough, 1831.

Mariner's Library or Voyager's Companion. Containing Narratives of the Most Popular Voyages from the Time of Columbus to the Present Day.... Boston: Lilly, Wait, Colman & Holden, 1833.

Marshall, Elihu. *A Spelling Book of the English Language Intended for "Common Schools."* Saratoga Springs, N.Y.: G. M. Danson, 1820.

Mavor, William Fordyce. *Universal History, Ancient and Modern; from Earliest Records of Time to the General Peace of 1801.* 25 vols. New York: Isaac Collins, 1804.

"Memoirs of the Board of Agriculture of the State of New York."

Milton, John. *The Works of John Milton.* 8 vols. London, n.d.

Milwaukee Advertiser.

Missionary Herald at Home and Abroad. Boston: American Board of Commissioners for Foreign Missions (the missions council of the Congregational and Christian churches), 1805–1951.

Mitchell, Samuel L. *The Picture of New York; or, The Traveller's Guide through the Commercial Metropolis of the United States.* New York: I. Riley & Co., 1807.

Mitchell and Miller's Repository & Review of Medical, Surgical, and Scientific Knowledge. New York: Collins & Perkins, 1809.

Montague, Edward Wortley. *Reflections on the Rise and Fall of the Ancient Republics.* Philadelphia: C. P. Wayne, 1806.

Moore, Thomas. *Letters and Journals of Lord Byron.* 2 vols. New York: J. & J. Harper, 1830.

Morcet, Mrs. James (Haldimand). *Conversations on Chemistry.* 2 vols. in 1. New Haven, Conn.: Sidney's Press, 1809.

More, Hannah. *Coelebs in Search of a Wife, Comprehending Observations on Domestic Habits and Manners, Religion and Morals.* New York: David Carlisle, 1809.

Morgan, Miss Sydney Owenson. *The Wild Irish girl, a National Tale.* New York: D. & G. Bruce, 1807.

Morse, Jedidiah. *The American Gazetteer.* Boston: S. Hall, Thomas & Andrews, 1797.

————. *The American Geography.* Elizabeth Town: Printed by Shepard Kollock for the author, 1789.

————. *A New Gazeteer of the Eastern Continent.* Charlestown, Mass.: Samuel Etheridge, 1802.

Mosheim, Johann L. *Mosheim's Church History, Ancient & Modern.* 2 vols. Baltimore: Phoenic N. Ward, 1832.

Murray, Lindley. *English Grammar.* There is a vast number of editions and abridgments.

National Intelligencer.

Newsletter. A Federalist paper published in Bennington 1811–15.

New York American.

New York Columbian.

New York Evening Star.

New York Observer. Merged into *Christian Work.*

New York Spectator.

New York Standard.

New York Statesman.

New York Weekly Constellation. 1830–32.

Nicholson, John. *The Farmer's Assistant.* Albany, N.Y.: H. C. Southwick, 1814.

Niles, John Milton. *The Life of Oliver Hazard Perry.* Hartford, Conn.: William S. Marsh, 1820.

North American Review.

An Old Friend with a New Face #1. London: Sherwood, 18__.

Paley, William. *Works of William Paley.* 5 vols. New York: S. King, 1824.

Parley's Magazine. New York and Boston. A children's or youth's *Penny Magazine* or *Family Magazine.*

Payne, John. *A New and Complete System of Universal Geography.* 4 vols. New York: John Low, 1798–1800.

Penny Magazine. Boston.

Perry, William. *The Royal Standard English Dictionary.* Worcester, Mass., 1788.

Philadelphia Aurora

Phillippe, Louis. *Memoirs and Recollections of Count Segur.* Boston: Wells & Lily, 1825.

Pierce, Sarah. *Sketches of Universal History, Complied from Several Authors for the Uses of Scholars.* New Haven, Conn.: Joseph Barber, 1811. See Mavor, *Universal History,* above.

Pike, Nicholas. *A New and Complete System of Arithmetic, Composed for the Use of the Citizens of the United States.* Newburyport, Mass.: John Mycall, 1786.

Pindar, Peter.

Pittsfield (Mass.) Sun.

Plutarch. *Lives.*

Polite Learning.

Political Observatory.

Pollock, Robert. *The Course of Time, a Poem in Two Books.* New York, 1828.

Pope, Alexander. *An Essay on Man.* London, 1732–33.

———. *The Poetical Works of Alexander Pope.* Many editions.

Porter, Jane. *Thaddeus of Warsaw.* 2 vols. Boston: Lemuel Blake, 1809.

Pratt, Samuel Jackson. *Pity's Gift; A Collection of Interesting Tales, to Excite the Compassion of Youth for the Animal Creations.* Philadelphia: B. & J. Johnson, 1801.

Prentiss, Charles. *The Life of the Late Gen. William Eaton.* Brookfield, Mass.: E. Merriam, 1813.

Preston, Daniel R. *The Wonders of Creation; Natural and Artificial. . . .* Boston: John M. Dunham, 1807.

Priestley, Joseph. *Lectures on History, and General Policy.* 2 vols. Philadelphia: P. Byrne, 1803.

Pye, Henry J. *The Democrat; or, Intrigues and Adventures of Jean Le Noir.* New York: James Rivington, 1795.

Ramsay, Andrew M. *The Travels of Cyrus, to Which Is Annexed a Discourse upon the Theology and Mythologies of the Ancients.* London: Woodward, 1727.

Ramsay, David. *The History of South Carolina, from Its First Settlement in 1670, to the Year 1808.* 2 vols. Charleston, S.C.: David Longworth, 1809.

———. *The Life of General Washington.* New York: Hopkins & Seymour, 1807.

———. *Universal History Americanized.* 2 vols. Philadelphia: M. Carey & Son, 1819.

Ray, William. *The Horrors of Slavery: or, The American Tars in Tripoli.* Troy, N.Y.: Oliver Lyon, 1806.

Rees, Abraham. *Cyclopedia; or, An Universal Dictionary of Arts and Sciences.* 30 vols. London: W. Strahan, 1778–88.

Reid, Thomas. *Essays on the Intellectual and Active Powers of Man.* Philadelphia: William Young, 1793.

Richmond (Va.) Enquirer.

Riley, James. *An Authentic Narrrative of the Loss of the American Brig Commerce, Wrecked on the Western Coast of Africa, in the Month of August, 1818.* Hartford, Conn.: Author, 1817.

Robertson, William. *The History of America*. 2 vols. New York: Robert Wilson, 1798.

Roche, Mrs. Reginia Maria (Dalton). *The Children of the Abbey, a Tale*. 4 vols. Philadelphia: John Bioren, 1800.

Rollins, Charles. *The Ancient History of the Egyptians*. 4 vols. Hartford, Conn.: Silas Andrus, 1815.

————. *The Ancient History of the Egyptians, Carthegenians, Assyrians, Babylonians, Medes & Persians, Macedonians, and Greecians*. 8 vols. Boston: Munroe & Evans, 1805.

Rush, Benjamin. *Medical Inquiries and Observations upon the Diseases of the Mind*. Philadelphia: Kimber & Richardson, 1812.

Russell, William. *The History of Modern Europe*. 5 vols. Philadelphia: H. Maxwell, 1800. Vol. 5 was published in 1809.

Saint-Pierre, Jacques Henri Bernardin de. *Voyages of Amasis*. Boston: I. Thomas & E. T. Andrews, 1795.

Sampson, William. *Memoirs of William Sampson*. New York: George Farmer, 1807.

Sandy Hill (N.Y.) Temperance Advocate.

Scott, William. *Lessons in Elocution: or, A Selection of Pieces in Prose & Verse, for the Improvement of Youth in Reading and Speaking*. Philadelphia: W. Young, 1788.

Scruprier's Biography.

Sedgwick, Catherine Maria. *A New England Tale; or, Sketches of New England Character and Manners*. N.Y.: E. Bliss & E. White, 1822.

Shakespeare, William. *Macbeth*.

————. *Richard II*.

————. *Works*.

Silliman, Benjamin. *A Journal of Travels in Europe, Holland, and Scotland, and of Two Passages over the Atlantic in the Years 1805 and 1806*. 2 vols. New York: D.& G. Bruce, 1810.

Sketch of the Life and Literary Career of Augustus Von Kotzabue; with the Journal of His Tour to Paris, at the Close of the Year 1790. New York: M. Ward & Co., 1801.

Slade, William. *Vermont State Papers*. Middlebury, Vt.: J. W. Copeland, 1823.

Sloan, James. *Rambles in Italy; in the Years 1816–17*. Baltimore: N. G. Maxwell, 1818.

Smellie, William. *Philosophy of Natural History*. Philadelphia, 1832.

Smith, Frederick. *Reason and Revelation Considered as Connected with Christian Faith and Experience*. London: Richard Taylor, 1811.

Smith, Thomas. *Wonders of Nature and Art, or, A Concise Account of Whatever Is*

Most Curious and Remarkable in the World. . . . 14 vols. Philadelphia: Robert Carr, 1806–7.

Smollett, Tobias George. *The Adventures of Roderick Rando.* 2 vols. Philadelphia: Mathew Carey, 1794.

———. *The History of England from the Revolution to the End of the American War, and Peace of Versailles in 1783.* 6 vols. Philadelphia: Henry Sweitzer, 1796–98.

Spafford, Horatio Gates. *A Gazeteer of the State of New York.* Albany, N.Y.: H. C. Southwick, 1813.

Spafford's Magazine.

Staunton, Sir George Leonard. *An Authentic Account of an Embassy from the King of Great Britain to the Emperor of China.* 2 vols. in 1. Philadelphia: John Bioren, 1799.

Sterne, Laurence. *The Works of Laurence Sterne.* 5 vols. Philadelphia: James Humphreys, 1774.

Stevens, John Hathaway. "A Discourse Delivered in Stoneham [Mass.] April 8, 1813. Being the Day of the State Fast." *Green Mountain Farmer,* August 1813.

Stevens, Samuel C. *The New England Manuscript, or Writing-Book for Writing Down the Rules and Operations of the Scholar, on Fine Paper, instead of Disfiguring the Arithmetic, Thereby Destroying Its Usefulness to a Scholar, or Even Himself in the Future.* . . . Dover, N.H.: S. C. Stevens, 1827.

Stewarton; Lewis Goldsmith. *Secret History of the Court of St. Cloud.* Philadelphia: John Watts, 1806.

Sully, Maximillien de Bethune, duc de. *The Memoirs of the Duke of Sully.* . . . 5 vols. Philadelphia: J. Maxwell, 1817.

Swan, Timothy. *The Songster's Museum; or, A Trip to Elysium.* Northampton, Mass.: Andrew Wright, 1803.

Swift, Jonathan. *A Tale of a Tub.* London, many editions.

Swift, Samuel. *An Oration, Delivered in Middlebury, at the Celebration of the Fourth of July, A.D. 1809.* Middlebury, Vt.: J. D. Huntington, 1809.

A Tablet of Memory; Shewing Every Memorable Event in History, from the Earliest Period to the Year 1774. . . . London: J. Bew, 1774.

Taggart, Samuel. *God's Visitation of Sinful Nations.* Greenfield, Mass.: D. Phelps, 1812.

Thacher, James. *A Military Journal of the American Revolutionary War, from 1775 to 1783.* Boston: Cottons, 1827.

Thomas, Isaiah. *The History of Printing in America.* Worcester, Mass.: Isaiah Thomas Jr., Isaac Sturtevant, 1810.

Travels of Captains Lewis & Clark. Philadelphia: Hubbard Lester, 1809.

Troy Botanical Thompsonian Advocate.

Troy New York Journal.

Trumbull, Benjamin. *A Complete History of Connecticut.* Hartford, Conn.: Hudson & Goodwin, 1797.

Trumbull, Henry. *History of the Discovery of America.* . . . Brooklyn: J. W. Carew, 1810.

Tucker, Benjamin. *Sacred & Profane History Epitomized.* Philadelphia: Jacob Johnson, 1806.

U.S. Musical Notes, U.S. Musical Book.

Vermont Gazette. Same as *Green Mountain Farmer;* the name changed over the years.

Voltaire. *The Philosophical Dictionary, for the Pocket.* Catskill, N.Y.: T. & M. Croswell, 1796.

Waldie's Literary Omnibus. Philadelphia: A. Waldie, 1837.

Waldie's Select Circulatng Library: The Journal of Belles Lettres. Philadelphia.

Waldo, Samuel Putnam. *Memoirs of Andrew Jackson.* Hartford, Conn.: John Russell, 1818.

Walker, John. *A Critical Pronouncing Dictionary.* Philadelphia: Budd & Bartram, 1803.

Walton's Vermont Register. St. Albans, Vt., 1820–34. An almanac.

Washington (D.C.) Globe.

Washington (D.C.) Mirror.

Watson, Elkanah. *Mr. Watson's Address, Delivered to the Members of the Berkshire Agricultural Society, at the Townhouse in Pittsfield, September 24, 1811.* Troy: Francis Adamcourt, 1813.

Webster, Noah. *An American Selection in Reading and Speaking.* Philadelphia: Young & McCulloch, 1787.

The Wild Irish Rose.

Windsor Vermont Chronicle.

Windsor (Vt.) Washingtonian.

Weems, Mason. *A History of the Life and Death, Virtues and Exploits of General George Washington.* Philadelphia: 1800?

Whipple's Compendium.

Why Am I a Christian? Likely a tract for one of the Bible or tract societies; *Why Am I a Baptist? Why Am I a Presbyterian?* and *Why Am I an Old School Presbyterian?* are examples of such tracts.

Wilkinson, James. *Memoirs of General Wilkinson.* 3 vols. Washington, D.C.: Author, 1811.

Williams, Samuel. *The Natural and Civil History of Vermont.* Walpole, N.H.: Isaiah Thomas, 1794.

Wirt, William. *The Old Bachelor.* Richmond: Thomas Ritchie, 1814.

————. *Sketches of the Life and Character of Patrick Henry.* Philadelphia: James Webster, 1818.

Wittman, William. *Travels in Turkey, Asia-Minor, Syria.* . . . Philadelphia: James Humphreys, 1804.

Woodbridge, William C. *Rudiments of Geography.* Hartford, Conn.: O. D. Cooke and Co., 1822.

————. *Rudiments of Geography, on a New Plan.* . . . Hartford, Conn., 1821.

Woodbridge's Elements of History.

Woodstock Constitution. An anti-Masonic Whig paper.

Wright, Frances D'Arusmont. *Views of Society and Manners in America, by an Englishwoman.* London: Hurst, Rees, Orno & Brown, 1821.

The Young Lady's Own Book: A Manual of Intellectual Improvement and Moral Deportment. Philadelphia: Key & Biddle, 1833.

Young Man's Own Book: A Manual of Politeness, Intellectual Improvement, and Moral Deportment, Calculated to Form the Character on a Solid Basis, and to Insure Respectability and Success in Life. Philadelphia: Key, Meikle & Biddle, 1832.

Young Mill Wright & Miller's Guide. Philadelphia: O. Evans, 1795.

A Hypothetical Analysis of
Hiram Harwood's Medical Problems

The symptoms manifested by Hiram since suffering severe trauma to the head during his reckless trip to Berlin, New York, October 28, 1835, clearly baffled him and his family. They had no way of knowing, or even suspecting, that the aged appearance noted by the two young travelers and the peddler might be intimately related to the physical pain he was suffering. Nearly a hundred years would pass before medical science would recognize his headaches, vomiting, dizziness, and fainting spells as classic symptoms of chronic subdural hematoma (a blood clot between the dura and the brain that can gradually expand and exert undue pressure on the brain).[1] By then it would also be understood that severe depression — many times associated with the appearance of a sad, lined face, stooped posture, and a generally wearied, deteriorated appearance — often accompanied this physical condition.[2]

Although it is difficult to declare with any certainty the precise cause of Hiram's "fainting spell" of July 29, 1837, it is quite possible that Hiram began suffering from partial seizures related to chronic subdural hematoma.[3] Given Hiram's temperament — his lifelong feelings of anxiety and tension regarding first his own personal development and then the success of the dairy venture — he might also have suffered from hypertension. If so, his "fainting spell" might have been a transient ischemic stroke. Such strokes, which generally last but a few minutes, are confined to an area of the brain perfused by a specific artery. In Hiram's case, given his repeated mention of problems on the left side of the head running down the neck, one might suppose it to be the left carotid artery.[4]

Hiram's unease over the "frightful sensations" he experienced and his feelings of impending doom may have been related to his depressed state. Such panic attacks—often accompanied by palpitations, sweating, trembling or shaking, sensations of shortness of breath or smothering, feelings of choking, chest pains, nausea, and dizziness—are often characteristic of this condition.[5] The precipitous weight loss Hiram discovered on August 18, 1837, too, is characteristic of individuals suffering from a major depressive disorder of the type often accompanying chronic subdural hematomas.[6]

The cry of "O' my right leg" and Hiram's subsequent "wailing and lamenting" about his increasingly sore and debilitating leg are a puzzle. He never mentioned injuring his leg in any way. This might have been simply an oversight, but the increased intracranial pressure caused by an enlarging hematoma might also have caused pain in others parts of his body to be "referred" to his right leg.[7] While in the throes of such pain and distress, when his family thought it "mostly hypo on my part," Hiram wistfully wrote: "I think I am correct—hope I am not." The fact that Hiram could still see alternatives indicated that his depression was not yet psychotic.[8] At the same time, though, he did fall deeper and deeper into depression.[9]

It is clear that at the time of his admission to the Vermont Insane Asylum, Hiram suffered from a severe depression. It is also clear that Rockwell's manner of treating him did not help; it very likely exacerbated Hiram's condition.[10] Convinced that Hiram suffered from monomania brought on by hypochondriasis, Rockwell continually administered stronger and stronger narcotics to "calm" Hiram so that the asylum's moral regime might "cure" him.[11] Thus, he prescribed stramonium, an extremely powerful yet commonly prescribed narcotic, which, employed in small doses, helps soothe the smooth-muscle tissue of the stomach. Rockwell had no way of knowing this at the time, but stramonium taken in too large a dose or ingested over too long a time often causes mental confusion in the patient. Physicians at the time also commonly prescribed calomel, a submuriate of mercury, as a cathartic. To prevent complete purging, they often blended it with opium. Again, Rockwell—like so many of his colleagues—remained unaware of the consequences of prescribing too large a dose over an extended period of time. In this case mercury, or heavy metal, poisoning could result.[12] Then he added yellow bark, which taken internally serves as a tonic meant to induce a sense of warmth and a feeling of calm. In too large a dose, however, it often creates considerable gastric and intestinal irritation. Taken over too long a period, it can lead to an increase in the pulse rate and bring about severe tension and feelings of anxiety. Tincture of cantharidis, another powerful narcotic, was intended to sedate the patient and to calm the stomach. Given in small doses, this is often the result; taken in too large a dose, it can produce sickness, vertigo, great anxiety, dimness of vision, and delirium.

As a consequence of ingesting such large amounts of these strong narcotics, the "red mixture" Hiram mentioned might well have resulted from gastric and intestinal irritation caused by prolonged use of yellow bark. And too strong a dose of tincture of lyttae (cantharidis) was capable of producing a sense of stricture of the throat. Consequently, Hiram's "swallow" could very well have been "stopped up." In any event, Rockwell claimed that his patient was "much as usual."[13]

Even though familiar with Burrows' analysis of "melancholia," Rockwell remained oblivious to the signs of severe depression being manifested by Hiram. Neither did he reveal any awareness that the heavy doses of narcotics he administered daily to Hiram could have contributed to his increasing sense of despair; instead, he remained intently focused on a physiological cure for hypochondriasis and the resulting monomania. A century hence, psychiatrists would not only be aware of the side effects of the narcotics being prescribed by Rockwell but would also recognize the somatic and persecutory illusions manifested by Hiram — his fear that Rockwell was "authorized by law to put him out of the way soon" and that he had "putrified and smells so no one can come near him" — as classic signs that the major depressive order from which he suffered had progressed to become "severe with psychotic features."[14]

Upon his dismissal and return to the farm and family, Hiram clearly suffered from a major depressive order with severe psychotic features. Chronic subdural hematoma, if left untreated, often leads to such a condition. Quite often the resulting depression leads to suicide. Alfred Alvarez believes there is "a whole class of suicides . . . who take their own lives not in order to die but to escape confusion, to clear their heads."[15] This may be as close as anyone can come to determining the cause of Hiram's death.

NOTES

1. For standard analyses of this condition, see Lawrence F. Marshall, "Injury to the Head and Spinal Cord," in J. Claude Bennett and Fred Plum, eds., *Cecil Textbook of Medicine*, 2 vols., 20th ed. (Philadelphia: W. B. Saunders, 1996), 2:2135–40; J. Donald Easton, "Cranial Trauma," in Jay Stein and Martin J. Cline, eds., *Internal Medicine* (Boston: Little, Brown, 1983), 867–69; Allan H. Ropper, "Traumatic Injuries of the Head and Spine," in Anthony S. Fauci, Eugene Braunwald, Kurt J. Isselbacher, Jean D. Wilson, Joseph B. Martin, Dennis L. Kasper, Stephen Hauser, and Dan L. Longo, eds., *Harrison's Principles of Internal Medicine*, 14th ed. (New York: McGraw-Hill, 1998), 2390–98.

Chronic subdural hematomas often give rise to a complex range of symptoms. For insight into those that appear to be particularly relevant to Hiram's condition, see Michel Elie, François Primeau, and Martin G. Cole, "Chronic Subdural Hematoma in the Elderly: A Case Report," *Journal of Geriatric Psy-*

chiatry and Neurology 9 (1996): 100–101; Daniel R. Weinberger, "Brain Disease and Psychiatric Illness: When Should a Psychiatrist Order a CAT Scan?" *American Journal of Psychiatry* 141 (1984): 1521–27; Jane R. Potter and Alan H. Fruin, "Chronic Subdural Hematoma: The 'great imitator,'" *Geriatrics* 32 (1977): 61–66; Linda M. Luxon and M. J. G. Harrison, "Chronic Subdural Haematoma," *Quarterly Journal of Medicine*, new ser., 48 (1979): 43–53; Donald W. Black, "Mental Changes Resulting from Subdural Haematoma," *British Journal of Psychiatry* 145 (1984): 200–203; Parvis Malek-Ahmadi, Jose R. Beceiro, B. Wayne McNeil, and Richard L. Weddige, "Electroconvulsive Therapy and Chronic Subdural Hematoma," *Convulsive Therapy* 6 (1990): 38–41.

2. The clinical literature on chronic subdural hematomas indicates that this condition is quite often accompanied by severe depression. The literature on depression is immense. That which I found most helpful includes Paul Willner, *Depression: A Psychobiological Synthesis* (New York: John Wiley & Sons, 1985); Paul Gilbert, *Depression: The Evolution of Powerlessness* (New York: Guilford Press, 1992); D. P. B. Goldberg, *Depression* (Edinburgh, Scotland: Churchill Livingstone, 1984); Brana Lobel and Robert M. A. Hirschfeld, *Depression: What We Know* (Rockville, Md.: National Institute of Mental Health, 1984); and Dorothy Rowe, *The Experience of Depression* (Chichester, N.Y.: Wiley, 1978). The single book that speaks most cogently to Hiram's life and condition is Mortimer Ostow, *The Psychology of Melancholy* (New York: Harper & Row, 1970). Ostow notes the relationship between depression and an aged appearance on 10–11.

3. For a discussion of the relationship between chronic subdural hematomas and seizures, see M. Cole and E. Spatz, "Seizures in Chronic Subdural Hematoma," *New England Journal of Medicine* 265 (1961): 628–31; and Sidney Levin, "Psychomotor Epilepsy as a Manifestation of Subdural Hematoma," *American Journal of Psychiatry* 107 (1951): 501–2.

4. For a discussion of transient ischemic strokes, see J. Donald Easton, Stephen L. Hauser, and Joseph B. Martin, "Cerebrovascular Diseases," in *Harrison's Principles of Internal Medicine*, 2325–48.

5. For a discussion of anxiety syndromes that include panic attack and panic disorder, see *Diagnostic and Statistical Manual of Mental Disorders*, 4th ed. (Washington, D.C.: American Psychiatric Association, 1994), 345–49 (hereafter cited as DSM-IV).

6. Such a precipitous loss of weight—nearly 15 percent of his normal body weight—in a period of six months is characteristic of individuals suffering from a major depressive disorder. See DSM-IV, 339–45, for a clinical analysis of this condition. At the same time, chronic subdural hematomas are often bilateral and can produce misleading clinical syndromes. As they gradually expand, they

often behave clinically like a tumor. The appearance of systemic symptoms such as weight loss or anxiety suggests the presence of a tumor. For discussions of the behavior of chronic subdural hematomas and brain tumors, see Ropper, "Traumatic Injuries of the Head and Spine," 2393; and Stephen M. Sagar and Mark A. Israel, "Tumors of the Nervous System," in *Harrison's Principles of Internal Medicine*, 2398–498. See esp. 2398.

7. For a discussion of pain referral, see Howard L. Fields and Joseph B. Martin, "Pain: Pathophysiology and Management," in *Harrison's Principles of Internal Medicine*, 53–58. Hiram's "increasing weakness of limbs" is, however, also a prominent characteristic of chronic subdural hematoma. See Weinberger, "Brain Disease and Psychiatric Illness"; Potter and Fruin, "Chronic Subdural Hematoma"; and Luxon and Harrison, "Chronic Subdural Haemotoma."

8. For the distinction between depression without psychotic features and depression with psychotic features, see DSM-IV, 339–45.

9. Much of the literature on shame and depression speaks to the circumstances of Hiram's life. D. P. B. Goldberg notes that in adolescence the parents of depressive individuals often employed verbal shaming as a method of discipline. *Depression*, 25. Helen B. Lewis observes that shame is often central to the maintenance of lifelong attachments to people. Shame (turning feelings of anger or frustration inward) is a means by which individuals try to preserve their loving relationships to others. Lewis, "Introduction: Shame — the 'Sleeper' in Psychopathology," in Helen B. Lewis, ed., *The Role of Shame in Symptom Formation* (Hillsdale, N.J.: LEA, 1987), 1–28. Ostow contends that an "individual who is forced to be dependent [upon another] by circumstances beyond his control becomes angry with the individual upon whom he becomes dependent even if the compulsion arises from his own instinctual needs and his own inability to achieve independence." *Psychology of Melancholy*, 85. Such feelings of intense anger (hatred) coexist with a deeply dependent love for the same person. Consequently, whatever anger he or she feels toward that person is not only concealed from the object of his or her anger, but the individual actually sublimates it in such a way that it exists only in his unconscious. At times an individual otherwise disposed toward depression is protected from it by acting out some identification with the one she or he is dependent upon. "This acting out requires a continuing series of successes and does not tolerate rebuffs or failures. Therefore any significant failure or rebuff may undo the defense and precipitate depression" (81). Simultaneously it may weaken the defensive effort to sublimate the anger or hostility felt toward the dependent other (79–91).

10. To identify the content as well as the side effects of the various prescriptions employed by Rockwell during Hiram's residence at the asylum, I have

relied upon various editions of *The Pharmacopoeia of the United States of America, by the Authority of the Medical Societies and Colleges* (Washington, D.C.: General Medical Convention, 1820, 1830, 1840); *A Translation of the New Pharmacopoeia of the Royal Colleges of Physicians of London: With Notes and Criticisms, by G.F. Collier* (London, 1837); *Gray's Supplement to the Pharmacopoeia; Being a Concise but Comprehensive Dispensatory and Manual of Facts and Formulae, for the Chemist and Druggist and Medical Practitioner* (London: Longman & Co., 1848); and Horatio C. Wood, *A Treatise on Therapeutics, Comprising materia medica and Toxicology, with Especial Reference to the Application of the Physiological Action of Drugs to Clinical Medicine* (Philadelphia: J. B. Lippincott & Co., 1874).

11. For insight into the influence that monomania wielded among physicians at this time, see Jan Goldstein, *Console and Classify: The French Psychiatric Profession in the Nineteenth Century* (New York: Cambridge University Press, 1987), 152–96. By this time, too, hypochondriasis exerted an equally powerful hold on alienists. See especially George Man Burrows, *Commentaries on the Causes, Forms, Symptoms, and Treatment, Moral and Medical, of Insanity* (London: Thomas & George Underwood, 1828), 466–83. My discussion of medical diagnoses as cultural constructs that "filter" the manner in which physicians encounter their patients draws upon Arthur Kleinman, *The Illness Narratives: Suffering, Healing, and the Human Condition* (New York: Basic Books, 1988), 194–208; Atwood D. Gaines, "Cultural Definitions, Behavior, and the Person in American Psychiatry," in Anthony Marsella and Geoffrey White, eds., *Cultural Conceptions of Mental Health and Therapy* (London: D. Reidel, 1982), 167–92; Atwood D. Gaines, "From DSM-I to III-R; Voices of Self Mastery and the Other: A Cultural Constructivist Reading of U.S. Psychiatric Classification," *Social Science and Medicine* 36 (1992): 3–24; and Juan Mezzich, Arthur Kleinman, Horatio Fabrega, and Delores Parron, eds., *Culture and Psychiatric Diagnosis: A DSM-IV Perspective* (Washington, D.C.: American Psychiatric Press, 1996).

12. Woodward made extensive use of these same drugs. See Gerald Grob, "Samuel B. Woodward and the Practice of Psychiatry in Early Nineteenth-Century America," *Bulletin of the History of Medicine* 36 (1962): 430–31.

13. MR, 27 Jan. 1838.

14. DSM-IV, 298, 339–45, 376–77. One of the most common somatic delusions associated with a major depressive disorder is the belief "that he or she emits a foul odor from the skin, mouth, rectum, or vagina" (298). Ostow maintains that it is not uncommon for severely melancholic patients to insist that "my liver is disintegrating and this disease will kill me" or that "my organs are decaying." *The Psychology of Melancholy*, 44, 59.

15. *The Savage God: A Study of Suicide* (New York: Random House, 1970), 131.

Notes

Relying primarily on the voluminous Harwood diaries located at the Bennington Museum, in Bennington, Vermont, *A Tale of New England* attempts to view the world of early-nineteenth-century America through the eyes of Hiram Harwood. Although the book's focus is on Hiram's thoughts and actions throughout, it is impossible to separate his life from that of the larger Bennington community. He and his family could not avoid the religious, social, economic, and political tensions affecting the town during his lifetime. Since I have discussed these issues fully in *Bennington and the Green Mountain Boys: The Emergence of Liberal Democracy in Vermont, 1760–1850* (Baltimore: Johns Hopkins University Press, 1996), I touch upon them in the present work only to the extent necessary to clarify Hiram's thought and behavior. In this regard *Bennington and the Green Mountain Boys* serves as a template providing the necessary background for understanding the Harwood family experience. Consequently, in an effort to avoid excessive repetition, no references to *Bennington and the Green Mountain Boys* appear in the notes below.

In many ways the Harwood family is representative of a great many rural New Englanders living at the time. In their day-to-day lives, their social interactions, their farming methods and involvement with a market economy, their desire to better themselves, and their participation in the civic life of their community, family members mirrored or exemplified the attitudes and behavior of thousands of other Americans living in the early nineteenth century. At the same time, though, they were distinctly unrepresentative in other important ways. Their allegiance to a patriarchal family structure; their commitment to impartible inheritance; their adherence to traditional communal practices and family values; Hiram's peculiar path to achieving manhood; the political activities of Hiram, his father, Benjamin, and his Uncle Jonas all fly in

the face of current historical orthodoxy. Scholarly treatment of these issues —
whether representative or unrepresentative of the Harwood experience — has
become prodigious in recent decades. *A Tale of New England* is deeply embedded in this scholarship, and yet, to keep the narrative sharply focused on the
Harwoods, historiographical discussions appear in the endnotes rather than in
the body of the text. Further, since the literature on such issues as patriarchy,
market values, masculinity, and the emergence of the middle class is so vast, no
effort has been made in the notes to be exhaustive. Instead, only works particularly relevant to the life experiences of the Harwoods have been included.

INTRODUCTION

1. Harwood Diary, Bennington Museum, Bennington, Vt., March 3, 1808
(hereafter cited as HD).

2. HD, 14 April, 7 Dec. 1808.

3. The first mention of Nathaniel Harwood in any official records occurs on
May 9, 1670, when he purchased six acres of land, including a house, apple
trees, and fences, "in consideration of a valluable sume in hand." Middlesex
County Deed Book 4, Middlesex County Courthouse, Cambridge, Mass., pp.
100–101. Nathaniel was made a freeman March 21, 1690.

4. Nathaniel Harwood left his homestead and farm to his third son, Peter,
who sold it and then purchased an extensive property in Littleton. Middlesex
County Deed Book 37, pp. 536–37. Peter, in turn, willed his entire estate to his
fourth son, Joseph. Middlesex County Probate Records, Massachusetts State
Archives, Boston, no. 10631. Peter's brother Nathaniel and his wife, Mary,
made over all their landed property to their son Jonathan on the condition that
"They were to have the best room in the now dwelling house, with the best
chamber, and a good, convenient cellar, without any let, stint, or hindrance.
And deed not to take place 'till their, the said Nathaniel and Mary Harwood's
decease." Twelve years later they willed the same to Jonathan. Middlesex
County Probate Records, no. 10629.

5. Lawrence Stone maintains that the modern nuclear family, characterized
by liberal rather than patriarchal values, emerged in England well before the
nineteenth century. *The Family, Sex, and Marriage in England 1500–1800* (New
York: Harper & Row, 1977). Stone's hypothesis pervades American scholarship
as well. See, for example, James Henretta, *The Evolution of American Society, 1700–1815: An Interdisciplinary Analysis* (Lexington, Mass.: D. C. Heath,
1973); Jay Fliegelman, *The American Revolution against Patriarchal Authority,
1750–1800* (Cambridge: Cambridge University Press, 1982).

6. Since this bargain took place before Benjamin began keeping a journal,
the agreement itself does not appear in the journal. Benjamin's most specific

reference to the agreement appears on September 13, 1809. In May 1814 Peter deeded the farm over to Benjamin in return for five thousand dollars, "received to my full satisfaction." Bennington County Deed Book 5, Bennington, Vt., p. 329. Since no money changed hands, Peter must have accepted Benjamin's thirty years of labor on the farm as payment in full. Peter's other children received portable property as their settlement.

CHAPTER I. A MAN OF BUSINESS

1. HD, 23 Oct. 1809.

2. HD, 15 Feb.; 7, 20, 28 March 1806; 31 March 1808; 23 June 1805.

3. HD, 16 July, 12 Aug. 1806.

4. HD, 28 June 1810; 5 Aug. 1809; 10 Aug. 1810.

5. Watson H. Harwood, *A Genealogical History of the Concord Harwoods Descendants of Nathaniel Harwood, son of John Harwood of London, England* (Chasm Fall, N.Y.: 1912), 10, 13–14. Middlesex County Land Book 37, p. 537; Book 38, pp. 297–98; Book 40, pp. 270–71. All these transactions involved transfers of four acres or less.

6. On November 3, 1739, Benjamin sold the one and one-half acres in Concord given to him by his father, Peter, prior to his death. Peter Harwood's will, dated 25 Oct. 1738, Middlesex County Probate Records, Massachusetts State Archives, Boston, no. 10631. At that time Benjamin described himself as a "Weaver" residing in Grafton Township, Worcester County. A deed to land in Grafton dated November 3, 1740, described Benjamin as a "Worsted Weaver." Worcester County Land Book 13, Worcester County Courthouse, Worcester, Mass., p. 290. Benjamin is mentioned only one other time in the Worcester County Land Books. This involved the sale of fifteen acres of land on February 13, 1748. At that time he is listed as a resident of Hardwick. Worcester County Land Book 33, p. 36.

In his will Benjamin left several rights of land in Westminster, New Hampshire, to his sons. Hampshire County Probate Court, Northampton, Mass., box 68, no. 4. Since the deeds to this property are not recorded in the Exeter County (N.H.) Courthouse, it is likely that Benjamin purchased these rights from a none-too-honest speculator in lands on the New Hampshire Grants. They would eventually prove worthless to the holders.

7. Quoted in Alan Heimert, *Religion and the American Mind from the Great Awakening to the Revolution* (Cambridge, Mass.: Harvard University Press, 1966), 305.

8. These quotations from the church record appear in Lucius R. Paige, *History of Hardwick, Massachusetts* (Boston, 1883), 225–26, 388.

9. Quoted in ibid., 182.

10. Edward W. Carpenter, *The History of the Town of Amherst, Massachusetts* (Amherst, Mass.: Carpenter & Morehouse, 1896), 19; James Avery Smith, *A Genealogical Outline of Individuals and Families Residing at Amherst, Massachusetts from circa 1728 through 1850*, 4 vols. (Amherst, Mass.: James A. Smith, 1984), 2:345–46.

11. Benjamin Harwood's will, Hampshire County Probate Court, Northampton, Mass., box 68, no. 4.

12. The legal status of the farm is uncertain. There is no recorded deed in the Hampden County Courthouse.

13. Harwood, *Concord Harwoods*, 17–18.

14. Peter paid £10 16s. 11p. for this land, December 7, 1761. Deed Book A-1, Town Clerk's Office, Bennington, Vt., pp. 214–15.

15. On April 13, 1785, Eleazer sold this land to Peter. Bennington County Deed Book 3, Bennington, Vt., p. 462.

16. Harwood, *Concord Harwoods*, 17–19, 25–26.

17. Ibid., pp. 17–18, 25–26.

18. Bennington County Deed Book 5, p. 329. This included 100 acres of the original 190 acres that Peter Harwood purchased from Samuel Robinson and the 55 acres that he purchased from Asa Harwood in 1785. The records do not indicate what became of the other 90 acres of Peter's original purchase. This land may have gone to Benjamin's brothers Clark and Ebenezer as partial settlement of Peter's estate when it was decided that Benjamin would inherit the farm.

19. Benjamin kept a very precise record of the number of acres he planted annually with each crop, as well as the annual yield per acre. He also kept a close accounting of his oxen, horses, cattle, and sheep. These numbers varied with each year and even according to the seasons of each year. See, for example, HD, 9 Aug., 3 Sept., 21 Nov. 1805; 21 Nov. 1806; 5 May, 14 Nov. 1807; 24 March, 7 May 1808; 11 March, 8 May, 27 Nov. 1809; 17 May 1810. For some reason Benjamin did not keep a record of his hogs, nor did he include them on the list he turned in with his annual poll. On April 17, 1806, he did mention that he had 15 young pigs born to 3 sows, and on November 10, 1808, he referred to 27 hogs of all sizes.

20. Benjamin never recorded the specific terms of this agreement. He did, however, make note from time to time of the days of labor that Ira had lost for one reason or another. See HD, 30 May, 26 June, 7 July, 18 July 1805. By this last date, including July 4, Ira had lost a total of eighteen and one-half days.

21. Greg Dening discusses the "silences of self" that help reveal the "closed-down-but-full-of-possibilities nature of self" in "Texts of Self," in Ronald Hoffman, Mechal Sobel, and Fredrika Teute, eds., *Through a Glass*

Darkly: Reflections on Personal Identity in Early America (Chapel Hill: University of North Carolina Press, 1997), 157–62.

22. Colossians 3:18 reads, "Wives, submit yourselves unto your own husbands, as it is fit in the Lord." All Bible quotations are from the King James Version.

23. Although other farmers may not have kept the precise records that Benjamin did, his choice of crops and methods of cultivation followed traditional beliefs and customs commonly practiced by farmers in New England for over a century. Percy Bidwell and John Falconer, *History of Agriculture in the Northern United States, 1620–1860* (Washington, D.C.: Carnegie Institution, 1925); Howard Russell, *A Long, Deep Furrow: Three Centuries of Farming in New England* (Hanover, N.H.: University Press of New England, 1976); Jeremy Attack and Fred Bateman, *To Their Own Soil: Agriculture in the Antebellum North* (Ames, Iowa: Iowa State University Press, 1987); and Clarence Danhof, *Change in Agriculture: The Northern United States, 1820–1870* (Cambridge, Mass.: Harvard University Press, 1969).

24. In one form or another, this phrase appears more often than any other throughout Benjamin's journal.

25. HD, 8 May; 20, 6 June 1807.

26. HD, 19 May 1807, 24 June 1806, 18 June 1808.

27. HD, 8, 9, 10 June 1807; 13 June 1808.

28. HD, 4 Oct 1808.

29. HD, 7 Oct 1807.

30. HD, 5 July 1806.

31. HD, 1 June 1805; 8, 11 June 1808.

32. HD, 21, 27 May 1808.

33. HD, 16 July 1808.

34. HD, 4 Aug. 1809.

35. HD, 29 Aug.; 1, 5 Sept. 1806.

36. This custom, originating in medieval England, persisted among those in America who adhered to traditional religious customs. Clare Gittings, *Death, Burial, and the Individual in Early Modern England* (London: Croom & Helm, 1984); David Cressy, *Birth, Marriage & Death: Ritual, Religion, and the Life-Cycle in Tudor and Stuart England* (New York: Oxford University Press, 1997); Gary Laderman, *The Sacred Remains: American Attitudes toward Death, 1799–1883* (New Haven, Conn.: Yale University Press, 1996); and James K. Crissman, *Death and Dying in Central Appalachia: Changing Attitudes and Practices* (Urbana, Ill.: University of Illinois Press, 1994).

37. HD, 24 Nov. 1807.

38. Bennington's Congregational Church, like other Strict Congregational

churches, drew a clear distinction between the "church" and the "society." The church consisted solely of individuals who had undergone the experience of saving grace, whereas the society included those who had not yet been saved. Only church members could participate in the sacrament of Communion and take part in the governance of the church.

39. HD, 18 Nov. 1805, 6 July 1806, 4 March 1810.

40. HD, 29 May 1808.

41. HD, 8 Dec. 1808.

42. HD, 2, 16, 22 Aug. 1808.

43. HD, 16 Sept. 1807, 29 Sept. 1808.

44. HD, 5 Sept. 1809.

45. HD, 3 Sept. 1805.

46. HD, 24 March 1807.

47. For a full discussion of the embargo, see Bradford Perkins, *Prologue to War: England and the United States, 1805–1812* (Berkeley: University of California Press, 1963), 140–83.

48. HD, 12 July 1808.

49. HD, 16 Aug. 1809.

50. HD, 13 Oct. 1806.

51. HD, 7 Oct. 1809, 15 Oct. 1807, 15 Oct. 1808, 15 Oct. 1807.

52. HD, 5 Oct. 1808, 11 Oct. 1806, 26 Oct. 1807.

53. HD, 11 Nov. 1807.

54. HD, 18 June, 10 Aug. 1808.

55. Benjamin's beliefs reveal the continued power of eighteenth-century perceptions of masculinity. His attitudes locate him much closer to the traditional male described in Lisa Wilson, *Ye Heart of a Man: The Domestic Life of Men in Colonial New England* (New Haven, Conn.: Yale University Press, 1999), than to the "self-made men" found in Michael Kimmel, *Manhood in America: A Cultural History* (New York: Free Press, 1996); E. Anthony Rotundo, *American Manhood: Transformations in Masculinity from the Revolution to the Modern Era* (New York: Basic Books, 1993); and Mark Kann, *A Republic of Men: The American Founders, Gendered Language, and Patriarchal Politics* (New York: New York University Press, 1998).

56. HD, 4 Sept. 1806.

57. HD, 6, 7, Nov. 1806; 6, 7, Feb. 1808. The Harwoods clearly had important ties to the world market through their grain trade in Troy. At the same time they remained immersed in an elaborate web of local exchange and home production. Their farm is an excellent example of what Richard Bushman refers to as a "composite farm"—one in which production for use and production for exchange were imperceptibly blended. Bushman's essay sheds wonderful

new light on the subsistence/commercial, traditional/modern, precapitalist/capitalist arguments that have engaged American historians for the last several decades. See Bushman, "Markets and Composite Farms in Early America," *William and Mary Quarterly*, 3d ser., 40 (1998): 451–74.

58. HD, 30 May 1809. Laurel Thatcher Ulrich provides excellent insight into women's contribution to the economic welfare of farm families in "Martha Ballard and Her Girls: Women's Work in Eighteenth-Century Maine," in Stephen Innes, ed., *Work and Labor in Early America* (Chapel Hill: University of North Carolina Press, 1988), 83–86; and in "Housewife and Gadder: Themes of Self-Sufficiency and Community in Eighteenth-Century New England," in Carol Groneman and Mary Beth Norton, eds., *"To Toil the Livelong Day": America's Women at Work, 1780–1980* (Ithaca, N.Y.: Cornell University Press, 1987), 21–34.

59. It is difficult to reach an exact calculation of the farm's annual income, but from the records Benjamin kept for 1807, 1808, and 1809, an average of $250 appears reasonable.

60. HD, 7 Feb. 1808, 12 June 1809, 19 April 1810.

61. HD, 20 July 1810, 25 Feb. 1809, 11 Aug. 1810.

62. HD, 27 July 1810; 19 June, 19 March 1807; 4 June 1808.

63. HD, 13 Jan. 1806.

64. HD, 7 March 1807.

65. HD, 30 Jan. 1809, 10 Feb. 1806, 4 March 1809.

66. HD, 6, 7, Nov. 1806. Bibliographical citations of all books and other writings mentioned in the text may be found in Appendix 1.

67. HD, 9 May 1807, 25 May 1808.

68. HD, 12, 27 Dec. 1807.

69. HD, 27 Dec. 1809.

70. Many New Englanders perceived a close relationship between a knowledge of grammar and an improved social and economic status. Kenneth Cmiel, *Democratic Eloquence: The Fight over Popular Speech in Nineteenth-Century America* (New York: William Morrow, 1990), 36–82.

71. HD, 30 May 1809, 16 May 1810.

72. HD, 2 Feb; 5 March; 1, 20 June 1807.

73. HD, 27, 28 June; 17 Sept. 1807.

74. HD, 22 Sept. 1807.

75. HD, 23 Sept. 1807.

76. HD, 28 April 1809.

77. HD, 18, 19, 20 Feb. 1809.

78. HD, 14 Sept. 1809.

79. Catherine Kelly analyzes the "specter of spinsterhood" in *In the New*

England Fashion: Reshaping Women's Lives in the Nineteenth Century (Ithaca, N.Y.: Cornell University Press, 1999). See esp. 115–22.

80. HD, 6 Feb. 1809.

81. HD 13 Sept. 1809.

82. HD, 14 Sept., 1 Dec. 1809; 24 May 1810.

83. HD, 1 Dec. 1809.

CHAPTER 2. A MAN OF PLEASURE

1. HD, 23 Oct. 1810.

2. HD, 23 Oct. 1810. Earlier Benjamin had observed that he overlooked Hiram's "childish scribblings" in the journal because "it keeps him out of mischief." HD, 29 Sept. 1809.

3. Commonplace books are private journals into which individuals copied letters, poems, essays, and other public documents in an attempt to make these words or thoughts their own. Kenneth Lockridge, *On the Sources of Patriarchal Rage: The Commonplace Books of William Byrd and Thomas Jefferson and the Gendering of Power in the Eighteenth Century* (New York: New York University Press, 1992); and Susan Miller, *Assuming the Positions: Cultural Pedagogy and the Politics of Commonplace Writing* (Pittsburgh: University of Pittsburgh Press, 1998).

4. Greg Deming discusses "texts of self" in Ronald Hoffman, Mechal Sobel, and Fredrika Teute, eds., *Through a Glass Darkly: Reflections on Personal Identity in Early America* (Chapel Hill: University of North Carolina Press, 1997), 157–62. Regarding the material copied into commonplace books, Lockridge observes that "beneath their surface sheen of public knowledge, then, these are profoundly instruments of personal identity." *Patriarchal Rage*, 4.

5. Diaries often result from efforts to deal with personal tensions in the life of the diarist. Steven Kagle, *American Diary Literature, 1620–1799* (Boston: Twayne, 1979); Suzanne Bunkers and Cynthia Huff, *Inscribing the Daily: Critical Essays on Women's Diaries* (Amherst, Mass.: University of Massachusetts Press, 1996). In his discussion of texts of self, Greg Deming asserts that such texts "come mostly in those moments of cultural edginess when contradictory demands are made on the individual." Deming, "Texts of Self," in Hoffman, Sobel, and Teute, *Through a Glass Darkly*, 157. Such personal tension is central to Kenneth Lockridge's argument in "Colonial Self-Fashioning: Paradoxes and Pathologies in the Construction of Genteel Identity in Eighteenth-Century America," in ibid., 274–339.

6. The stages of life — dependent, semidependent, independent — described in Joseph Kett, *Rites of Passage: Adolescence in America, 1790 to the Present* (New York: Basic Books, 1977), although more helpful in understanding the matura-

tion process of young people in nineteenth-century America than terms such as *childhood, adolescence,* and *adulthood,* have little relevance to the Harwoods' family experience. Their adherence to traditional patriarchal attitudes left Hiram suspended in a state between dependence and semidependence for most of his adult life. John Gillis's description of the preindustrial peasant family, in *Youth and History: Tradition and Change in European Age Relations, 1770–Present* (New York: Academic Press, 1981), comes much closer to the life experience of the Harwood family throughout the first third of the nineteenth century.

7. HD, 22 Oct., 14 Jan. 1811; 27 May, 9 April 1812.

8. HD, 9, 28, 27 April 1811.

9. HD, 9 Aug. 1811, 24 July 1812.

10. HD, 18 April 1812, 10 Oct. 1811, 15 May 1812.

11. HD, 18 May 1812, 15 April 1811.

12. HD, 27 May 1812. In the early nineteenth century, the stigma of boyishness carried with it an association with frivolous behavior, the lack of worthy aims, and the want of self-control. Consequently, any action characterized by a man as boyish was viewed with extreme contempt. Anthony Rotundo, *American Manhood: Transformations in Masculinity from the Revolution to the Modern Era* (New York: Basic Books, 1993), 20; Michael Kimmel, *Manhood in America: A Cultural History* (New York: Free Press, 1996), 18; and Mark Kann, *A Republic of Men: The American Founders, Gendered Language, and Patriarchal Politics* (New York: New York University Press, 1998), 20–21.

13. HD, 19 Feb. 1834.

14. HD, 28, 20 April; 7 Jan. 1811.

15. John Demos, "Shame and Guilt in Early New England," in Carol Z. Stearns and Peter N. Stearns, eds., *Emotion and Social Change: Toward a New Psychohistory* (New York: Holmes & Meier, 1988), 69–85.

16. HD, 5 Feb., 1 Nov. 1811.

17. Although Hiram always referred to Mary Doty as his grandmother, she was Peter's second wife and not Benjamin's mother. She had a number of children of her own, whose families became close with the Harwoods.

18. HD, 27, 29 Oct. 1819.

19. HD, 16 Nov. 1810.

20. HD, 5 Aug. 1811.

21. HD, 5 Oct. 1811.

22. HD, 10 Nov. 1811.

23. Kett suggests that religious conversion could be one means of laying aside youth and embracing the new associations of adulthood. *Rites of Passage,* 80. Living as he did within a patriarchal family situation, however, Hiram knew full well that religious conversion or no, he would remain in a semi-

dependent status within the Harwood household. This may have contributed to his passive-aggressive behavior.

24. HD, 23 Oct. 1810, 10 May 1811.

25. HD, 31 Oct. 1810.

26. HD, 6 Dec. 1810.

27. HD, 28, 29 Sept. 1811.

28. Joyce Appleby offers a provocative discussion of a cohort of men born in New England between 1765 and 1804 whose lives stand in stark contrast with that of Hiram. See "New Cultural Heroes in the Early National Period," in Thomas Haskell and Richard Teichgraeber, eds., *The Culture of the Market: Historical Essays* (New York: Cambridge University Press, 1993), 163–88; and Joyce Appleby, *Inheriting the Revolution: The First Generation of Americans* (Cambridge, Mass.: Harvard University Press, 2000). The principal common characteristic she discerns among these men is that they had all broken free from their parents and struck out on their own to forge new careers amid the burgeoning opportunities provided by the economic and social transformations taking place within the new nation.

29. Even though they were of different generations, Ira and Hiram were of the same age cohort and thus experienced similar tensions and anxieties within the Harwood family. Conflict resulting from age stratification was quite common during this time. Ann Foner, "Age Stratification and the Changing Family," in John Demos and Sarane Spence Boocock, eds., *Turning Points: Historical and Sociological Essays on the Family* (Chicago: University of Chicago Press, 1978), 340–65.

30. HD, 29 Oct. 1810.

31. Haswell, the original editor of the *Vermont Gazette*, was prosecuted by Federalist authorities under the provisions of the Sedition Act and forced to serve a sentence in the local jail as a result.

32. HD, 29 Nov. 1810, 21 Sept. 1811.

33. HD, 23 April 1812, 20 Nov. 1811.

34. HD, 8 Nov. 1811. Hannah More, the author of *Coelebs*, intended to convey proper middle-class values in her stilted, moralistic novel. Annette M. B. Meakin, *Hannah More: A Biographical Study* (London: John Murray, 1919), 337–75; Elizabeth Kowaleski-Wallace, *Their Fathers' Daughters: Hannah More, Maria Edgeworth, and Patriarchal Complicity* (New York: Oxford University Press, 1991), 56–93. In terms of understanding Hiram's attraction to *Coelebs*, Leonore Davidoff and Catherine Hall offer the most trenchant analysis. *Family Fortunes: Men and Women of the English Middle Class, 1780–1850* (Chicago: University of Chicago Press, 1987), 167–72.

35. Ronald J. Zboray, *A Fictive People: Antebellum Economic Development and*

the American Reading Public (New York: Oxford University Press, 1993); William J. Gilmore, *Reading Becomes a Necessity of Life: Material and Cultural Life in Rural New England, 1780–1835* (Knoxville: University of Tennessee Press, 1989); Richard D. Brown, *Knowledge Is Power: The Diffusion of Information in Early America, 1700–1865* (New York: Oxford University Press, 1989); and Christopher Clark, "The Diary of an Apprentice Cabinetmaker: Edward Jenner Carpenter's 'Journal,' 1844–45," *Proceedings of the American Antiquarian Society* 98 (1988): 303–94.

For a comprehensive list of the books, magazines, and other pieces of literature mentioned in the Harwood diaries, see Appendix 1.

36. Hiram's reading interests were strikingly similar to those of Edward Jenner Carpenter, a cabinetmaker's apprentice analyzed by David Gross in "The History of the Book: Research Trends and Source Materials," *Book* 31 (Nov. 1993): 3–7.

37. In many ways the figures Hiram so frequently read about were representative of the aggressive, mobile, free individuals that Michael Kimmel and Anthony Rotundo hold to be representative of the nineteenth-century American male. These individuals, as well as those portrayed by Joyce Appleby, vigorously pursued careers entirely closed off to Hiram.

38. HD, 2 Dec. 1810, 21 Jan. 1811.

39. HD, 23 Dec. 1810; 8 Jan., 12 April 1811.

40. HD, 20 Nov. 1810.

41. HD, 21 Nov. 1810.

42. HD, 12, 16, 25 Nov. 1810.

43. HD, 30 Nov. 1811; 19, 21 Feb. 1812.

44. HD, 12 Jan. 1810.

45. HD, 30 March 1812.

46. HD, 17 Nov. 1810.

47. HD, 22 Nov. 1810.

48. HD, 14 Aug. 1811, 26 April 1812.

49. HD, 26 Feb. 1811, 28 Nov. 1810.

50. HD, 3 July 1812.

51. HD, 24 Oct. 1811.

52. HD, 26 Dec. 1810, 11 Jan. 1811.

53. HD, 16 Jan. 1811.

54. HD, 2 Dec. 1810.

55. HD, 4 Oct. 1811.

56. HD, 1 Jan. 1811.

57. HD, 23 Sept. 1811; 2 Dec., 7 Nov. 1810; 13 Jan. 1811; 2 Dec. 1810; 7 March, 23 Jan. 1811.

58. HD, 7, 11 March 1811.

59. HD, 12 March 1811.

60. HD, 27, 28 March; 1 June 1811.

61. HD, 3 May 1811.

62. HD, 19 July 1811.

63. HD, 10 Dec. 1810; 13 April, 29 Jan. 1811; 8 Feb. 1812.

64. HD, 8 Dec. 1811; 14 Feb., 21 March, 13 April 1812.

65. HD, 20 Aug. 1811.

66. HD, 28 Aug. 1811.

67. HD, 27 Sept. 1811.

68. HD, 27 Sept. 1811.

69. HD, 28 Sept., 8 Oct. 1811.

70. HD, 14, 15 Oct. 1811.

71. HD, 17 Oct. 1811.

72. In her analysis of manhood in the greater Revolutionary period (1740–1840), Mechal Sobel writes that many men "came to feel that they could improve their insecure sense of manhood by becoming soldiers." *Teach Me Dreams: The Search for Self in the Revolutionary Era* (Princeton, N.J.: Princeton University Press, 2000), 135.

73. Reginald Horseman, *The Causes of the War of 1812* (Philadelphia: University of Pennsylvania Press, 1962), 30. The legislation calling for troops appears in the *Annals of the Congress of the United States, 1789–1824*, 42 vols. (Washington, D.C., 1834–56), 12th Cong., 1st sess., 1811–12, 2267–69.

74. HD, 14 June, 7 Oct. 1811; 23 July 1812.

CHAPTER 3. A SOLDIER'S LIFE

1. HD, 5 Sept. 1812.

2. The secretary of war ordered regularly organized militia units all over the country to supply a specific number of men to make up the one-hundred-thousand-man army called for by President Madison. Volunteers or draftees from these militia companies, said to be "detached" from their local companies, served in newly formed regiments. Men from the various town militia companies throughout Bennington County made up the "detached regiment" in which Hiram served. The law calling for the formation of such regiments appears in the *Annals of the Congress of the United States, 1789–1824*, 42 vols. (Washington, D.C., 1834–56), 12th Cong., 1st sess., 1811–12, 2267–69.

3. HD, 7 Sept. 1812.

4. HD, 8 Sept. 1812.

5. The quotations appear under the date 10 Sept. 1812 in Hiram's military journal — the "blank book" purchased on September 7. To avoid confusion

with the Harwood Diary (HD), the military journal, also in the Bennington Museum, is cited hereafter as MJ.

6. MJ, 10 Sept. 1812.

7. Herbert Johnson mistakenly assumed the two Hiram Harwoods to be the same man and therefore recorded Zechariah's son as serving in both the detached militia and the Eleventh Regiment of Vermont regulars. *Roster of Soldiers in the War of 1812–14* (St. Albans, Vt.: Messenger Press, 1933), 204.

8. As early as July, Hiram had asked Captain Samuel Blackmer if he might serve as a fifer in the new company. HD, 7 July 1812. As a result, Blackmer may have intervened on Hiram's behalf with Captain Samuel Cross.

9. It was standard military policy, from colonial times through the Civil War, to allow men to provide substitutes or to pay to exempt themselves from service. Lawrence D. Cress, *Citizens in Arms: The Army and the Militia in American Society to the War of 1812* (Chapel Hill: University of North Carolina Press, 1982), 3–14.

10. MJ, 10 Sept. 1812.

11. MJ, 11 Sept. 1812.

12. MJ, 11 Sept. 1812.

13. MJ, 12 Sept. 1812.

14. Zechariah's sons Silas, Abel, Oliver, and Joseph lived in Rupert.

15. This was an adaptation of a popular tune, "Mortality," that emerged with the enthusiasm for taking Canada.

16. MJ, 12 Sept. 1812.

17. MJ, 13 Sept. 1812.

18. MJ, 14 Sept. 1812.

19. MJ, 14 Sept. 1812.

20. MJ, 15 Sept. 1812. Brigadier-General William Hull led an abortive American invasion of Canada and surrendered his entire garrison at Detroit on August 16, 1812, without firing a shot.

21. MJ, 15 Sept. 1812.

22. MJ, 16 Sept. 1812.

23. MJ, 17 Sept. 1812.

24. MJ, 17 Sept. 1812.

25. MJ, 18 Sept. 1812.

26. The "college" later became the University of Vermont.

27. MJ, 19 Sept. 1812.

28. MJ, 20, 21 Sept. 1812.

29. MJ, 22 Sept. 1812.

30. MJ, 23 Sept. 1812.

31. MJ, 24 Sept. 1812.

32. MJ, 25 Sept. 1812.

33. MJ, 26 Sept. 1812.

34. MJ, 26 Sept. 1812.

35. MJ, 26 Sept. 1812.

36. MJ, 26 Sept. 1812.

37. MJ, 29, 30 Sept. 1812.

38. MJ, 1 Oct. 1812.

39. MJ, 3 Oct. 1812.

40. MJ, 3 Oct. 1812.

41. MJ, 5 Oct. 1812.

42. MJ, 5 Oct. 1812.

43. MJ, 6 Oct. 1812.

44. MJ, 7, 8 Oct. 1812.

45. Members of the detached militia were to receive their pay every two months.

46. MJ, 9 Oct. 1812.

47. MJ, 10 Oct. 1812.

48. MJ, 11 Oct. 1812.

49. MJ, 14 Oct. 1812.

50. MJ, 13 Oct. 1812.

51. MJ, 14 Oct. 1812.

52. After landing at Plattsburgh, Hiram did not make daily entries; instead he lumped together observations with only occasional mention of specific dates. For this reason, references to the journal from this point on note page numbers rather than dates. The quotations in this paragraph of the text appear on page 49.

53. MJ, 50.

54. MJ, 50.

55. MJ, 51.

56. MJ, 52–53.

57. MJ, 54.

58. MJ, 52, 53.

59. MJ, 57.

60. MJ, 58.

61. MJ, 60.

62. MJ, 60, 61.

63. MJ, 62.

64. MJ, 64.

65. MJ, 55, 56.

66. MJ, 67, 68.

67. MJ, 68.

68. MJ, 69–70.

69. MJ, 70.

CHAPTER 4. A COMPACT OF SUCH VITAL IMPORTANCE

1. HD, 6 Dec. 1812.

2. In the first edition of *An American Dictionary of the English Language* (1828), Noah Webster defined manliness as involving the qualities of man — dignity, bravery, boldness. To be manly was to be manlike — firm, brave, undaunted. For an excellent discussion of nineteenth-century American cultural attitudes toward courage and manliness, see Gerald Linderman, *Embattled Courage: The Experience of Combat in the American Civil War* (New York: Free Press, 1987), 7–16. Although he contended that masculine ideals changed over time, Anthony Rotundo identified three — courage, rationality, and steadiness — that persisted over time. "Body and Soul: Changing Ideals of American Middle-Class Manhood, 1770–1920," *Journal of Social History* 16 (1983): 23–38.

3. HD, 7 Dec. 1812.

4. HD, 9 Dec. 1812.

5. HD, 11, 25 Dec. 1812; 17 Jan. 1813.

6. HD, 20–24 Dec. 1812.

7. HD, 2 Jan. 1813.

8. HD, 10, 17 Dec. 1812; 24 Feb. 1813.

9. HD, 14 Jan. 1813.

10. HD, 21 Feb. 1813.

11. HD, 12 Feb., 12 July 1813.

12. HD, 2 April 1813.

13. HD, 8 Feb. 1815.

14. HD, 2 Jan. 1813.

15. HD, 21, 12 April 1813.

16. HD, 6, 11 May 1813; 16 Feb. 1815.

17. HD, 6, 7 April 1814.

18. HD, 25 Feb. 1813.

19. HD, 25 March 1814.

20. HD, 25 March 1814.

21. HD, 7 June 1814.

22. HD, 21 Jan. 1815.

23. HD, 26, 27 March 1814. Jonas and Hiram appear to be signal exceptions to the thesis propounded by Glen Altschuler and Stuart Blumin, who claim that average citizens in the nineteenth century had little interest in politics and

displayed minimal if any loyalty to political parties. *Rude Republic: Americans and Their Politics in the Nineteenth Century* (Princeton, N.J.: Princeton University Press, 2000). At the same time, their close ties to Tanbrook confirm Paul Bourke and Donald De Bats's findings regarding the influence of neighborhoods in American politics. *Washington County: Politics and Community in Antebellum America* (Baltimore: Johns Hopkins University Press, 1995). See esp. 247–322.

24. HD, 30 March, 4 April 1814.

25. HD, 19, 29 Aug. 1814. The British suffered 360 men killed or wounded and nearly 540 men captured when they attempted to storm Ft. Erie on August 15, 1814. The Americans suffered only about 130 casualties. Donald R. Hickey, *The War of 1812: A Forgotten Conflict* (Urbana: University of Illinois Press, 1985), 188–89.

26. HD, 6 Sept. 1814.

27. There was no popular majority in the gubernatorial election of 1813. As a result, the newly elected Federalist majority in the general assembly named Martin Chittenden to be governor.

28. HD, 14 Sept. 1814. For a discussion of this engagement, see Hickey, *War of 1812*, 190–93.

29. HD, 18 Oct. 1814.

30. HD, 25 Oct. 1814.

31. Record Book of the Sons of Liberty of Bennington, Vermont, Vermont Historical Society, Montpelier, Vt., 5 Sept. 1813 (hereafter cited as Record Book).

32. HD, 11 Sept. 1813.

33. Record Book, 11 Sept. 1813.

34. Record Book, 21 Sept. 1813. For insight into Masonic rituals in Bennington, see John Spargo, *Anthony Haswell: Printer, Patriot, Ballader* (Rutland, Vt.: Tuttle Co., 1925), 171–88. Steven Bullock provides a full discussion of Masonic practices throughout the nation in *Revolutionary Brotherhood: Freemasonry and the Transformation of the American Social Order, 1730–1840* (Chapel Hill: University of North Carolina Press, 1996).

35. Record Book, 21, 29 Sept. 1813.

36. Their desire to support the war apparently stopped short of any active participation on their own part. Of the original members of the association, only Hiram and Nathaniel Locke served in the detached militia. The rest had either escaped the lottery or had supplied substitutes.

37. Record Book, 17 Nov. 1813.

38. HD, 17 April 1814. The address does not appear in the Record Book.

Hiram copied it, along with the subscriptions of numerous women, into his journal after he had taken the notice around the neighborhood.

39. HD, 4 July 1814; Record Book, 4 July 1814.

40. Here the reference is to Martin Chittenden, the governor chosen by a Federalist-dominated legislature. The Council of Censors, also composed of a Federalist majority, had recommended that judges of the Vermont Supreme Court be named for life rather than appointed each year.

41. These toasts and poems appear in Record Book, 4 July 1814.

42. HD, 14 Jan. 1814.

43. HD, 29 Jan. 1814.

44. HD, 6, 12, 13, 19 Feb. 1814. The records of the association reveal nothing beyond the fact that Hiram delivered an address. Record Book, 19 Feb. 1814.

45. HD, 7, 29 March; 7 Oct. 1814.

46. HD, 7 Oct. 1814. "G.M.F'r" refers to the *Green Mountain Farmer*, the local newspaper published in Bennington.

47. HD, 27 Jan, 1 May 1814.

48. HD, 2 March 1815, 31 May 1814, 11 Feb. 1815.

49. HD, 4, 5, 6 Feb. 1815.

50. HD, 21 Jan. 1813; 12 Aug., 20 July 1814.

51. HD, 13 Jan, 15 May, 13 Sept., 29 Dec. 1814.

52. HD, 10 March 1814.

53. HD, 6, 27 June 1813; 30 Jan. 1815.

54. HD, 14 July 1814.

55. HD, 29 May 1814.

56. HD, 30 July 1814.

57. HD, 19 June; 5, 8, Aug. 1814.

58. HD, 21 Aug. 1814.

59. This authentic self, when united with another individual willing to reveal his or her true essence, became the basis of romantic love. For a discussion of the growing influence of this ideal in nineteenth-century America, see Ellen K. Rothman, *Hands and Hearts: A History of Courtship in America* (New York: Basic Books, 1984); Karen Lystra, *Searching the Heart: Women, Men, and Romantic Love in Nineteenth-Century America* (New York: Oxford University Press, 1989); and Steven Seidman, *Romantic Longings: Love in America, 1830– 1980* (New York: Routledge, 1991).

60. Lucia McMahon employs this term to describe the relationship between a male teacher and female student; it bears striking similarities to that emerging between Hiram and Clarissa. McMahon provides provocative insights into the

manner in which two individuals could reveal intimate feelings without having intimate personal contact. " 'While Our Souls Together Blend': Narrating a Romantic Readership in the Early Republic," in Peter N. Stearns and Jan Lewis, eds., *An Emotional History of the United States* (New York: New York University Press, 1998), 66–90.

61. HD, 22 Feb. 1815.

62. HD, 23 Feb. 1815.

63. HD, 22 June 1813.

64. HD, 2 Dec. 1813; 30 March, 21 April; 4, 9 May 1814.

65. HD, 21, 22 Dec. 1814.

66. HD, 22, 23, Jan.; 8 Feb. 1815. James Newcomer, *Lady Morgan the Novelist* (Lewisburg, Pa.: Bucknell University Press, 1990); and Lionel Stevenson, *The Wild Irish Girl: The Life of Sydney Owenson, Lady Morgan* (New York: Russell & Russell, 1969), provide interesting insight into both the author and the novel itself.

67. HD, 7 Feb. 1815.

68. HD, 6 Dec. 1813.

69. HD, 12 Feb. 1815.

70. HD, 14, 15 Feb. 1815.

71. HD, 15, 16, Feb. 1815.

72. HD, 14 March, 1815; 21 Oct., 11 Sept. 1814.

73. HD, 15 March 1815.

74. HD, 18 March 1815.

75. HD, 19, 13 March 1815.

76. HD, 19 March 1815.

77. Catherine Kelly employs the term *reciprocal marriage* to describe the manner in which provincial New England men and woman joined one another in wedlock. In these marriages the practical values of the household economy took precedence over the more ephemeral ideals of romantic love. By no means, however, did such a marriage preclude the presence of feelings of true affection between the individuals being joined in marriage. Catherine Kelly, *In the New England Fashion: Reshaping Women's Lives in the Nineteenth Century* (Ithaca, N.Y.: Cornell University Press, 1999), 128–37.

78. HD, 19 March 1815.

79. HD, 19 March 1815.

80. HD, 20 March 1815.

81. The tradition of the second-day wedding very likely resulted from the time during the 1740s and 1750s when Separate Congregationalists suffered persecution at the hands of orthodox Congregational authorities. Forced to have their wedding ceremonies performed by these authorities, Separates en-

dured the official ceremony (the first-day wedding) and held their own celebration among friends (the second-day wedding) the following day.

82. HD, 20 March 1815.

83. HD, 23 March 1815.

84. HD, 24 March 1815. In his study of Abraham Lincoln, David Donald suggests that such feelings may have been common among young men in the early nineteenth century. David Donald, *Lincoln* (New York: Simon & Schuster, 1995), 86–87.

CHAPTER 5. HUSBAND, FATHER, NEIGHBOR

1. HD, 11 April 1815.

2. HD, 6 April; 27, 29 March 1815.

3. HD, 28, 30 March; 10, 13 April 1815.

4. HD, 14, 15 April 1815.

5. HD, 16, 21 April; 18 May 1815.

6. HD, 21, 26 April; 7, 14 May; 11, 26 June; 27 Aug. 1818.

7. HD, 12 May 1815.

8. HD, 16, 17, 19 June 1815.

9. HD, 30 July 1815.

10. HD, 14 Aug. 1815.

11. HD, 10 Sept. 1815.

12. HD, 14 Sept. 1815.

13. HD, 15 Sept. 1815.

14. Hiram's intense interest in technological innovations is representative of a much broader attitude toward these developments in the nineteenth century. John F. Kasson analyzes the relationship between republican attitudes and technology during this time in his *Civilizing the Machine: Technology and Republican Values in America, 1776–1900* (New York: Grossman, 1976). See particularly 3–51.

15. HD, 15, 16 Sept. 1815.

16. HD, 20 Sept. 1815.

17. HD, 20 Sept. 1815.

18. HD, 21 Sept. 1815.

19. HD, 21 Sept. 1815. It is interesting to note the parallels between the contrasts Hiram drew between town and country at this early date and the idealization or romanticization of the New England town described by Joseph S. Wood in *The New England Village* (Baltimore: Johns Hopkins University, 1997); and by Stephen Nissenbaum in "New England as Region and Nation," in Edward Ayers, Patricia Nelson Limerick, Stephen Nissenbaum, and Peter S. Onuf, eds., *All Over the Map: Rethinking American Regions* (Baltimore: Johns

Hopkins University, 1996), 38–61. Catherine Kelly discusses this early senti-
mentalization of the countryside; see Catherine Kelly, *In the New England
Fashion: Reshaping Women's Lives in the Nineteenth Century* (Ithaca, N.Y.: Cornell University Press, 1999), 1–11, 185–87, 240–41.

20. HD, 25 Sept. 1815.

21. HD, 26 Sept. 1815.

22. HD, 27 Sept. 1815.

23. HD, 2 Oct. 1815.

24. HD, 8 Jan. 1816.

25. HD, 17, 25 Feb. 1816.

26. HD, 28 Feb., 13 March 1816.

27. HD, 30 March, 6 Aug. 1816.

28. HD, 5 May 1816.

29. HD, 28 Sept. 1816.

30. HD, 24, 29 Nov. 1816.

31. HD, 1 Oct., 23 Nov. 1816; 1 Jan., 28 March 1817.

32. HD, 17, 20 April; 23, 28 May; 1 June 1817.

33. HD, 19 Feb., 18 June 1817.

34. HD, 1 Oct. 1817.

35. HD, 23 Oct. 1817.

36. HD, 9 Dec. 1817.

37. Leonore Davidoff and Catherine Hall analyze the relationship between
marriage and adulthood in the early nineteenth century. *Family Fortunes: Men
and Women of the English Middle Class, 1780–1850* (Chicago: University of
Chicago Press, 1987), 323–29.

38. HD, 8 Sept. 1819.

39. HD, 13, 17 Sept. 1819.

40. HD, 30 Sept. 1819.

41. HD, 2 Dec. 1819, 25 Aug. 1820.

42. HD, 20 Oct. 1821.

43. HD, 23 April; 16 June; 20, 27 Aug. 1820; 23 Sept. 1821; 7 July 1824.

44. HD, 3 March, 24 June 1821; 28 Aug. 1819.

45. HD, 23 Oct.; 1, 4, 12 April 1822.

46. HD, 16 May, 13 Oct. 1822.

47. HD, 19 Oct. 1815.

48. Jack Larkin, *The Reshaping of Everyday Life, 1790–1840* (New York:
Harper & Row, 1988), 232–57; Jon Finson, *The Voices That Are Gone: Themes
in Nineteenth-Century American Popular Songs* (New York: Oxford University
Press, 1994); Charles Hamm, *Yesterdays: Popular Songs in America* (New York:
Norton, 1979).

49. HD, 14 Jan. 1818.

50. HD, 26 Oct. 1816, 27 Aug. 1818, 31 May 1819, 31 Aug. 1821, 12 May 1817, 21 Feb. 1823.

51. HD, 2 March; 15, 16 June 1821.

52. HD, 17 June 1817. Davidoff and Hall note how reading assumed a central place in the lives of the emerging middle class. See *Family Fortunes*, esp. 155–92. In addition, the authors contend that the middle-class male's "claims for new forms of manliness found one of their most powerful expressions in formal associations" (416). This was particularly true of literary societies.

53. For insight into this phenomenon, see David Jaffee, "The Village Enlightenment in New England, 1760–1820," *William and Mary Quarterly*," 3d ser., 47 (1990): 327–46.

54. HD, 13 Aug. 1821.

55. HD, 9 Aug. 1818.

56. HD, 15 April 1819, 15 Nov. 1821, 4 July 1822.

57. HD, 13 March 1822.

58. HD, 17 April 1819, 11 Aug. 1821, 16 Aug. 1819.

59. HD, 14 Jan. 1817, 6 March 1821. George Dangerfield presents a comprehensive analysis of the events that attracted Hiram's attention in *The Awakening of American Nationalism, 1815–1828* (New York: Harper & Row, 1965).

60. HD, 25 Oct. 1819.

61. HD, 9 March 1821.

62. HD, 25 July 1821.

63. HD, 25, 26, 28 Sept. 1822.

64. HD, 29, 30 Sept. 1822.

65. HD, 15 Oct. 1816.

66. HD, 1, 7–10 Jan. 1815.

67. HD, 20 June 1816, 18 Aug. 1817, 4 Aug. 1819.

68. HD 16 May, 17 Nov. 1820.

69. HD, 14 June 1816.

70. HD, 1 Sept. 1820. Jaffee notes a tendency among participants in the Village Enlightenment, as "custodians of culture," to "set themselves above less enlightened neighbors." "Village Enlightenment," 346.

71. HD, 12, 14 Feb. 1822.

72. HD, 9 April 1817.

73. HD, 23 April, 30 July 1817.

74. HD, 31 Jan. 1818, 13 Feb. 1821, 1 Jan. 1819.

75. HD, 4 Jan. 1819.

76. HD, 9 Feb. 1819, 30 March 1822.

77. HD, 3, 4 Aug. 1817.

78. HD, 28 Aug. 1817.

79. HD, 30 Sept. 1817; 16 Oct., 8 Dec. 1815.

80. HD, 16 May 1817, 7 Dec. 1822, 31 Jan. 1823.

81. HD, 29 Dec. 1815; 28 Feb. 1816; 2 Aug. 1819; 8, 9 Jan.; 16 Nov. 1820.

82. HD, 1, 29 March, 20 Dec. 1816; 22 July 1817.

83. HD, 4, 20, 21, 24 Aug. 1816.

84. HD, 9 June, 1 July 1819; 9 April 1822.

85. HD, 23 March 1820.

86. HD, 7 Jan. 1823.

CHAPTER 6. ENTREPRENEUR

1. HD, 18 May 1823. "Y'k" refers to York money—New York money of account, in which one dollar equaled eight shillings.

2. Sally McMurry, *Transforming Rural Life: Dairying Families and Agricultural Change, 1820–1885* (Baltimore: Johns Hopkins University Press, 1995).

3. HD, 1 March 1819.

4. HD, 15 April, 24 July 1818; 30 July 1819; 23 Oct. 1818.

5. HD, 27 Feb. 1819, 16 Nov. 1822, 7 Nov. 1820.

6. HD, 22 Jan. 1818.

7. Hiram entered precise figures for the family's yearly income for four of these years, a record of their yearly expenses for three years, and the total of the great debt (including lists of the individuals who held these notes and the amount owed to each person) for five years. The averages given in the text are drawn from these years.

8. HD, 20 July, 23 Aug. 1819; 21 Aug., 2 June 1821; 11 Nov. 1822.

9. HD, 5 Aug., 17 May 1819; 20 Jan. 1822.

10. HD, 16 June 1821.

11. HD, 20 April, 23 May 1822.

12. Nancy Grey Osterud, *Bonds of Community: The Lives of Farm Women in Nineteenth-Century New York* (Ithaca, N.Y.: Cornell University Press, 1991); and Joan M. Jensen, *Loosening the Bonds: Mid-Atlantic Farm Women, 1750–1850* (New Haven, Conn.: Yale University Press, 1986).

13. HD, 11 Oct. 1823.

14. Christopher Clark, *The Roots of Rural Capitalism: Western Massachusetts, 1780–1860* (Ithaca, N.Y.: Cornell University Press, 1990); and the essays in Steven Hahn and Jonathan Prude, eds., *The Countryside in the Age of Capitalist Transformation: Essays in the Social History of Rural America* (Chapel Hill: University of North Carolina Press, 1985).

15. HD, 15 Oct. 1823.

16. HD, 16 Oct. 1823.

17. HD, 18 Oct. 1823.

18. HD, 12 Dec. 1823; 15, 17 March 1824.

19. HD, 15 Jan., 12 July 1824.

20. HD, 27 March 1824.

21. HD, 5, 15, 17 May 1824.

22. HD, 8 Oct. 1825.

23. HD, 4 Jan. 1828; 9 Dec. 1827; 23, 30 April; 5, 27 Oct. 1826.

24. HD, 14 Oct. 1827.

25. HD, 12, 20 Nov. 1827.

26. HD, 12 Jan. 1828.

27. HD, 13 Nov. 1829.

28. HD, 10, 21 May 1831.

29. HD, 4, 13 Feb. 1829; 8 July 1832; 2 June 1835; 19 June 1837; 4 June 1835.

30. HD, 1 March 1833, 6 Dec. 1834, 10 Oct. 1836.

31. HD, 7 July 1832, 19 May 1835. McMurry, *Transforming Rural Life*, 72–99.

32. HD, 9 Aug. 1829; 6, 7 Sept. 1834; 16 Sept. 1833.

33. HD, 18, 19 April 1835.

34. HD, 8 Dec. 1832, 18 May 1835.

35. HD, 29 Oct. 1835.

36. HD, 29 Oct. 1835.

37. HD, 31 Oct. 1835, 2 Jan. 1836, 3 Jan. 1837 (quotations in the first two entries).

38. Leonore Davidoff and Catherine Hall analyze this perception of manliness in *Family Fortunes: Men and Women of the English Middle Class, 1780–1850* (Chicago: University of Chicago Press, 1987). See particularly 107–48.

39. For Nina Silber, the urge to attain "respectability" distinguished the male persona in the North from that in the South. She believes this perception of masculinity dovetailed with the emerging free-labor ideology that spread throughout the North in the early nineteenth century. *The Romance of Reunion: Northerners and the South, 1865–1900* (Chapel Hill: University of North Carolina Press, 1993), 20–22.

40. Although he lacked the geographical mobility characteristic of so many individuals of the immediate post-Revolution generation, Hiram shared their desire to tap the creative potential that abounded in the new republic. In this way he is quite like the individuals studied in Joyce Appleby's *Inheriting the Revolution: The First Generation of Americans* (Cambridge, Mass.: Harvard University Press, 2000).

41. The "self-made" middle-class men described by Anthony Rotundo and

Michael Kimmel, having broken free of the restraints of family and community, forged their identities in the urban workplace, which was invariably separated from the home. As they did so, fathers increasingly surrendered their influence within the family to their wives. E. Anthony Rotundo, *American Manhood: Transformations in Masculinity from the Revolution to the Modern Era* (New York: Basic Books, 1993); Michael Kimmel, *Manhood in America: A Cultural History* (New York: Free Press, 1996). This simply was not the case with the Harwoods. Their family circumstances more closely resemble the analyses found in Catherine Kelly, *In the New England Fashion: Reshaping Women's Lives in the Nineteenth Century* (Ithaca, N.Y.: Cornell University Press, 1999); Karen Hansen, *A Very Social Time: Crafting Community in Antebellum New York* (Berkeley: University of California Press, 1994); McMurry, *Transforming Rural Life*; and Osterud, *Bonds of Community*.

42. HD, 14, 20 March 1833.

43. HD, 29 June 1833.

44. HD, 29 June 1833.

45. HD, 5 June, 28 Aug. 1833; 3 Oct. 1834; 21 April, 7 Oct. 1836.

46. HD, 2 June 1836; 9 June 1837.

47. HD, 4 Sept. 1824.

48. HD, 6, 30 June; 23 Sept. 1826.

49. HD, 9 March 1828, 12 March 1835, 4 Jan. 1836.

50. HD, 4 Nov. 1825; 19 Nov. 1827.

51. HD, 1 July 1828; 17 Nov. 1835; 9, 11 June 1836.

52. Hiram's account of his first trip, November 10-16, 1833, has been lost. He recorded his next two trips, October 26-31, 1834, and October 18-24, 1836, in a small separate journal, located in the Bennington Museum. This record is cited as New York Journal (NYJ).

53. NYJ, 29, 30 Oct. 1834.

54. NYJ, 19 Oct. 1836.

55. NYJ, 20 Oct. 1836.

56. NYJ, 21 Oct. 1836.

57. HD, 22 March 1831, 22 March 1832.

58. HD, 10 Dec. 1834.

59. HD, 10, 29 Jan. 1835. Tamara Plakins Thornton contends that early-nineteenth-century fathers desirous of improving their sons' opportunities in the business world often sent them to a handwriting master. *Handwriting in America: A Cultural History* (New Haven, Conn.: Yale University Press, 1996).

60. HD, 7 Sept. 1835.

61. HD, 9 Feb. 1835. Hiram often referred to his sister as Damia.

62. HD, 27 Nov., 4 Dec. 1835.

63. HD, 6, 8 Dec. 1835.

64. HD, 12 Feb. 1836. Catherine Kelly notes that it was quite customary for students to attend female academies for only a single term. *In the New England Fashion*, 175 n. 18.

65. Catherine Kelly discusses the manner in which singing and dancing schools not only fostered sociability among young men and women but also promoted the development of "middle-class" attitudes and behavior in the small villages of New England. *In the New England Fashion*, 195–99.

66. HD, 3 Dec. 1832; 20 May, 21 July 1836. For an analysis of this transformation in rural villages, see Kelly, *In the New England Fashion*, 214–51. Richard Bushman provides a wonderful analysis of these changes in a much broader context in *The Refinement of America: Persons, Houses, Cities* (New York: Knopf, 1992). See also David Jaffee, "Peddlers of Progress and the Transformation of the Rural North, 1760–1860," *Journal of American History* 78 (1991): 511–35.

67. Historians associate these values with the emergence of the "middle class" in nineteenth-century America. See particularly Stuart Blumin, "The Hypothesis of Middle-Class Formation in Nineteenth-Century America: A Critique and Some Proposals," *American Historical Review* 90 (1985): 299–338; and Stuart Blumin, *The Emergence of the Middle Class: Social Experience in the American City, 1760–1900* (New York: Cambridge University Press, 1989).

A number of historians have recently taken issue with Blumin's identification of the middle class with particular socioeconomic categories associated with nonmanual labor that emerged in response to nineteenth-century urbanization and industrialization. Two essays that discover aspects of middle-class social values and practices prior to the nineteenth century that bear no relationship to occupational categories are C. Dallett Hemphill, "Middle Class Rising in Revolutionary America: The Evidence From Manners," *Journal of Social History* 30 (1996): 317–44; and Jacquelyn Miller, "An 'Uncommon Tranquility of Mind': Emotional Self-Control and the Construction of a Middle-Class Identity in Eighteenth-Century Philadelphia," *Journal of Social History* 30 (1996): 129–48. Hemphill greatly expands her discussion in *Bowing to Necessity: A History of Manners in America, 1620–1860* (New York: Oxford University Press, 1999).

68. The three most prominent works dealing with the origins of middle-class manners — Karen Halttunen, *Confidence Men and Painted Women: A Study of Middle-Class Culture in America, 1830–1870* (New Haven, Conn.: Yale University Press, 1982); John Kasson, *Rudeness and Civility: Manners in Nineteenth-Century Urban America* (New York: Hill and Wang, 1990); and Hemphill, *Bowing to Necessities* — claim that the emergence of middle-class manners and values drew upon a multitude of etiquette books published throughout the

nineteenth century. All of these authors provide a list of the etiquette books they used to support their findings. A single composite list (accounting for a great deal of overlap) includes more than five hundred books. Hiram read only three of these: *The Young Lady's Own Book*, *The Young Man's Own Book*, and Adolf Knigge, *Practical Philosophy of Social Life* (see Appendix 1). The great majority of such books were published after Hiram's death.

    69. *Walton's Vermont Register and Farmer's Almanac for the Year of our Lord 1828* (St. Albans, Vt.), September entry. At another point, the almanac noted that "Capt. Cleanly" always "wears a clean white frock when he comes to market himself, and his butter is always clean, bright and sweet." As a result, he was always the first to sell his product (*Walton's Vermont Register . . . 1827*, November entry). Also readers were advised to "see that your sons and your daughters have dress that is neat, tidy and respectable" (*Walton's Vermont Register . . . 1821*, March entry).

    Webster's speller, for which Hiram had a particular fondness, was replete with similar advice. Although he was critical of the Bible because of its archaic grammatical constructions, Webster incorporated a great many biblical homilies in the stories he employed as examples of "easy standards of pronunciation."

    70. HD, 3 April 1826; 28 Nov., 15 Dec. 1827; 19, 24 July 1830.

    71. HD, 9 March, 1829.

    72. HD, 14 Jan., 8 May 1828; 11 June, 24 Dec. 1829.

    73. HD, 2 Sept. 1828, 16 March 1829, 1 March 1834, 8 Nov. 1833.

    74. HD, 28 Jan. 1834, 8 Dec. 1833, 31 Jan. 1834.

    75. HD, 15, 16, 17 Feb. 1834.

    76. HD, 30 March 1834, 22 July 1835.

    77. HD, 5 Dec. 1829, 7 Dec. 1836.

    78. HD, 14 Oct. 1835.

    79. HD, 4 July 1833, 12 March 1834.

    80. HD, 2, 22 June 1836. For an understanding of the changing nature of contracts in the larger national setting, see Morton Horwitz, *The Transformation of American Law, 1780–1860* (Cambridge, Mass.: Harvard University Press, 1977); and William Nelson, *Americanization of the Common Law: The Impact of Legal Change on Massachusetts Society, 1760–1830* (Cambridge, Mass.: Harvard University Press, 1975).

    81. HD, 4 Nov. 1836.

CHAPTER 7. BIRTH OF A WHIG

    1. HD, 4 Sept. 1815.

    2. HD, 15 Sept. 1815.

    3. HD, 29 March 1815.

4. HD, 26, 30 Aug. 1815.

5. HD, 23 June, 1816.

6. HD, 30 Aug. 1817.

7. HD, 1, 2 Sept. 1817.

8. HD, 19 Feb. 1920, 4 Sept. 1821, 27 March 1822.

9. HD, 2 Sept. 1823.

10. The names Pioneer and Old Line referred to stage lines running through Bennington. The Pioneer Line was a Sabbath-keeping stage and boat line formed in New York in 1828. The Old Line ran from Boston to Albany every day of the week. See Paul E. Johnson, *A Shopkeeper's Millennium: Society and Revivals in Rochester, New York, 1815–1837* (New York: Hill & Wang, 1978), for a fuller discussion of the Pioneer Line.

11. HD, 10 Jan. 1824.

12. HD, 17 Jan. 1824.

13. *Vermont Gazette*, 27 Jan., 3 Feb. 1824.

14. HD, 7 Sept. 1824.

15. HD, 19 Feb.; 4, 18 March; 8, 18 May 1825.

16. HD, 21 Sept. 1825.

17. HD, 5 Sept. 1826.

18. HD, 11 Sept. 1826.

19. HD, 27 Dec. 1826, 26 Jan. 1827.

20. HD, 22 Aug., 4 Sept. 1827.

21. HD, 4 Sept. 1827.

22. HD, 30 July, 30 Nov. 1827; 20 Jan., 8 Feb. 1826.

23. HD, 20 Nov. 1827.

24. HD, 18, 28 Aug.; 2 Sept. 1828.

25. HD, 28 Oct., 29 Dec. 1827; 14 March 1828.

26. HD, 29 Oct. 1828.

27. HD, 12 Nov. 1828.

28. HD, 1 June 1829.

29. HD, 31, 3 July 1830.

30. HD, 8, 14 Dec. 1829.

31. HD, 24 Feb.; 8, 9 March; 25 July 1830.

32. HD, 26 July 1830.

33. HD, 11, 6 Sept. 1831.

34. The opposition to Andrew Jackson assumed the title National Republicans, or "Nationals," whereas Jackson's party took the title Democratic Republicans.

35. HD, 20 Nov.; 2, 9 Dec. 1831; 13 Feb.; 16, 18 March; 27 May; 16 June 1832.

36. HD, 7 June, 4 Sept. 1832.

37. HD, 14, 19 July; 6, 12 Oct. 1832.

38. This series, reprinted from the *Boston Daily Advertiser and Patriot*, appeared throughout the months of September and October 1832.

39. HD, 21, 24 Oct.; 4, 10, 26 Nov. 1832.

40. HD, 13, 14, 15 Dec. 1832; 29 Jan., 26 March 1833.

41. HD, 29 Jan. 1833; 18 Dec. 1832; 4, 5 Jan. 1833; 5 Jan. 1835.

42. HD, 7, 13 Feb. 1833.

43. *North Adams (Mass.) Berkshire Advocate*, 13 Feb. 1833.

44. HD, 18 Feb. 1833. See, for example, the speeches of William Wilkins and John M. Clayton, printed in the *Spectator*, 4, 13 Feb. 1833.

45. HD, 19 Feb. 1833.

46. HD, 22 Feb. 1833.

47. HD, 25 Aug. 1837, 3 Sept. 1833. Antimasonry became a dominant force in Vermont politics at this time, although the party never gained acceptance in Bennington. For a discussion of Antimasonry in Vermont, see Paul Goodman, *Towards a Christian Republic: Antimasonry and the Great Transition in New England, 1826–1836* (New York: Oxford University Press, 1988).

48. HD, 26 Dec. 1833. For insight into the Bank War, see Charles Sellers, *The Market Revolution: Jacksonian America, 1815–1846* (New York: Oxford University Press, 1991), 321–26; Robert Remini, *Andrew Jackson and the Bank War: A Study in the Growth of Presidential Power* (New York: Norton, 1967); Bray Hammond, *Banks and Politics in America, from the Revolution to the Civil War* (Princeton, N.J.: Princeton University Press, 1957).

49. HD, 26 Dec. 1833; 6, 10 Jan. 1834.

50. HD, 11 Jan. 1834.

51. *Spectator*, 30 Dec. 1833.

52. HD, 31 Jan., 2 Feb. 1834.

53. *Spectator*, 31 Jan. 1834.

54. For these observations, see the *Spectator*, Dec. 1833; Jan., Feb., March, April 1834.

55. Major Jack Downing is the pseudonym adopted by Seba Smith, who wrote humorous columns satirizing politics and politicians. For an analysis of Smith, see Milton Rickels and Patricia Rickels, *Seba Smith* (Boston: Twayne, 1977).

56. HD, 11 Jan., 28 April 1834.

57. On February 3, 1834, Hiram received a pamphlet, *Speech of the Hon. Horace Binney on the Question of the Removal of the Deposits*, from Hall that subsequently served as his reference point on this issue.

58. Hiland Hall to David Robinson Jr., 8 March 1834, Hiland Hall Papers, Park-McCullough House, North Bennington, Vermont.

59. Hiland Hall to David Robinson Jr., 2 April 1838, Hall Papers.

60. *Register of Debates in Congress*, 23rd Cong., 1st sess., 1834, vol. 10, pt. 3, 3944.

61. Ibid., 3944–45.

62. Ibid., 3945–46.

63. HD, 2 Sept. 1834.

64. HD, 1 May 1834, 12 Oct. 1833.

65. HD, 15 Dec. 1836, 16 March 1833.

66. For editorials favoring these principles, see *Vermont Gazette*, 17, 24 Jan.; 7 Nov.; 26 Dec. 1826; 9 Jan., 16 Oct. 1827; 8 April, 27 May 1828. Colonel Merrill pressed Hiram to read a copy of the "Addresses of a Society of Philadelphia for the Promotion of National Industry" that he loaned him. HD, 6 Jan. 1827.

67. During these years Hiram signed a wool grower's petition to Congress, supported a movement to construct a canal linking Bennington to Albany, and maintained a constant interest in the possibility of a railroad passing through or near Bennington in the hopes of increasing the town's commercial prosperity. HD, 5 Jan., 17 Aug., 1 Sept. 1827; 11 Oct. 1836.

68. HD, 9 Dec. 1834.

69. HD, 9 Feb, 1 Sept. 1835.

70. HD, 18, 19, 21 Feb.; 24 July; 7, 8 Nov. 1836.

71. HD, 26 Nov. 1836.

72. HD, 12 Jan. 1836; 10, 20 Jan. 1837.

73. Robert Remini, *Andrew Jackson and the Course of American Democracy, 1833–1845* (New York: Harper & Row, 1984), 376–81.

74. HD, 27, 31 Jan. 1837.

75. HD, 3 Feb., 17 June 1837.

76. *Vermont Gazette*, 3 Sept. 1839.

77. Hiland Hall, draft of speech, Hall Papers.

78. *Register of Debates in Congress*, 23rd Cong., 1st sess., 1834, 10, pt. 3, 3948–49.

79. Ibid., 3945.

80. HD, 10 Feb. 1837. Hinsdill had been instrumental in establishing the Bennington Seminary in opposition to the Bennington Academy and in separating a large segment of the congregation away from Old First Church in order to establish a Presbyterian church in Hinsdillville, where he built a large stone edifice in which to conduct services.

81. Michael Holt, *The Rise and Fall of the American Whig Party: Jacksonian Politics and the Onset of the Civil War* (New York: Oxford University Press, 1999); and Daniel W. Howe, *The Political Culture of the American Whigs* (Chicago: University of Chicago Press, 1979), provide helpful discussions of the formation of the Whig Party throughout the nation.

82. In many ways, Hiram represented an amalgam of the "venturous conservative" devoted to old republican principles described by Marvin Meyers in *The Jacksonian Persuasion: Politics and Belief* (Palo Alto, Calif.: Stanford University Press, 1957), 33–56, and the Whig inclined toward character-building and self-improvement that Howe believes to be most clearly epitomized by Abraham Lincoln. *Political Culture of the American Whigs*, 263–98.

83. HD, 2 March 1837.

84. HD, 18 July 1834, 21 Jan. 1836.

85. For a discussion of McDuffie's stance, as well as insight into the political culture of South Carolina at this time, see William Freehling, *Prelude to Civil War: The Nullification Controversy in South Carolina, 1816–1836* (New York: Oxford University Press, 1966), 301–60; and William Freehling, *The Road to Disunion: Secessionists at Bay, 1776–1854* (New York: Oxford University Press, 1990), 271–336.

86. HD, 28 Dec. 1836; 17 March, 5 Jan. 1837. For Van Buren's address, see James D. Richardson, *A Compilation of the Messages and Papers of the Presidents, 1789–1897*, 10 vols. (Washington, D.C.: Government Printing Office, 1896–99), 3:313–20. In this speech Van Buren referred to his campaign promise to remain "the inflexible and uncompromising opponent of every attempt on the part of Congress to abolish slavery in the District of Columbia against the wishes of the slaveholding States, and also with a determination equally decided to resist the slightest interference with it in the States where it exists." He also warned against "dangerous agitation" of the issue (318).

87. HD, 11, 16 May 1837.

CHAPTER 8. H. HARWOOD

1. HD, 22 Sept. 1825.

2. HD, 11 Jan. 1827, 22 June 1829, 7 March 1830.

3. HD, 13 May 1826.

4. HD, 30 Sept. 1826.

5. HD, 15 Oct., 6 Sept. 1826.

6. HD, 19 Dec. 1826.

7. HD, 13 Jan. 1827.

8. HD, 2, 23 March; 2 April 1827.

9. HD, 17 April 1827.

10. HD, 29 May, 24 Dec. 1827.

11. HD, 9 April; 14, 16 March; 24, 25 Aug. 1828.

12. HD, 19 July 1829.

13. HD, 14 Oct. 1830.

14. Gridley's conduits to Finney were Rev. Nathaniel Beman, pastor of the First Presbyterian Church in Troy, and Rev. Horatio Foote, a fiery evangelist active throughout eastern New York, Vermont, and Massachusetts. For a full account of Finney and his co-workers, see Keith J. Hardman, *Charles Grandison Finney, 1792–1875: Revivalist and Reformer* (Syracuse, N.Y.: Syracuse University Press, 1987). For a discussion of Finney's techniques, see Paul E. Johnson, *A Shopkeeper's Millennium: Society and Revivals in Rochester, New York, 1815–1837* (New York: Hill & Wang, 1978).

15. HD, 16 March; 28, 29 June 1831.

16. HD, 4 July, 3 Sept. 1831.

17. HD, 7 Jan., 22 Feb. 1832.

18. Jon Butler, *Awash in a Sea of Faith: Christianizing the American People* (Cambridge, Mass.: Harvard University Press, 1990); Nathan Hatch, *The Democratization of American Christianity* (New Haven, Conn.: Yale University Press, 1989); and Johnson, *Shopkeeper's Millennium*.

19. HD, 3, 4, 8, 11 Dec. 1833.

20. HD, 24 Dec. 1833.

21. HD, 2 Feb., 13 May 1834.

22. HD, 3 Jan. 1836.

23. Hiram's first notation of the fact that Benjamin and Damia joined the church does not come until February 1, 1836.

24. HD, 3 Feb., 26 March, 10 May 1835. Paul Johnson and Sean Wilentz provide a fascinating discussion of Robert Matthews, the Prophet Matthias, in *The Kingdom of Matthias* (New York: Oxford University Press, 1994).

25. HD, 2 Feb. 1827, 10 April 1830, 29 Sept. 1832.

26. HD, 19 Feb., 26 March 1827; 5 July 1831.

27. David B. Davis, *Homicide in American Fiction, 1798–1860* (Ithaca, N.Y.: Cornell University Press, 1957); Karen Halttunen, *Murder Most Foul: The Killer and the American Gothic Imagination* (Cambridge, Mass.: Harvard University Press, 1998); David S. Reynolds, *Beneath the American Renaissance: The Subversive Imagination in the Age of Emerson and Melville* (New York: Knopf, 1988); Andie Tucher, *Froth and Scum: Truth, Beauty, Goodness, and the Ax Murder in America's First Mass Medium* (Chapel Hill: University of North Carolina Press, 1994); and John D. Stevens, *Sensationalism and the New York Press* (New York: Columbia University Press, 1991).

28. Louis C. Jones, *Murder at Cherry Hill: The Strang-Whipple Case, 1827* (Albany, N.Y.: Historical Cherry Hill, 1982).

29. HD, 21, 22 May 1827.

30. HD, 4 June 1827.

31. HD, 14 Aug. 1827.

32. HD, 20, 23, 25, 30 Aug. 1827.

33. *Confessions, Trials, and Biographical Sketches of the Most Cold-Blooded Murderers* (Boston: G. N. Thomson & E. Littlefield, 1840), 303. See Halttunen, *Murder Most Foul*, for references to the Joel Clough case.

34. *The Trial and Sentence of Joel Clough Who Was Eexecuted on the 26th of July, 1833 for the Murder of Mary W. Hamilton of Bordentown, N.J.* (Philadelphia: J. Scarlet, 1833); and *Trial, Sentence, Confession and Execution of Joel Clough* (New York: Christian Brown, [1833]).

35. HD, 14, 16, 25 June 1837.

36. For a full analysis of Sarah Cornell's murder and the subsequent trial, see David Kasserman, *Fall River Outrage: Life, Murder, and Justice in Early Industrial New England* (Philadelphia: University of Pennsylvania Press, 1986). William McLoughlin analyzes the divisive furor raised by the Avery trial in terms of the larger social, political, economic, and religious transformations affecting New England society at the time. "Untangling the Tiverton Tragedy: The Social Meaning of the Terrible Haystack Murder of 1833," *Journal of American Culture* 7 (1984): 75–84.

37. Quoted in Halttunen, *Murder Most Foul*, 185–86.

38. HD, 16 June 1833.

39. Quoted in Halttunen, *Murder Most Foul*, 186.

40. HD, 18 June 1833.

41. Patricia Cline Cohen, *The Murder of Helen Jewett: The Life and Death of a Prostitute in Nineteenth-Century New York* (New York: Knopf, 1998).

42. HD, 20 July, 29 Sept. 1833.

43. HD, 13 Feb. 1837, 28 Dec. 1836. John R. McDowall was a young divinity student who investigated the problem of prostitution in New York City and published his findings in *McDowall's Journal*. He also published two pamphlets, the *Magdalen Report* and the *Magdalen Facts*, which were considered to be "disgraceful" and "indecent" by many of his opponents. For a discussion of McDowell in this context, see Barbara Berg, *The Remembered Gate: Origins of American Feminism: The Woman and the City, 1800–1860* (New York: Oxford University Press, 1978), 178–79.

44. HD, 3 Aug., 12 Sept. 1835.

45. HD, 27 Aug. 1834.

46. HD, 2 July 1825.

47. HD, 7 March 1824. William Slade, *Vermont State Papers* (Middlebury, Vt.: J. W. Copeland, 1823), included a great deal of material dealing with the struggle between settlers on the New Hampshire Grants (present-day Vermont) and New York authorities that gave rise to the Green Mountain Boys.

48. HD, 25 Oct., 7 March 1824; 17 Aug. 1828; 8 Jan. 1829.

49. HD, 25 Feb. 1824.

50. HD, 18 Aug., 6 Jan. 1828. Hiram was clearly an exception to Michael Kammen's generalization that the post-Revolutionary generations felt themselves "burdened too much with the past." *Mystic Chords of Memory: The Transformation of Tradition in American Culture* (New York: Knopf, 1991), 40–61.

51. HD, 9 April 1829, 31 Aug. 1825, 14 July 1827, 25 Dec. 1833.

52. HD, 22 Aug. 1827.

53. HD, 14 July 1827; 15 June 1830; 8 July, 4 Oct. 1834; 18 June 1835; 20 June 1836.

54. HD, 1 Feb. 1837. Deacon Samuel Chandler revised and enlarged Hiram's list in 1870. Chandler's son and C. F. Sears added to it in 1919, and in 1930 Richard S. Bayhan elaborated, enlarged, and completed the list and published it under the title *Historical Sketch of Buildings Now or Once Located in the Village on the Hill at Bennington, Vermont, Formerly Known as Bennington Center, and Now Called Old Bennington* (Cleveland: Central Publishing House, 1930). Hiram received credit on the title page for compiling the original list.

55. HD, 1 Aug. 1829, 2 May 1830.

56. HD, 2 Aug. 1832, 30 Nov. 1834.

57. HD, 13 Jan. 1835.

58. HD, 16 June 1835, 25 Jan. 1837.

59. HD, 16 Nov. 1825, 16 April 1832.

60. HD, 13 Jan. 1831, 12 Jan. 1835.

61. HD, 5 May 1834.

62. HD, 13 Jan. 1826, 14 Feb. 1828.

63. HD, 20 June 1824, 28 Aug. 1828.

64. HD, 9 March 1836.

65. HD, 13 Nov. 1824, 24 July 1825, 13 Sept. 1827, 19 March 1824, 19 March 1835, 19 March 1836, 15 Sept. 1830.

66. HD, 21 Nov. 1829; 9, 21 Sept. 1835.

67. HD, 19 Sept. 1829, 6 May 1836.

68. HD, 9 Nov. 1836.

69. HD, 3 Feb. 1836.

70. HD, 10, 28 March; 17 April; 11 Dec. 1824; 14 May 1825; 26 Feb. 1827; 26 Dec. 1829.

71. HD, 1 April, 5 Oct. 1834; 8 Feb. 1836.

72. HD, 29 July 1835; 19 March, 25 Nov. 1836.

73. Damia's account book is in the Joseph Downs Manuscript Collection, Henry Francis du Pont Winterthur Museum, Winterthur, Del.

74. HD, 29 Aug. 1829, 1 Feb. 1831.

75. HD, 19 Feb. 1834.

76. HD, 9 Dec. 1828.

77. HD, 9 Sept. 1829; 22, 25 Jan. 1831.

78. HD, 5 Feb. 1835.

79. HD, 23 April 1837.

CHAPTER 9. A MISERABLE MAN

1. HD, 29 July 1837.

2. HD, 24 Nov. 1835; 1 April, 8 May 1836.

3. HD, 19 Dec. 1836, 17 April 1837.

4. HD, 3 March, 26 July 1836; 17 March 1837.

5. Benjamin Rush, *Medical Inquiries and Observations upon the Diseases of the Mind* (Philadelphia: Kimber & Richardson, 1812), 104, 105.

6. The *Journal of Health*, "conducted by an association of physicians," was published in Philadelphia during the years 1829–33.

7. HD, 1 Dec. 1832; 30 July, 28 Sept. 1836; 2 Feb. 1837. For an analysis of Thomsonian medical practices, see William G. Rothstein, *American Physicians in the Nineteenth Century: From Sects to Science* (Baltimore: Johns Hopkins University Press, 1972).

8. Hiram was by no means alone in his interest in hypochondriasis. For a discussion of the widespread prevalence of such interest at the time, see Susan Baur, *Hypochondria: Woeful Imaginings* (Berkeley: University of California Press, 1988).

9. HD, 30 Sept. 1832. This entry, which synthesized a wide range of medical authorities on the subject, consumed six double-column pages. Abraham Rees, *The Cyclopaedia: or Universal Dictionary of Arts, Sciences, and Literature*, 30 vols. (London: Longman, Hurst, Rees, Orme, & Brown, 1819), vol. 18 (not paginated).

10. HD, 28 Nov. 1825, 5 Nov. 1832, 20 Feb. 1834.

11. HD, 1 Aug. 1837.

12. HD, 3 Aug. 1837.

13. HD, 4 Aug. 1837.

14. HD, 4 Aug. 1837.

15. HD, 7, 9, 8, 13, 14 Aug. 1837.

16. HD, 15, 17, 18 Aug. 1837.

17. HD, 18 Aug. 1837.

18. HD, 18, 19 Aug. 1837.

19. HD, 20 Aug. 1837.

20. HD, 21, 22, 24 Aug. 1837.

21. HD, 26, 27 Aug. 1837.

22. HD, 28, 29, 31 Aug. 1837.

23. HD, 1, 3 Sept. 1837.

24. HD, 3, 4, 5 Sept. 1837.

25. HD, 6 Sept. 1837.

26. HD, 1 Oct. 1837.

27. HD, 2 Oct. 1837.

28. HD, 7 Oct. 1837.

29. HD, 7, 8 Oct. 1837.

30. HD, 9, 10, 11, 12 Oct. 1837.

31. HD, 13 Oct. 1837.

32. HD, 14 Oct. 1837. Hiram continually commented on the manner that "pain & inquietude" affected his hand, and yet his handwriting in the journal is just as clear and concise as always. Apparently Hiram suffered such intense nervous tension within his body that he felt writing to be a struggle.

33. HD, 16 Oct. 1837.

34. HD, 22, 23 Oct. 1837.

35. The circular appears in the *First Annual Report of the Trustees of the Vermont Asylum for the Insane* (Montpelier: E. P. Walton, 1837), 18–22.

36. Ibid., 21–22.

37. For a biographical sketch of Dr. Rockwell, as well as a history of the institution, see Esther Swift and Mona Beach, *Brattleboro Retreat, 1834–1984: 150 Years of Caring* (Brattleboro, Vt.: Bock Press, 1984).

38. For insights into Woodward's career and methods of dealing with the insane, see Gerald Grob, "Samuel B. Woodward and the Practice of Psychiatry in Early Nineteenth-Century America," *Bulletin of the History of Medicine* 36 (1962): 420–43; Gerald Grob, *The State and the Mentally Ill: A History of Worcester State Hospital in Massachusetts, 1830–1920* (Chapel Hill: University of North Carolina Press, 1966).

39. For a discussion of moral treatment, see especially Andrew Scull, "Moral Treatment Reconsidered: Some Sociological Comments on an Episode in the History of British Psychiatry," in Andrew Scull, ed., *Madhouses, Mad-Doctors, and Madmen: The Social History of Psychiatry in the Victorian Era* (Philadelphia: University of Pennsylvania Press, 1981), 105–18; Andrew Scull, "Madness and Segregative Control: The Rise of the Insane Asylum," *Social Problems* 24 (1977): 337–51; and Grob, *The State and the Mentally Ill*, 43–79.

40. *First Annual Report*, 5.

41. *Second Annual Report of the Trustees of the Vermont Asylum for the Insane* (Brattleboro, Vt.: Wm. E. Ryther, 1838), 7.

42. *First Annual Report*, 7

43. Grob, *The State and the Mentally Ill*, 66.

44. Andrew Scull, *Museums of Madness: The Social Organization of Insanity in Nineteenth-Century England* (New York: St. Martin's Press, 1979); and David J. Rothman, *Discovery of the Asylum: Social Order and Disorder in the New Republic* (Boston: Little, Brown, 1971), present the clearest explication of this model in Europe and America.

45. Michel Foucault, *Madness and Civilization: A History of Insanity in the Age of Reason* (New York: Random House, 1965), 252–55. My discussion of the superintendent as patriarch draws upon Foucault's insights.

46. First Annual Report, 15.

47. Ibid., 15–16.

48. Ibid., 16.

49. *Second Annual Report*, 13.

50. Ibid., 13.

51. Burrows' *Commentaries on the Causes, Forms, Symptoms, and Treatment, Moral and Medical, of Insanity* (London: Thomas and George Underwood, 1828) was one of the single most important treatises on the subject available at this time.

52. These quotations appear in Rockwell's inaugural address, delivered upon the opening of the asylum, December 12, 1836, and printed in the *Twelfth Annual Report of the Board of Managers of the Prison Discipline Society, Boston, May, 1837* (Boston: The Society, 1837), 95.

53. *Second Annual Report*, 14.

54. Ibid., 14–15.

55. Upon visiting Worcester State Hospital, a prominent physician noted that Woodward prescribed medicine to be taken three times a day "even when it was required but twice." Grob, "Samuel B. Woodward and the Practice of Psychiatry," 431.

56. The patient records of the Vermont Asylum for the Insane have been transcribed to standard forms of the Brattleboro Retreat, Brattleboro, Vermont, where the records are now stored. Hiram's medical record is filed as case number 61, serial number 62. Hereafter his file is cited as Medical Record (MR).

57. MR, 17 Nov. 1937. Jan Goldstein presents an insightful analysis of Esquirol's conception of monomania in *Console and Classify: The French Psychiatric Profession in the Nineteenth Century* (New York: Cambridge University Press, 1987), 152–96. For Burrows' analysis of hypochondriasis, which Rock-

well followed quite closely, see Burrows, *Commentaries*, 466–83. See Appendix 2 for an analysis of Hiram's illness and Rockwell's treatment from a modern medical perspective.

58. For Woodward's attitudes toward such systems, see Grob, *The State and the Mentally Ill*, 57–60.

59. MR, 18, 19, 20 Nov. 1837.

60. MR, 21 Nov. 1837.

61. MR, 22, 29 Nov. 1837.

62. MR, 4 Dec. 1837.

63. MR, 6, 13, 28 Dec. 1837. Burrows wrote, "Uninterrupted confidence of the patient in his physician is the sure basis of success in the treatment of all mental affections." In addition, "the hypochondriac's chief solace is in a detail of all his feelings and pains, real and imaginary. Hence the physician must listen with great attention and apparent interest to the long enumeration of symptoms and sympathise with all his patient's sufferings." *Commentaries*, 480. Woodward, too, followed this advice closely. Grob, "Samuel B. Woodward and the Practice of Psychiatry," 433.

64. MR, 3 Jan. 1838.

65. MR, 4, 14, 15, 17, 16 Jan.; 19 Feb. 1838.

66. MR, 20, 21 Jan. 1838.

67. MR, 22 Jan. 1838.

68. MR, 23, 25, 26, 27 Jan. 1838.

69. MR, 29, 30, 31 Jan.; 1 Feb. 1838.

70. MR, 5, 6, 7, 8, 11 Feb. 1838. Samuel Woodward, considering his patients "more calm under the influence of medicine," did not hesitate to prescribe opium. Grob discusses the record of one of Woodward's patients that bears a striking resemblance to Rockwell's treatment of Hiram. *The State and the Mentally Ill*, 70–71.

71. MR, 9, 10, 12, 14 Feb. 1838.

72. MR, 14, 20, 15, 19 Feb. 1838. For Burrows on melancholia, see *Commentaries*, 352–56. Ironically, Burrows concluded his discussion of hypochondriasis with the observation that "it may continue months or years, and then end happily. But it sometimes terminates in melancholia or mania, especially if there exist an hereditary predisposition in the patient; then desire of self-preservation, which at first characterises this affection, is often converted into the desire of self-destruction" (83).

73. MR, 23, 25 Feb.; 9, 10, 15, 26, 29 March 1838.

74. This notation appears on page 2 of Hiram's medical records as transcribed to the standard forms employed by the Brattleboro Retreat.

75. In his first report to the legislature, Rockwell included a chart showing

the number of patients who were discharged "recovered" or "improved," as well as the condition of those remaining in the asylum. He was clearly interested in showing positive results. *First Annual Report*, 10–12. Woodward was also constantly concerned about showing successful results. Indeed, his statistical reports eventually came under considerable criticism. Grob, *The State and the Mentally Ill*, 74–76. The case history of an excitable woman printed by Grob reveals that Woodward, too, released a patient even though she was "still disposed to be talkative and feeling excitable" (71).

76. *Vermont Gazette*, 12 March 1839.

EPILOGUE

1. Benjamin's will, dated December 26, 1839, appears in the Bennington Town Records, book 33, Town Clerk's Office, Bennington, Vt., pp. 484–86.

2. The lease, dated March 1, 1842, appears in the Bennington Town Records, book 21, pp. 349–51.

3. Edwin Bigelow and Nancy Otis, *Manchester Vermont: A Pleasant Land among the Mountains* (Town of Manchester, 1961), 276.

4. Probate Records, Bennington County Courthouse, Manchester, Vt., book 28, pp. 462–63.

5. Bennington Town Records, book 45, pp. 95–96.

6. Ibid., book 48, pp. 330, 473; book 49, p. 330; book 53, p. 284; book 54, p. 449; book 55, pp. 289, 293, 643; book 57, p. 616.

7. Ibid., book 48, pp. 473–75.

8. Ibid., book 57, p. 616.

9. Hopkins' obituary appears in the Day Papers, Bennington Museum, Bennington, Vt., H-103.

Index